W9-CFC-469

enVisionMATH 2.0

Scott Foresman · Addison Wesley

Volume 1 Topics 1-8

Authors

Randall I. Charles
Professor Emeritus
Department of Mathematics
San Jose State University
San Jose, California

Janet H. Caldwell
Professor of Mathematics
Rowan University
Glassboro, New Jersey

Juanita Copley
Professor Emerita, College of Education
University of Houston
Houston, Texas

Warren Crown
Professor Emeritus of Mathematics
Education
Graduate School of Education
Rutgers University
New Brunswick, New Jersey

Francis (Skip) Fennell
L. Stanley Bowlsbey Professor
of Education and Graduate and
Professional Studies
McDaniel College
Westminster, Maryland

Stuart J. Murphy
Visual Learning Specialist
Boston, Massachusetts

Kay B. Sammons
Coordinator of Elementary Mathematics
Howard County Public Schools
Ellicott City, Maryland

Jane F. Schielack
Professor of Mathematics
Associate Dean for Assessment and
Pre K-12 Education, College of Science
Texas A&M University
College Station, Texas

Mathematicians

Roger Howe
Professor of Mathematics
Yale University
New Haven, Connecticut

Gary Lippman
Professor of Mathematics and Computer
Science
California State University East Bay
Hayward, California

PEARSON

Glenview, Illinois   Boston, Massachusetts   Chandler, Arizona   Upper Saddle River, New Jersey

Contributing Authors

Zachary Champagne
District Facilitator, Duval County Public Schools
Florida Center for Research in Science,
Technology, Engineering, and Mathematics
(FCR-STEM)
Jacksonville, Florida

Jonathan A. Wray
Mathematics Instructional Facilitator
Howard County Public Schools
Ellicott City, Maryland

ELL Consultants

Janice Corona
Retired Administrator
Dallas ISD, Multi-Lingual Department
Dallas, Texas

Jim Cummins
Professor
The University of Toronto
Toronto, Canada

Texas Reviewers

Theresa Bathe
Teacher
Fort Bend ISD

Chrissy Beltran
School Wide Project Coordinator
Ysleta ISD

Renee Cutright
Teacher
Amarillo ISD

Sharon Grimm
Teacher
Houston ISD

Esmeralda Herrera
Teacher
San Antonio ISD

Sherry Johnson
Teacher
Round Rock ISD

Elvia Lopez
Teacher
Denton ISD

Antoinese Pride
Instructional Coach
Dallas ISD

Joanna Ratliff
Teacher
Keller ISD

Courtney Jo Ridehuber
Teacher
Mansfield ISD

Nannie D. Scurlock-McKnight
Mathematics Specialist
A.W. Brown Fellowship-Leadership Academy
Dallas, TX

Brian Sinclair
Math Instructional Specialist
Fort Worth ISD

ISBN-13: 978-0-328-76719-9
ISBN-10: 0-328-76719-0

Look for these digital resources in every lesson!

Digital Resources

 Go to PearsonTexas.com

 **Solve**
Solve & Share problems plus math tools

 Learn
Visual Learning Animation Plus with animation, interaction, and math tools

A-Z **Glossary**
Animated Glossary in English and Spanish

 Tools
Math Tools to help you understand

Check
Quick Check for each lesson

Games
Math Games to help you learn

eText
The pages in your book online

PearsonTexas.com
Everything you need for math anytime, anywhere

Key

Number and Operations

Algebraic Reasoning

Geometry and Measurement

Data Analysis

Personal Financial Literacy

Mathematical Process Standards are found in all lessons.

Digital Resources at PearsonTexas.com

Solve

Learn

A-Z Glossary

Check

Tools

Games

And remember the pages in your book are also online!

Contents

✦ Topics

VOLUME 1

TOPIC 1   Numbers 0 to 5

TOPIC 2   Comparing Numbers 0 to 5

TOPIC 3   Numbers 6 to 10

TOPIC 4   Comparing Numbers 0 to 10

TOPIC 5   Numbers to 20

TOPIC 6   Numbers to 30

TOPIC 7   Understanding Addition

TOPIC 8   Understanding Subtraction

VOLUME 2

TOPIC 9   Money

TOPIC 10   More Addition and Subtraction

TOPIC 11   Counting to 100

TOPIC 12   Two-Dimensional Shapes

TOPIC 13   Three-Dimensional Solids

TOPIC 14   Measurement

TOPIC 15   Data

TOPIC 16   Personal Financial Literacy

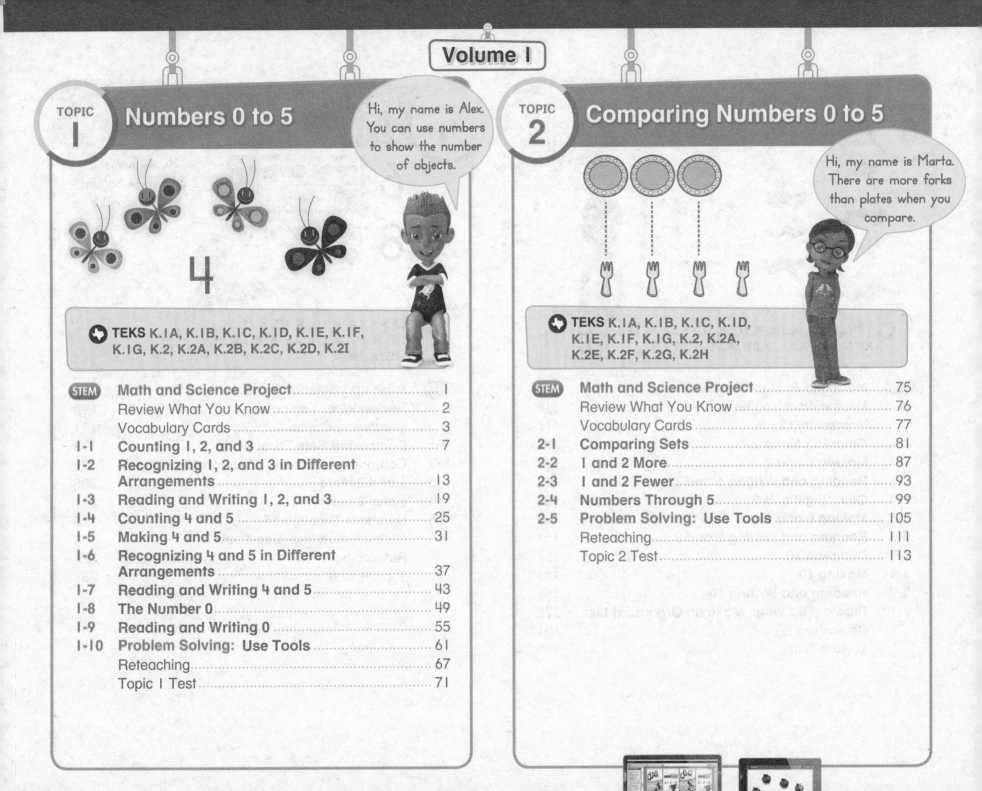

TOPIC 1 — Numbers 0 to 5

Hi, my name is Alex. You can use numbers to show the number of objects.

4

TEKS K.1A, K.1B, K.1C, K.1D, K.1E, K.1F, K.1G, K.2, K.2A, K.2B, K.2C, K.2D, K.2I

STEM Math and Science Project 1
Review What You Know 2
Vocabulary Cards 3
1-1 Counting 1, 2, and 3 7
1-2 Recognizing 1, 2, and 3 in Different Arrangements 13
1-3 Reading and Writing 1, 2, and 3 19
1-4 Counting 4 and 5 25
1-5 Making 4 and 5 31
1-6 Recognizing 4 and 5 in Different Arrangements 37
1-7 Reading and Writing 4 and 5 43
1-8 The Number 0 49
1-9 Reading and Writing 0 55
1-10 Problem Solving: Use Tools 61
Reteaching 67
Topic 1 Test 71

TOPIC 2 — Comparing Numbers 0 to 5

Hi, my name is Marta. There are more forks than plates when you compare.

TEKS K.1A, K.1B, K.1C, K.1D, K.1E, K.1F, K.1G, K.2, K.2A, K.2E, K.2F, K.2G, K.2H

STEM Math and Science Project 75
Review What You Know 76
Vocabulary Cards 77
2-1 Comparing Sets 81
2-2 1 and 2 More 87
2-3 1 and 2 Fewer 93
2-4 Numbers Through 5 99
2-5 Problem Solving: Use Tools 105
Reteaching 111
Topic 2 Test 113

TOPIC 3

Numbers 6 to 10

Hi, my name is Jackson. You can show the parts that make the whole.

TEKS K.1A, K.1B, K.1C, K.1D, K.1E, K.1F, K.1G, K.2, K.2A, K.2B, K.2C, K.2I

STEM **Math and Science Project** 115
Review What You Know 116
Vocabulary Cards 117
3-1 **Counting 6 and 7** 121
3-2 **Making 6 and 7** 127
3-3 **Reading and Writing 6 and 7** 133
3-4 **Counting 8 and 9** 139
3-5 **Making 8 and 9** 145
3-6 **Reading and Writing 8 and 9** 151
3-7 **Counting 10** 157
3-8 **Making 10** 163
3-9 **Reading and Writing 10** 169
3-10 **Problem Solving: Make an Organized List** 175
Reteaching 181
Topic 3 Test 185

TOPIC 4

Comparing Numbers 0 to 10

6
8

Hi, my name is Emily. The bottom set has 2 more.

TEKS K.1A, K.1B, K.1C, K.1D, K.1E, K.1F, K.1G, K.2, K.2A, K.2E, K.2F, K.2G, K.2H

STEM **Math and Science Project** 189
Review What You Know 190
Vocabulary Cards 191
4-1 **Comparing Sets Through 10** 193
4-2 **Comparing Numbers Through 10** 199
4-3 **1 and 2 More** 205
4-4 **1 and 2 Fewer** 211
4-5 **Numbers Through 10** 217
4-6 **Problem Solving: Use Tools** 223
Reteaching 229
Topic 4 Test 231

TOPIC 5

Numbers to 20

Hi, my name is Carlos. I counted 19 objects and wrote 19.

19
nineteen

TEKS K.1A, K.1B, K.1C, K.1D, K.1E, K.1F, K.1G, K.2, K.2A, K.2B, K.2C, K.2E, K.2F, K.2G, K.2H

STEM	**Math and Science Project**	233
	Review What You Know	234
	Vocabulary Cards	235
5-1	**Counting, Reading, and Writing 11 and 12**	239
5-2	**Counting, Reading, and Writing 13, 14, and 15**	245
5-3	**Counting, Reading, and Writing 16 and 17**	251
5-4	**Counting, Reading, and Writing 18, 19, and 20**	257
5-5	**Problem Solving: Draw a Picture**	263
5-6	**Comparing Sets Through 20**	269
5-7	**Creating Sets to 20**	275
5-8	**Comparing Numbers Through 20**	281
5-9	**1 More Than and 1 Less Than**	287
5-10	**Problem Solving: Use Reasoning**	293
	Reteaching	299
	Topic 5 Test	303

TOPIC 6

Numbers to 30

Hi, my name is Jada. There are more apples than oranges.

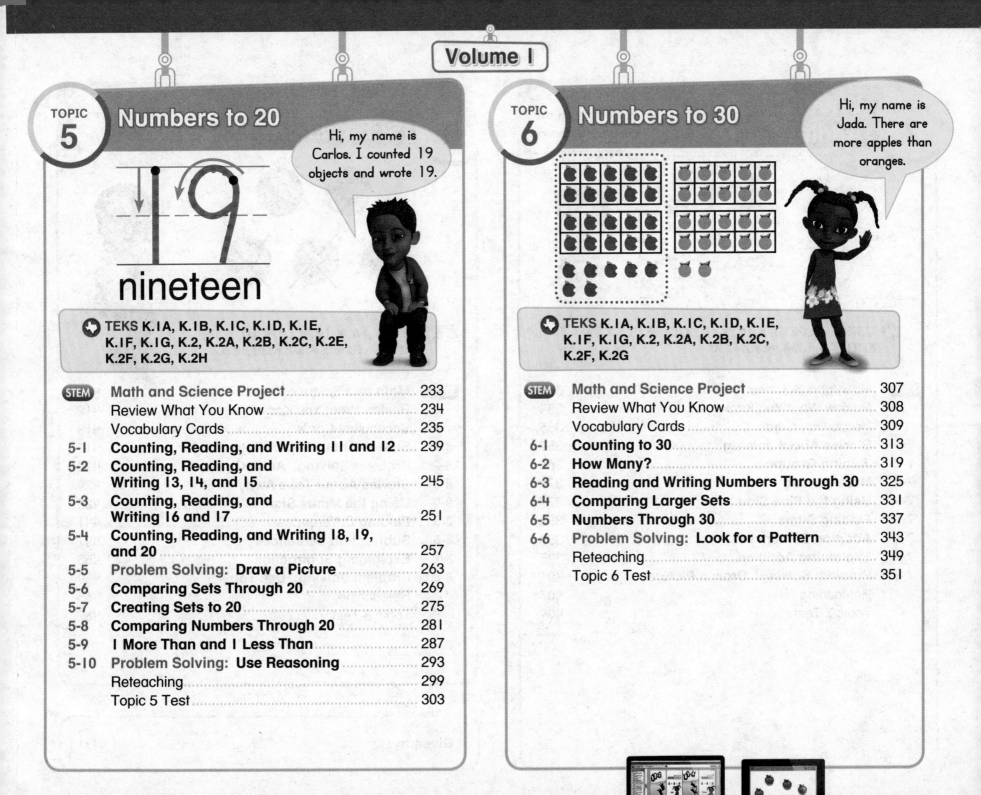

TEKS K.1A, K.1B, K.1C, K.1D, K.1E, K.1F, K.1G, K.2, K.2A, K.2B, K.2C, K.2F, K.2G

STEM	**Math and Science Project**	307
	Review What You Know	308
	Vocabulary Cards	309
6-1	**Counting to 30**	313
6-2	**How Many?**	319
6-3	**Reading and Writing Numbers Through 30**	325
6-4	**Comparing Larger Sets**	331
6-5	**Numbers Through 30**	337
6-6	**Problem Solving: Look for a Pattern**	343
	Reteaching	349
	Topic 6 Test	351

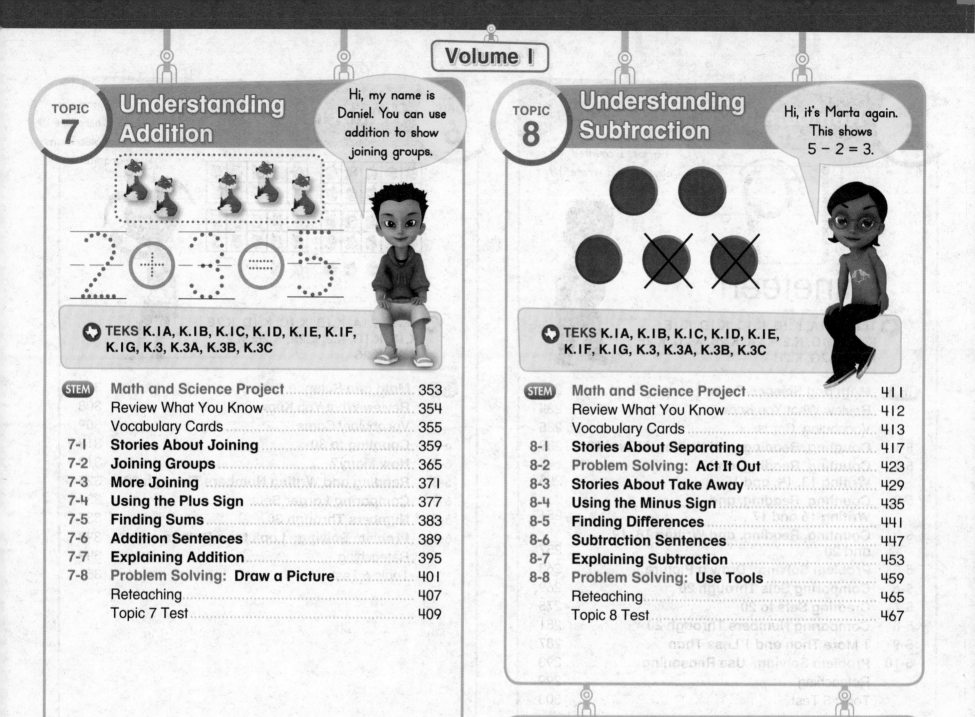

Volume 1

TOPIC **7** Understanding Addition

Hi, my name is Daniel. You can use addition to show joining groups.

⬥ TEKS K.IA, K.IB, K.IC, K.ID, K.IE, K.IF, K.IG, K.3, K.3A, K.3B, K.3C

STEM	**Math and Science Project**	353
	Review What You Know	354
	Vocabulary Cards	355
7-1	**Stories About Joining**	359
7-2	**Joining Groups**	365
7-3	**More Joining**	371
7-4	**Using the Plus Sign**	377
7-5	**Finding Sums**	383
7-6	**Addition Sentences**	389
7-7	**Explaining Addition**	395
7-8	**Problem Solving: Draw a Picture**	401
	Reteaching	407
	Topic 7 Test	409

TOPIC **8** Understanding Subtraction

Hi, it's Marta again. This shows 5 – 2 = 3.

⬥ TEKS K.IA, K.IB, K.IC, K.ID, K.IE, K.IF, K.IG, K.3, K.3A, K.3B, K.3C

STEM	**Math and Science Project**	411
	Review What You Know	412
	Vocabulary Cards	413
8-1	**Stories About Separating**	417
8-2	**Problem Solving: Act It Out**	423
8-3	**Stories About Take Away**	429
8-4	**Using the Minus Sign**	435
8-5	**Finding Differences**	441
8-6	**Subtraction Sentences**	447
8-7	**Explaining Subtraction**	453
8-8	**Problem Solving: Use Tools**	459
	Reteaching	465
	Topic 8 Test	467

Glossary	G1

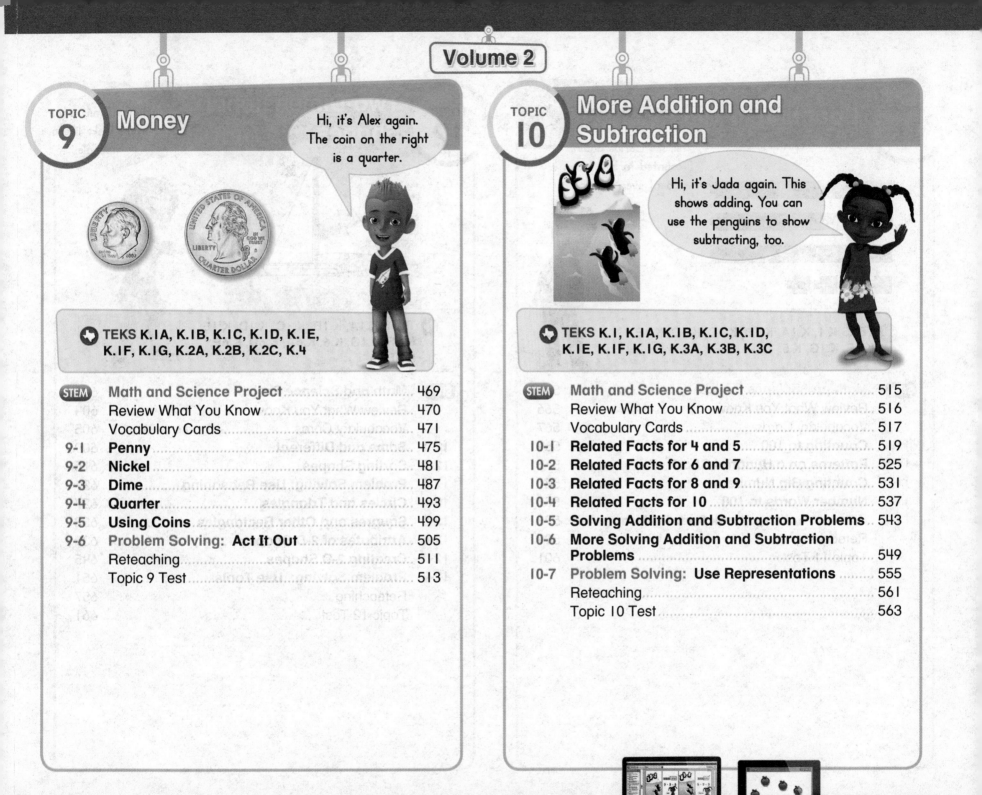

Volume 2

TOPIC 9 Money

Hi, it's Alex again. The coin on the right is a quarter.

⭐ TEKS K.1A, K.1B, K.1C, K.1D, K.1E, K.1F, K.1G, K.2A, K.2B, K.2C, K.4

STEM	Math and Science Project	469
	Review What You Know	470
	Vocabulary Cards	471
9-1	**Penny**	475
9-2	**Nickel**	481
9-3	**Dime**	487
9-4	**Quarter**	493
9-5	**Using Coins**	499
9-6	**Problem Solving: Act It Out**	505
	Reteaching	511
	Topic 9 Test	513

TOPIC 10 More Addition and Subtraction

Hi, it's Jada again. This shows adding. You can use the penguins to show subtracting, too.

⭐ TEKS K.1, K.1A, K.1B, K.1C, K.1D, K.1E, K.1F, K.1G, K.3A, K.3B, K.3C

STEM	Math and Science Project	515
	Review What You Know	516
	Vocabulary Cards	517
10-1	**Related Facts for 4 and 5**	519
10-2	**Related Facts for 6 and 7**	525
10-3	**Related Facts for 8 and 9**	531
10-4	**Related Facts for 10**	537
10-5	**Solving Addition and Subtraction Problems**	543
10-6	**More Solving Addition and Subtraction Problems**	549
10-7	**Problem Solving: Use Representations**	555
	Reteaching	561
	Topic 10 Test	563

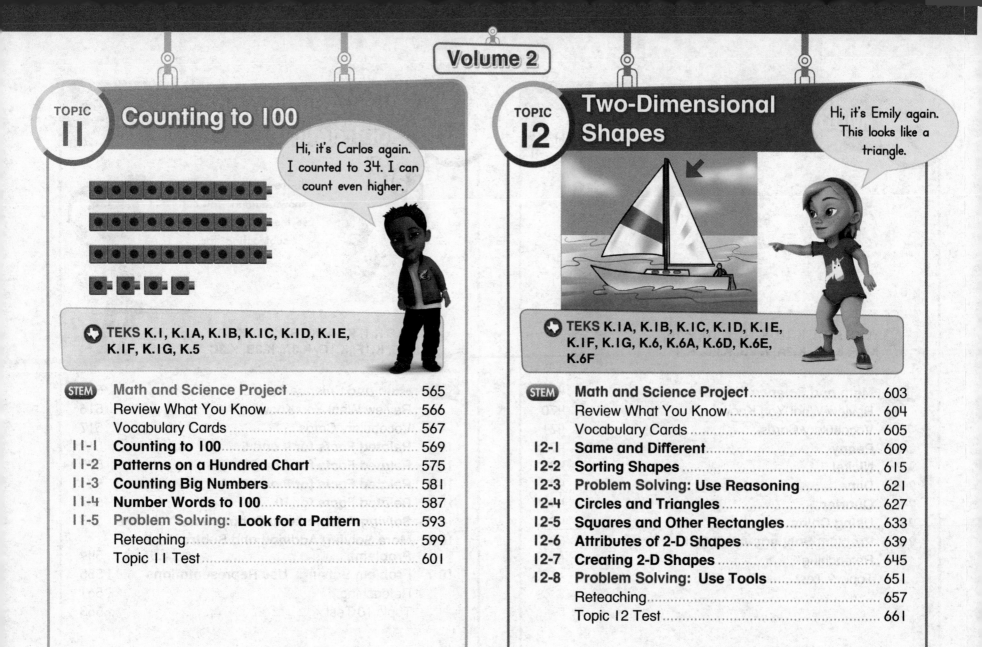

Volume 2

TOPIC 11 Counting to 100

Hi, it's Carlos again. I counted to 34. I can count even higher.

🌟 TEKS K.1, K.1A, K.1B, K.1C, K.1D, K.1E, K.1F, K.1G, K.5

STEM	Math and Science Project	565
	Review What You Know	566
	Vocabulary Cards	567
11-1	Counting to 100	569
11-2	Patterns on a Hundred Chart	575
11-3	Counting Big Numbers	581
11-4	Number Words to 100	587
11-5	Problem Solving: Look for a Pattern	593
	Reteaching	599
	Topic 11 Test	601

TOPIC 12 Two-Dimensional Shapes

Hi, it's Emily again. This looks like a triangle.

🌟 TEKS K.1A, K.1B, K.1C, K.1D, K.1E, K.1F, K.1G, K.6, K.6A, K.6D, K.6E, K.6F

STEM	Math and Science Project	603
	Review What You Know	604
	Vocabulary Cards	605
12-1	Same and Different	609
12-2	Sorting Shapes	615
12-3	Problem Solving: Use Reasoning	621
12-4	Circles and Triangles	627
12-5	Squares and Other Rectangles	633
12-6	Attributes of 2-D Shapes	639
12-7	Creating 2-D Shapes	645
12-8	Problem Solving: Use Tools	651
	Reteaching	657
	Topic 12 Test	661

TOPIC 13 — Three-Dimensional Solids

Hi, it's Jackson again. You can sort these 3-D figures in different ways.

🟦 **TEKS K.IA, K.IB, K.IC, K.ID, K.IE, K.IF, K.IG, K.6, K.6A, K.6B, K.6C, K.6D, K.6E**

STEM	**Math and Science Project**	665
	Review What You Know	666
	Vocabulary Cards	667
13-1	**Sorting 3-D Figures**	671
13-2	**Solid Figures**	677
13-3	**Flat Surfaces of Solid Figures**	683
13-4	**Comparing Solid Figures**	689
13-5	**Problem Solving: Use Reasoning**	695
	Reteaching	701
	Topic 13 Test	703

TOPIC 14 — Measurement

Hi, it's Marta again. You can compare the sizes of different objects.

🟦 **TEKS K.IA, K.IB, K.IC, K.ID, K.IE, K.IF, K.IG, K.7, K.7A, K.7B**

STEM	**Math and Science Project**	705
	Review What You Know	706
	Vocabulary Cards	707
14-1	**Describing Objects by More Than One Attribute**	711
14-2	**Comparing by Length**	717
14-3	**Problem Solving: Use Tools**	723
14-4	**Comparing by Height**	729
14-5	**Comparing Capacities**	735
14-6	**Comparing by Weight**	741
	Reteaching	747
	Topic 14 Test	751

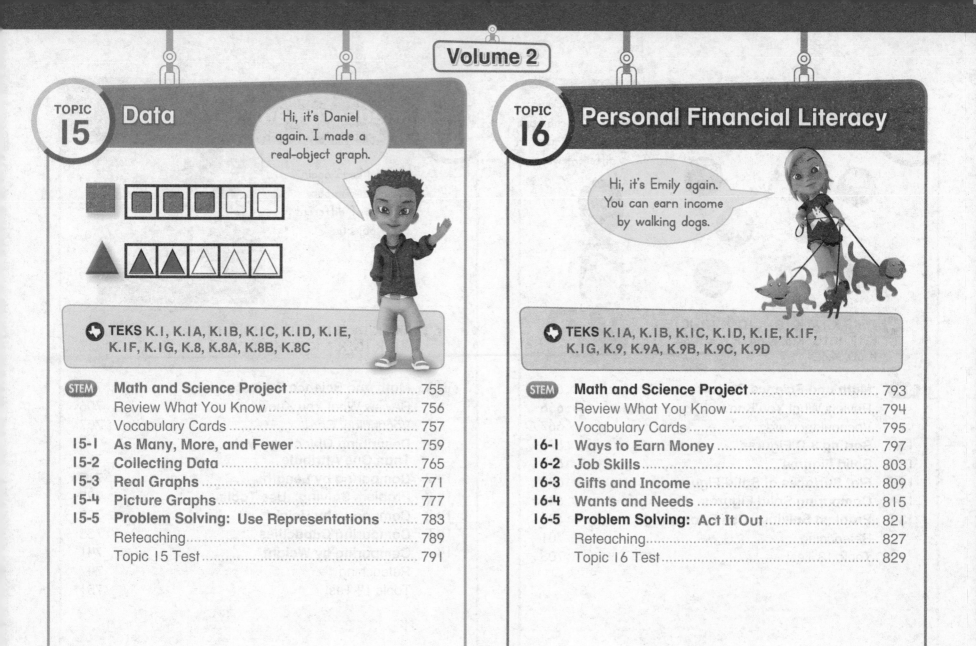

Volume 2

TOPIC 15 — Data

Hi, it's Daniel again. I made a real-object graph.

TEKS K.1, K.1A, K.1B, K.1C, K.1D, K.1E, K.1F, K.1G, K.8, K.8A, K.8B, K.8C

STEM	Math and Science Project	755
	Review What You Know	756
	Vocabulary Cards	757
15-1	**As Many, More, and Fewer**	759
15-2	**Collecting Data**	765
15-3	**Real Graphs**	771
15-4	**Picture Graphs**	777
15-5	**Problem Solving: Use Representations**	783
	Reteaching	789
	Topic 15 Test	791

TOPIC 16 — Personal Financial Literacy

Hi, it's Emily again. You can earn income by walking dogs.

TEKS K.1A, K.1B, K.1C, K.1D, K.1E, K.1F, K.1G, K.9, K.9A, K.9B, K.9C, K.9D

STEM	Math and Science Project	793
	Review What You Know	794
	Vocabulary Cards	795
16-1	**Ways to Earn Money**	797
16-2	**Job Skills**	803
16-3	**Gifts and Income**	809
16-4	**Wants and Needs**	815
16-5	**Problem Solving: Act It Out**	821
	Reteaching	827
	Topic 16 Test	829

Volume 2

Step Up to Grade 1

These lessons help prepare you for Grade 1.

★ TEKS 1.1A, 1.1B, 1.1C, 1.1D, 1.1E, 1.1F, 1.1G, 1.2, 1.2B, 1.2C, 1.2E, 1.3B, 1.5B, 1.5C, 1.5D, 1.5E, 1.6, 1.6A, 1.6C, 1.6D, 1.6E

	Table of Contents	831
	Grade 1 TEKS for Step-Up Lessons	832
1	Making 8 and 9	833
2	Introducing Addition Expressions and Number Sentences	837
3	Finding Missing Parts of 8 and 9	841
4	Introducing Subtraction Expressions and Number Sentences	845
5	Tens and Ones	849
6	Making 120 with Tens	853
7	Comparing Numbers	857
8	Sorting Shapes	861
9	Identifying Plane Shapes	865
10	Identifying Solid Figures	869

Glossary	G1

Numbers 0 to 5

Essential Question: How can numbers from 0 to 5 be counted, read, and written?

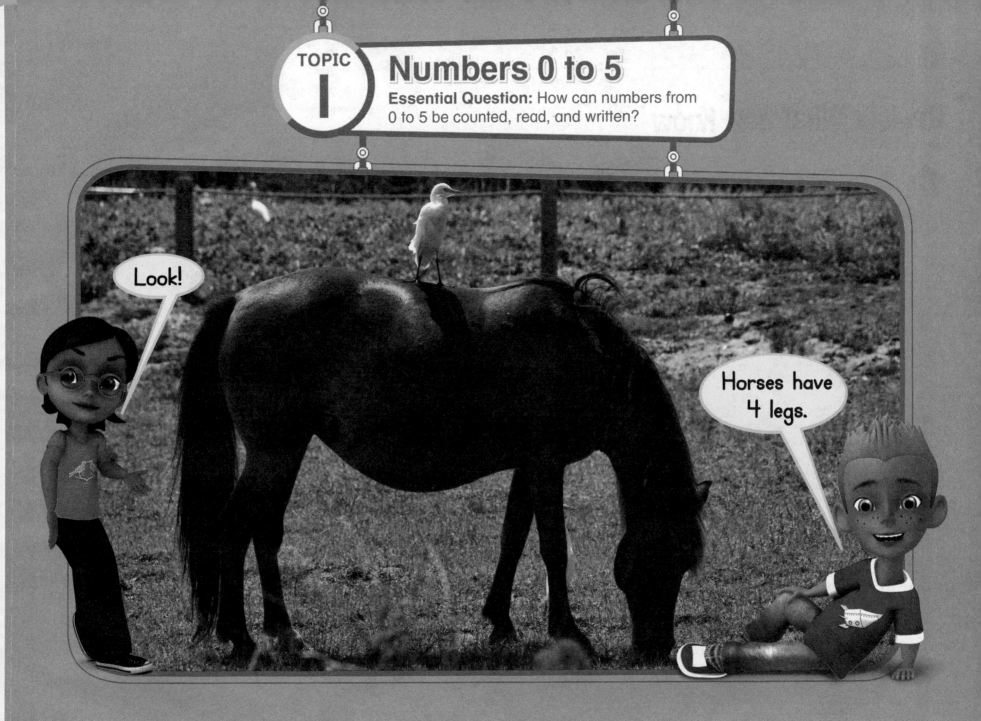

Math and Science Project: How Many Legs?

Directions Read the character speech bubbles to students. **Find Out!** Have students think about animals with 4 legs and animals with 2 legs. Say: *Talk to your friends and relatives about animals with 2 legs and animals with 4 legs. Ask them to help you think of an animal without any legs.* **Journal: Make a Poster** Then have students make a poster. Have them draw animals that have 4 legs, 2 legs, or 0 legs.

Name _____

Review What You Know

1

2

3

4

5

6

Directions Have students: **1** circle the animal that is on the right; **2** circle the animal that is on the left; **3** circle the animal that is green; **4–5** draw a line from each item in the top row to an item in the bottom row.

My Word Cards

Directions Have students cut out the vocabulary cards. Read the front of the card, and then ask them to explain what the word or phrase means.

A-Z

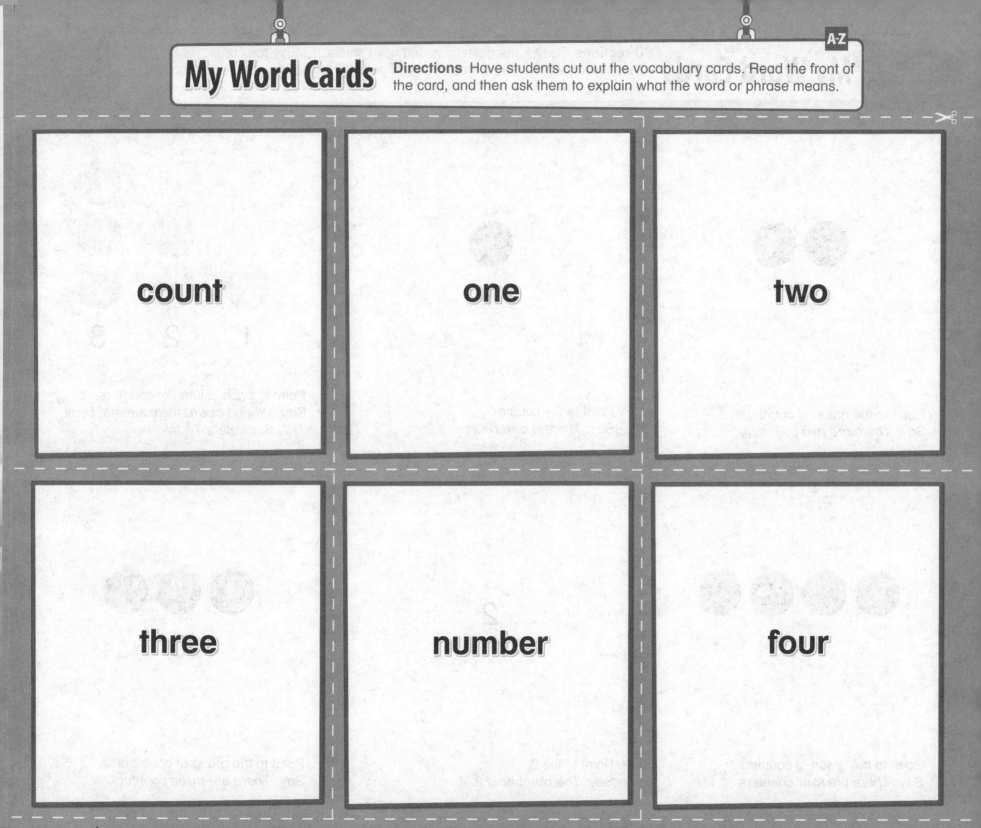

count

one

two

three

number

four

My Word Cards

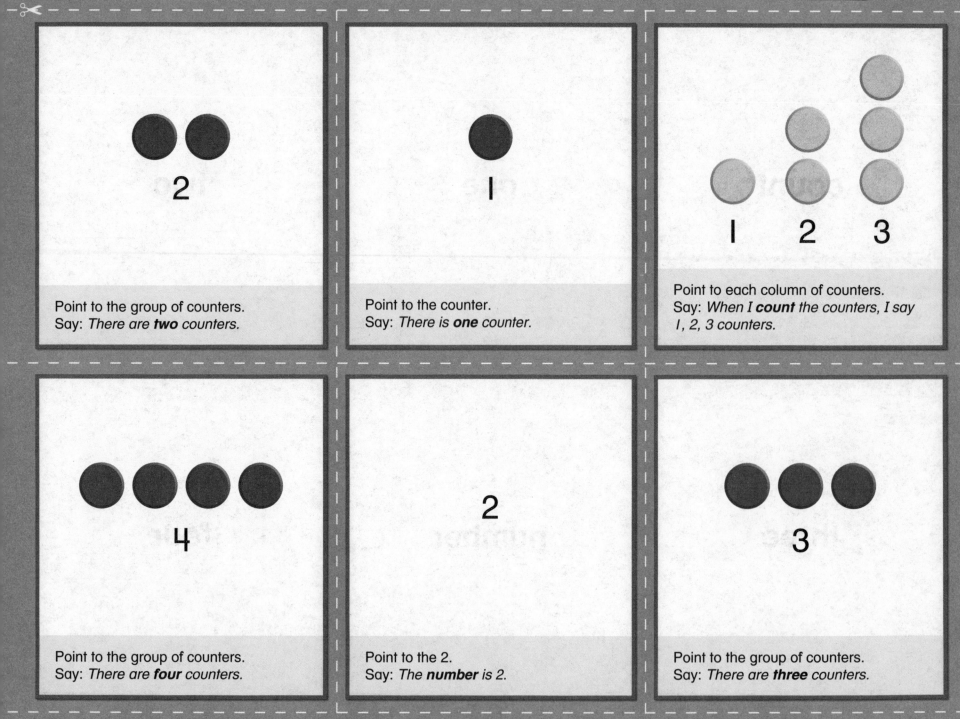

2

Point to the group of counters.
Say: *There are **two** counters.*

1

Point to the counter.
Say: *There is **one** counter.*

1 2 3

Point to each column of counters.
Say: *When I **count** the counters, I say 1, 2, 3 counters.*

4

Point to the group of counters.
Say: *There are **four** counters.*

2

Point to the 2.
Say: *The **number** is 2.*

3

Point to the group of counters.
Say: *There are **three** counters.*

My Word Cards

Directions Have students cut out the vocabulary cards. Read the front of the card, and then ask them to explain what the word or phrase means.

five

whole

part

zero

Directions Review the definitions and have students study the cards. Extend learning by having students draw pictures for each word on a separate piece of paper.

Point to the bananas on the left.
Say: *The 3 bananas are **part** of this group of 5 pieces of fruit.*

Point to the group of fruit.
Say: *The group of 5 pieces of fruit is the **whole** group.*

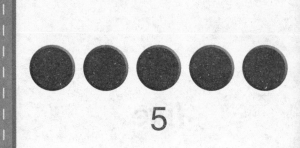

5

Point to the group of counters.
Say: *There are **five** counters.*

0

Point to the 0.
Say: *Another word for 0 is **none**.*

0

Point to the 0.
Say: *This number is **zero**.*

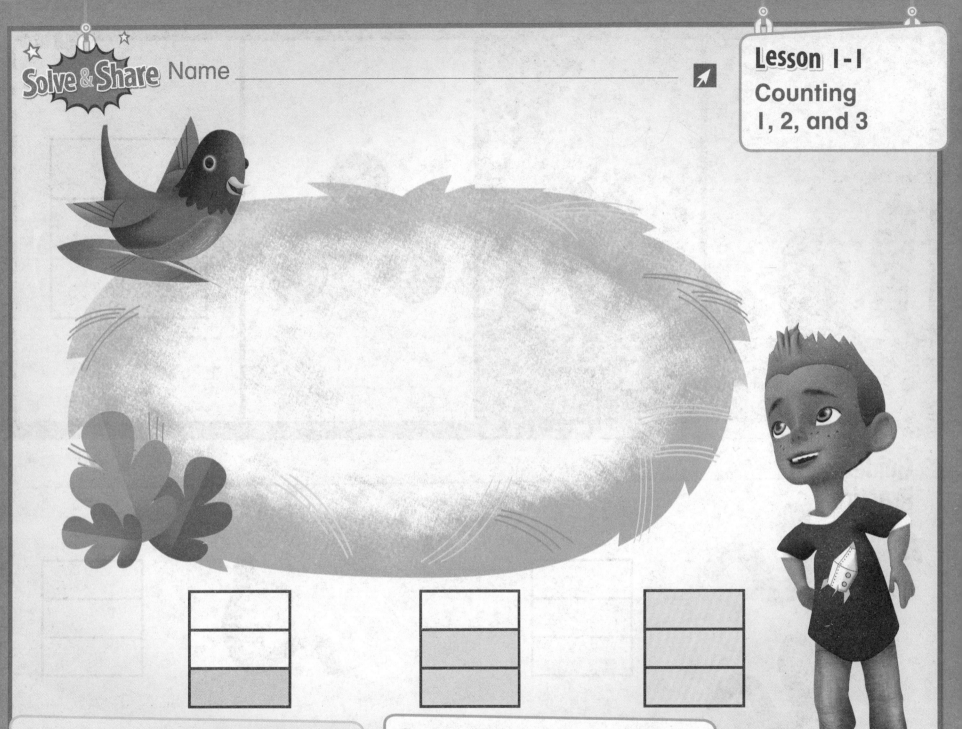

Solve & Share Name _____

Directions Have students place 2 counters in the nest on the workmat. Then, say: *Peeps the bird found these worms for her babies. Circle the colored box that shows how many worms Peeps found. Tell how you know you are correct. Then use digital tools to solve the problem.*

⭐ **TEKS K.2C** Count a set of objects up to at least 20 and demonstrate that the last number said tells the number of objects in the set regardless of their arrangement or order. Also, K.2, K.2A, K.2B. **Mathematical Process Standards** K.1C, K.1D, K.1E, K.1F.

Digital Resources at PearsonTexas.com

Solve   Learn   A-Z Glossary   Check   Tools   Games

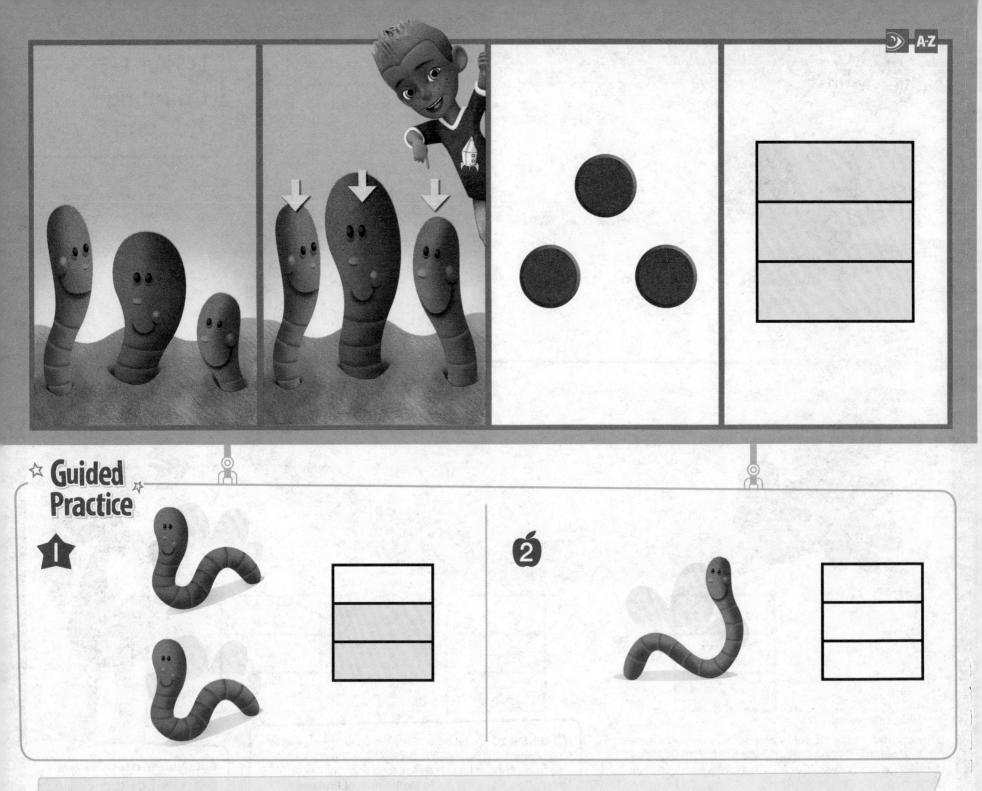

☆ Guided Practice ☆

1

2

Directions Have students count the worms, and then color the boxes to show how many.

Name _____

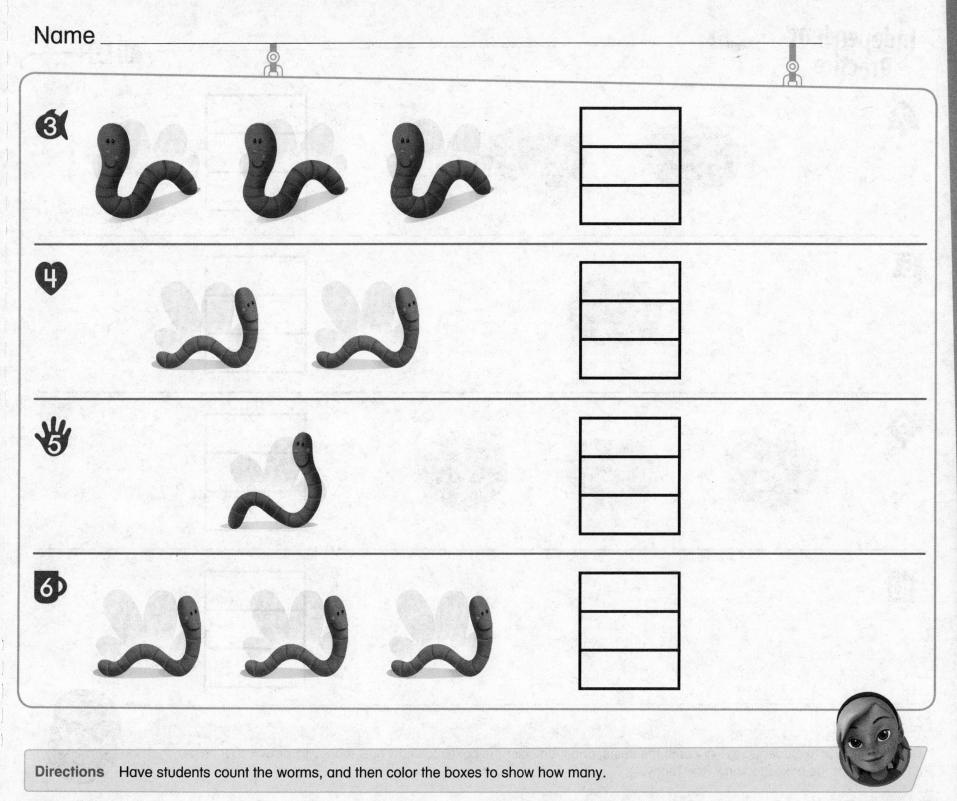

Directions Have students count the worms, and then color the boxes to show how many.

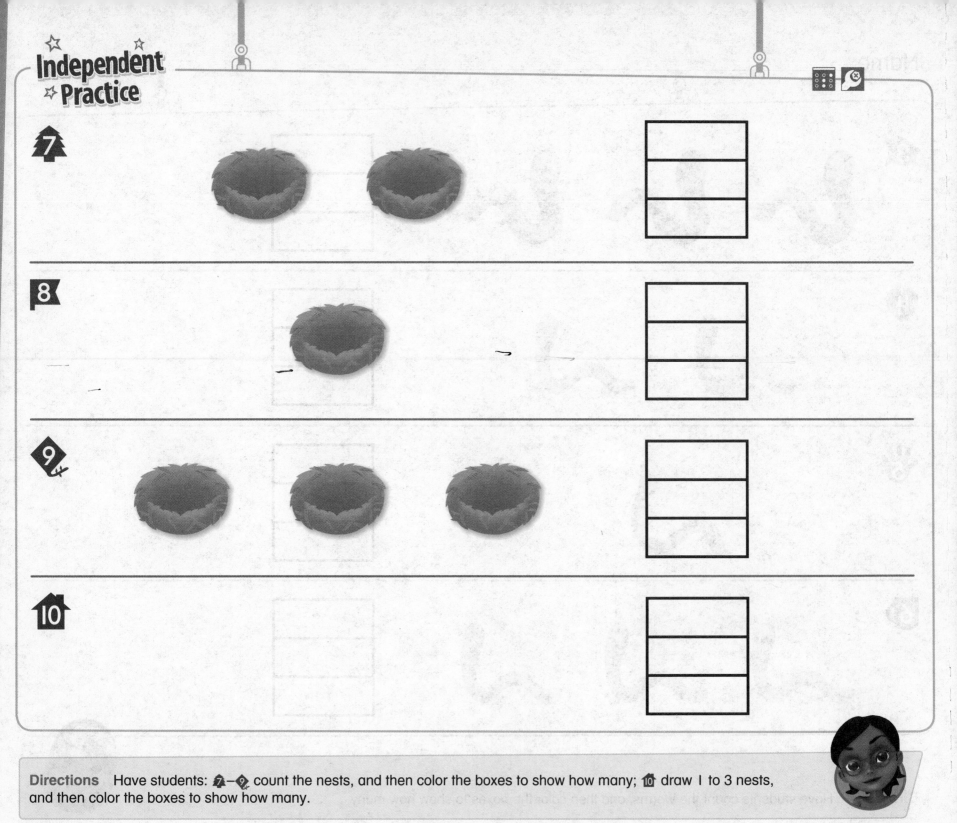

7

8

9

10

Directions Have students: **7–9** count the nests, and then color the boxes to show how many; **10** draw 1 to 3 nests, and then color the boxes to show how many.

Topic 1 | **Lesson 1**

Name _____

Another Look

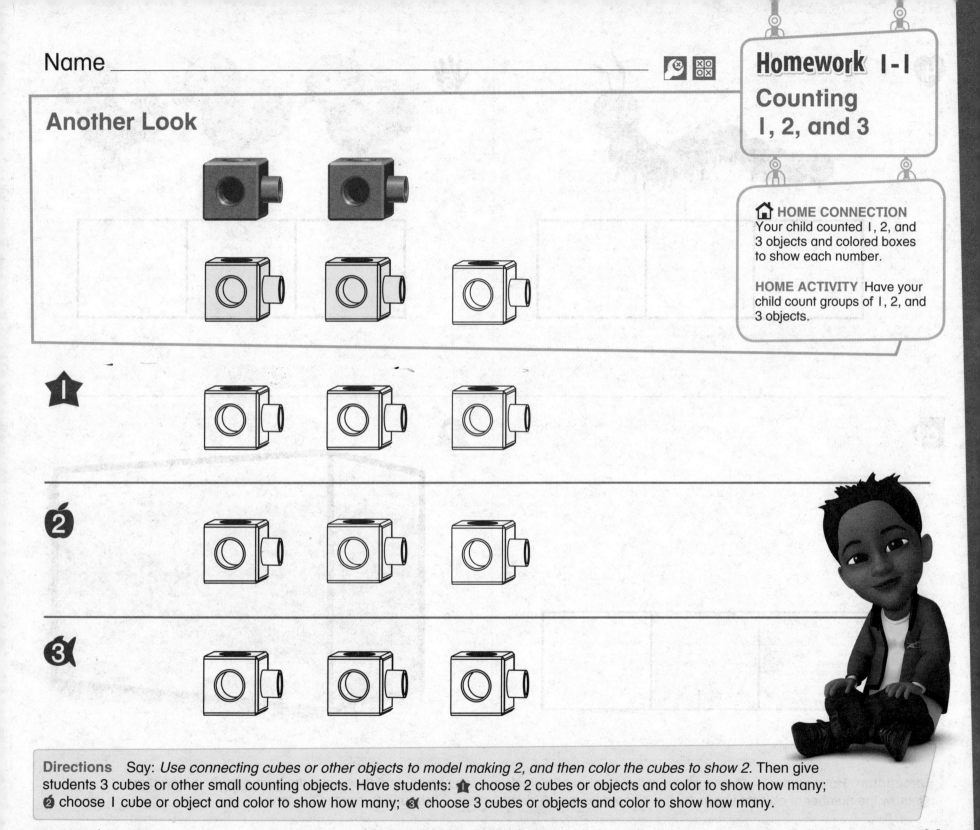

HOME CONNECTION
Your child counted 1, 2, and 3 objects and colored boxes to show each number.

HOME ACTIVITY Have your child count groups of 1, 2, and 3 objects.

★ 1

★ 2

★ 3

Directions Say: *Use connecting cubes or other objects to model making 2, and then color the cubes to show 2*. Then give students 3 cubes or other small counting objects. Have students: ★ choose 2 cubes or objects and color to show how many; ★ choose 1 cube or object and color to show how many; ★ choose 3 cubes or objects and color to show how many.

4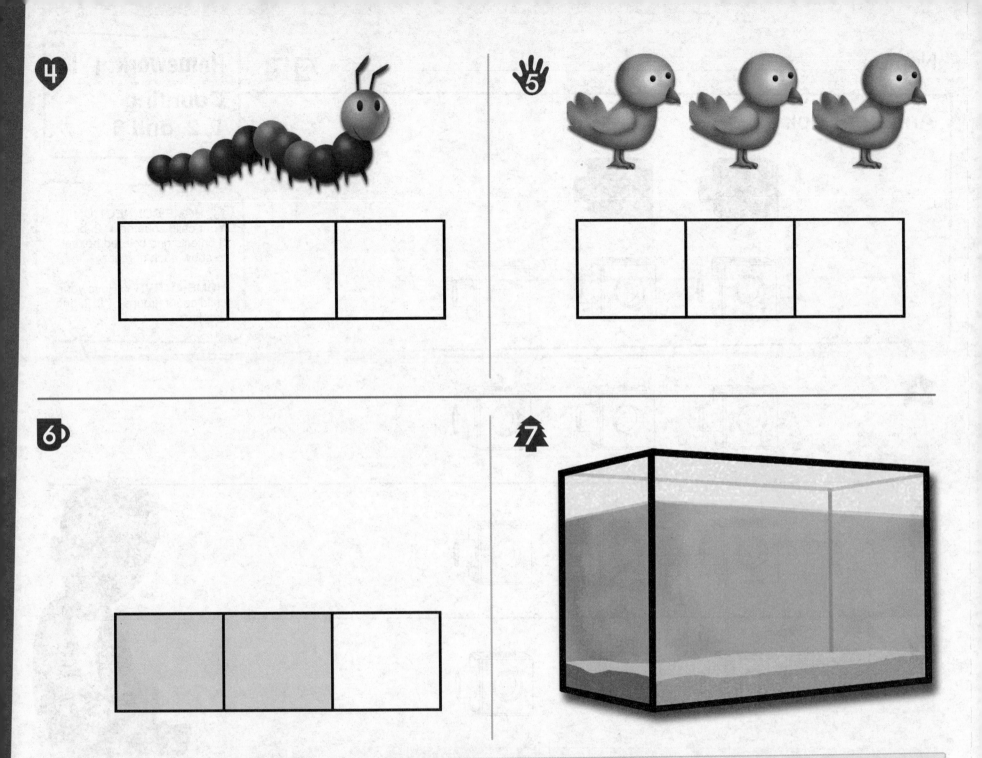

5

6

7

Directions Have students: **4** and **5** count the number of animals in each picture, and then color the boxes to show how many; **6** draw the number of objects shown by the colored boxes; **7** draw 1 plant, 2 fish, and 3 rocks in the tank.

12 twelve   © Pearson Education, Inc. K   **Topic 1** | Lesson 1

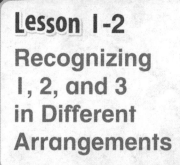

Solve & Share Name _____

Directions Have students place counters in the empty circles on the workmat to show how many worms each bird found. Then, say: *Each bird found some worms for their babies. Did they find the same or different number of worms? Color the boxes to show how you know.*

TEKS K.2D Recognize instantly the quantity of a small group of objects in organized and random arrangements. Also, K.2, K.2C. **Mathematical Process Standards** K.1C, K.1D, K.1F.

Digital Resources at PearsonTexas.com

Solve Learn Glossary Check Tools Games

Guided Practice

1

2

Directions Have students place a counter over each bird as they count it, and then color the boxes to show how many.

© Pearson Education, Inc. K

Name _____

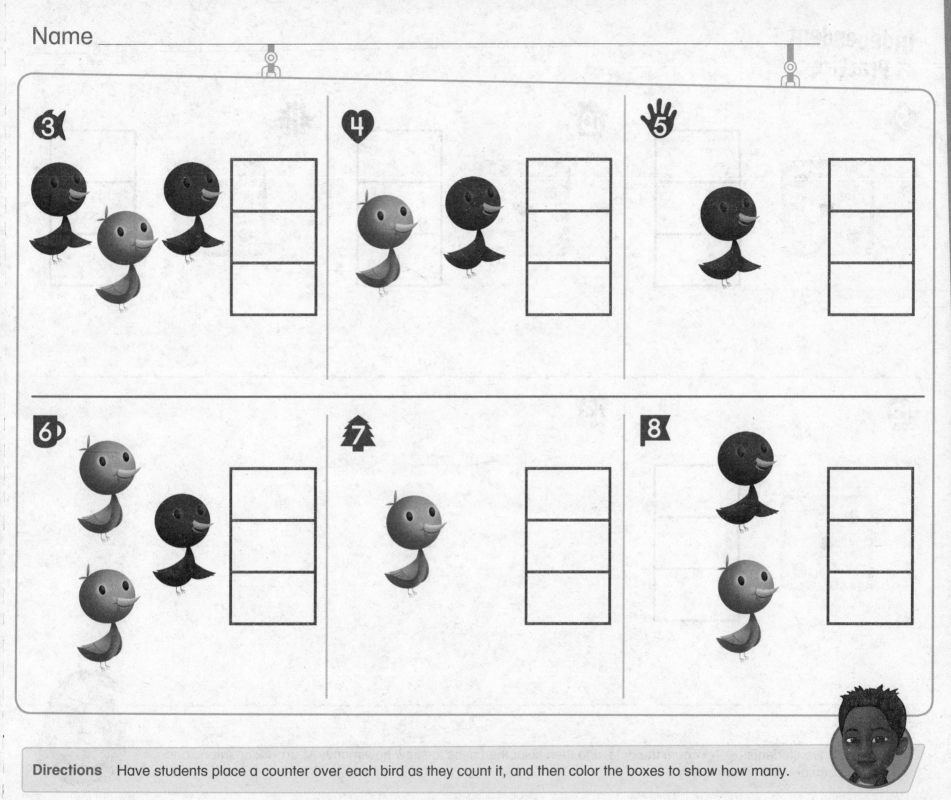

Directions Have students place a counter over each bird as they count it, and then color the boxes to show how many.

Topic 1 | Lesson 2

fifteen 15

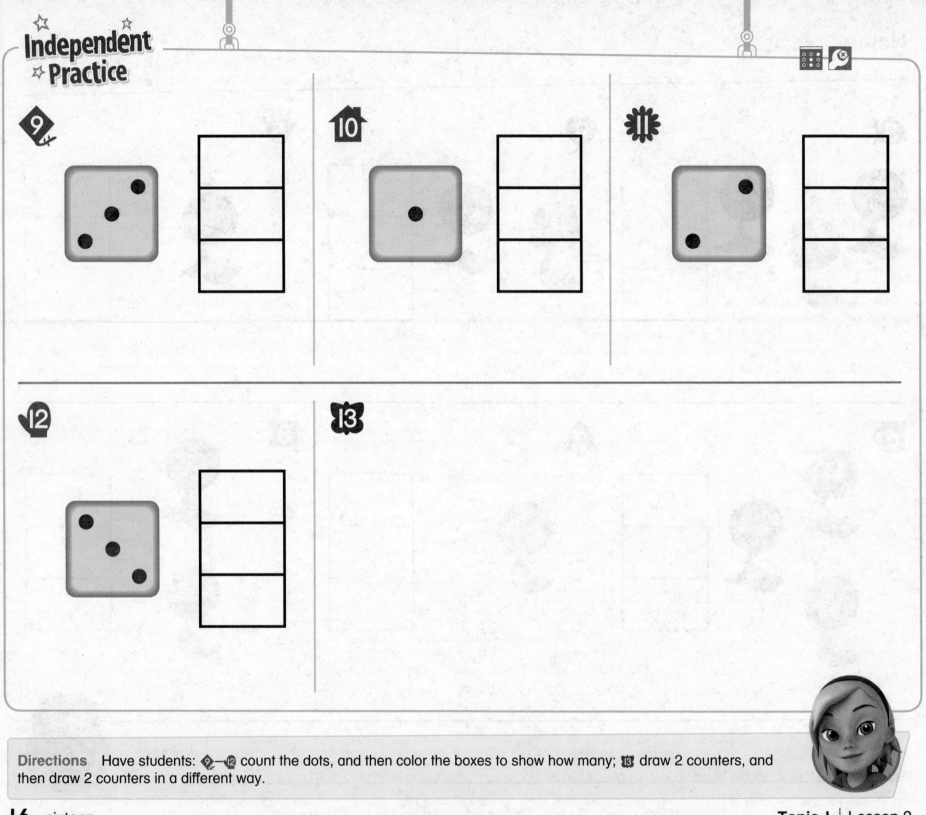

9

10

11

12

13

Directions Have students: **9**—**12** count the dots, and then color the boxes to show how many; **13** draw 2 counters, and then draw 2 counters in a different way.

Topic 1 | Lesson 2

Name _____

Another Look

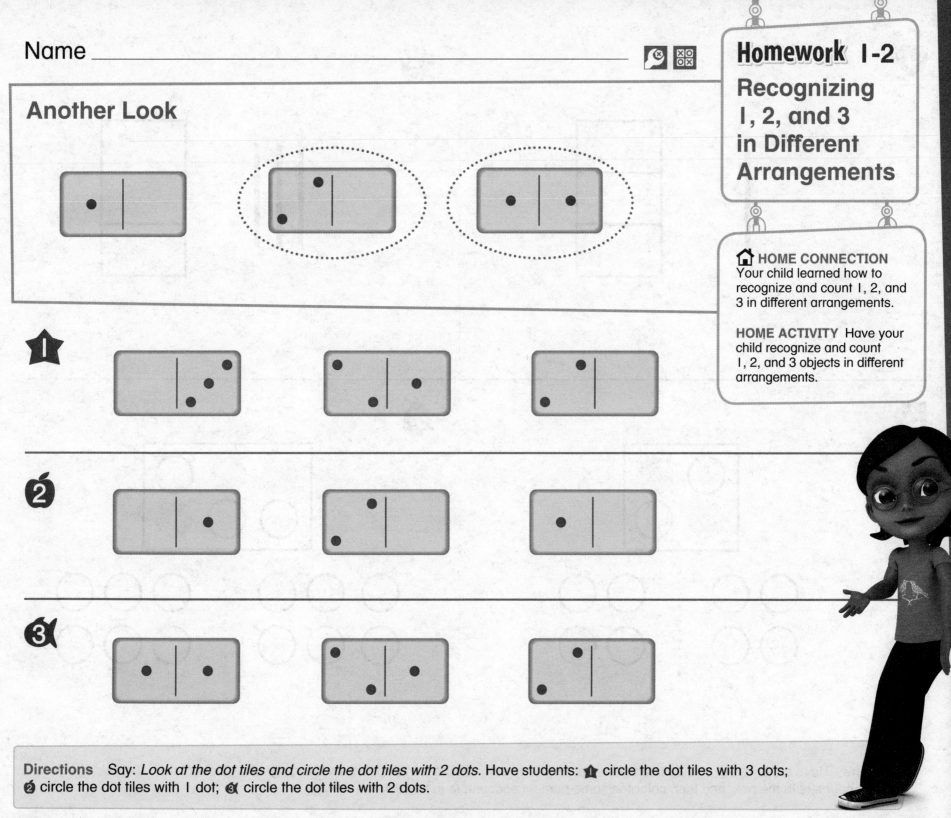

Directions Say: *Look at the dot tiles and circle the dot tiles with 2 dots.* Have students: ⭐ circle the dot tiles with 3 dots; 🍎 circle the dot tiles with 1 dot; 🐟 circle the dot tiles with 2 dots.

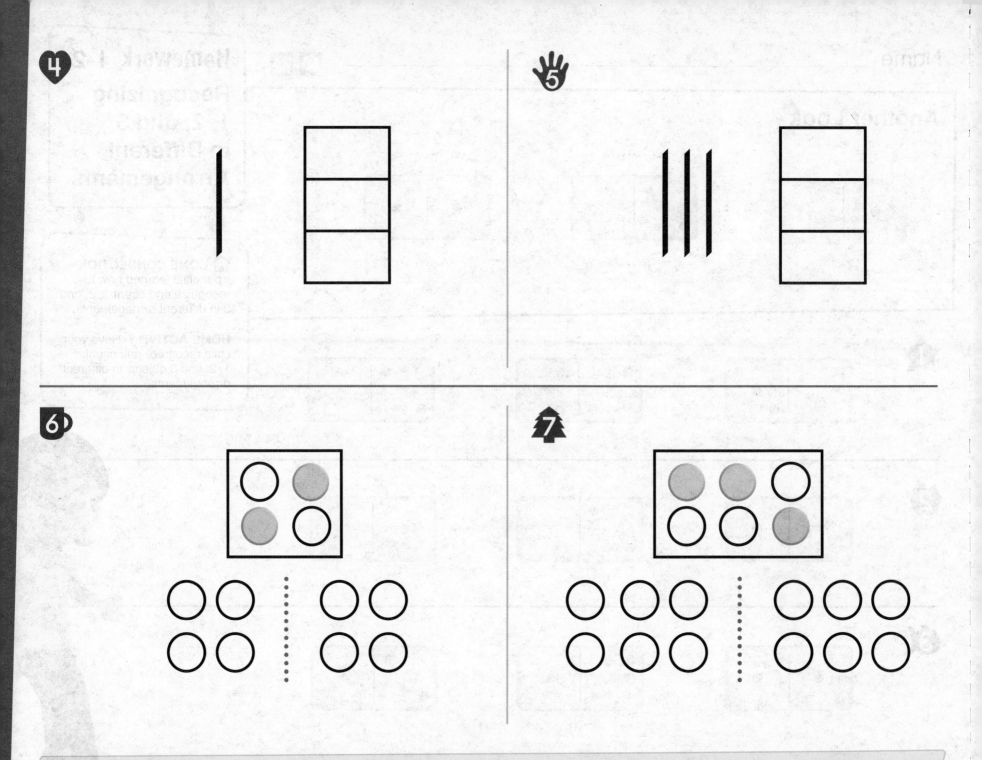

4 |

5 |||

6

7

Directions Have students: **4** and **5** count the lines, and then color the boxes to show how many; **6** and **7** count the number of yellow counters in the box, and then color the same number of counters in two different ways.

© Pearson Education, Inc. K

three

3

Directions Have students place two counters in the large cloud on the left side of the workmat. Then, say: *Alex sees two stars in the sky. He draws two stars on one cloud. How can he show how many stars in another way? Draw the other way in the empty cloud.*

⭐ **TEKS K.2B** Read, write, and represent whole numbers from 0 to at least 20 with and without objects or pictures. Also, K.2, K.2C. **Mathematical Process Standards** K.1C, K.1D, K.1G.

Digital Resources at PearsonTexas.com

Solve Learn Glossary Check Tools Games

☆ Guided Practice ☆

Directions Have students count the stars, and then write the number that tells how many.

© Pearson Education, Inc. K

Name _____

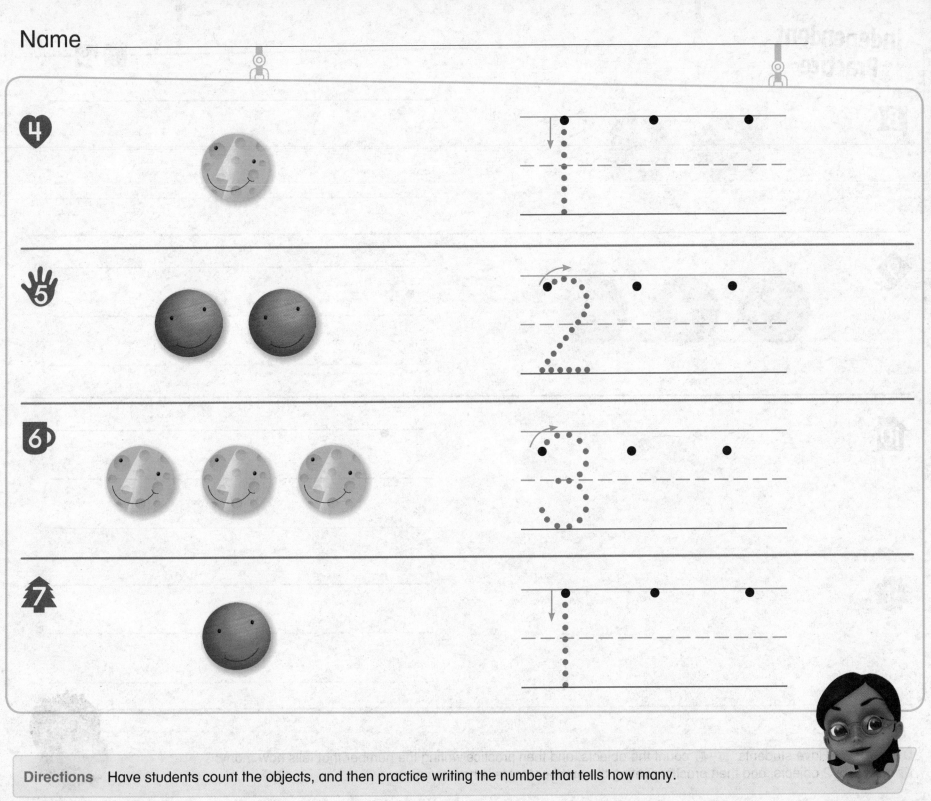

Directions Have students count the objects, and then practice writing the number that tells how many.

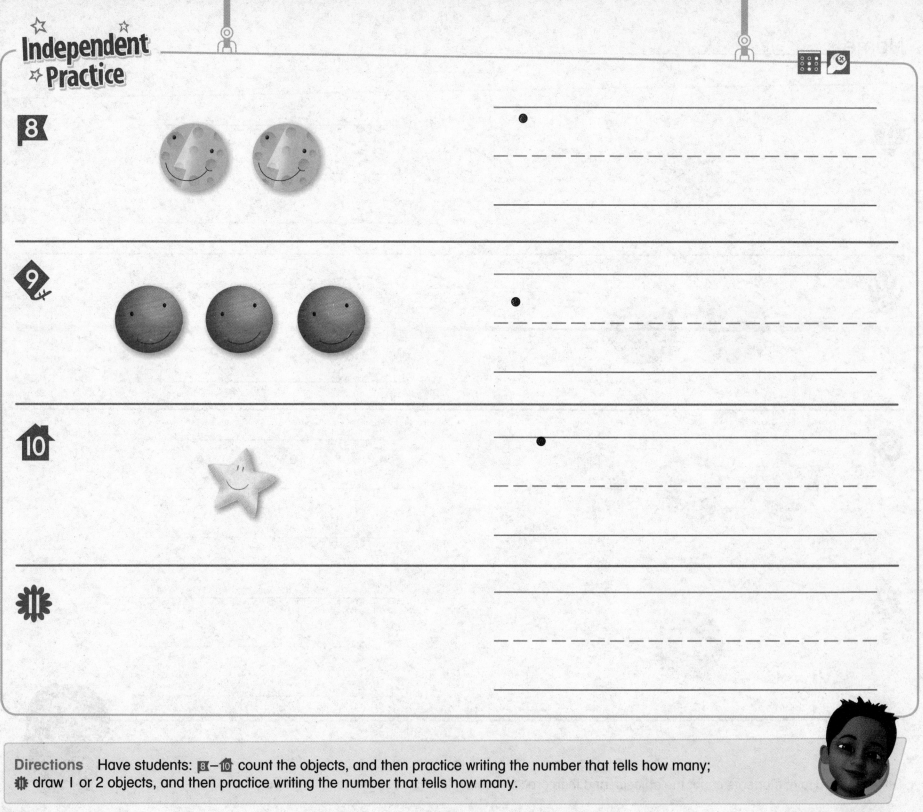

8

9

10

※

Directions Have students: **8**–**10** count the objects, and then practice writing the number that tells how many;
※ draw 1 or 2 objects, and then practice writing the number that tells how many.

22 twenty-two   © Pearson Education, Inc. K   **Topic 1** | Lesson 3

Name _____

Another Look

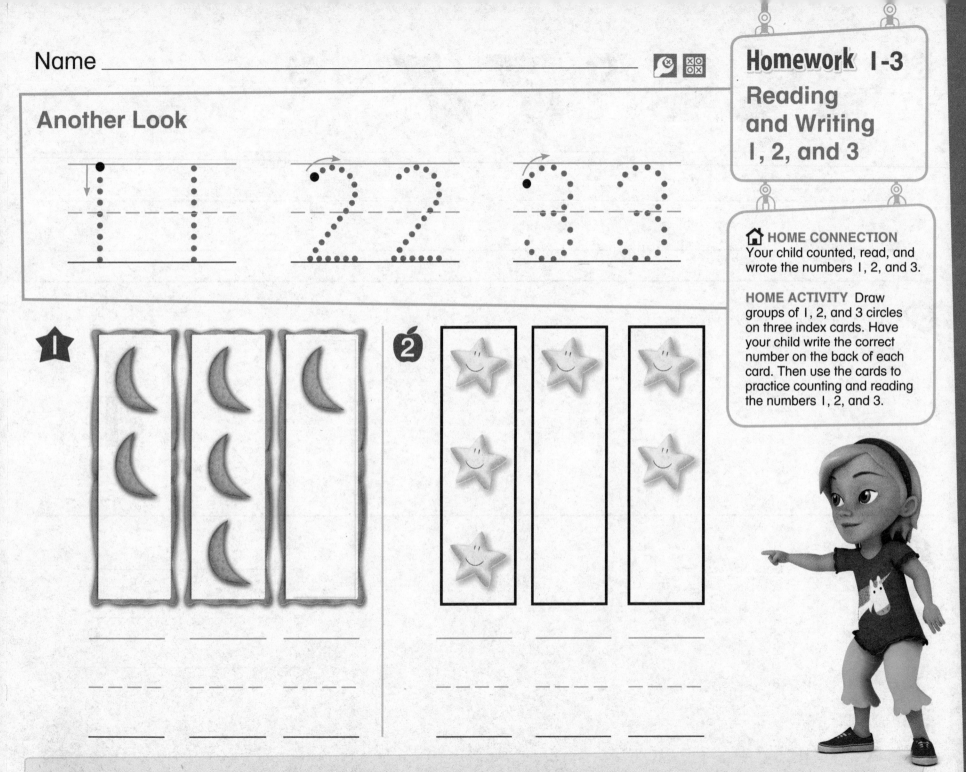

🏠 **HOME CONNECTION**
Your child counted, read, and wrote the numbers 1, 2, and 3.

HOME ACTIVITY Draw groups of 1, 2, and 3 circles on three index cards. Have your child write the correct number on the back of each card. Then use the cards to practice counting and reading the numbers 1, 2, and 3.

Directions Say: *Write each number, and then write each number again.* Then have students: ⭐ count the moons, and then write the number of moons under each picture; 🍎 count the stars, and then write the number of stars under each picture.

3

_____

– – – – – – – – –

_____

4

_____

– – – – – – – – –

_____

5

_____

– – – – – – – – –

_____

6

I

– – – – – – –

7

_____

– – – – – – – – –

_____

Directions Have students: **3**–**5** count the objects, and then practice writing the number that tells how many; **6** draw objects to show the number; **7** draw 2 or 3 objects, and then practice writing the number that tells how many.

Solve & Share   Name _____

Directions Have students place 5 counters in the tree on the workmat. Then, say: *Chips the chipmunk found these nuts. Circle the colored box that shows how many nuts Chips found. Tell how you know you are correct.*

⭐ **TEKS K.2C** Count a set of objects up to at least 20 and demonstrate that the last number said tells the number of objects in the set regardless of their arrangement or order. Also, K.2, K.2A, K.2B. **Mathematical Process Standards** K.1C, K.1D, K.1E, K.1F.

Digital Resources at PearsonTexas.com

Solve   Learn   Glossary   Check   Tools   Games

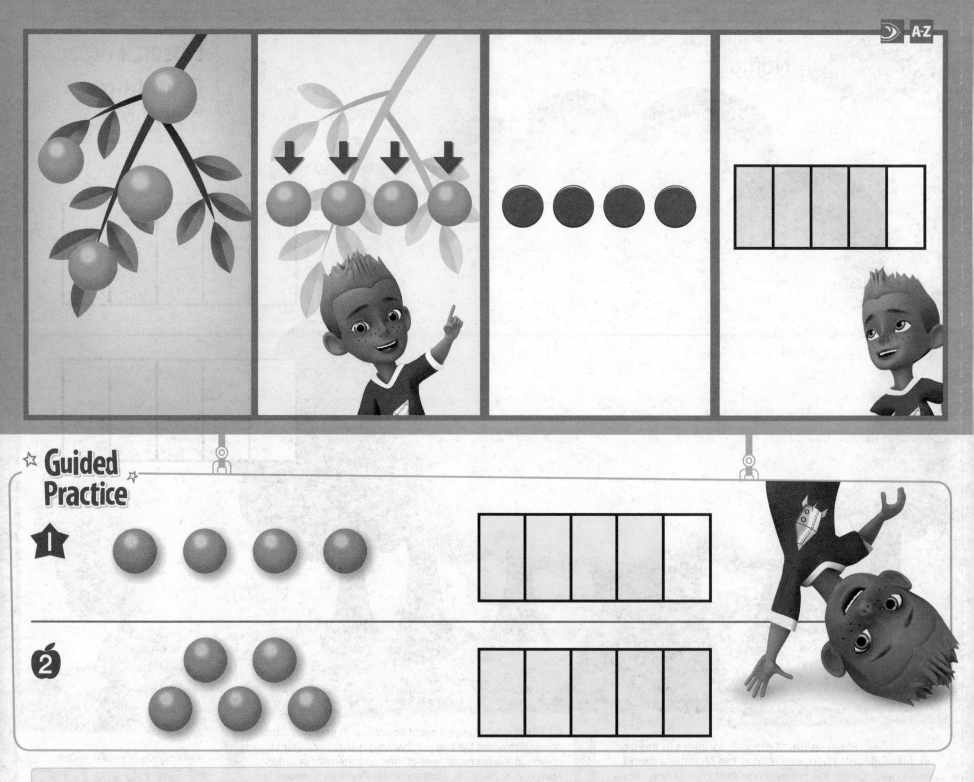

Guided Practice

⭐ 1

⭐ 2

Directions Have students count the oranges, and then color the boxes to show how many.

© Pearson Education, Inc. K

Name _____

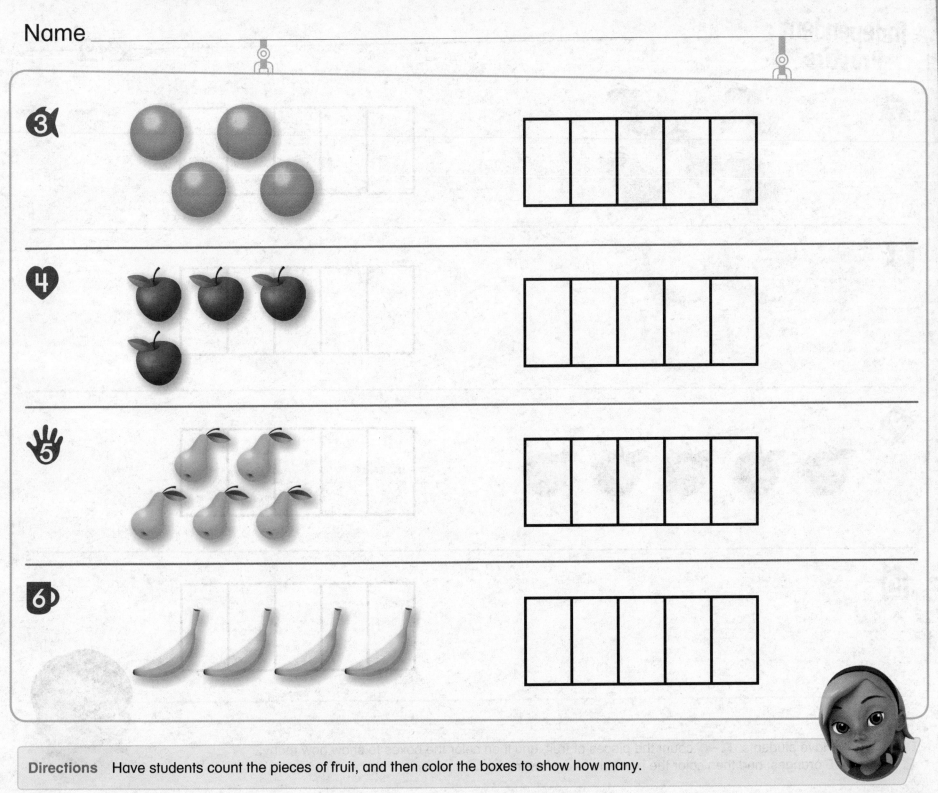

3

4

5

6

Directions Have students count the pieces of fruit, and then color the boxes to show how many.

Topic 1 | Lesson 4   twenty-seven **27**

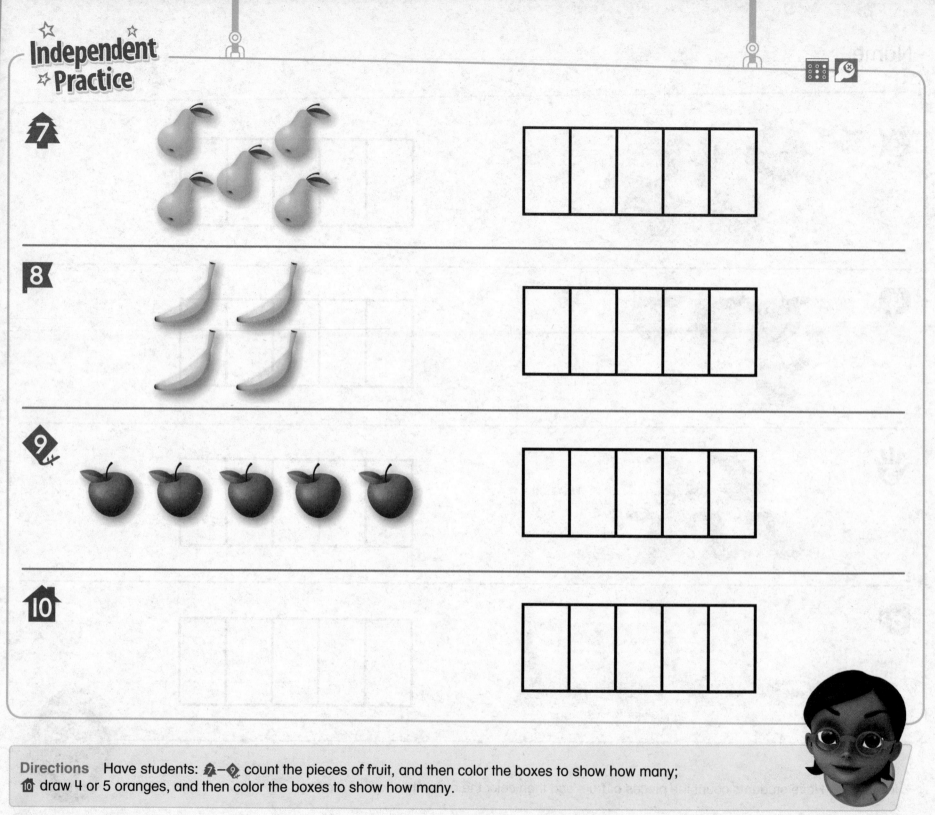

7

8

9

10

Directions Have students: 🌲—◆ count the pieces of fruit, and then color the boxes to show how many; 🏠 draw 4 or 5 oranges, and then color the boxes to show how many.

Topic I | Lesson 4

Name _____

Another Look

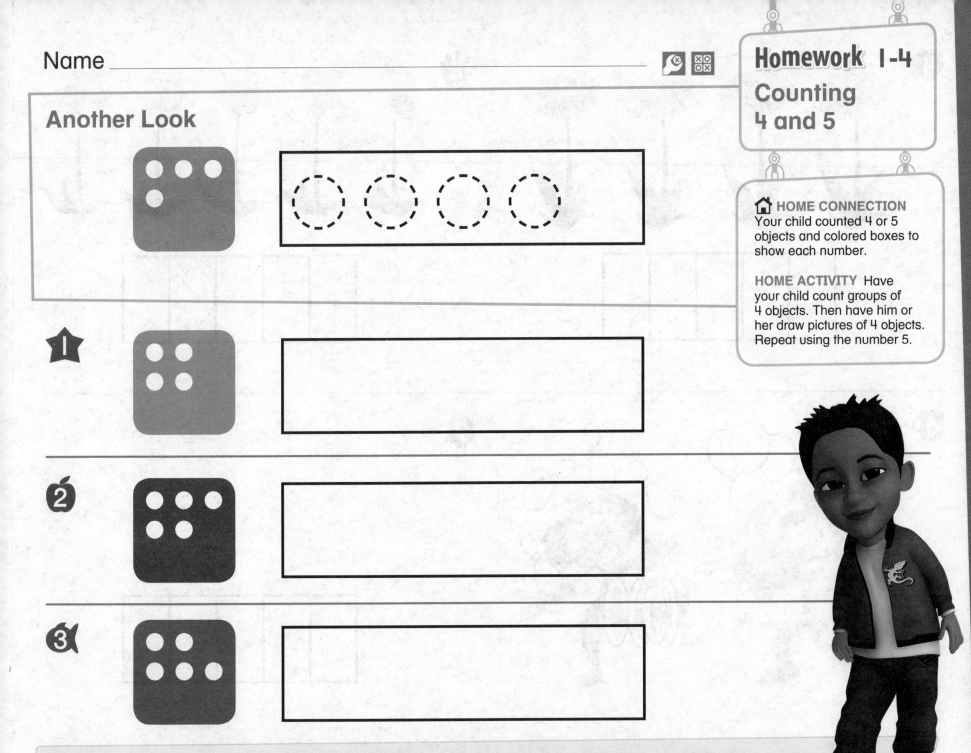

🏠 **HOME CONNECTION**
Your child counted 4 or 5 objects and colored boxes to show each number.

HOME ACTIVITY Have your child count groups of 4 objects. Then have him or her draw pictures of 4 objects. Repeat using the number 5.

Directions Say: *Count the dots and use counters or objects to show that number. Then draw counters in the box to show the same number of dots.* Have students: ★–❸ count the number of dots, use counters or objects to show that number, and then draw counters in the box to show the same number of dots.

Directions Have students: ❤ and ✋ count the number of flowers, and then color the boxes to show how many; ☕ color red each set of 4 items the clowns have and color yellow each set of 5 items the clowns have; 🌲 draw 4 or 5 flowers and color the number of boxes to show how many.

© Pearson Education, Inc. K

Solve & Share Name _____

Directions Say: *5 daisies are in a flowerpot. How can you use counters to show 5 in different ways? Color the daisies red and yellow to show your work. Has the total number of counters changed? Why or why not?*

⭐ **TEKS K.2I** Compose and decompose numbers up to 10 with objects and pictures. Also, K.2. Mathematical Process Standards K.1C, K.1D, K.1F.

Digital Resources at PearsonTexas.com

Solve Learn Glossary Check Tools Games

☆ Guided Practice ☆

1

2

Directions Have students use counters to find these two different ways to make 4, and then color the daisies to show these ways.

Name _____

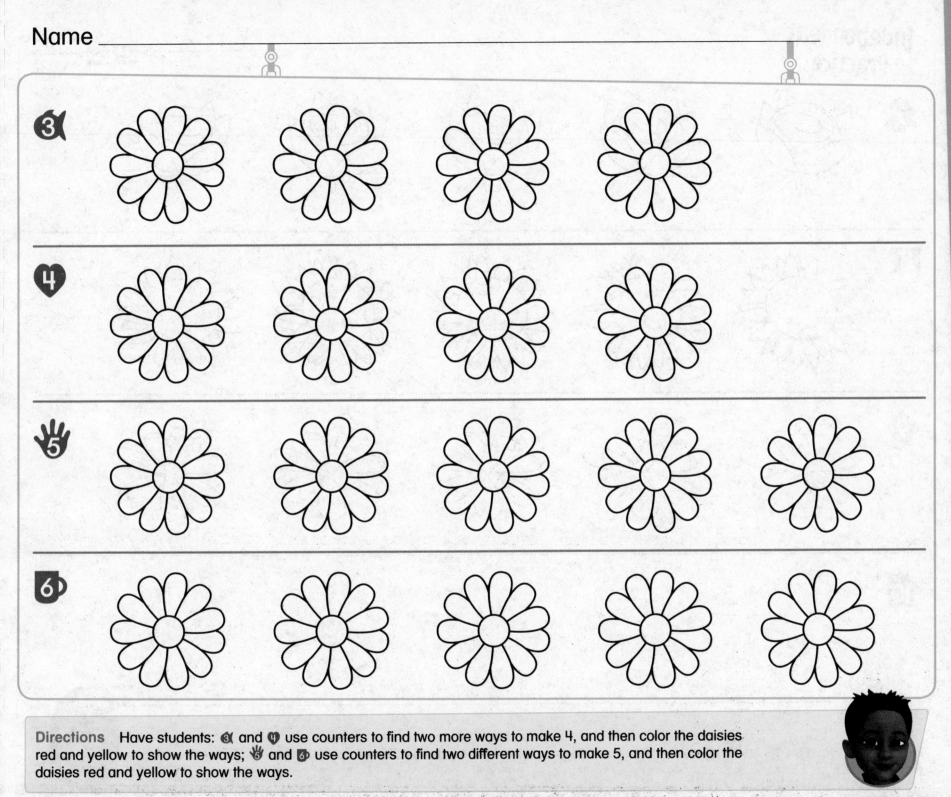

Directions Have students: ③ and ④ use counters to find two more ways to make 4, and then color the daisies red and yellow to show the ways; ✋ and ⑥ use counters to find two different ways to make 5, and then color the daisies red and yellow to show the ways.

Topic 1 | Lesson 5   thirty-three **33**

7

8

9

10

Directions Have students: **7–9** color the flowers red and yellow to show three different ways to make 5; **10** draw another way to make 5.

Another Look

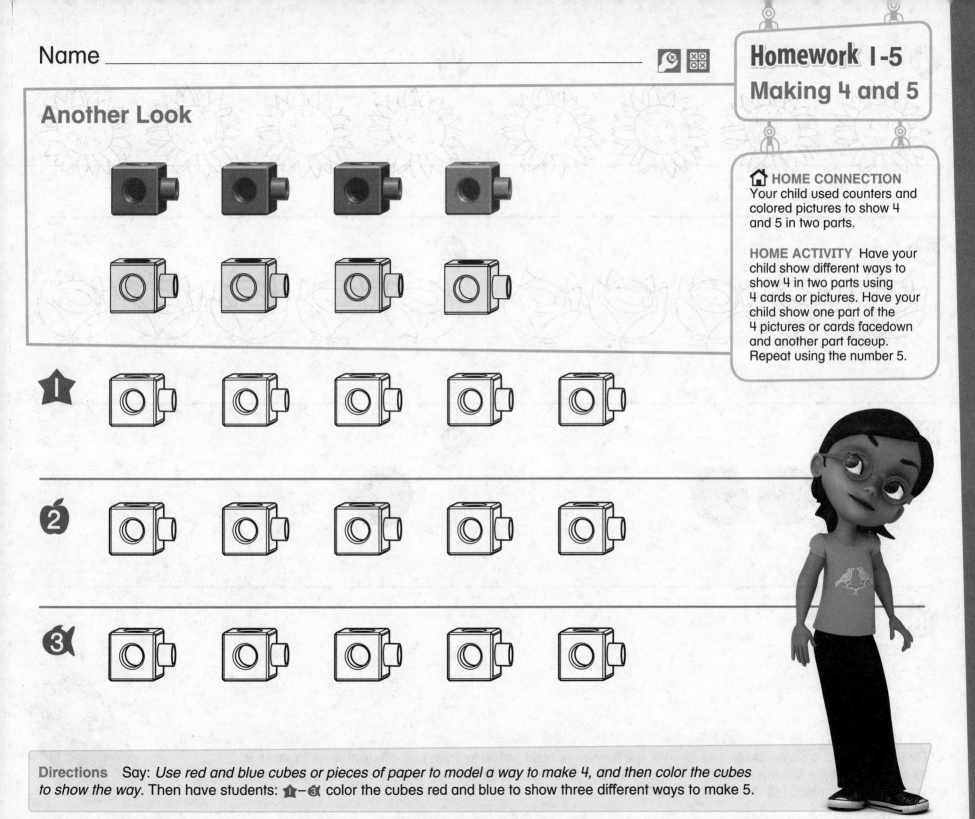

🏠 **HOME CONNECTION**
Your child used counters and colored pictures to show 4 and 5 in two parts.

HOME ACTIVITY Have your child show different ways to show 4 in two parts using 4 cards or pictures. Have your child show one part of the 4 pictures or cards facedown and another part faceup. Repeat using the number 5.

⭐1

🍎2

✫3

Directions Say: *Use red and blue cubes or pieces of paper to model a way to make 4, and then color the cubes to show the way.* Then have students: ⭐–✫ color the cubes red and blue to show three different ways to make 5.

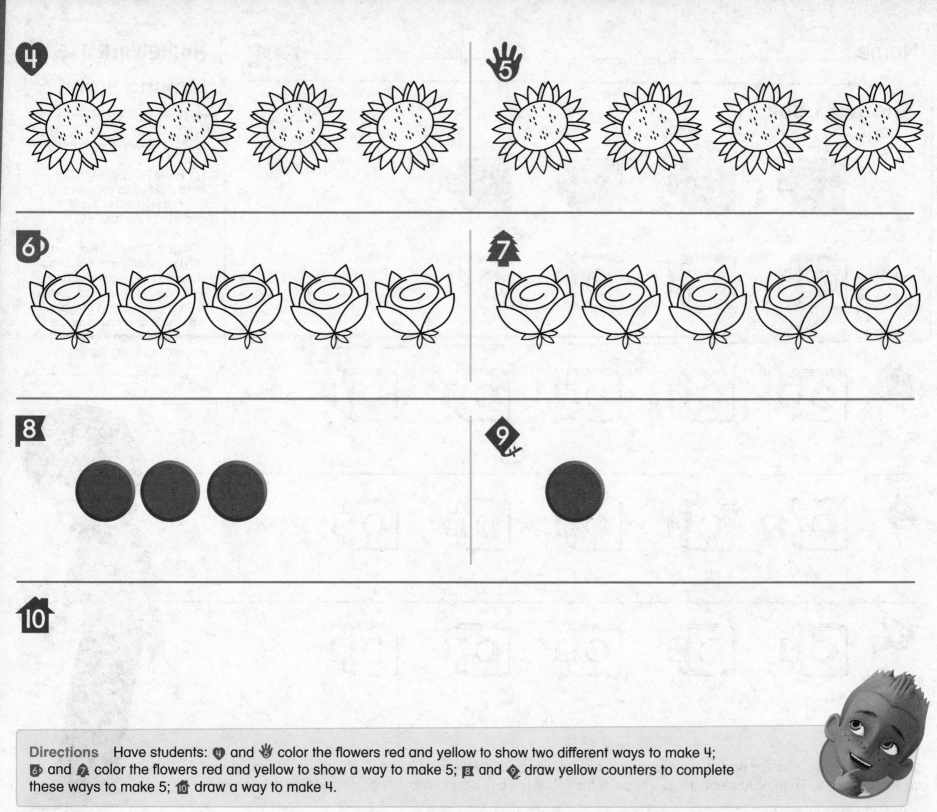

© Pearson Education, Inc. K

Solve & Share Name _____

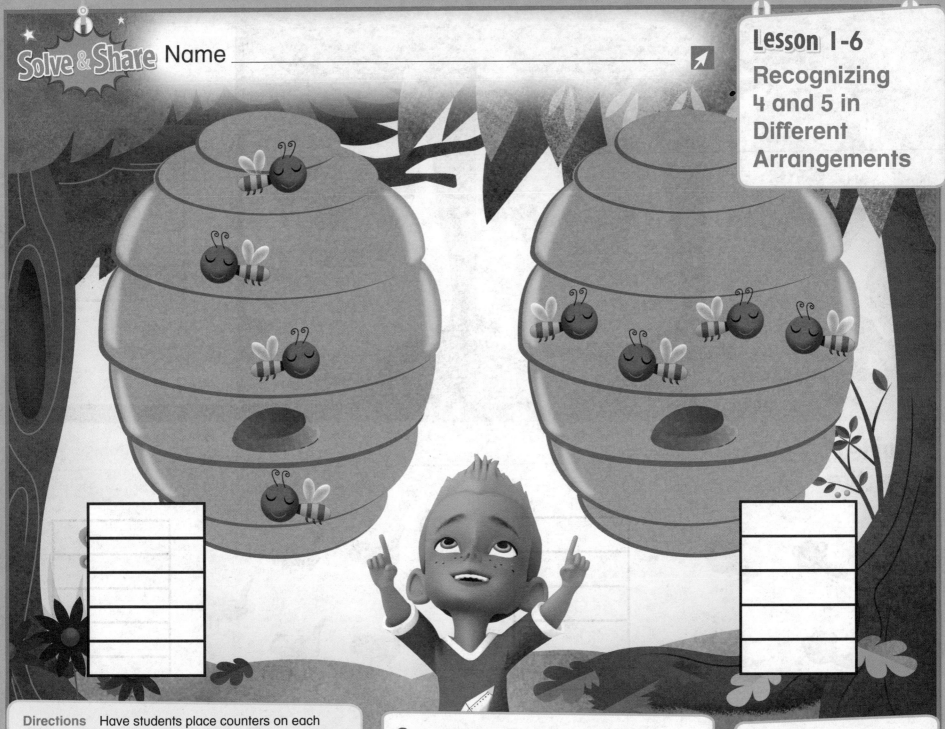

Directions Have students place counters on each bee to show how many bees there are. Then, say: *The beekeeper has 2 hives full of bees. Do the 2 hives have the same or different number of bees flying in front of them? Color the boxes to show how you know.*

⭐ **TEKS K.2D** Recognize instantly the quantity of a small group of objects in organized and random arrangements. Also, K.2, K.2C. **Mathematical Process Standards** K.1C, K.1D, K.1F, K.1G.

Digital Resources at PearsonTexas.com

Solve Learn Glossary Check Tools Games

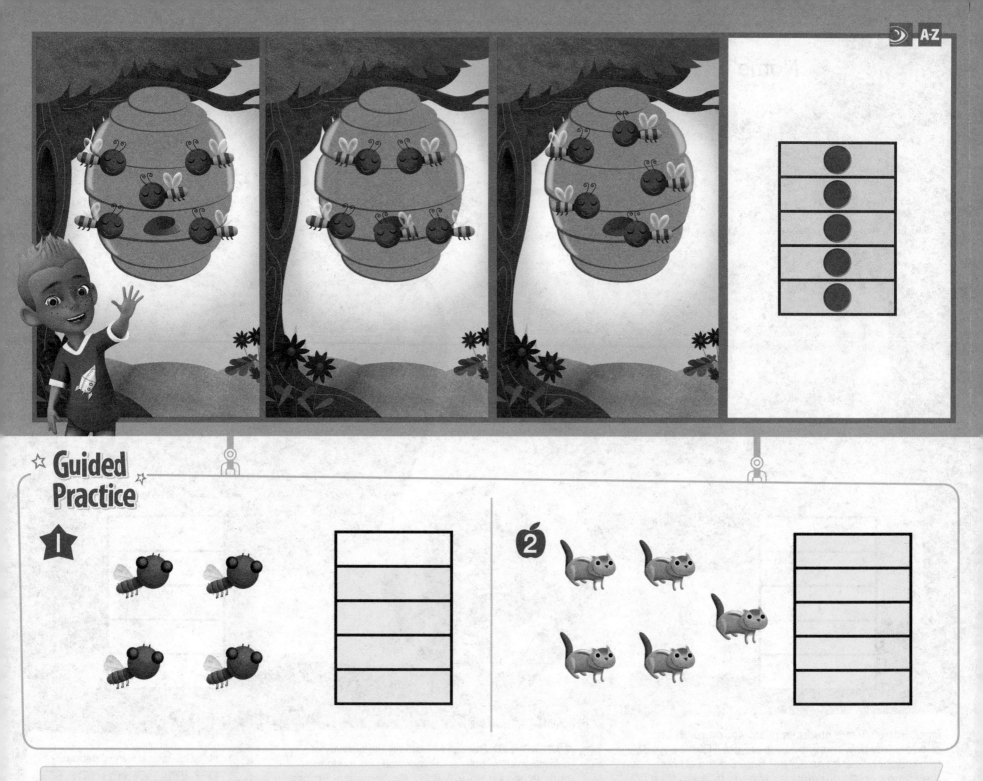

Guided Practice

1

2

Directions Have students place a counter over each animal as they count it, and then color the boxes to show how many.

© Pearson Education, Inc. K

Topic I | **Lesson 6**

Name _____

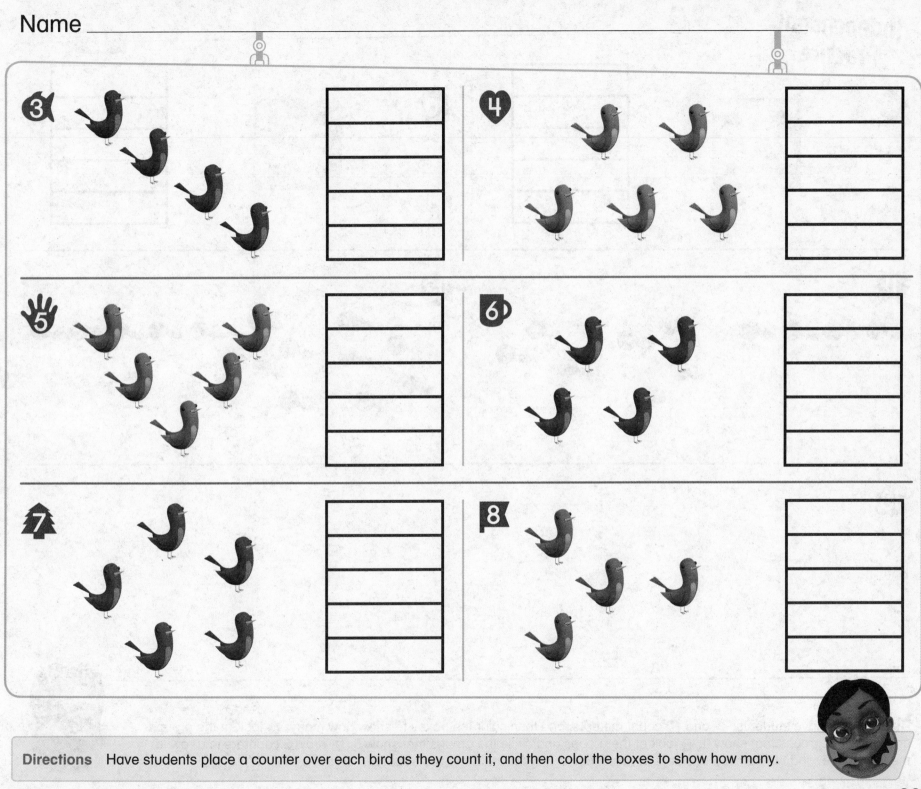

Directions Have students place a counter over each bird as they count it, and then color the boxes to show how many.

Topic 1 | Lesson 6

thirty-nine **39**

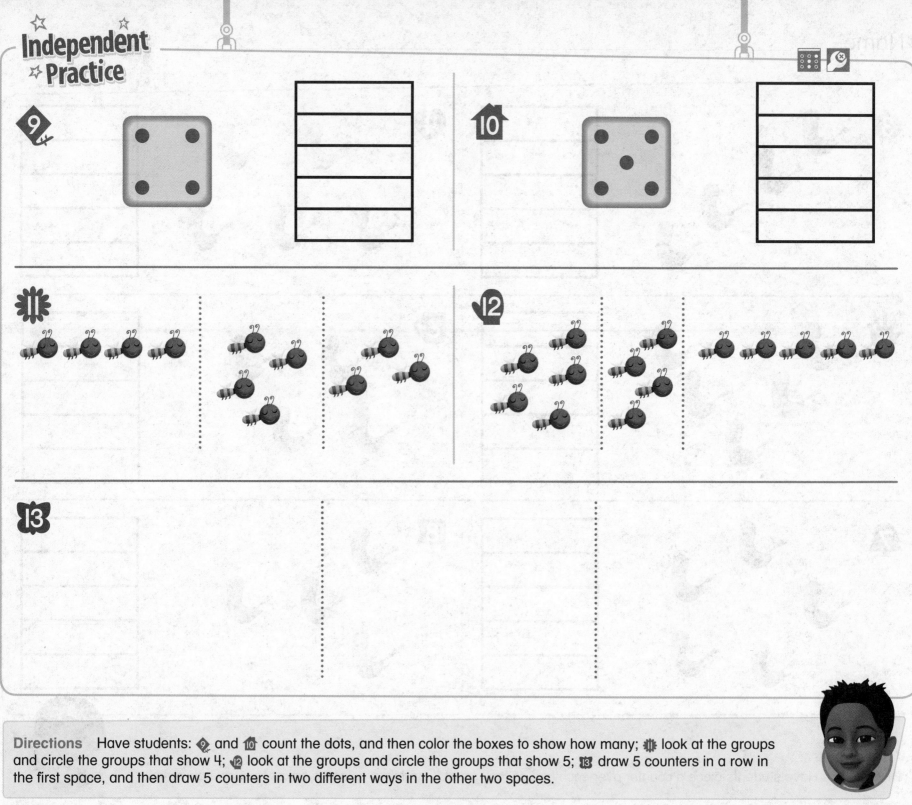

9

10

11

12

13

Directions Have students: **9** and **10** count the dots, and then color the boxes to show how many; **11** look at the groups and circle the groups that show 4; **12** look at the groups and circle the groups that show 5; **13** draw 5 counters in a row in the first space, and then draw 5 counters in two different ways in the other two spaces.

Name _____

Another Look

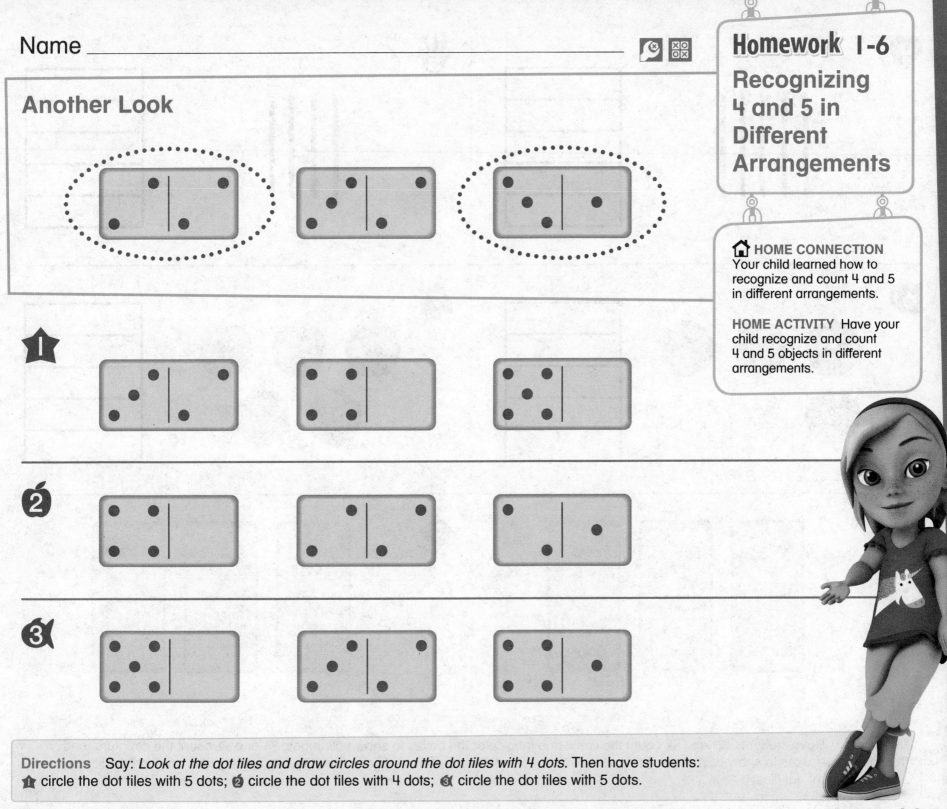

★ 1

② 2

③ 3

Directions Say: *Look at the dot tiles and draw circles around the dot tiles with 4 dots.* Then have students:
★ circle the dot tiles with 5 dots; ② circle the dot tiles with 4 dots; ③ circle the dot tiles with 5 dots.

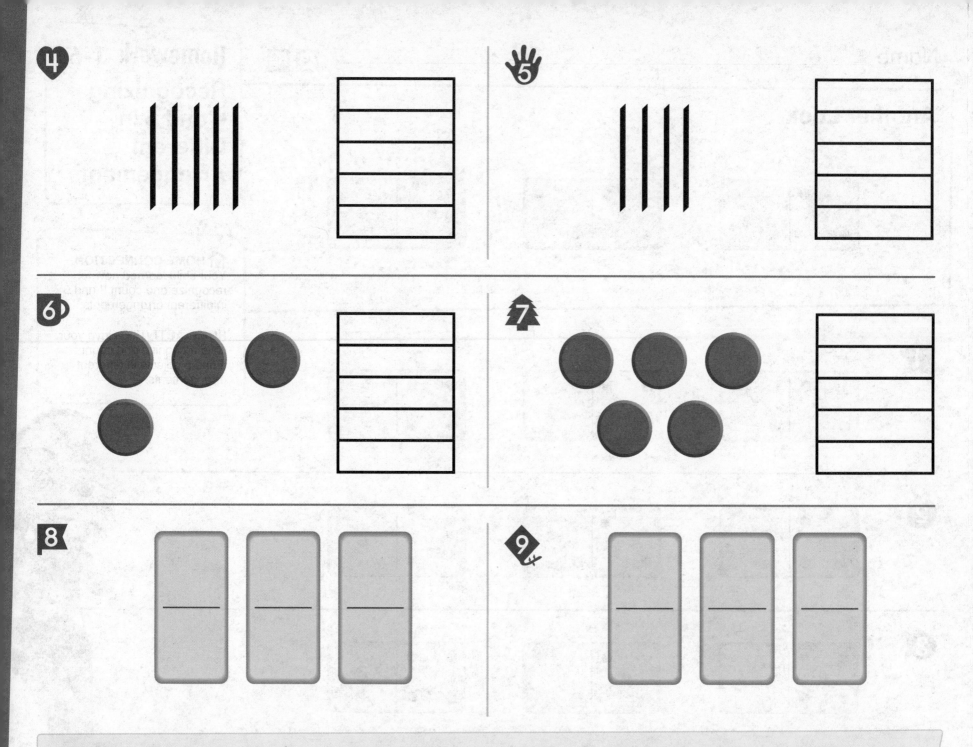

Directions Have students: ♥ and ✋ count the lines, and then color the boxes to show how many; ☕ and 🌲 count the counters, and then color the boxes to show how many; 🏴 draw 4 dots on each dot tile to show 3 different dot tiles; 🔶 draw 5 dots on each dot tile to show 3 different dot tiles.

© Pearson Education, Inc. K

Solve & Share Name _____

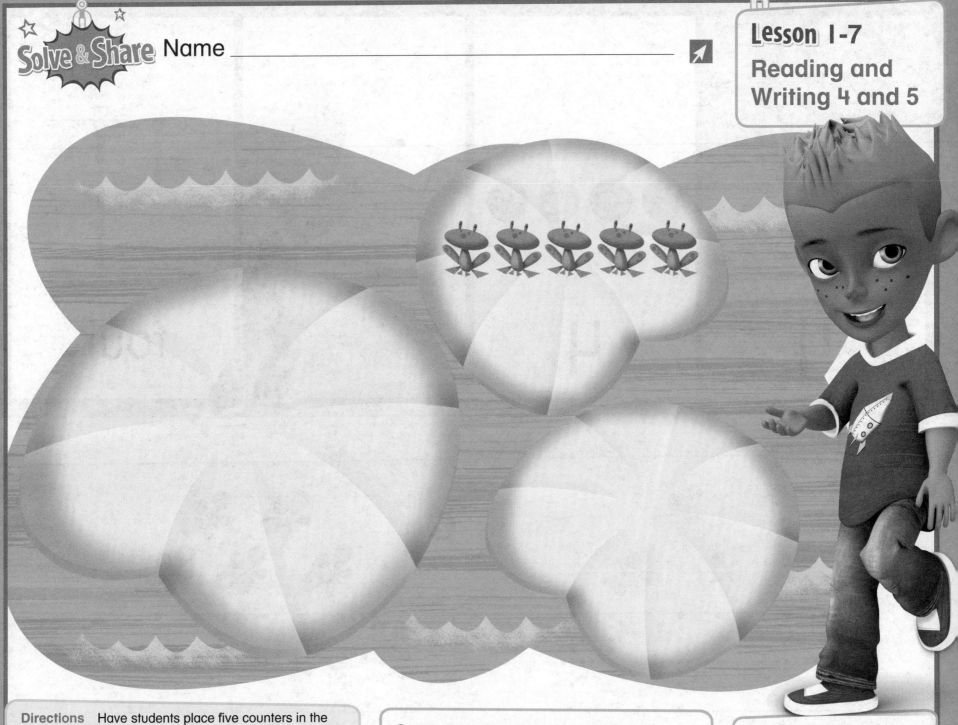

Directions Have students place five counters in the lily pad on the left side of workmat. Then, say: *Alex sees five frogs on the lily pad. He glues pictures of five frogs on one lily pad. How can he show how many frogs in another way? Draw the other way in the empty lily pad.*

⭐ **TEKS K.2B** Read, write, and represent whole numbers from 0 to at least 20 with and without objects or pictures. Also, K.2, K.2C. **Mathematical Process Standards** K.1C, K.1D, K.1F.

Digital Resources at PearsonTexas.com

Solve Learn Glossary Check Tools Games

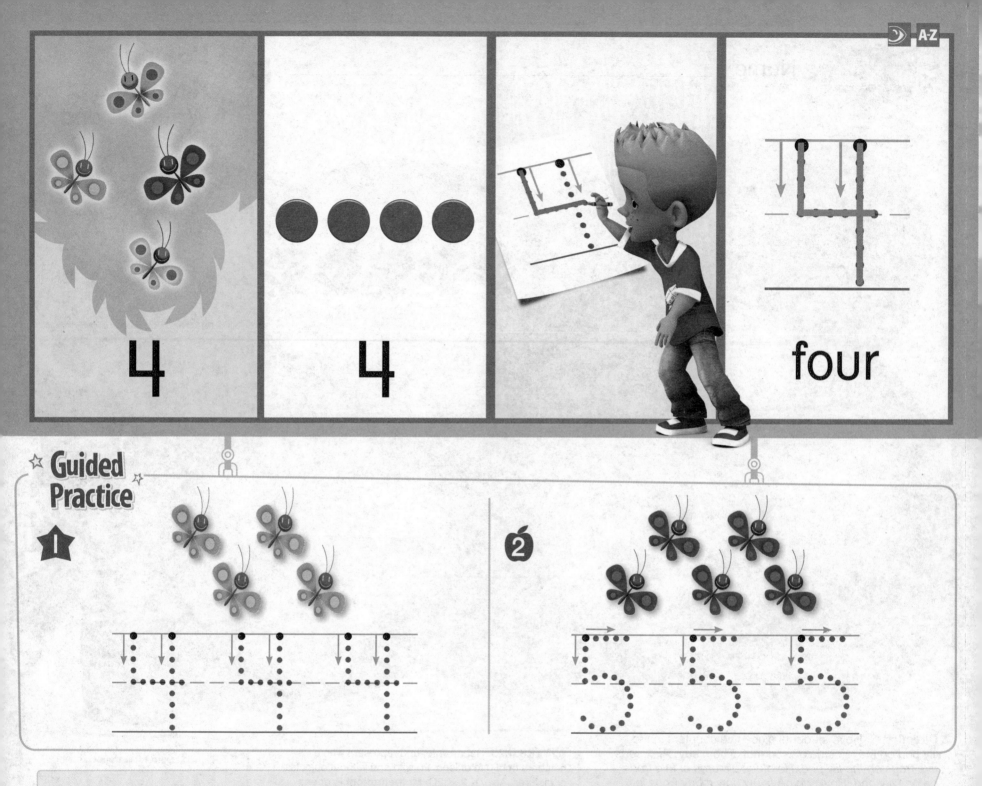

4

4

four

☆ **Guided Practice** ☆

1

2

Directions Have students count the butterflies, and then practice writing the number that tells how many.

© Pearson Education, Inc. K

Name _____

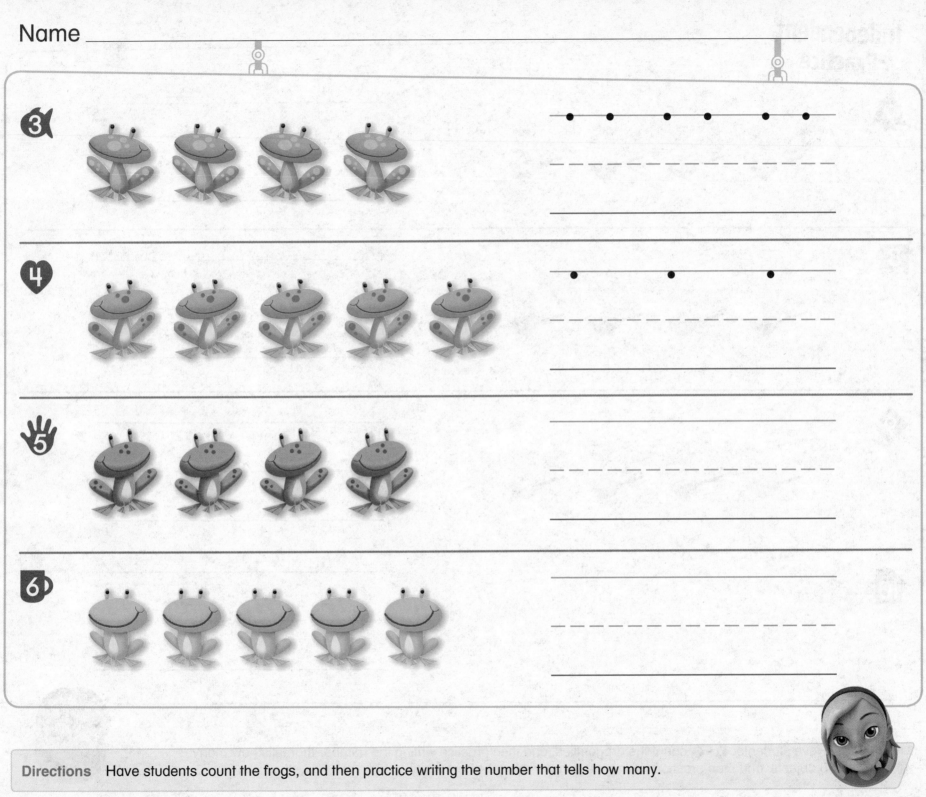

Directions Have students count the frogs, and then practice writing the number that tells how many.

Independent Practice

7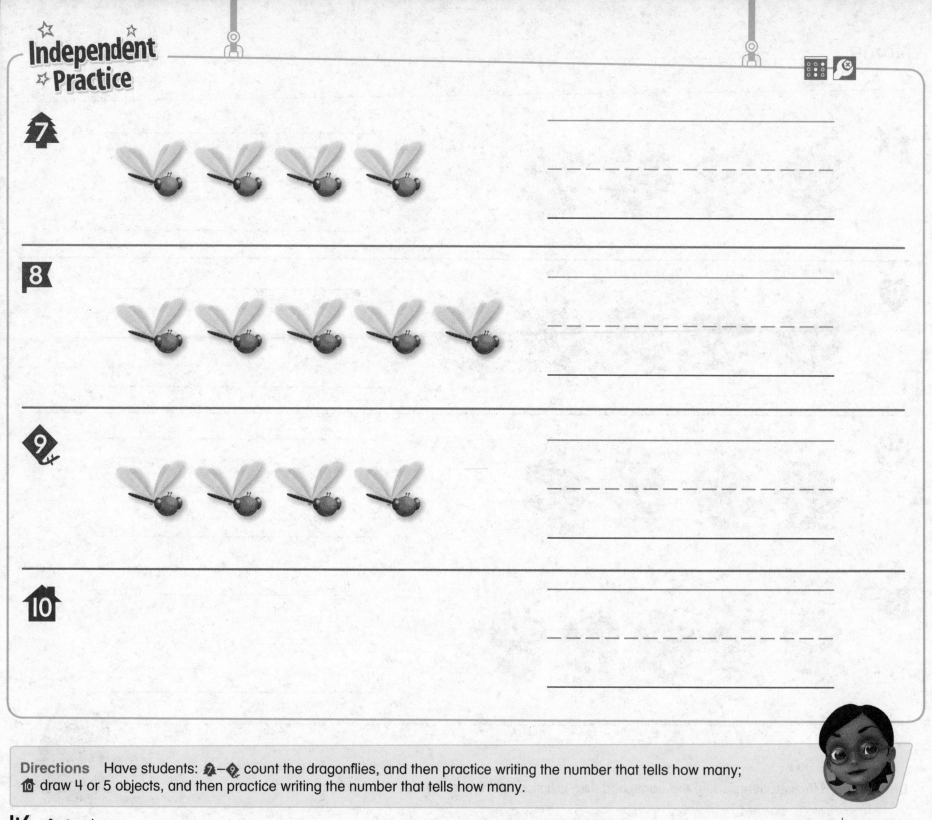

_____

- - - - - - - - - - - -

_____

8

_____

- - - - - - - - - - - -

_____

9

_____

- - - - - - - - - - - -

_____

10

_____

- - - - - - - - - - - -

_____

Directions Have students: **7–9** count the dragonflies, and then practice writing the number that tells how many; **10** draw 4 or 5 objects, and then practice writing the number that tells how many.

© Pearson Education, Inc. K

Name _____

Another Look

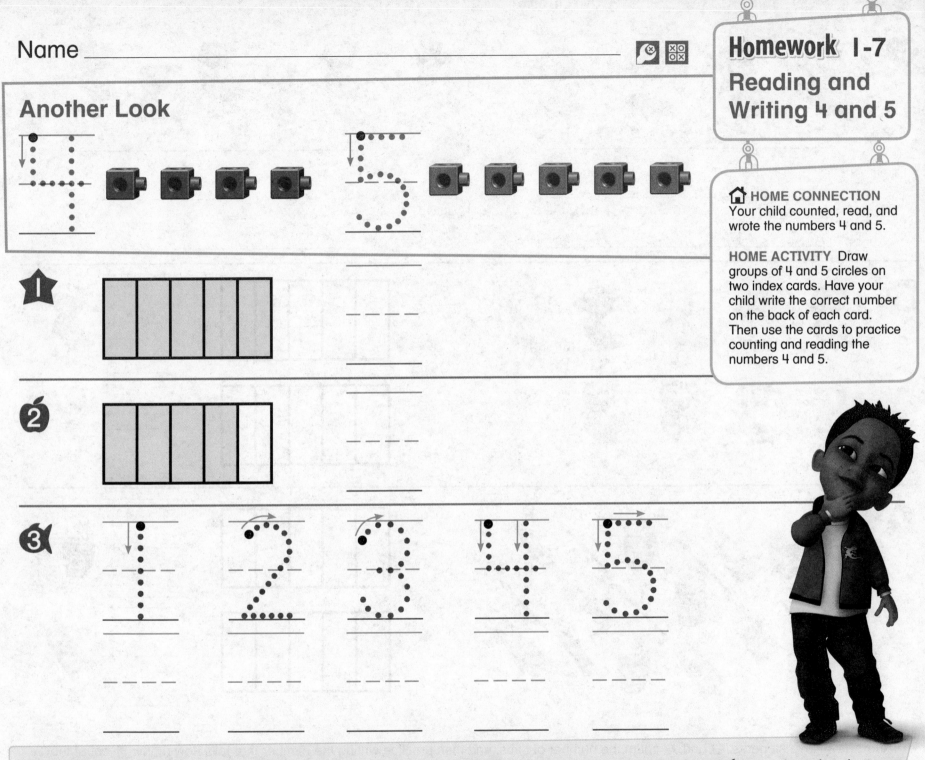

🏠 **HOME CONNECTION**
Your child counted, read, and
wrote the numbers 4 and 5.

HOME ACTIVITY Draw
groups of 4 and 5 circles on
two index cards. Have your
child write the correct number
on the back of each card.
Then use the cards to practice
counting and reading the
numbers 4 and 5.

Directions Say: *Count the cubes, and then write the numbers that tell how many.* Then have students: ⭐ and ❷ count the colored boxes, and then write the number that tells how many; ❸ practice writing the numbers as you count from 1 to 5.

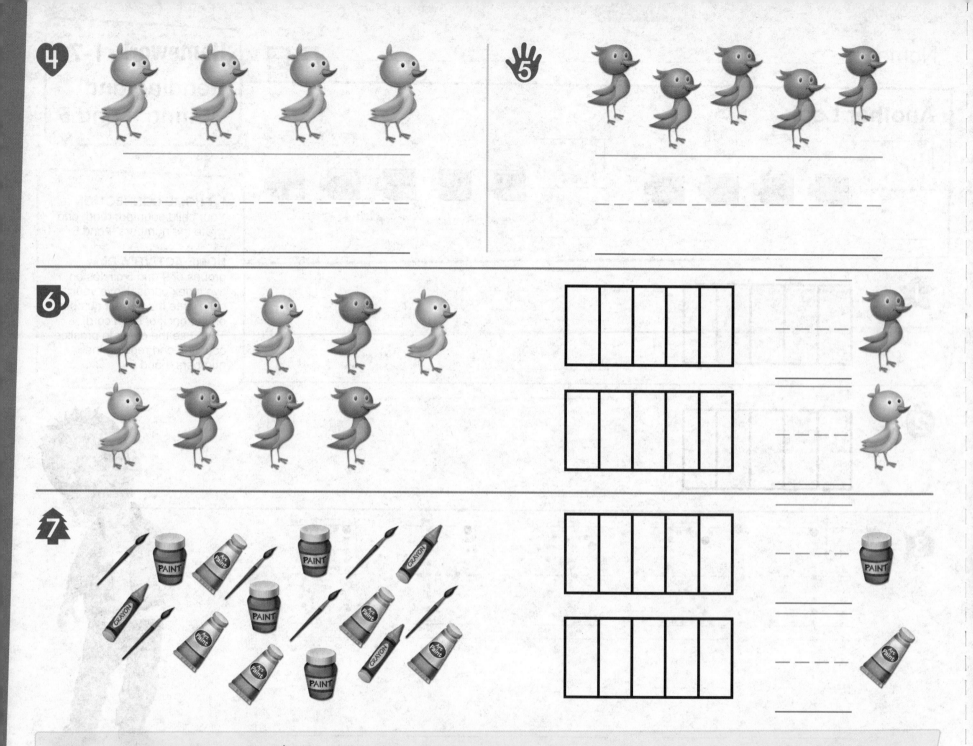

Directions Have students: ❤ and ✋ 5 count the number of birds, and then practice writing the number that tells how many; 6 count the blue birds and the yellow birds, color a box for each bird, and then write the numbers that tell how many; 7 count the tubes of paint and the jars of paint, color a box for each item, and then write the numbers that tell how many.

Name _____

Directions Say: *Alex is in his vegetable garden. He does not see any potatoes in the basket. The basket is empty. How can Alex color the boxes to show there are no potatoes in the basket?*

⭐ **TEKS K.2C** Count a set of objects up to at least 20 and demonstrate that the last number said tells the number of objects in the set regardless of their arrangement or order. Also, K.2, K.2A, K.2B. **Mathematical Process Standards** K.1A, K.1C, K.1D.

Digital Resources at PearsonTexas.com

Solve   Learn   Glossary   Check   Tools   Games

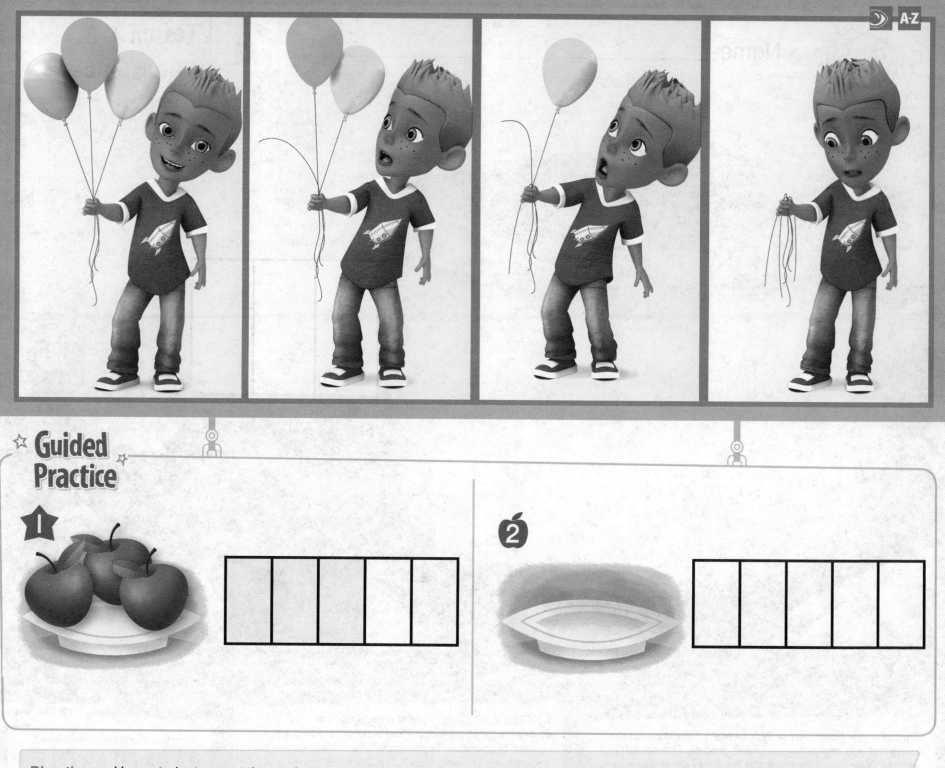

☆ Guided Practice ☆

1

2

Directions Have students count the apples on each plate, and then color the boxes to show how many.

Topic 1 | Lesson 8

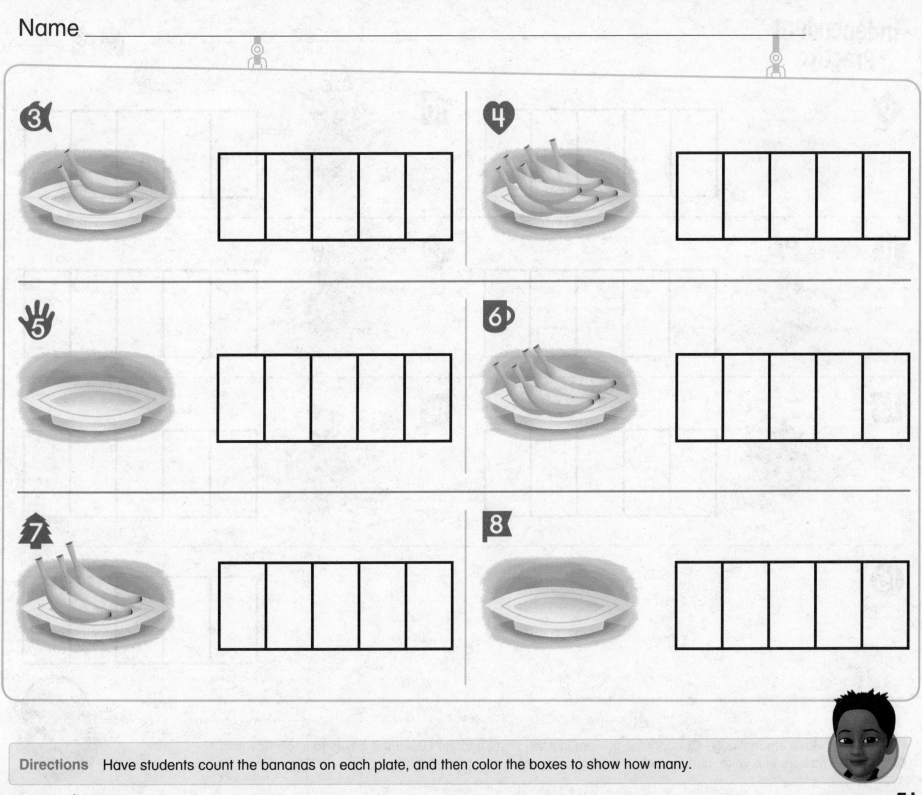

Directions Have students count the bananas on each plate, and then color the boxes to show how many.

Independent Practice

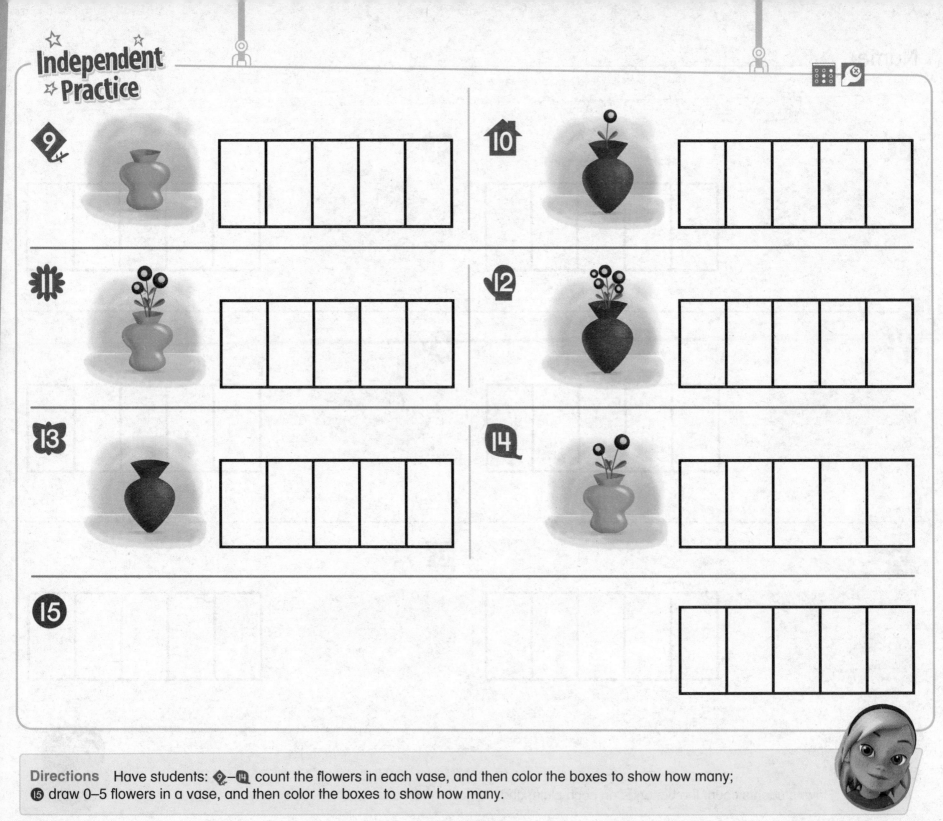

Directions Have students: 9–14 count the flowers in each vase, and then color the boxes to show how many; 15 draw 0–5 flowers in a vase, and then color the boxes to show how many.

52 fifty-two   © Pearson Education, Inc. K   **Topic I** | Lesson 8

Another Look

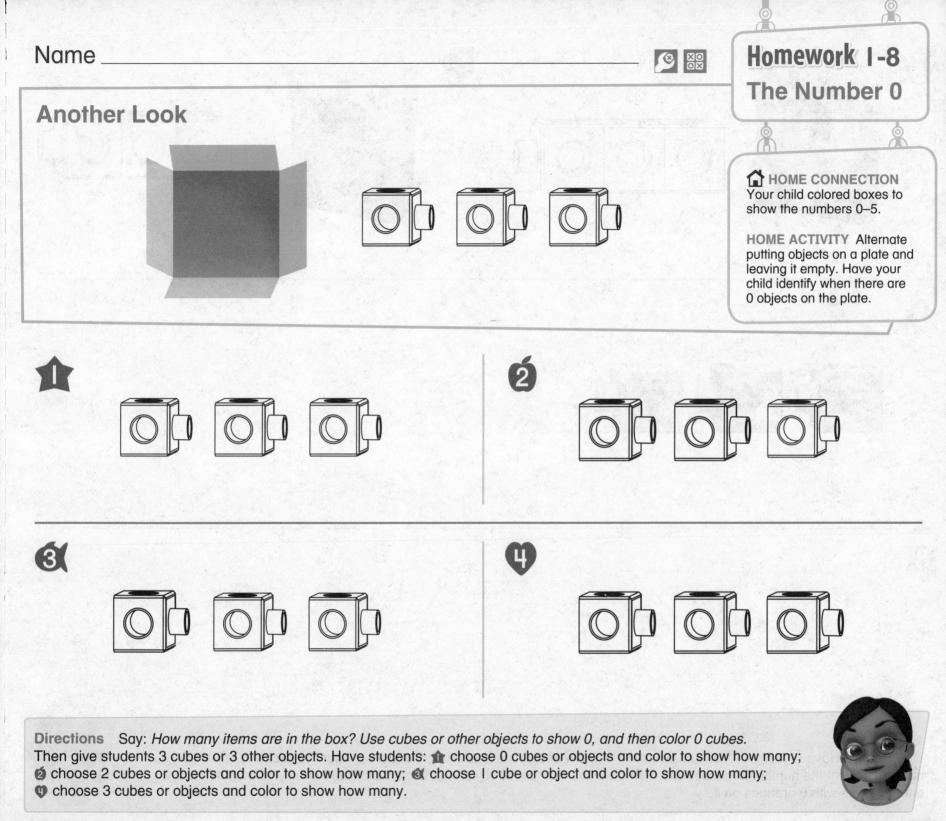

🏠 **HOME CONNECTION**
Your child colored boxes to show the numbers 0–5.

HOME ACTIVITY Alternate putting objects on a plate and leaving it empty. Have your child identify when there are 0 objects on the plate.

Directions Say: *How many items are in the box? Use cubes or other objects to show 0, and then color 0 cubes.*
Then give students 3 cubes or 3 other objects. Have students: ⭐ choose 0 cubes or objects and color to show how many;
❷ choose 2 cubes or objects and color to show how many; ❸ choose 1 cube or object and color to show how many;
❹ choose 3 cubes or objects and color to show how many.

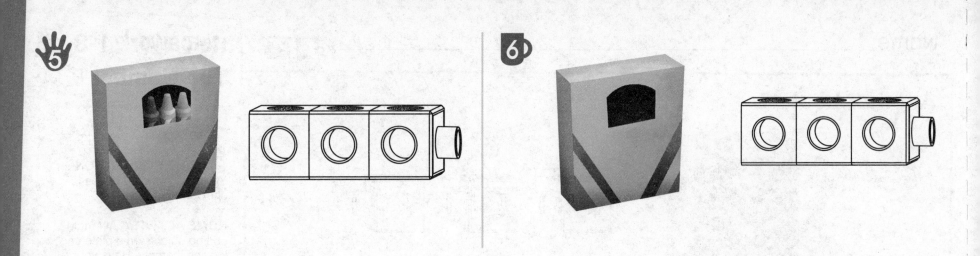

5

6

7

8

Directions   Have students: **5** and **6** count the number of crayons in each box, and then color the cubes to show how many; **7** count the number of cubes, and then draw that number of objects; **8** draw a plate with oranges, and then draw another plate with 0 oranges on it.

© Pearson Education, Inc. K

Solve & Share   Name _____

Directions Say: *Alex does not see any pencils. How can he use a number to show no pencils, or none?*

★ **TEKS K.2B** Read, write, and represent whole numbers from 0 to at least 20 with and without objects or pictures. Also, K.2, K.2C. **Mathematical Process Standards** K.1C, K.1D, K.1F.

Digital Resources at PearsonTexas.com

Solve Learn Glossary Check Tools Games

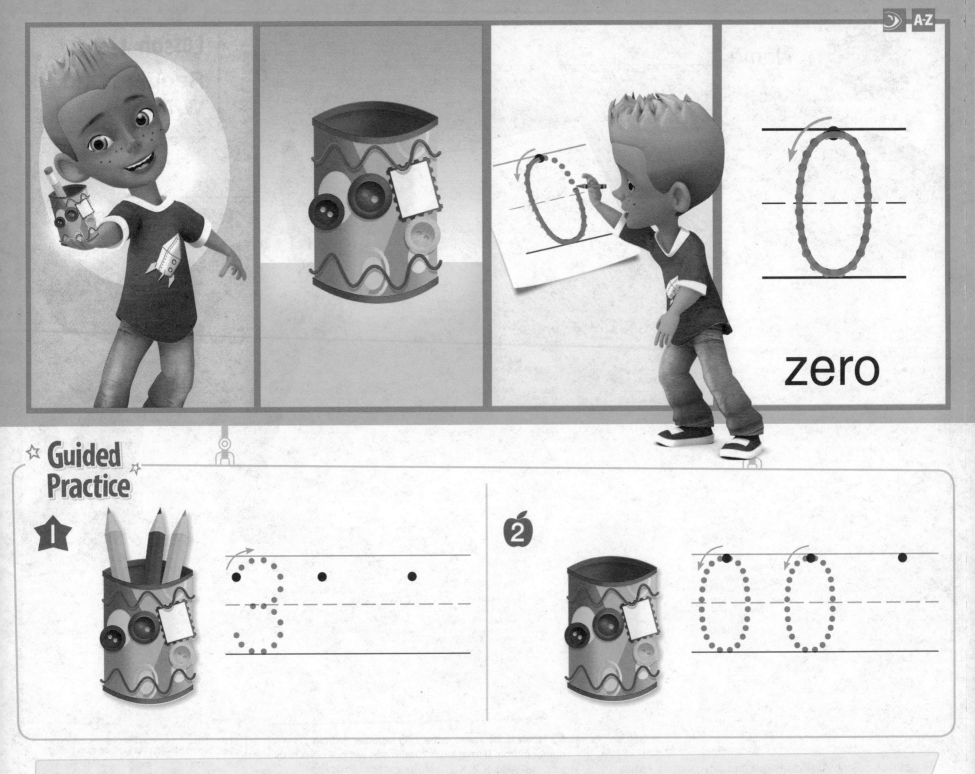

zero

☆ Guided Practice ☆

1

2

Directions Have students count the pencils in each pencil holder, and then practice writing the number that tells how many.

© Pearson Education, Inc. K

Name _____

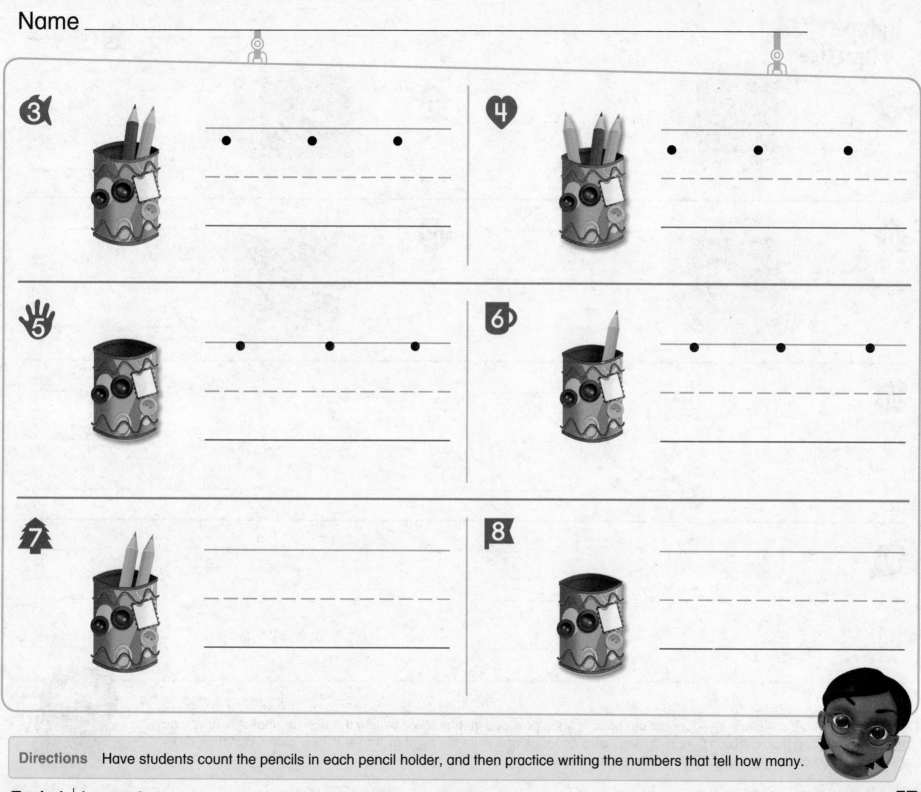

③ •   •   •

④ •   •   •

✋5 •   •   •

6 •   •   •

7

8

Directions Have students count the pencils in each pencil holder, and then practice writing the numbers that tell how many.

Topic 1 | Lesson 9

fifty-seven **57**

9

10

11

12

13

14

Directions Have students: 9—12 count the balls in each box, and then practice writing the number that tells how many; 13 practice writing the numbers 0 to 5; 14 draw zero counters and write the number that tells how many, and then draw 1 to 5 counters and write the number that tells how many.

© Pearson Education, Inc. K

Topic 1 | Lesson 9

Another Look

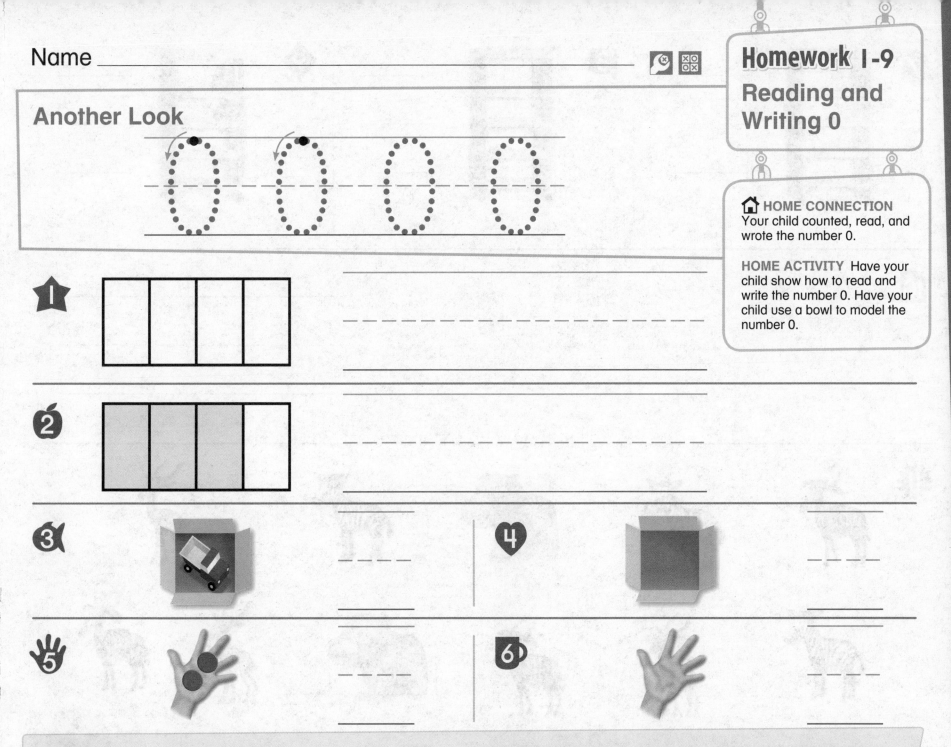

Directions Say: *Practice writing the number 0.* Then have students: ⭐ and 🍎 count the colored boxes, and then practice writing the number that tells how many; 🔷 and 💜 count the trucks in the box, and then write the number that tells how many; ✋ and ☕ count the counters in the hand, and then write the number that tells how many.

© Pearson Education, Inc. K

Topic 1 | Lesson 9

Directions Have students: ⑦–⑨ count the books on the bookshelf, and then write the number that tells how many; ⑩ draw 0 to 5 objects, and then practice writing the number that tells how many; ⑪ circle each animal that has 0 horns and draw Xs on each animal that has 0 stripes.

Solve & Share

Name _____

Directions Say: *Alex needs to count the group of shapes. How can you use counters to help him count these shapes? Write the number that tells how many shapes.*

TEKS K.1C Select tools, including real objects, manipulatives ... and techniques, including mental math, ... and number sense as appropriate, to solve problems. Also, **K.2. Mathematical Process Standards** K.1B, K.1D, K.1F.

Digital Resources at PearsonTexas.com

Solve | Learn | Glossary | Check | Tools | Games

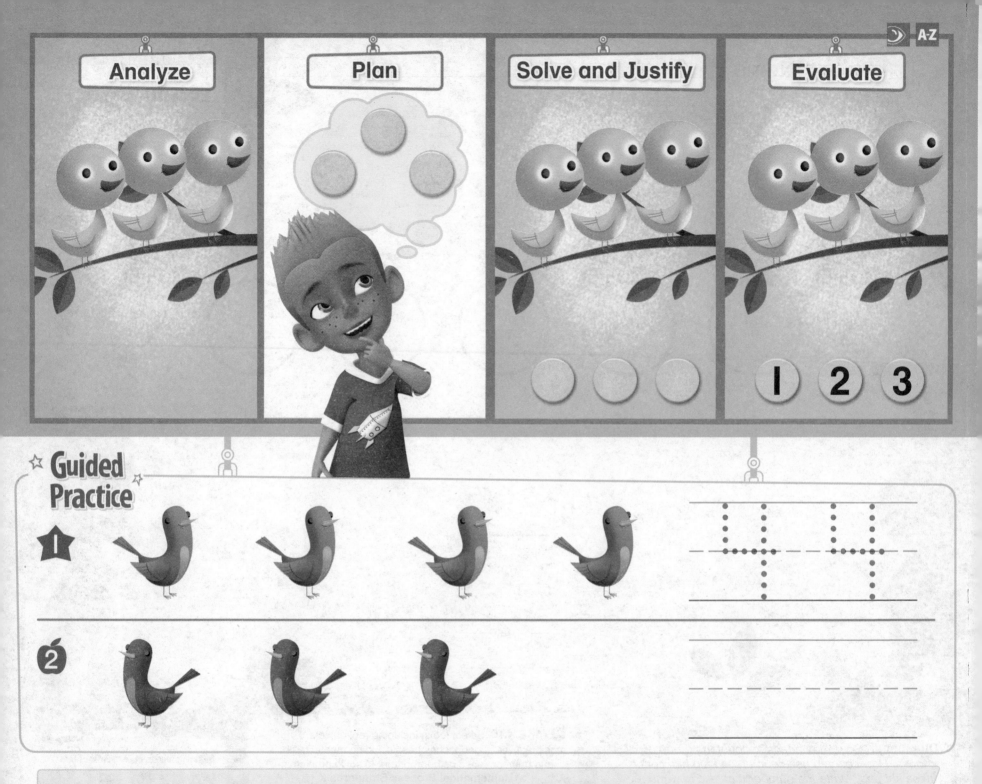

1 2 3

☆ Guided ☆
Practice

1

2

Directions Have students place a counter over each bird as they count it, and then practice writing the number that tells how many.

3

4

5

6

Directions Have students place a counter over each leaf as they count it, and then practice writing the number that tells how many.

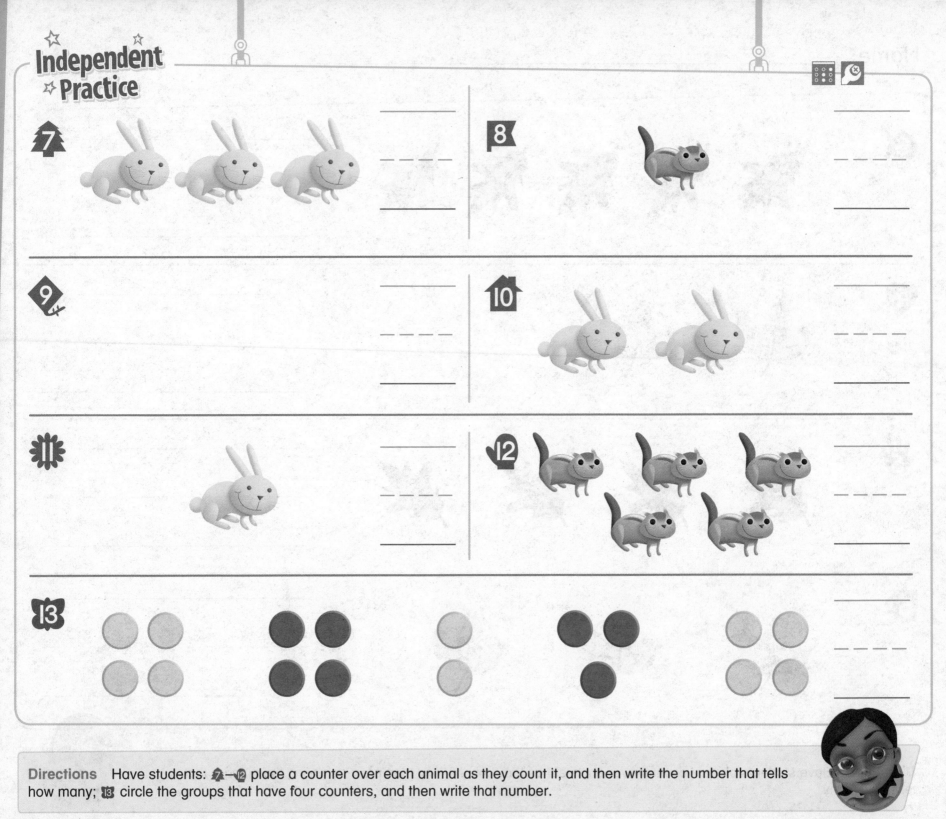

7 _____

8 _____

9 _____

10 _____

⚛ _____

12 _____

13 _____

Directions Have students: **7**—**12** place a counter over each animal as they count it, and then write the number that tells how many; **13** circle the groups that have four counters, and then write that number.

© Pearson Education, Inc. K

Name _____

Another Look

🏠 **HOME CONNECTION**
Your child used counters to count groups of up to 5 objects.

HOME ACTIVITY Place a row of up to 5 cups in front of your child. Have your child use coins to count the number of cups by dropping a coin in each cup. Repeat with different numbers of cups up to 5.

⭐ 1

🍎 2

🐟 3

Directions Say: *Place a counter or object over the chipmunk, and then practice writing the number that tells how many.* Then have students: ⭐–🐟 *place a counter or object on each chipmunk as they count it, and then write the number that tells how many.*

4 _____

_ _ _ _

_____

5 _____

_ _ _ _

6 _____

_ _ _ _

_____

7 _ _ _ _

_____

_ _ _ _

_____

8

Directions Have students: **4–6** place a counter or object over each acorn as they count it, and then write the number that tells how many; **7** use counters or objects to help find how many squirrels and how many acorns, and then write the numbers that tell how many next to the correct picture; **8** draw 1 to 5 objects in three different ways.

© Pearson Education, Inc. K

Set A

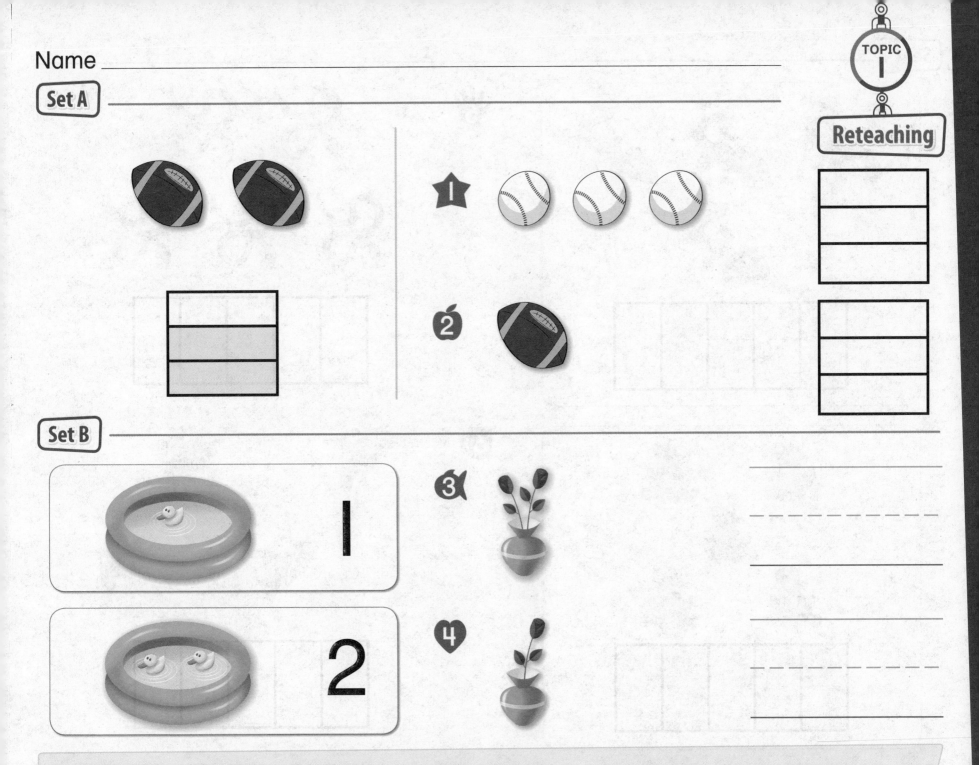

⭐ 1

🍎 2

Set B

1

2

★ 3

❤ 4

Directions Use digital tools to solve these and other Reteaching problems. Have students: ⭐ and 🍎 count the balls, and then color the boxes to show how many; ★ and ❤ count the flowers in the vase, and then practice writing the number that tells how many.

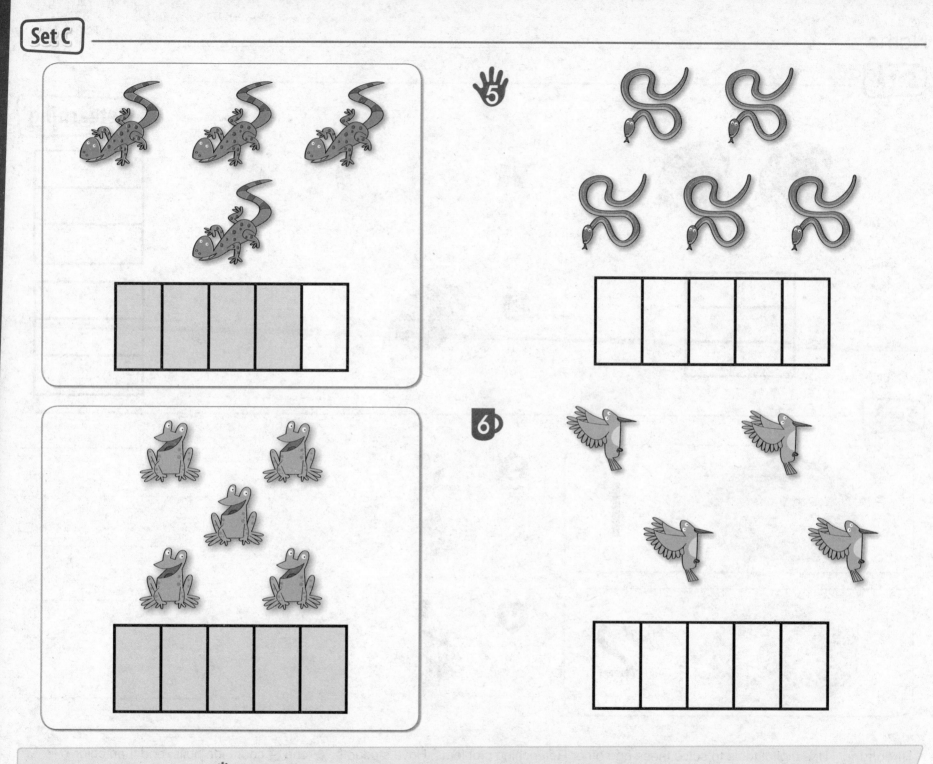

Directions Have students: 🖐 and ☕ count the animals, and then color the boxes to show how many.

© Pearson Education, Inc. K

Name _____

_____

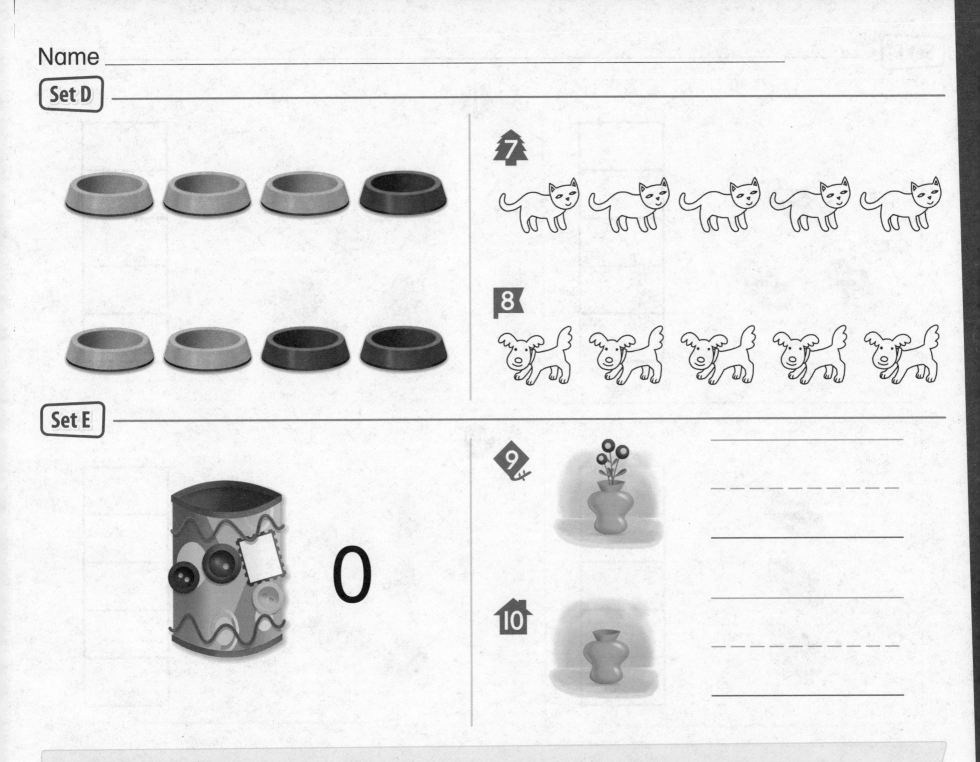

7

8

0

9

10

Directions Have students: 7 and 8 use red and yellow crayons to color the animals two different ways to make 5, and then tell what parts make 5; 9 and 10 count the flowers in the vase, and then practice writing the number that tells how many.

✳

〈12

Directions Have students: ✳ and 〈12 count the octopuses, and then color the boxes to show how many.

70 seventy © Pearson Education, Inc. K **Topic I**

⭐ 1

○ 🌷🌷

○ 🌷🌷🌷

○ 🌷🌷🌷🌷

○ 🌷🌷🌷🌷🌷

🍎 2

○ 5 🍃🍃🍃🍃🍃

○ 2 🍃🍃

○ 3 🍃🍃🍃

○ 4 🍃🍃🍃🍃

3

🍐🍐🍐🍐🍐

1	3	4	5
○	○	○	○

Directions Have students mark the best answer. ⭐ Which shows 4 flowers? 🍎 Which shows the number two?
3 How many pears are there?

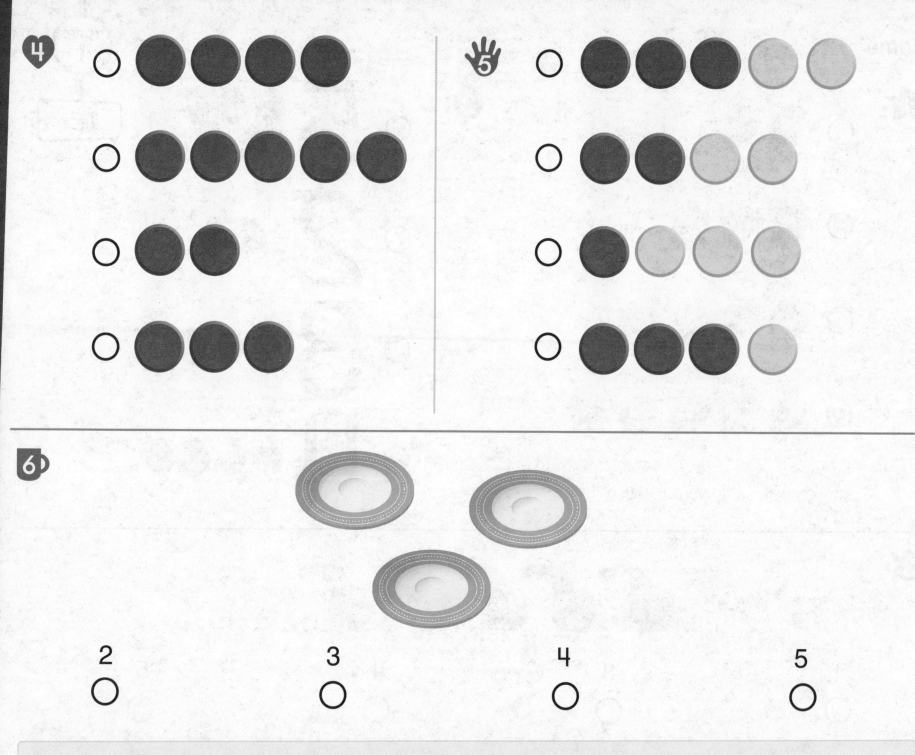

4

○ ⬤ ⬤ ⬤ ⬤

○ ⬤ ⬤ ⬤ ⬤ ⬤

○ ⬤ ⬤

○ ⬤ ⬤ ⬤

5

○ ⬤ ⬤ ⬤ ⚪ ⚪

○ ⬤ ⬤ ⚪ ⚪

○ ⬤ ⚪ ⚪ ⚪

○ ⬤ ⬤ ⬤ ⚪

6

2   3   4   5
○   ○   ○   ○

© Pearson Education, Inc. K

Topic 1

Name _____

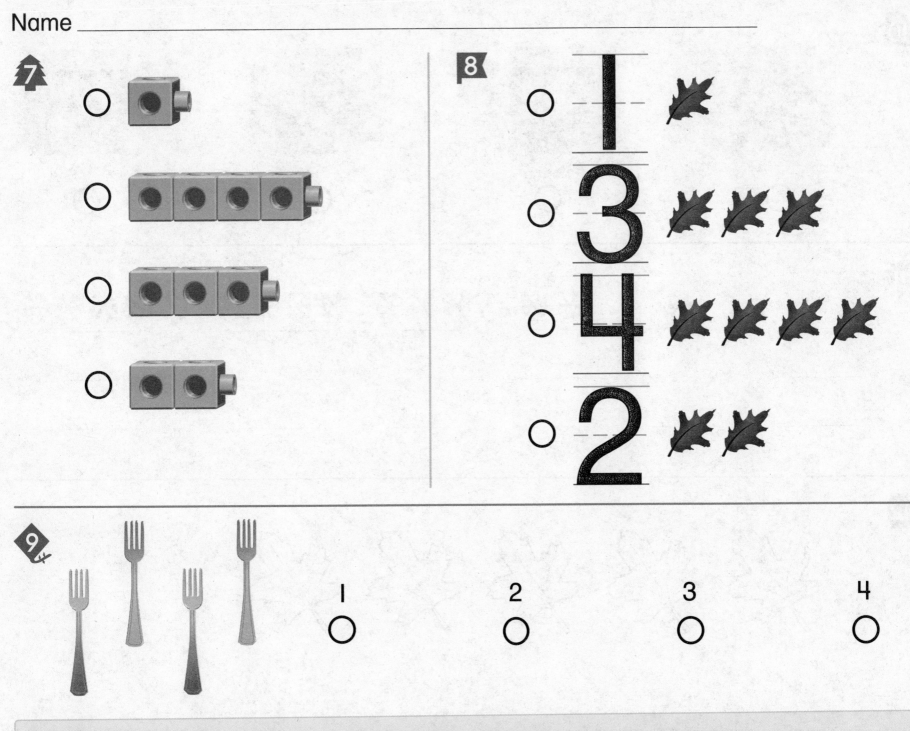

Directions Have students mark the best answer. Which shows 3 cubes? Which shows the number one? How many forks are there?

10

○   ○   ○   ○

❄

❄   ❄❄   ❄❄❄   ❄❄❄❄   ❄❄❄❄❄

_____   _____   _____   _____   _____

- - - - - - - - - - - - - - - - - - - - - - - - - - - - - -

_____   _____   _____   _____   _____

12

TOPIC 2

Comparing Numbers 0 to 5

Essential Question: How can numbers from 0 to 5 be compared and ordered?

Math and Science Project: Comparing Seeds and Plants

Directions Read the character speech bubbles to students. **Find Out!** Have students find out how seeds grow into plants. Say: *Not every seed grows into a plant. Even with lots of care, some seeds won't grow. Talk to your friends and relatives about how seeds grow. Ask if they ever planted a seed that never grew into a plant.* **Journal: Make a Poster** Then have students make a poster that shows more seeds than plants that grow. Have them use up to 5 seeds. Have them compare the number of seeds and plants.

Name _____

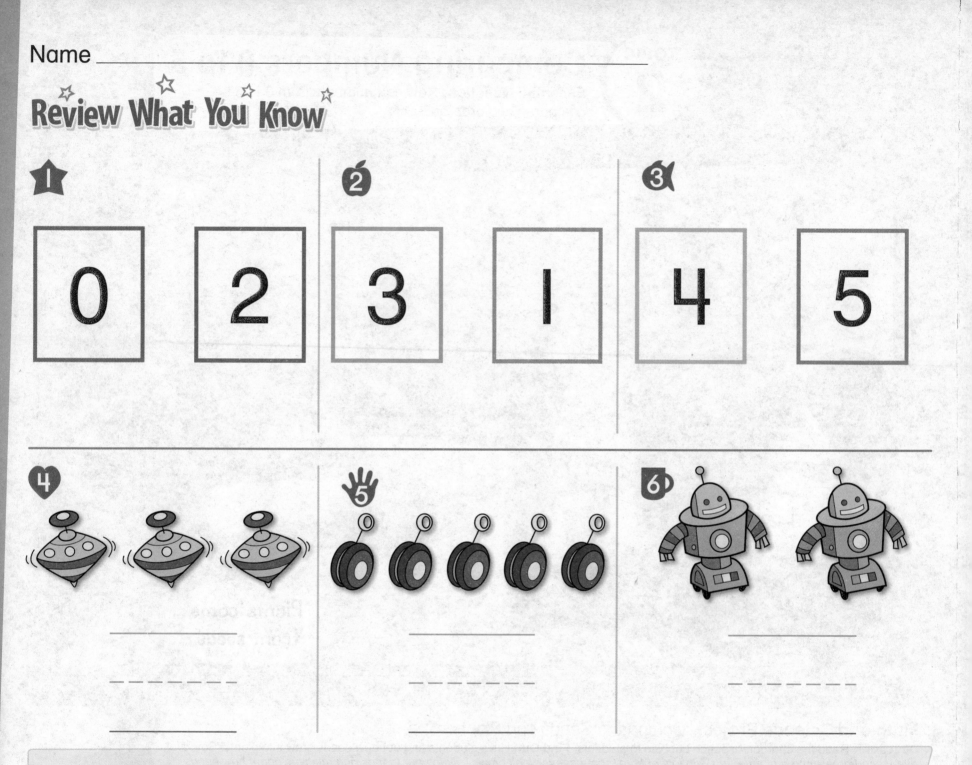

⭐ 1

| 0 | 2 |

🍎 2

| 3 | 1 |

🐟 3

| 4 | 5 |

❤️ 4

5 ✋

☕ 6

My Word Cards

Directions Have students cut out the vocabulary cards. Read the front of the card, and then ask them to explain what the word or phrase means.

more (than)	**fewer (than)**	**same number as**
compare	**column**	**row**

My Word Cards

Directions Review the definitions and have students study the cards. Extend learning by having students draw pictures for each word on a separate piece of paper.

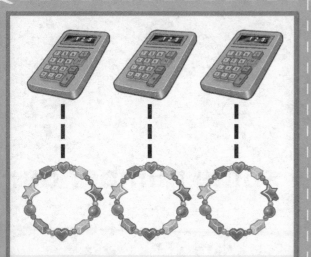

Point to the picture.
Say: *The top row has the **same number as** the bottom row.*

Point to the bottom row of counters.
Say: *This row has **fewer** counters than the top row.*

Point to the top row of counters.
Say: *This row has **more** counters than the bottom row.*

1	2	3	4	5
11	12	13	14	15
21	22	23	24	25
31	32	33	34	35

Point to the circled row.
Say: *This is a **row**. Rows go side to side.*

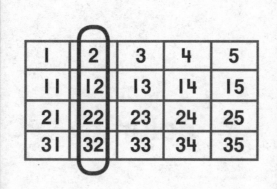

Point to the circled column.
Say: *This is a **column**. Columns go up and down.*

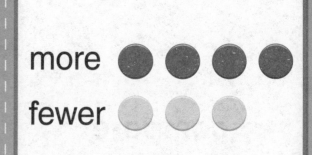

Point to the picture.
Say: *When we **compare** these two rows, we see one has more counters and one has fewer counters.*

My Word Cards

A-Z

order

My Word Cards

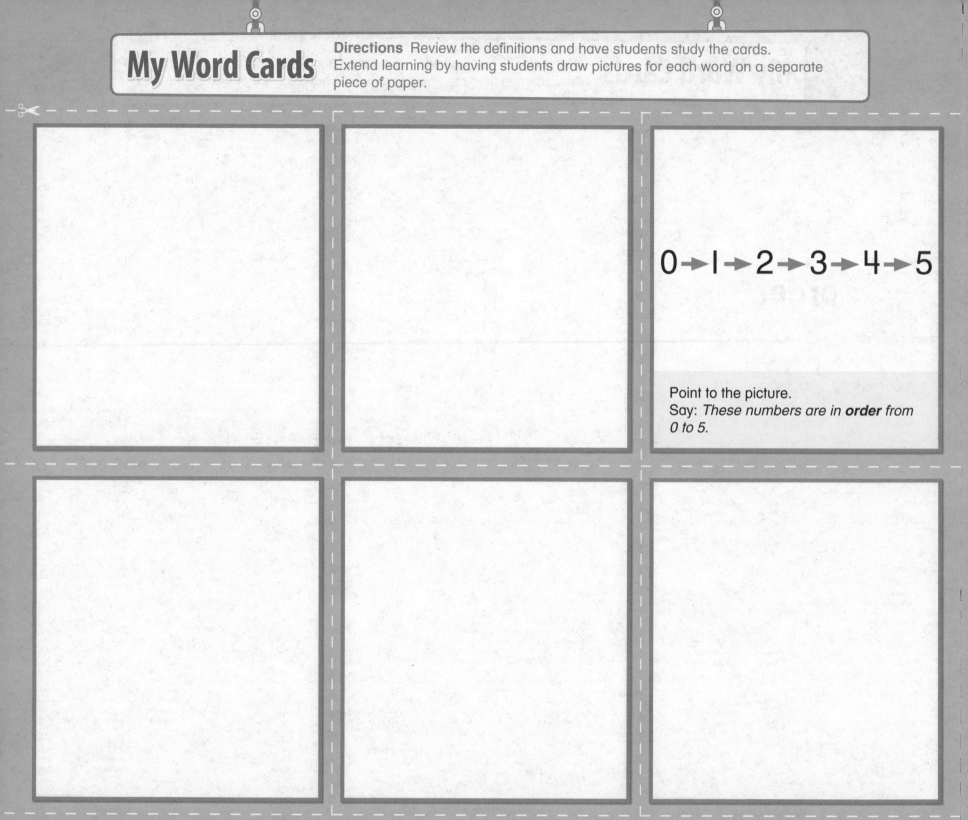

0 → 1 → 2 → 3 → 4 → 5

Point to the picture.
Say: *These numbers are in* **order** *from 0 to 5.*

Solve & Share Name _____

Directions Say: *Marta sees 4 tables. She sees 3 chairs. Does she see more tables or chairs? Use your connecting cubes to show how you know.*

⭐ **TEKS K.2G** Compare sets of objects up to at least 20 in each set using comparative language. Also, K.2, K.2E. **Mathematical Process Standards** K.1C, K.1D, K.1F, K.1G.

Digital Resources at PearsonTexas.com

Solve Learn Glossary Check Tools Games

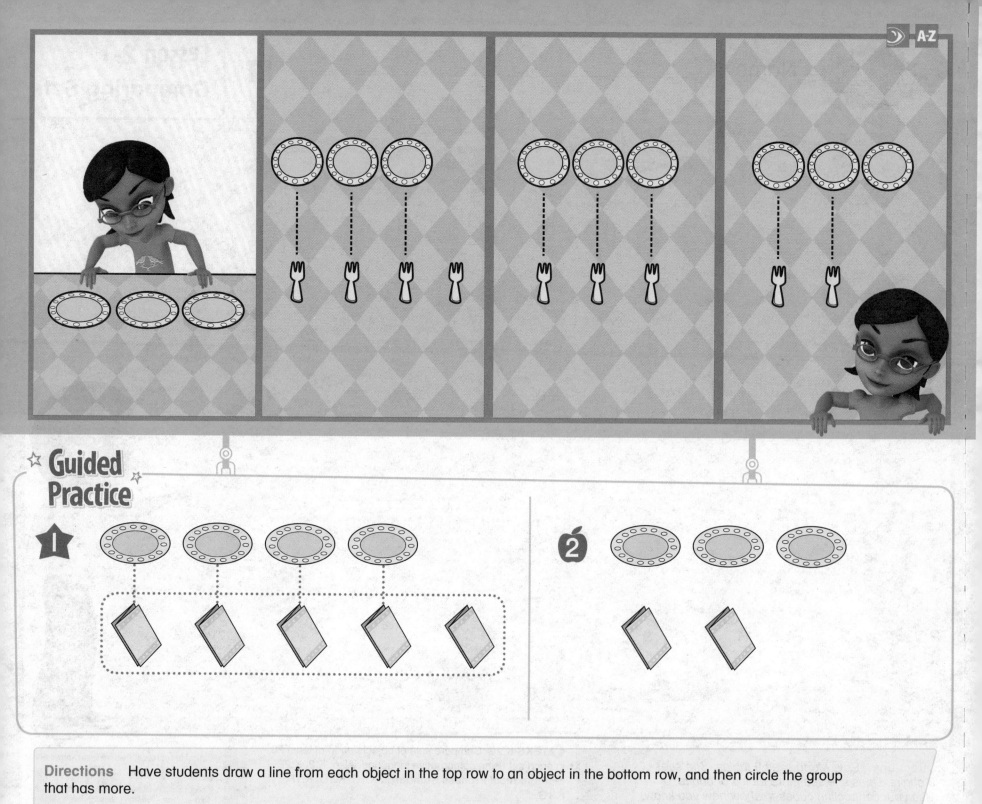

Guided Practice

1

2

Directions Have students draw a line from each object in the top row to an object in the bottom row, and then circle the group that has more.

Topic 2 | Lesson I

Directions Have students: ③ draw a line from each object on the left to an object on the right, and then circle the groups that have the same number of objects; ④ and ⑤ draw a line from each object in the top row to an object in the bottom row, and then circle the group that has fewer; ⑥ draw a line from each object in the top row to an object in the bottom row, and then circle the group that has more.

Independent Practice

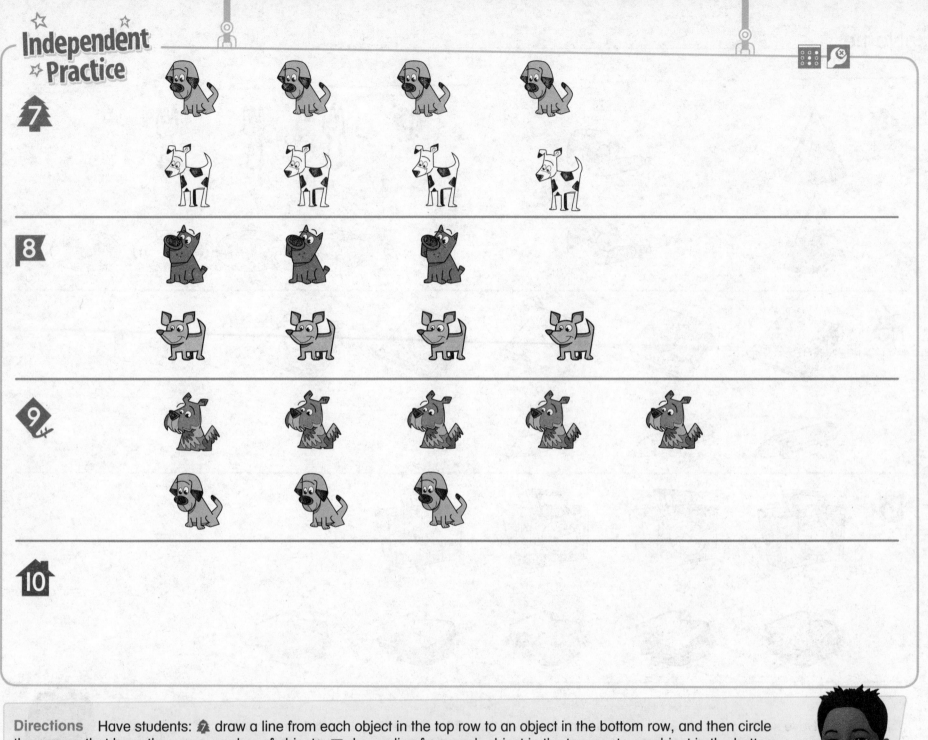

7

8

9

10

Directions Have students: **7** draw a line from each object in the top row to an object in the bottom row, and then circle the groups that have the same number of objects; **8** draw a line from each object in the top row to an object in the bottom row, and then circle the group that has more; **9** draw a line from each object in the top row to an object in the bottom row, and then circle the group that has fewer; **10** draw two groups of objects that have the same number of objects.

© Pearson Education, Inc. K

Another Look

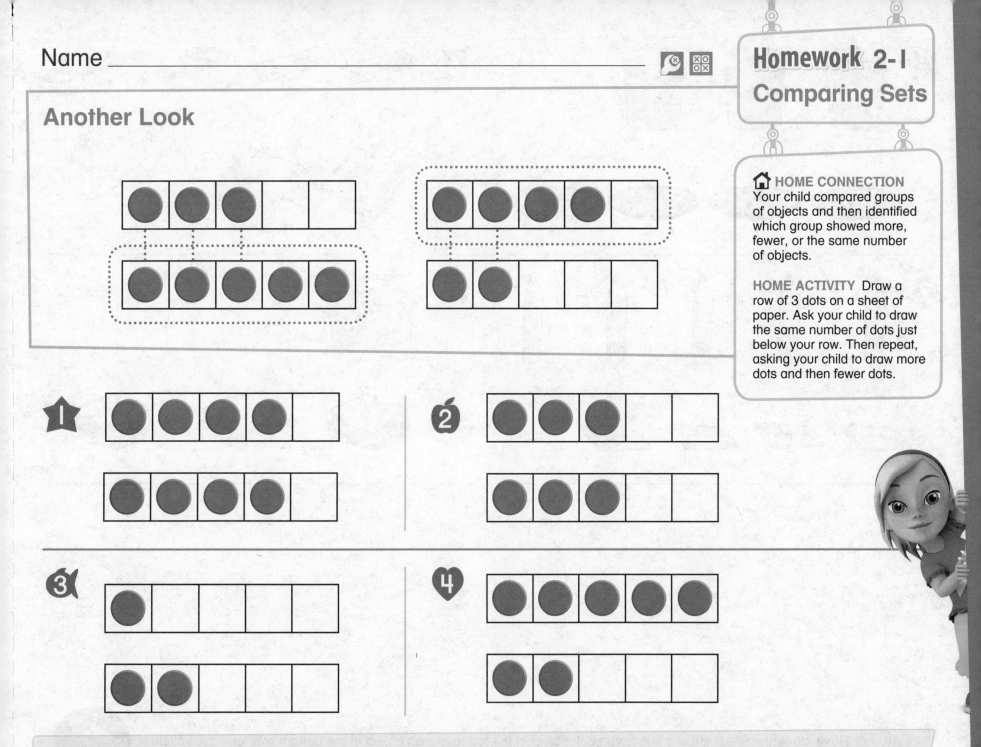

Directions Say: *Draw a line from each counter in the top frame to a counter in the bottom frame, and then draw a circle around the group that has more.* Then have students: ⭐ and 🍎 draw lines to match the counters, and then circle the groups that have the same number of objects; 🔄 and 💜 draw lines to match the counters, and then circle the group that has fewer.

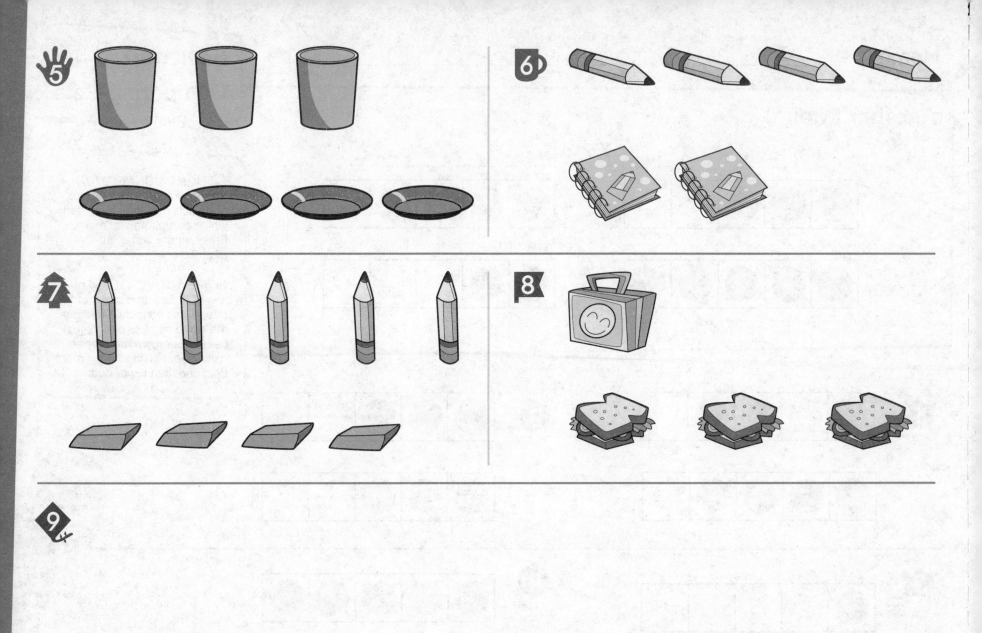

© Pearson Education, Inc. K

Directions Say: *Marta has 4 connecting cubes in her hand. Show a group with 1 more cube. Show how you know you are correct.*

⚙ **TEKS K.2E** Generate a set using concrete and pictorial models that represents a number that is more than, less than, and equal to a given number up to 20. Also, K.2. **Mathematical Process Standards** K.1C, K.1D, K.1E, K.1F.

Digital Resources at PearsonTexas.com

Solve Learn Glossary Check Tools Games

Guided Practice

1

2

Directions Have students: **1** color the yo-yos to show 1 more yo-yo than tops; **2** color the basketballs to show 2 more basketballs than toy planes.

© Pearson Education, Inc. K

Name _____

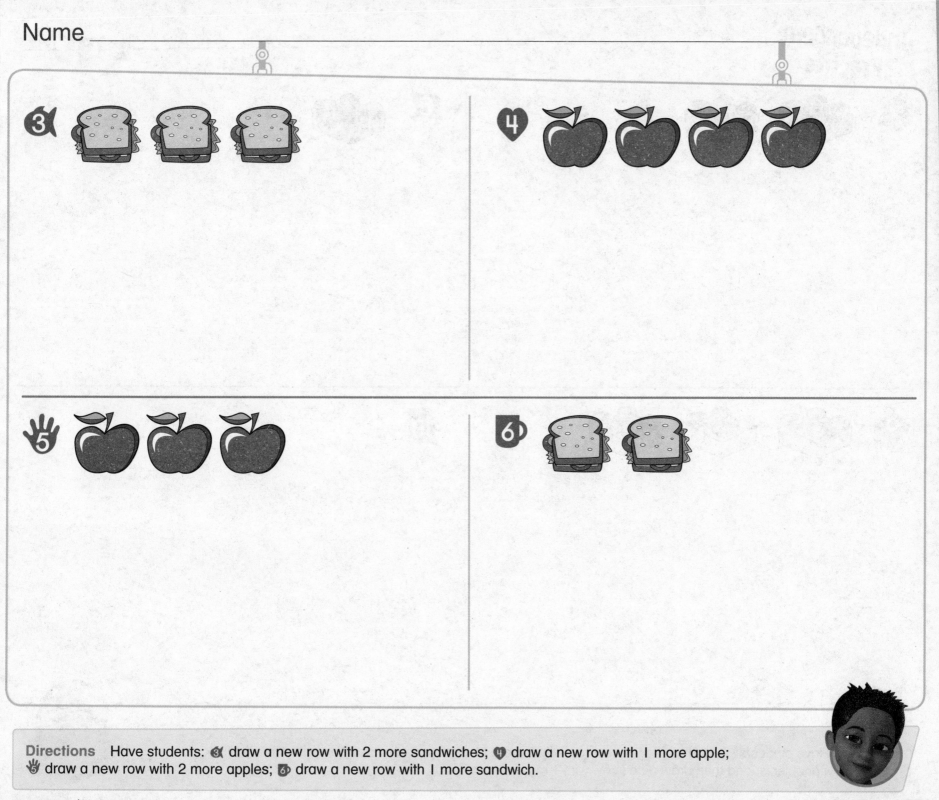

Directions Have students: ❸ draw a new row with 2 more sandwiches; ❹ draw a new row with 1 more apple; ❺ draw a new row with 2 more apples; ❻ draw a new row with 1 more sandwich.

Topic 2 | Lesson 2

eighty-nine **89**

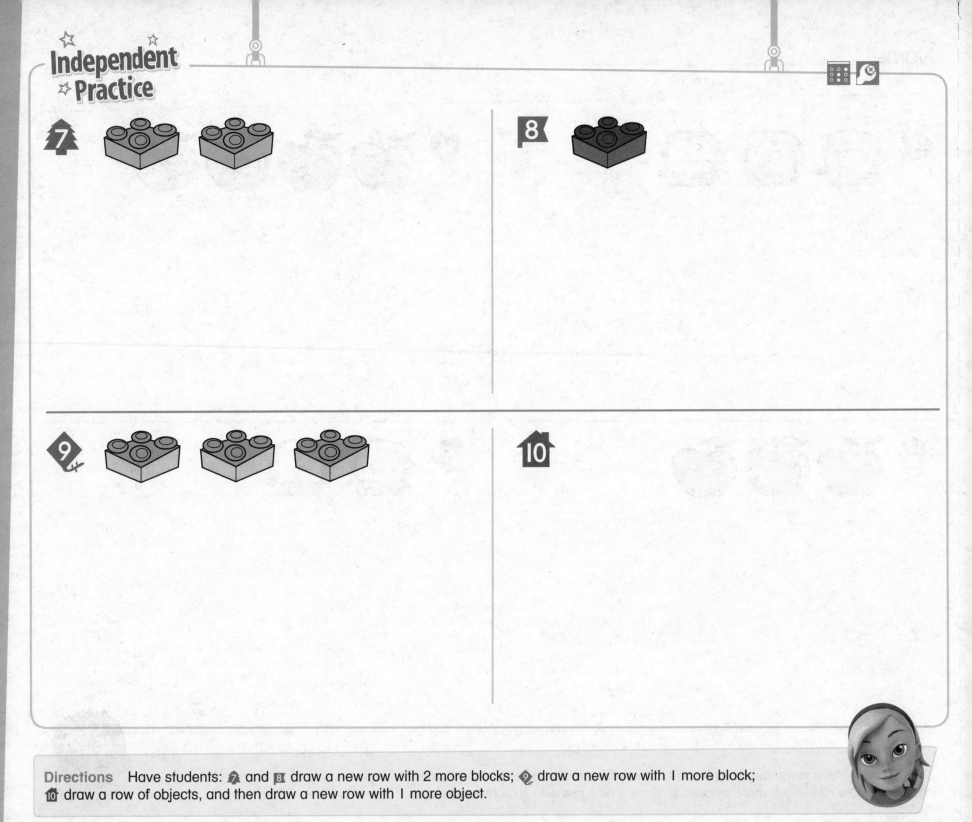

7 🌲

8 🚩

9 🔶

10 🏠

Directions Have students: **7** and **8** draw a new row with 2 more blocks; **9** draw a new row with 1 more block; **10** draw a row of objects, and then draw a new row with 1 more object.

Name _____

Another Look

🏠 **HOME CONNECTION**
Your child identified or drew groups with 1 more or 2 more.

HOME ACTIVITY Draw a row of 5 dots. Ask your child to draw a row of dots with 1 more dot below your row. Then ask your child to draw a row with 2 more dots below that row. Have your child talk about what he or she did using the terms *1 more* and *2 more*.

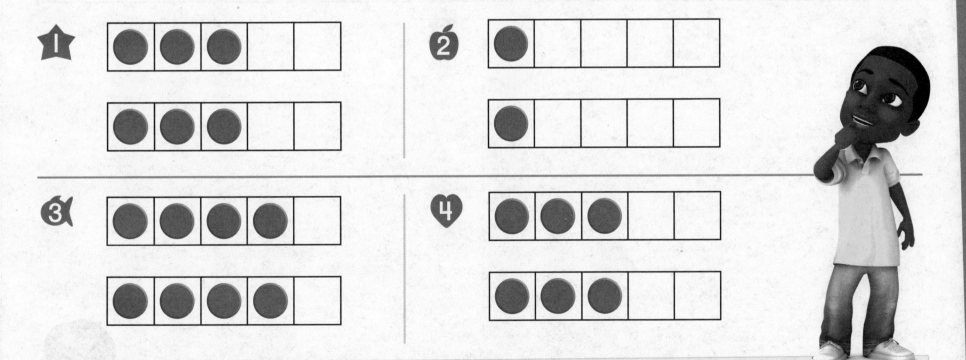

Directions Say: *Look at the top rows and then draw counters in the bottom rows to show 1 more and 2 more.* Then have students:
⭐ and ② look at the top row and draw 2 more in the bottom row; ③ and ④ look at the top row and draw 1 more in the bottom row.

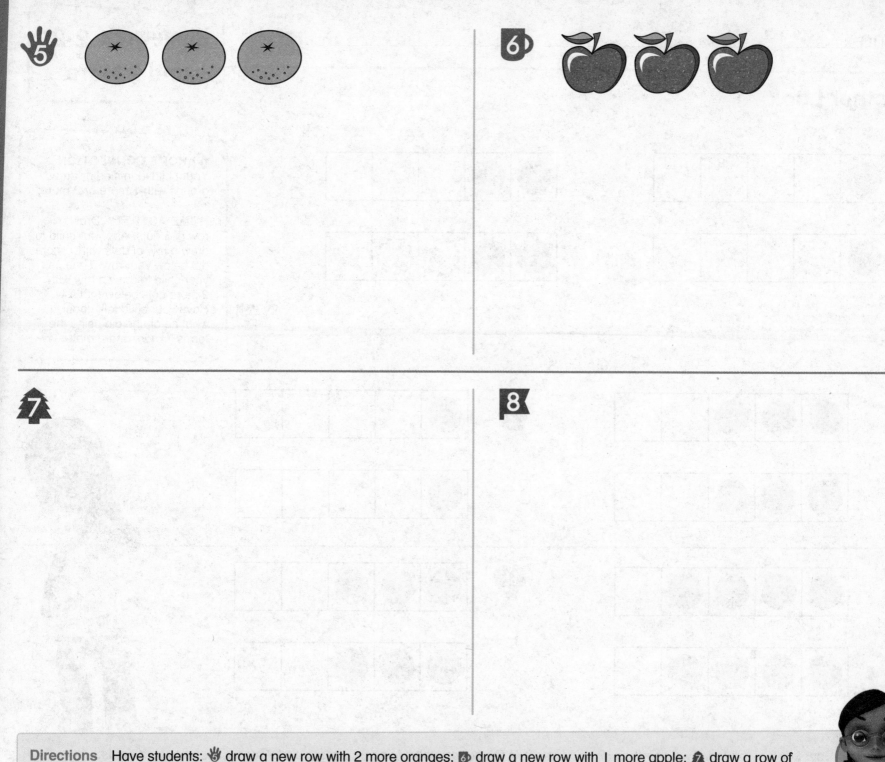

© Pearson Education, Inc. K

Solve & Share Name _____

Directions Say: *Marta has 3 connecting cubes in her hand. Show a group with 1 fewer cube. Show how you know you are correct.*

⭐ **TEKS K.2E** Generate a set using concrete and pictorial models that represents a number that is more than, less than, and equal to a given number up to 20. Also, K.2. **Mathematical Process Standards** K.1B, K.1C, K.1D, K.1F.

Digital Resources at PearsonTexas.com

Solve   Learn   Glossary   Check   Tools   Games

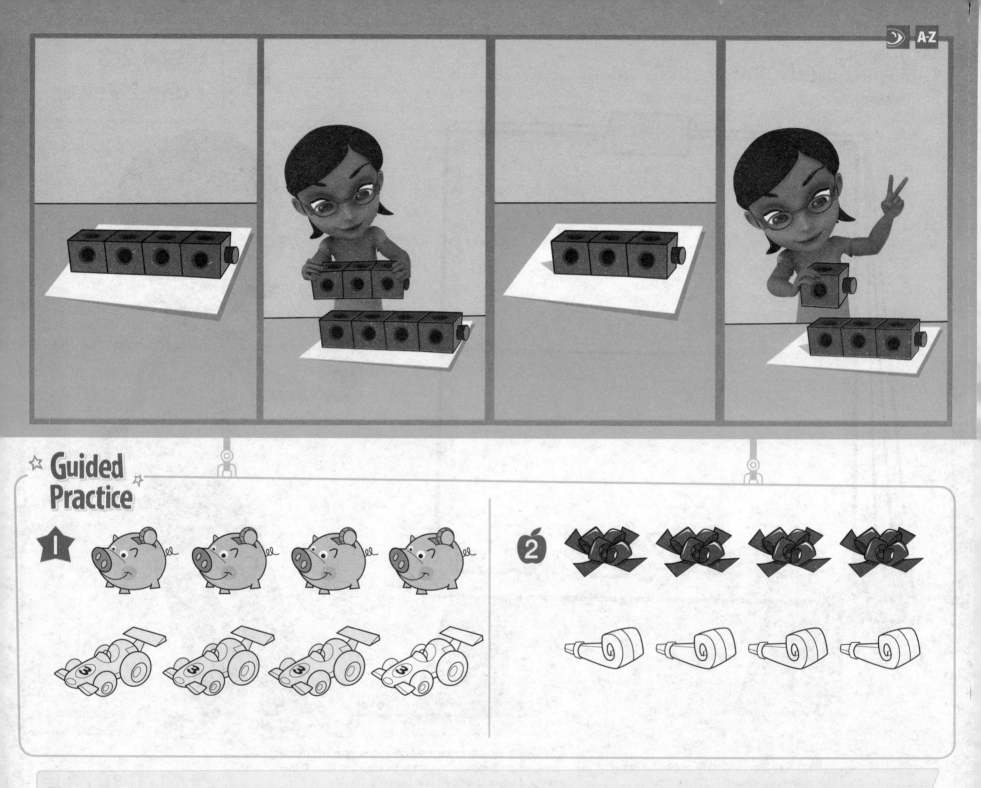

☆ Guided Practice ☆

1

2

Directions Have students: **1** color the cars to show 1 fewer car than banks; **2** color the party horns to show 2 fewer party horns than bows.

© Pearson Education, Inc. K

Name _____

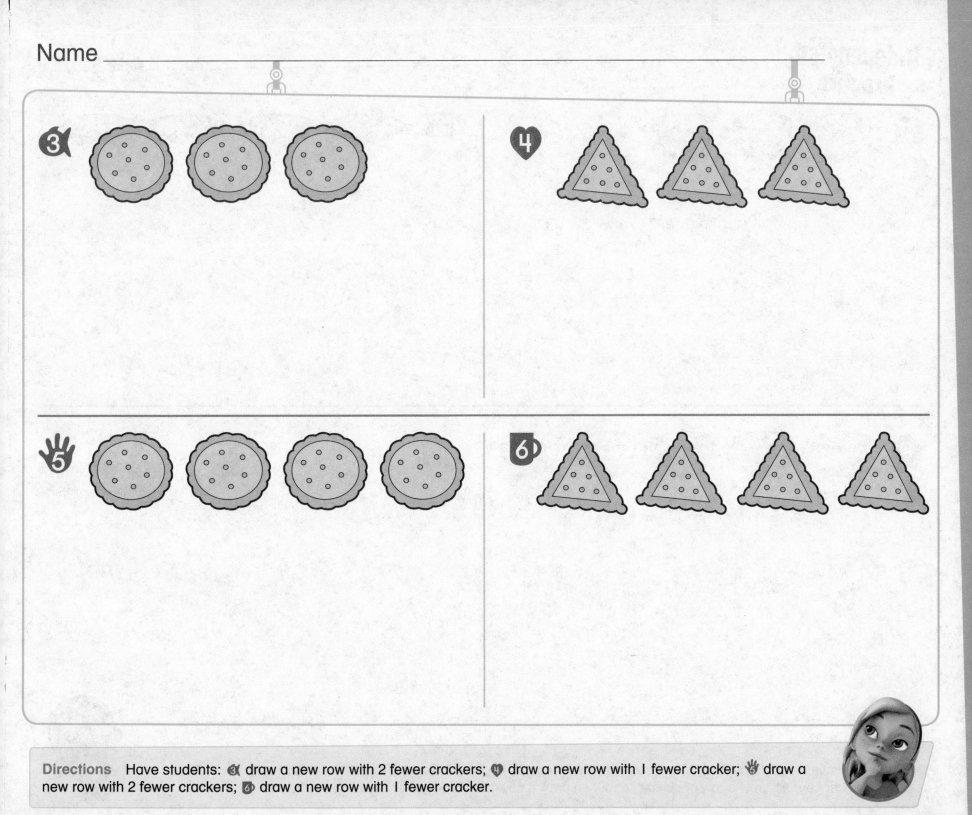

3

4

5

6

Directions Have students: 3 draw a new row with 2 fewer crackers; 4 draw a new row with 1 fewer cracker; 5 draw a new row with 2 fewer crackers; 6 draw a new row with 1 fewer cracker.

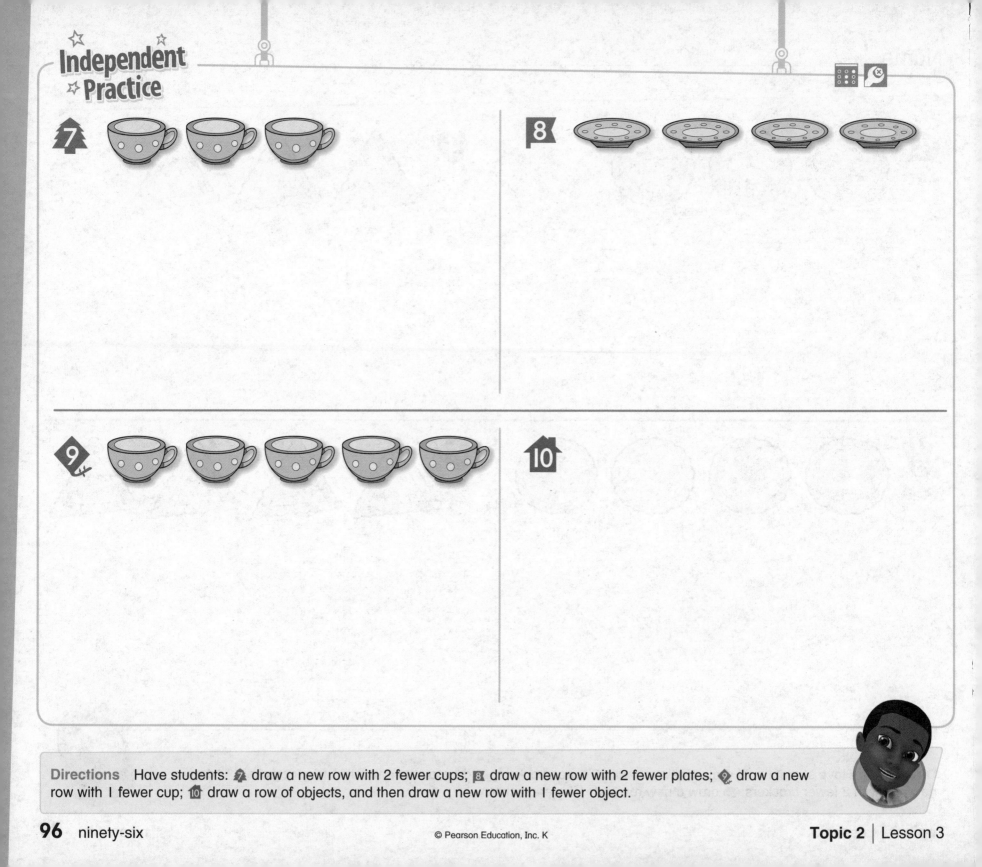

7

8

9

10

Directions Have students: **7** draw a new row with 2 fewer cups; **8** draw a new row with 2 fewer plates; **9** draw a new row with 1 fewer cup; **10** draw a row of objects, and then draw a new row with 1 fewer object.

96 ninety-six

Topic 2 | Lesson 3

Another Look

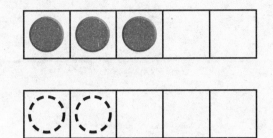

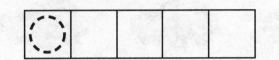

🏠 **HOME CONNECTION**
Your child identified or drew groups with 1 fewer or 2 fewer.

HOME ACTIVITY Draw a row of 5 dots. Ask your child to draw a row of dots with 1 fewer dot below your row. Then ask your child to draw a row with 2 fewer dots below that row. Have your child talk about what he or she did using the terms *1 fewer* and *2 fewer*.

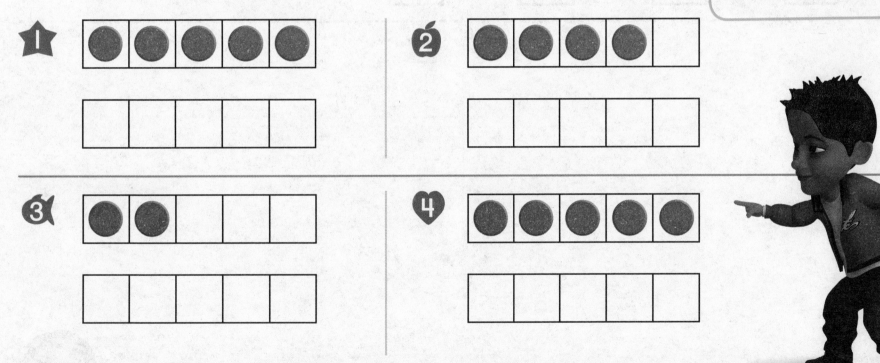

Directions Say: *Look at the top rows and draw counters in the bottom rows to show 1 fewer and 2 fewer.* Then have students:
⭐ and 🍎 look at the top row and draw 2 fewer in the bottom row; 🐟 and 💜 look at the top row and draw 1 fewer in the bottom row.

5

6

7

8

© Pearson Education, Inc. K

Solve & Share   Name _____

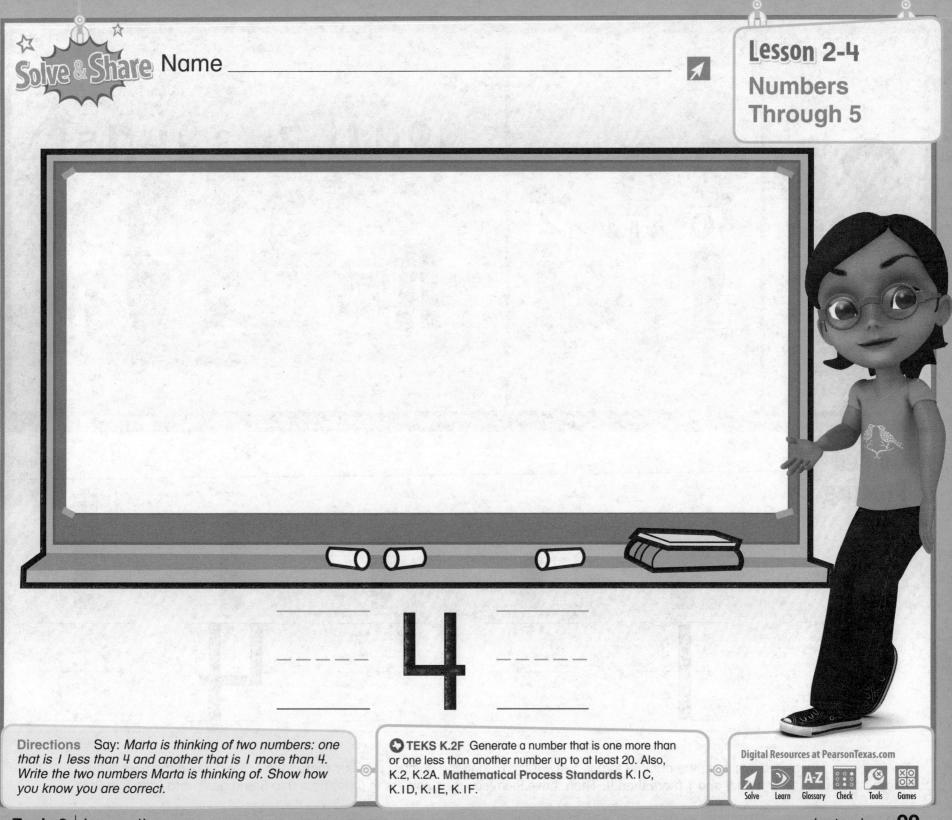

4

Directions Say: *Marta is thinking of two numbers: one that is 1 less than 4 and another that is 1 more than 4. Write the two numbers Marta is thinking of. Show how you know you are correct.*

⭐ **TEKS K.2F** Generate a number that is one more than or one less than another number up to at least 20. Also, K.2, K.2A. **Mathematical Process Standards** K.1C, K.1D, K.1E, K.1F.

Digital Resources at PearsonTexas.com

Solve Learn Glossary Check Tools Games

☆ Guided Practice ☆

1

0   1   2   3   4   5

Directions Have students write the number that is 1 fewer than 1 and the number that is 1 more than 1. Next, have them write the number that is 1 fewer than 4 and 1 more than 4. Then, have them say the numbers in order from 0 to 5 and backward from 5 to 0.

Name _____

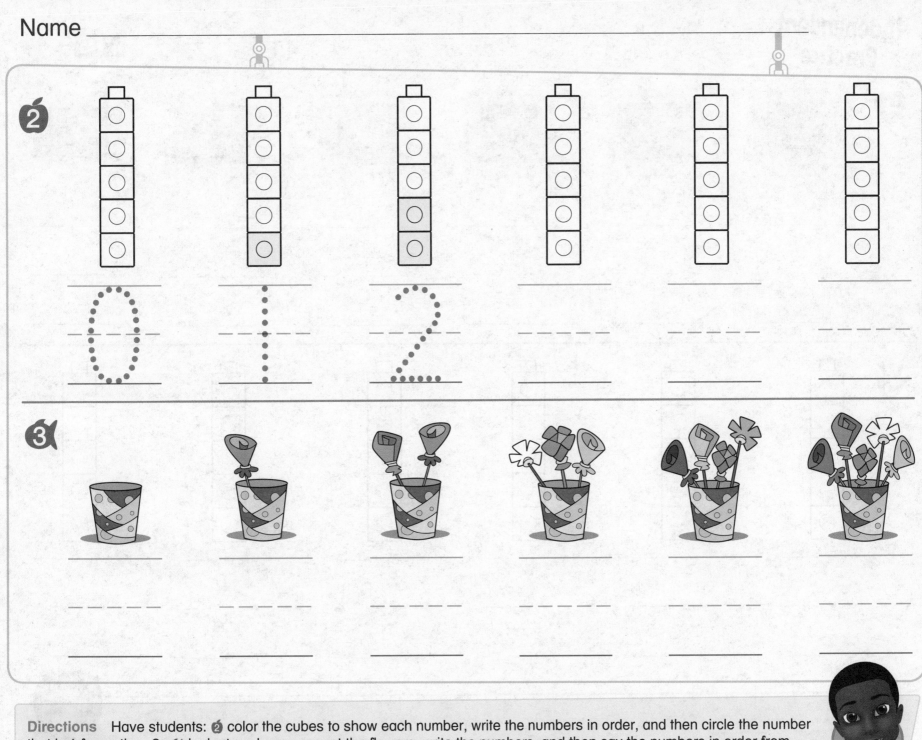

2

0   1   2

3

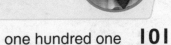

Topic 2 | Lesson 4

one hundred one   **101**

❤️ 4

_____ _____ _____ _____ _____ _____

- - - - - - - - - - - - - - - - - - - - - - - - - - - - - -

_____ _____ _____ _____ _____ _____

✋ 5

_____ _____ _____ _____ _____ _____

- - - - - - - - - - - - - - - - - - - - - - - - - - - - - -

_____ _____ _____ _____ _____ _____

Directions Have students: ❤️ look at each box, count the toys, write the numbers, and then circle the number that is 1 more than 4; ✋ color 5 cubes and write the number, and then color 1 fewer cube in each following tower and write the number.

© Pearson Education, Inc. K

Topic 2 | Lesson 4

Name _____

Another Look

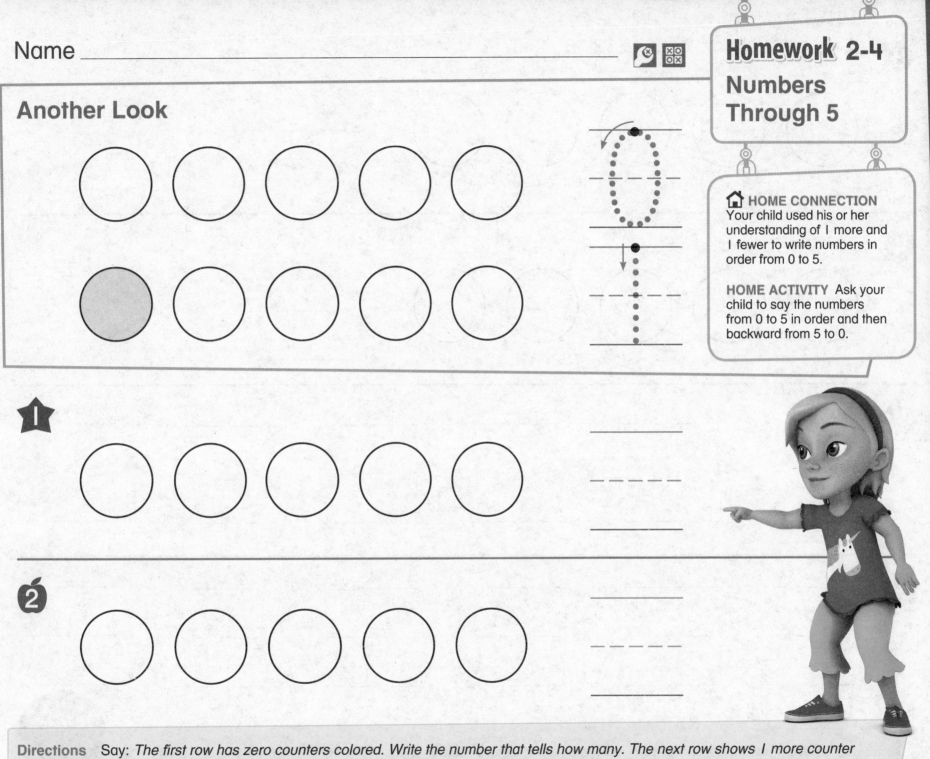

🏠 **HOME CONNECTION**
Your child used his or her understanding of I more and I fewer to write numbers in order from 0 to 5.

HOME ACTIVITY Ask your child to say the numbers from 0 to 5 in order and then backward from 5 to 0.

Directions Say: *The first row has zero counters colored. Write the number that tells how many. The next row shows I more counter colored. Write the number that tells how many.* Then have students: ⭐ and 🍎 *color counters to add I more counter to each row than the row before and write the number that tells how many.*

Topic 2 | Lesson 4   Digital Resources at PearsonTexas.com   one hundred three   **103**

3

⭕ ⭕ ⭕ ⭕ ⭕

_____

- - - - - - -

_____

4

⭕ ⭕ ⭕ ⭕ ⭕

_____

- - - - - - -

_____

5

_____ _____ _____ _____ _____ _____

- - - - - - - - - - - - - - - - - - - - - - - -

_____ _____ _____ _____ _____ _____

6

_____ _____ _____ _____ _____ _____

- - - - - - - - - - - - - - - - - - - - - - - -

_____ _____ _____ _____ _____ _____

Directions Have students: **3** and **4** color counters to add 1 more counter to each row than the row before, and then write the numbers that tell how many; **5** write the numbers in order from 0 to 5, and then circle the number that is 1 fewer than 1 and draw a box around the number that is 1 more than 1; **6** write the numbers in backward order from 5 to 0.

Topic 2 | Lesson 4

Solve & Share   Name _____

Directions Say: *Marta has 2 red marbles and 4 blue marbles. How can you find out which group has more? Color the connecting cubes and write the numbers that tell how many. Circle the marble that shows which group has more.*

✪**TEKS K.1C** Select tools, including real objects, manipulatives, ... and techniques, including mental math, ... and number sense as appropriate, to solve problems. Also, K.2, K.2G, K.2H. **Mathematical Process Standards K.1A, K.1B, K.1D, K.1G.**

Digital Resources at PearsonTexas.com

Solve   Learn   Glossary   Check   Tools   Games

Analyze

Plan

Solve, Justify, and Evaluate

1

5

1

5

☆ **Guided Practice** ☆

1

5

2

2 · 5

Directions Say: *Marta has 2 flamingo stickers and 5 fish stickers. Which group has fewer stickers? How can you use cubes to find out?* Have students create cube trains for each group, color the number of cubes, and then write the numbers that tell how many. Then have them rewrite the numbers in order and circle the number that is less.

© Pearson Education, Inc. K

Name _____

2

3

Directions Have students listen to each story, create cube trains for each group, color the number of cubes, and then write the numbers that tell how many. **2** *Carlos has 4 yellow blocks and 5 blue blocks. Which group has more blocks? How can you use cubes to find out? Rewrite the numbers in order and circle the greater number.* **3** *listen to this story: Carlos has 3 red blocks and 1 blue block. Which group has fewer blocks? How can you use cubes to find out? Rewrite the numbers in order and circle the number that is less.*

Topic 2 | Lesson 5   one hundred seven   **107**

4

5

Directions Have students: **4** listen to this story: *Emily has 2 dog stickers and 4 frog stickers. Which group has fewer stickers? How can you use cubes to find out?* Create cube trains for each group, color the number of cubes, and then write the numbers that tell how many. Then have them rewrite the numbers in order and circle the number that is less. **5** listen to this story: *Marta also has some dog and frog stickers. Which group has more stickers? How can you use cubes to find out?* Create cube trains for each group, write the numbers in order, and then circle the greater number.

© Pearson Education, Inc. K

Name _____

Another Look

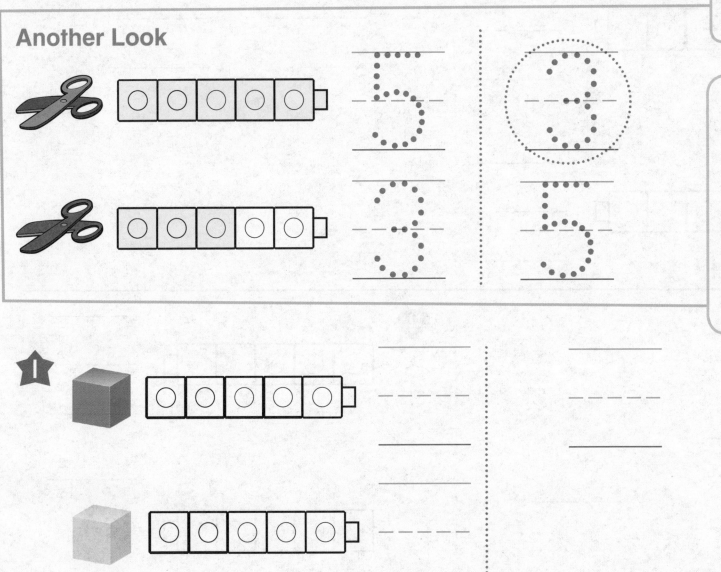

🏠 **HOME CONNECTION**
Your child used connecting cubes to act out stories, order numbers, and compare numbers.

HOME ACTIVITY Make a group of 4 raisins and write the number. Ask your child to make a group that has 3 raisins and write the number of raisins. Ask your child which number tells which group is greater. Repeat with different numbers from 0 to 5.

Directions Say: *Listen to the story. Mr. Davis has 5 green scissors and 3 red scissors for his class. Which group has fewer scissors? How can you use cubes or other objects to find out? Create cube or object trains for each group, color the number of cubes, and then write the numbers that tell how many. Now rewrite the numbers in order and circle the number that is less.* Have students repeat the steps for this story: ⭐ *Marta has 4 purple blocks and 2 yellow blocks. Which group of blocks has fewer?*

Topic 2 | Lesson 5   Digital Resources at PearsonTexas.com   one hundred nine **109**

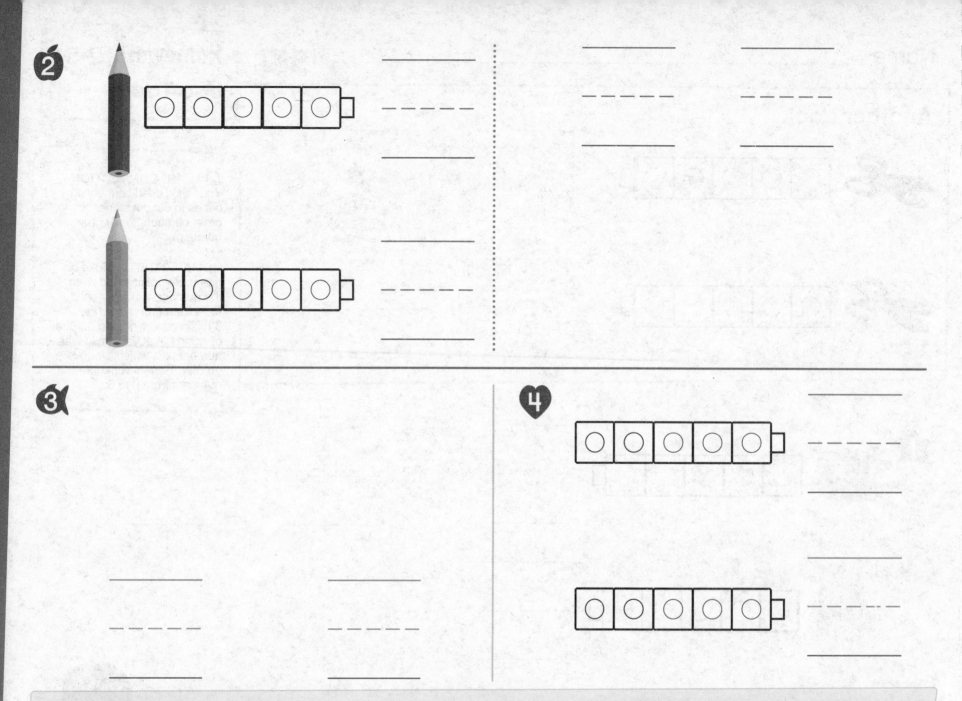

Directions Have students: ② listen to this story: *Adam has 4 purple pencils and 3 aqua pencils. Which group has more pencils? How can you use cubes to find out?* Create cube or object trains for each group, color the number of cubes, and then write the numbers that tell how many. Then have them rewrite the numbers in order and circle the greater number; ③ draw two groups that have different numbers of objects with up to 5 objects in each group. Write the numbers that tell how many are in each group in order, and then circle the number that is less; ④ tell a story about two groups that have different numbers of objects with up to 5 objects in each group. Color the number of cubes, write the numbers that tell how many, and then circle the greater number.

Topic 2 | Lesson 5

Name _____

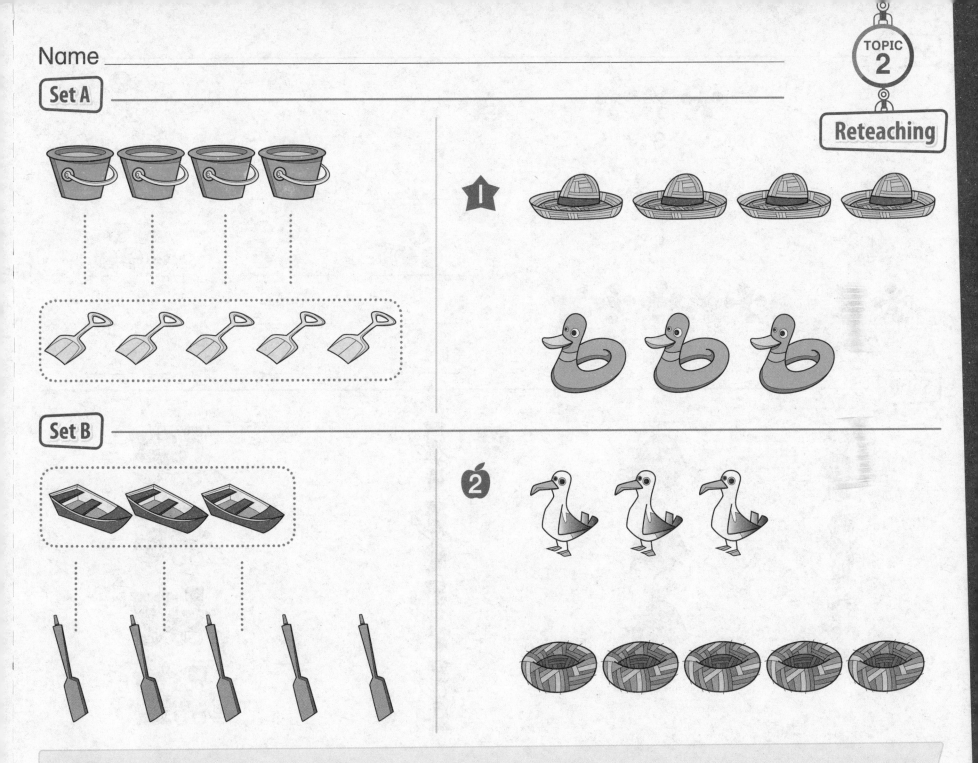

Set A

Set B

⭐ 1

🍎 2

Directions Have students: ⭐ draw lines to match each hat to a duck, and then circle the group that has 1 more; 🍎 draw lines to match each seagull to a nest, and then circle the group that has 2 fewer.

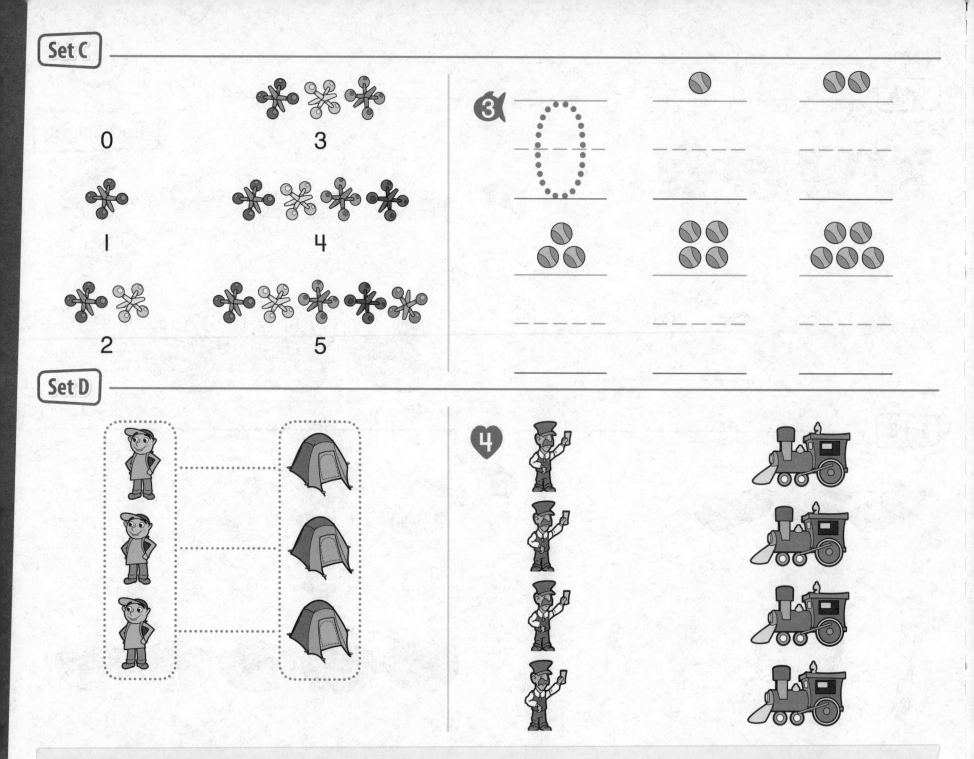

Set D

Directions Have students: ❸ count the balls and write the numbers in order from 0 to 5; ❹ match a conductor to a train, and then circle the groups to show they have the same number of items.

112   one hundred twelve   © Pearson Education, Inc. K   Topic 2

Name _____

⭐ 1

② 2

③ 3

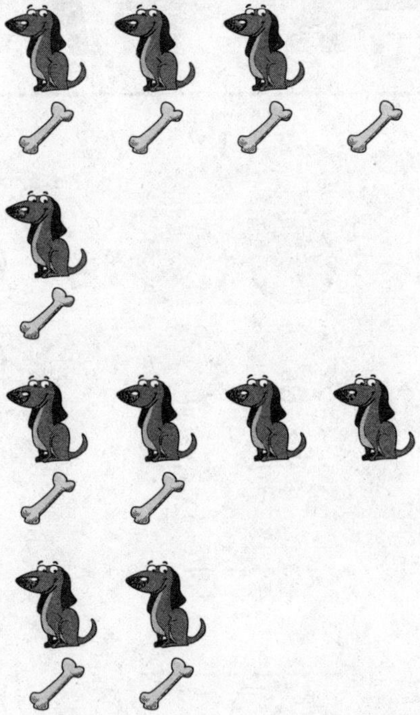

♥ 4

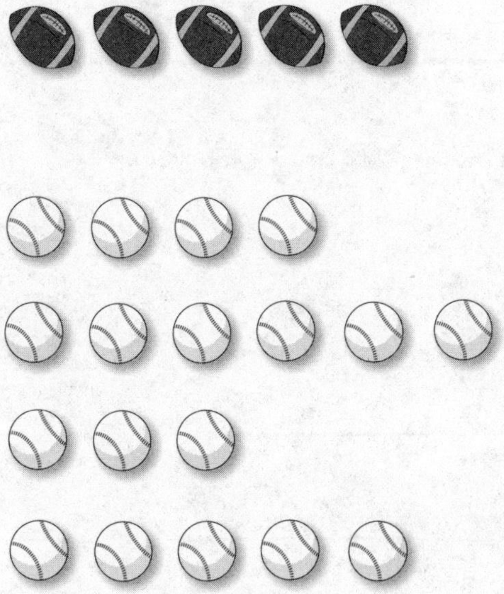

Directions Have students mark the best answer. ⭐ Which shows more cups than plates? ② Which shows 2 more colored dots than the group at the top? ③ Which shows 1 fewer dog than bones? ♥ Which shows the same number of baseballs as footballs?

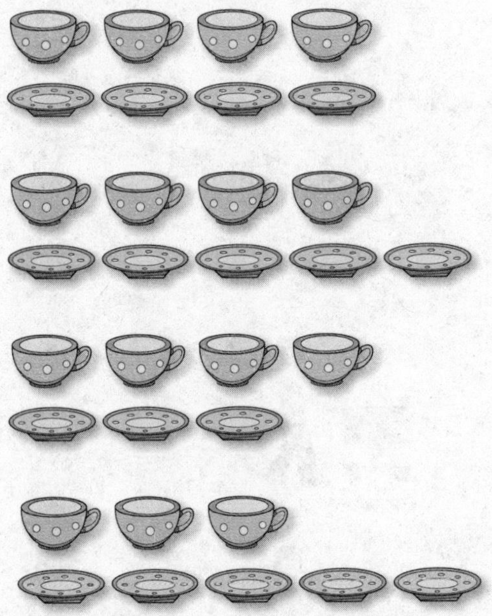

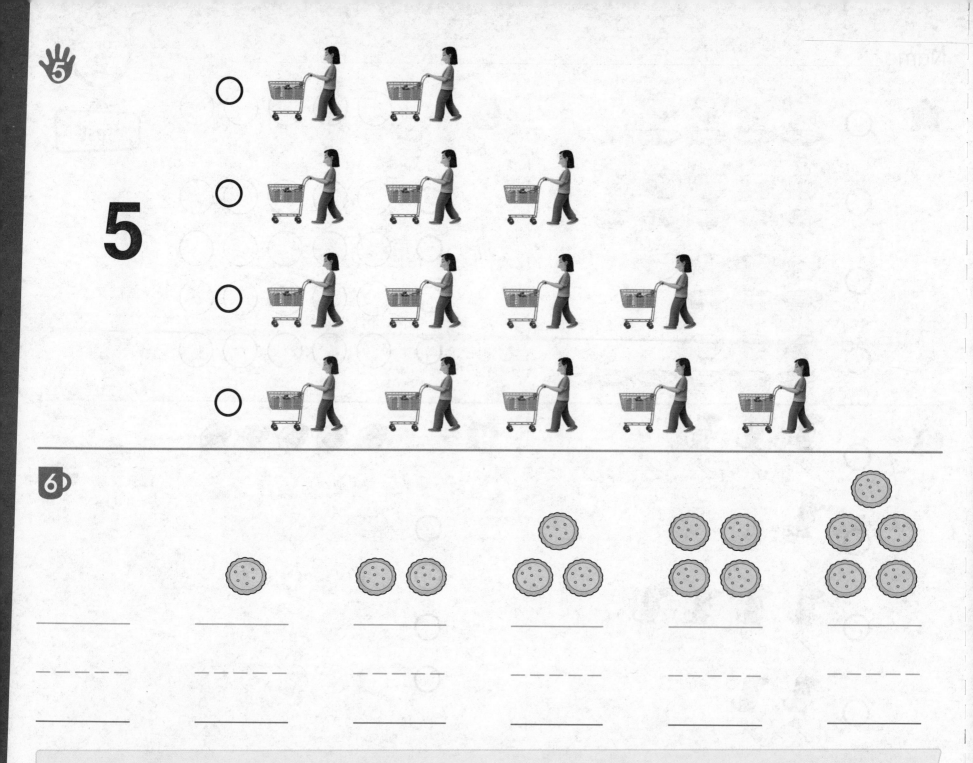

5

○

○

○

○

Directions Have students: ✋ mark the best answer. Which shows 2 fewer shoppers than 5? ☕ count the crackers, and then write the numbers in order from 0 to 5.

114 one hundred fourteen   © Pearson Education, Inc. K   **Topic 2**

TOPIC 3

Numbers 6 to 10

Essential Question: How can numbers from 6 to 10 be counted, read, and written?

Cows!

Some cows are brown and some are black.

Math and Science Project: Sorting Animals

Directions Read the character speech bubbles to students. **Find Out!** Have students find out about animals that can be sorted by color. Say: *Talk to friends and relatives about animals. Ask which types of animals come in two or more colors.* **Journal: Make a Poster** Then have students make a poster. Have them choose one animal they learned about. Ask them to draw a group with 6–10 of the animal they chose, color the animals using two different colors, and then write the number that tells how many animals.

Name _____

Review What You Know

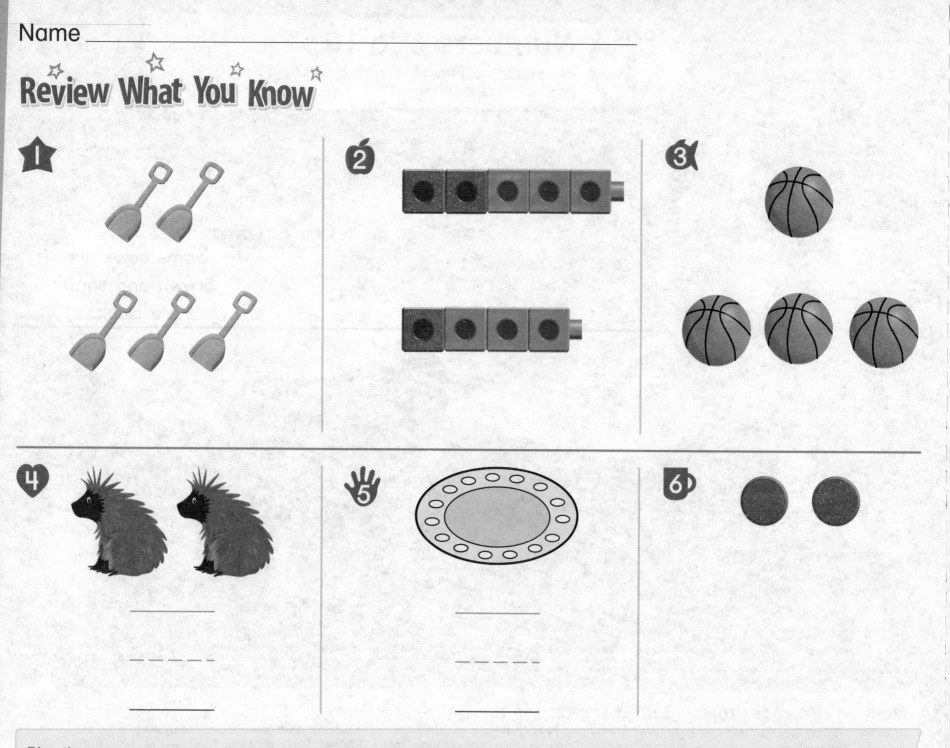

1 ⭐

2 🍎

3 🔄

4 ❤️

5 ✋

6 ☕

Directions Have students: ⭐ circle the group that shows 3; 🍎 circle the group that shows a way to make 5; 🔄 circle the group that has fewer; ❤️ count and write the number of hedgehogs; ✋ count and write the number of carrots on the plate; ☕ draw 2 more counters.

Topic 3

My Word Cards

Directions Have students cut out the vocabulary cards. Read the front of the card, and then ask them to explain what the word or phrase means.

A-Z

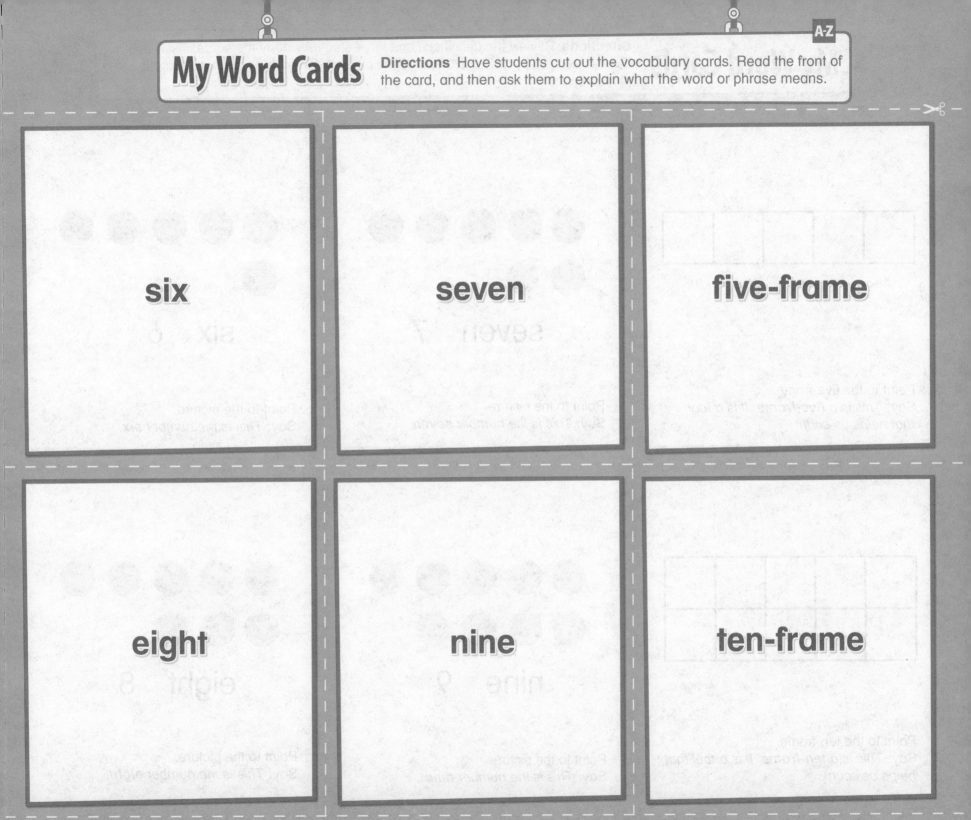

six

seven

five-frame

eight

nine

ten-frame

My Word Cards

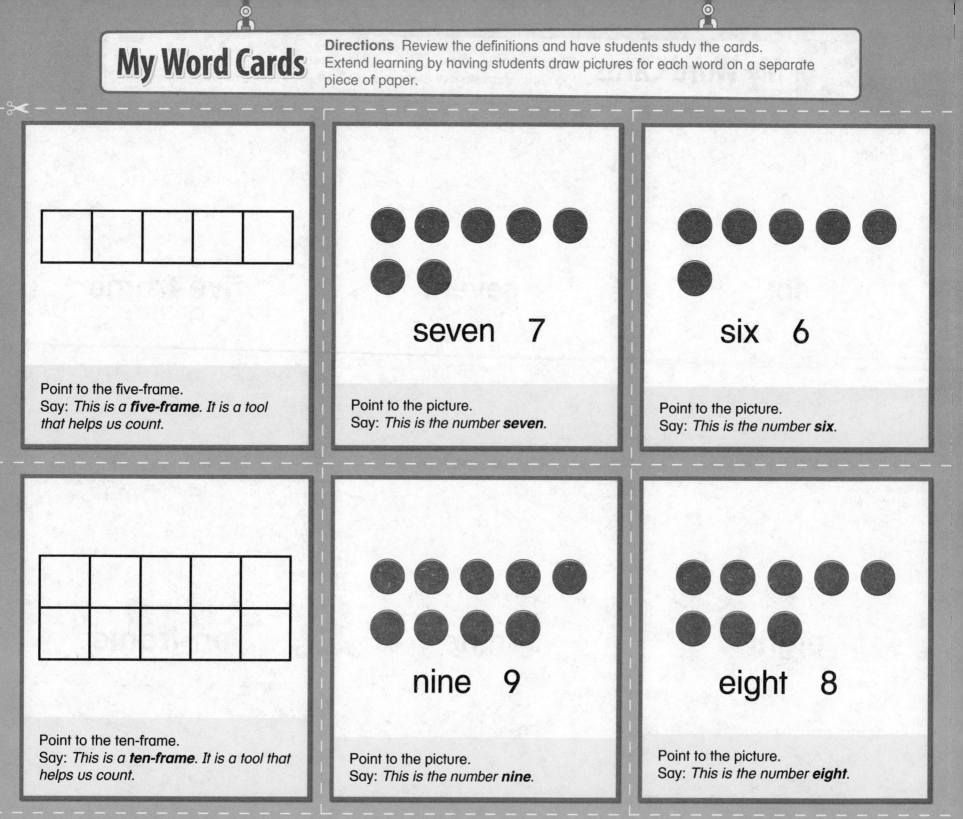

Point to the five-frame.
Say: *This is a **five-frame**. It is a tool that helps us count.*

seven   7

Point to the picture.
Say: *This is the number **seven**.*

six   6

Point to the picture.
Say: *This is the number **six**.*

Point to the ten-frame.
Say: *This is a **ten-frame**. It is a tool that helps us count.*

nine   9

Point to the picture.
Say: *This is the number **nine**.*

eight   8

Point to the picture.
Say: *This is the number **eight**.*

My Word Cards

Directions Have students cut out the vocabulary cards. Read the front of the card, and then ask them to explain what the word or phrase means.

A-Z

ten

My Word Cards

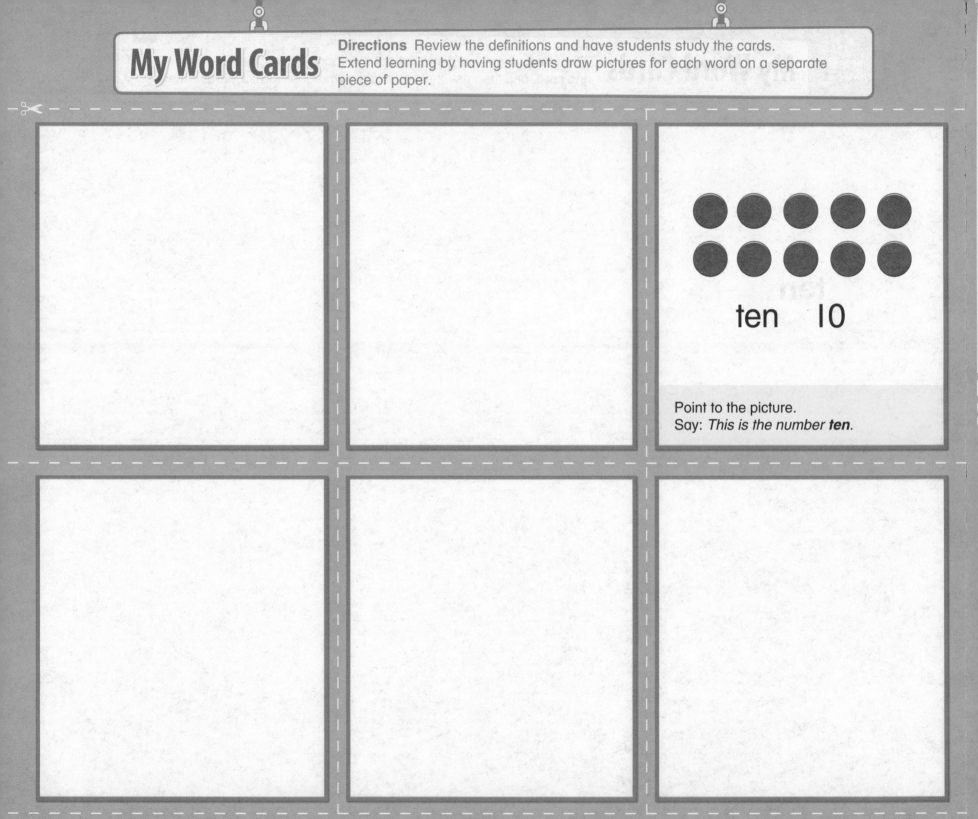

ten   10

Point to the picture.
Say: *This is the number **ten**.*

Solve & Share   Name _____

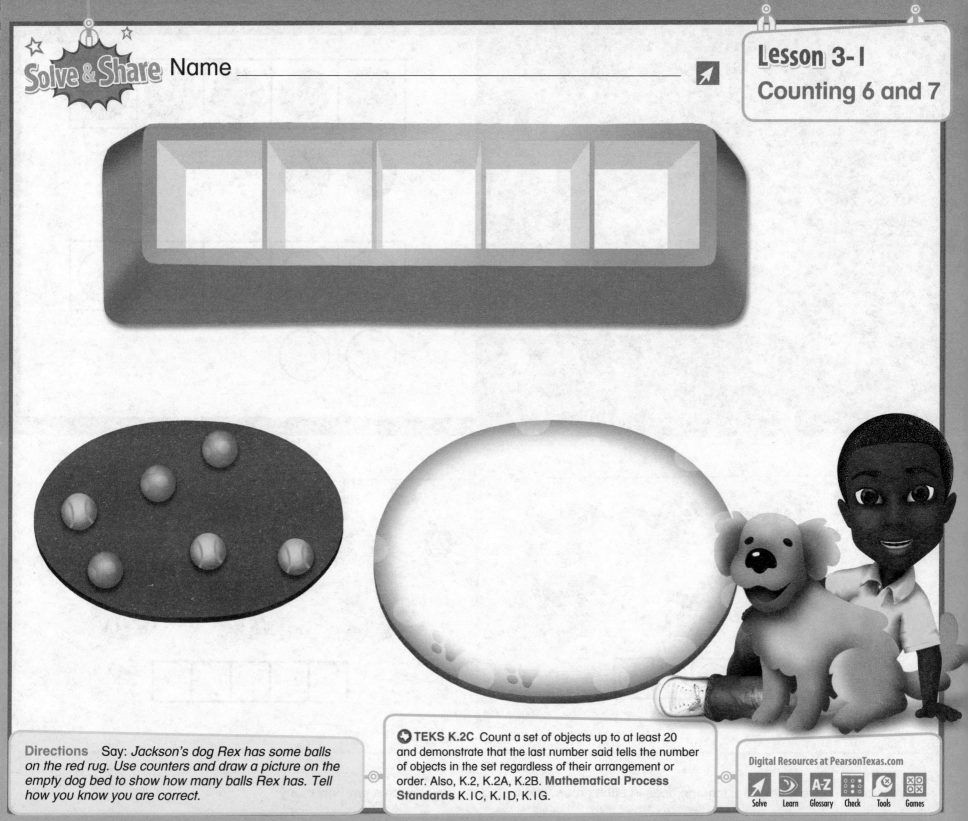

Directions   Say: *Jackson's dog Rex has some balls on the red rug. Use counters and draw a picture on the empty dog bed to show how many balls Rex has. Tell how you know you are correct.*

☆ TEKS K.2C Count a set of objects up to at least 20 and demonstrate that the last number said tells the number of objects in the set regardless of their arrangement or order. Also, K.2, K.2A, K.2B. **Mathematical Process Standards** K.1C, K.1D, K.1G.

Digital Resources at PearsonTexas.com

Solve   Learn   Glossary   Check   Tools   Games

☆ Guided Practice ☆

1

2

Directions Have students count the dogs in each group, and then draw counters to show how many.

© Pearson Education, Inc. K

Topic 3 | Lesson 1

Name _____

3

4

5

Directions Have students count the animals in each group, and then draw counters to show how many.

Topic 3 | Lesson 1

one hundred twenty-three **123**

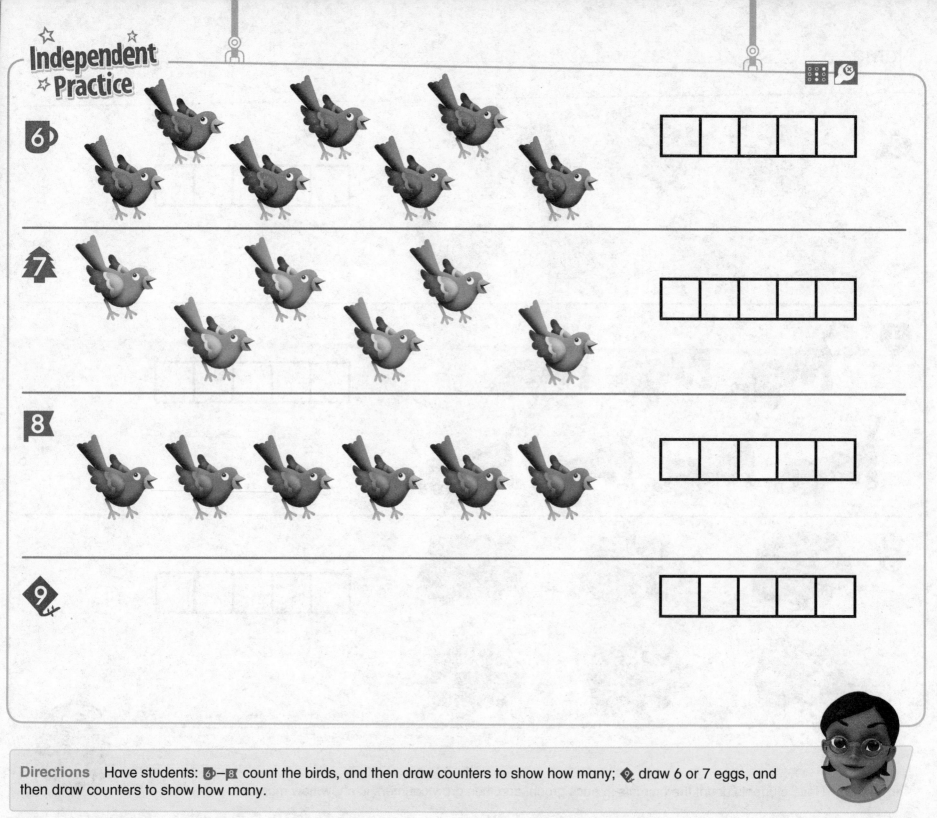

🥤 6

🌲 7

8

9

Directions Have students: 6–8 count the birds, and then draw counters to show how many; 9 draw 6 or 7 eggs, and then draw counters to show how many.

© Pearson Education, Inc. K

Name _____

Another Look

🏠 **HOME CONNECTION**
Your child counted 6 or 7 objects and drew counters to show each number.

HOME ACTIVITY Have your child count groups of 6 objects. Then he or she can draw pictures of 6 objects. Repeat using the number 7.

⭐ 1

🍎 2

★ 3

Directions Say: *Count the dots and use counters or other objects to show that number. Then draw counters in the box to show the same number of counters as dots.* Then have students: ⭐–★ count the number of dots, use counters or other objects to show that number, and then draw counters in the box to show the same number of counters as dots.

4

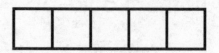

5

6

Solve & Share Name _____

Directions Say: *6 cars are on the road. How can you use counters to show 6 in different ways? Color the counters red and yellow to show your work.*

✪ **TEKS K.2I** Compose and decompose numbers up to 10 with objects and pictures. Also, K.2. **Mathematical Process Standards** K.1C, K.1D, K.1F.

Digital Resources at PearsonTexas.com

Solve Learn Glossary Check Tools Games

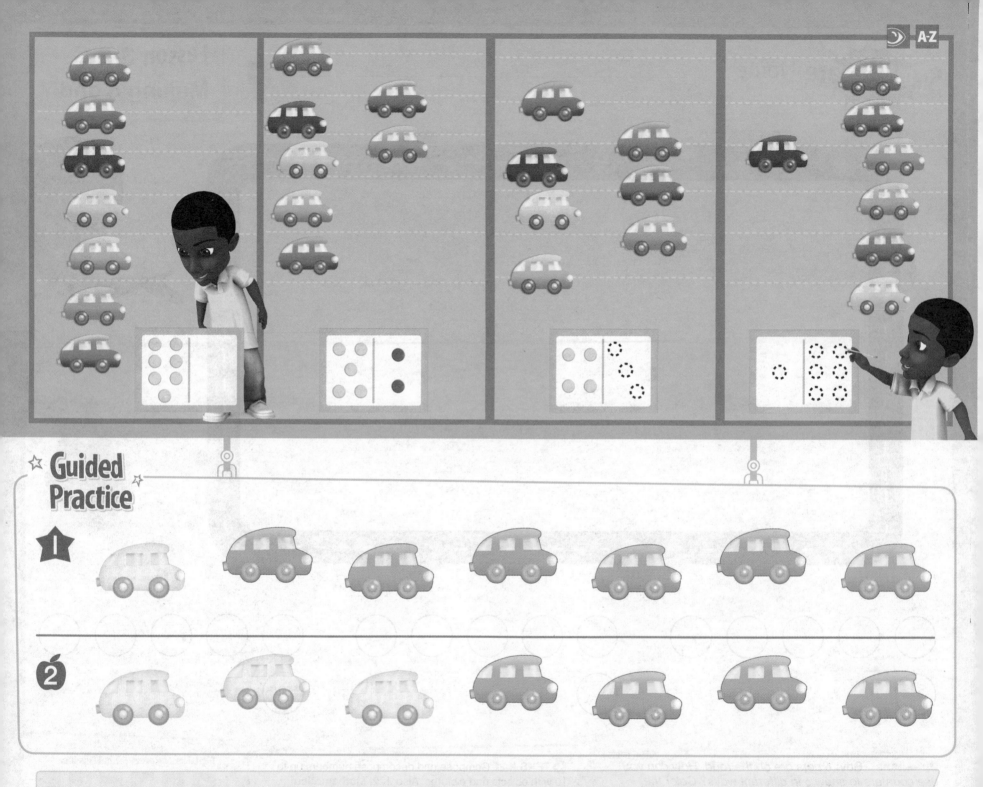

☆ Guided Practice ☆

1

2

Directions Have students use counters to find these two different ways to make 7, and then color the cars to show these ways.

© Pearson Education, Inc. K

Topic 3 | Lesson 2

Name _____

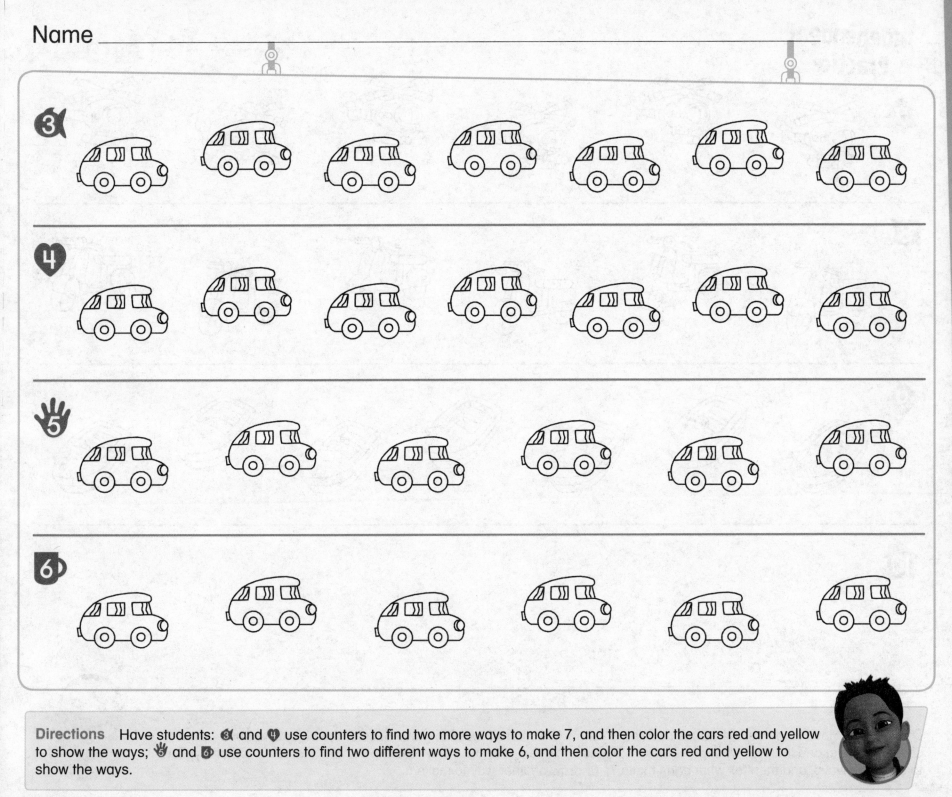

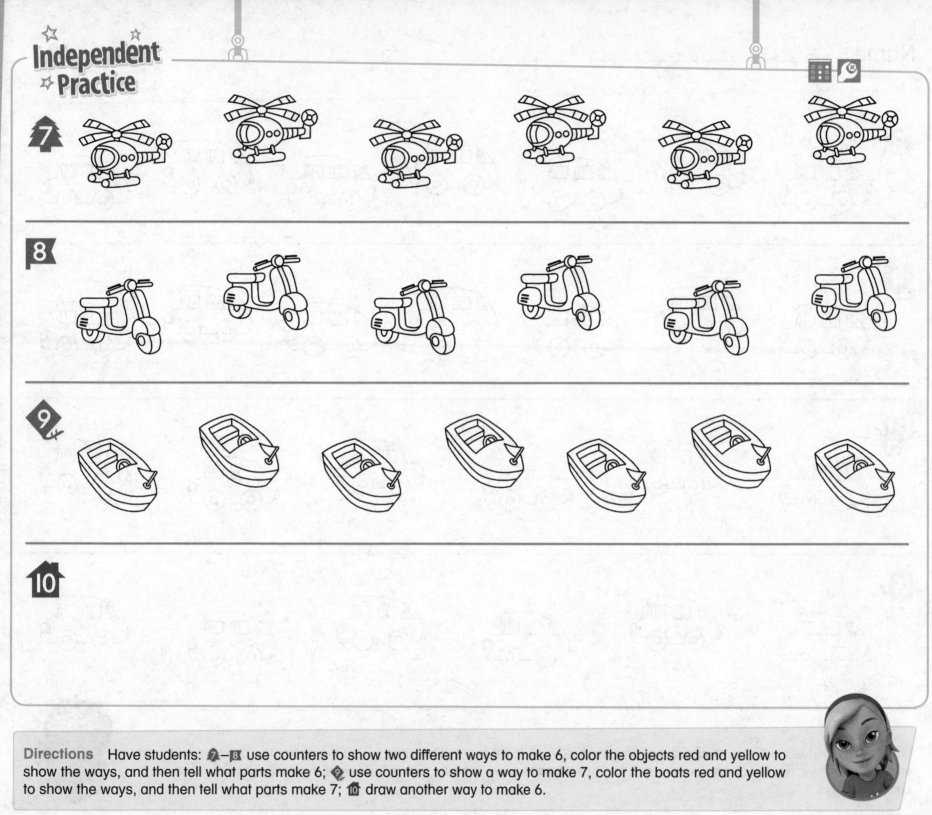

7

8

9

10

Directions Have students: **7**–**8** use counters to show two different ways to make 6, color the objects red and yellow to show the ways, and then tell what parts make 6; **9** use counters to show a way to make 7, color the boats red and yellow to show the ways, and then tell what parts make 7; **10** draw another way to make 6.

130 one hundred thirty   © Pearson Education, Inc. K   **Topic 3** | Lesson 2

Name _____

Another Look

🏠 **HOME CONNECTION**
Your child used counters and colored pictures to show 6 and 7 in two parts.

HOME ACTIVITY Take turns with your child showing 6 and 7 objects in different ways. For example, show 4 pennies showing heads on one side of a table and 3 showing tails on the other. Let your child flip the pennies to show a different way to show 7.

1

2

3

Directions Say: *Use red and blue cubes or pieces of paper to model this way to make 6, and then color the cubes to show the way.* Then have students: 1 use red and blue cubes or pieces of paper to find a different way to make 6, and then color the cubes to show the way; 2 and 3 use red and blue cubes or pieces of paper to find two different ways to make 7, and then color the cubes to show the ways.

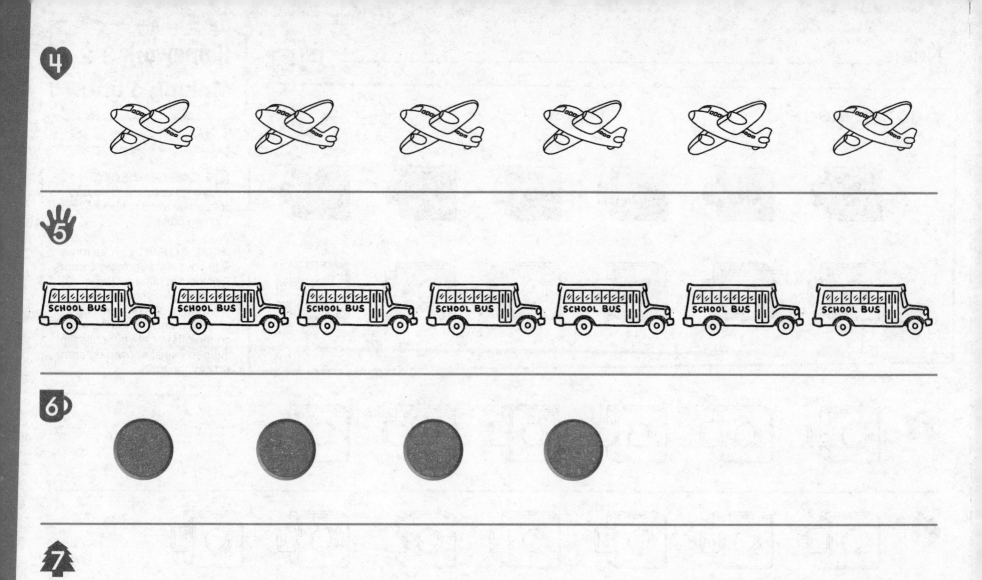

4

5

6

7

Directions Have students: **4** color the planes red and yellow to show a way to make 6; **5** color the buses red and yellow to show a way to make 7; **6** draw yellow counters to complete this way to make 6; **7** draw a way to make 7.

© Pearson Education, Inc. K

Topic 3 | Lesson 2

Directions Say: *Jackson sees seven beach balls. How can he show how many beach balls in two different ways? Draw the ways on the blankets.*

✪ **TEKS K.2B** Read, write, and represent whole numbers from 0 to at least 20 with and without objects or pictures. Also, K.2, K.2C. **Mathematical Process Standards** K.1A, K.1C, K.1D.

Digital Resources at PearsonTexas.com

Solve   Learn   Glossary   Check   Tools   Games

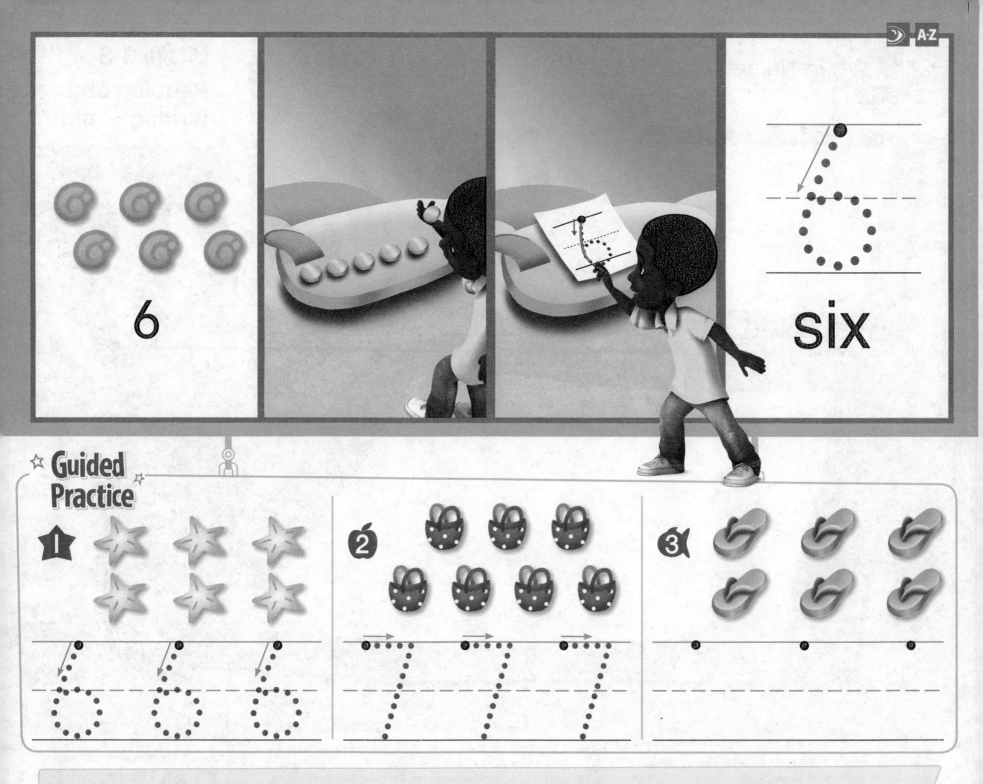

6

six

☆ **Guided Practice** ☆

1

2

3

Directions Have students count the items in each group, and then practice writing the number that tells how many.

© Pearson Education, Inc. K

Topic 3 | **Lesson 3**

Name _____

♥ 4

_____

- - - - - - - - - - - - - - - -

_____

🖐 5

_____

- - - - - - - - - - - - - - - -

_____

☕ 6

_____

- - - - - - - - - - - - - - - -

_____

🌲 7

_____

- - - - - - - - - - - - - - - -

_____

Directions Have students count the items in each group, and then practice writing the number that tells how many.

8

- - - -

9

- - - -

10

- - - -

❄

- - - -

Directions Have students: **8**–**10** count the fish, and then practice writing the number that tells how many; ❄ draw 6 or 7 objects, and then practice writing the number that tells how many.

© Pearson Education, Inc. K

Topic 3 | Lesson 3

Name _____

Another Look

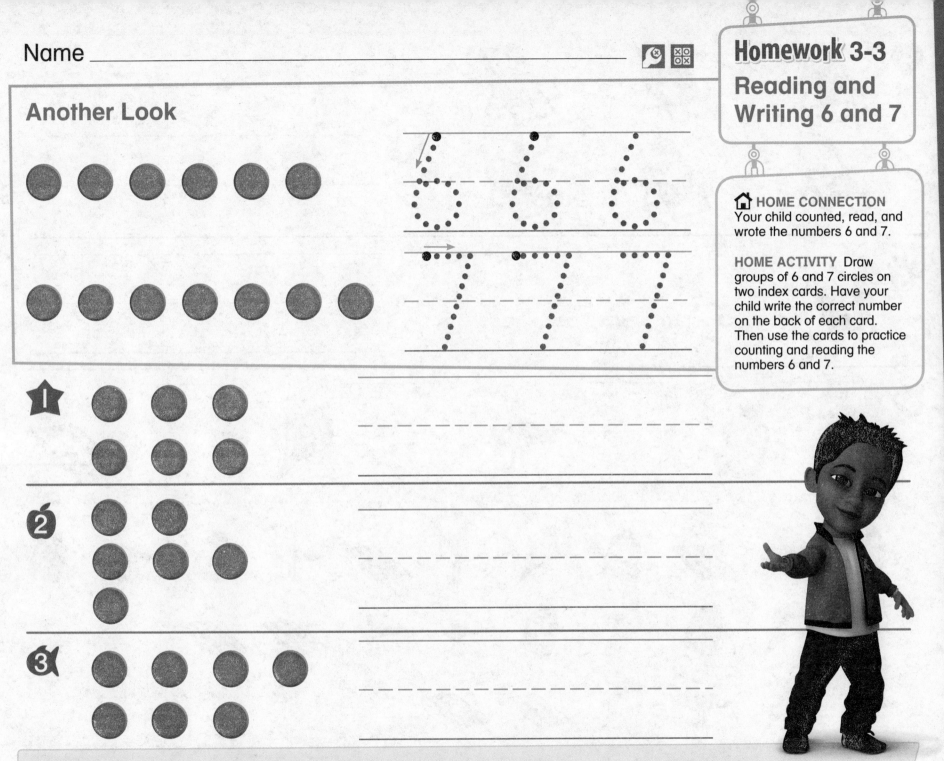

🏠 **HOME CONNECTION**
Your child counted, read, and wrote the numbers 6 and 7.

HOME ACTIVITY Draw groups of 6 and 7 circles on two index cards. Have your child write the correct number on the back of each card. Then use the cards to practice counting and reading the numbers 6 and 7.

1

2

3

Directions Say: *Count the counters, and then practice writing the numbers that tell how many.* Then have students: 1–3 count the counters, and then practice writing the number that tells how many.

© Pearson Education, Inc. K

Solve & Share Name _____

Directions Say: *Jackson made some sandwiches for lunch at the beach. Use counters and draw a picture on the blank sign to show how many sandwiches Jackson made. Tell how you know you are correct.*

⭐ **TEKS K.2C** Count a set of objects up to at least 20 and demonstrate that the last number said tells the number of objects in the set regardless of their arrangement or order. Also, K.2, K.2A, K.2B. **Mathematical Process Standards** K.1C, K.1D, K.1E, K.1G.

Digital Resources at PearsonTexas.com

Solve   Learn   Glossary   Check   Tools   Games

Topic 3 | Lesson 4

one hundred thirty-nine **139**

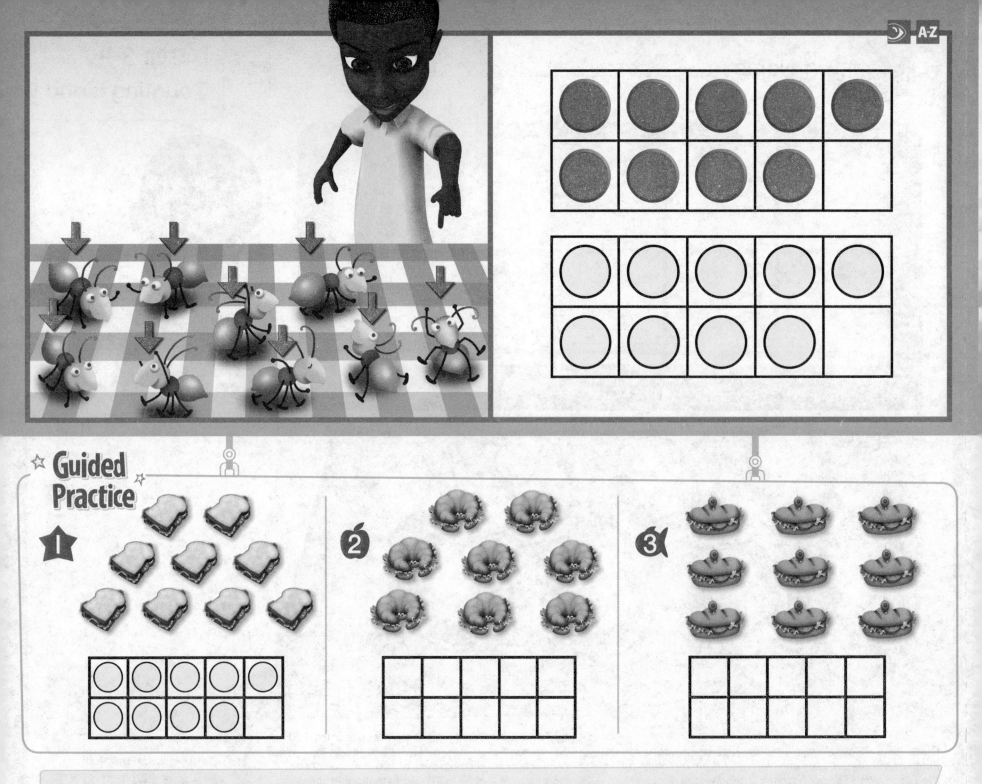

Guided Practice

1

2

3

Directions Have students count the sandwiches in each group, and then draw counters to show how many.

© Pearson Education, Inc. K

Name _____

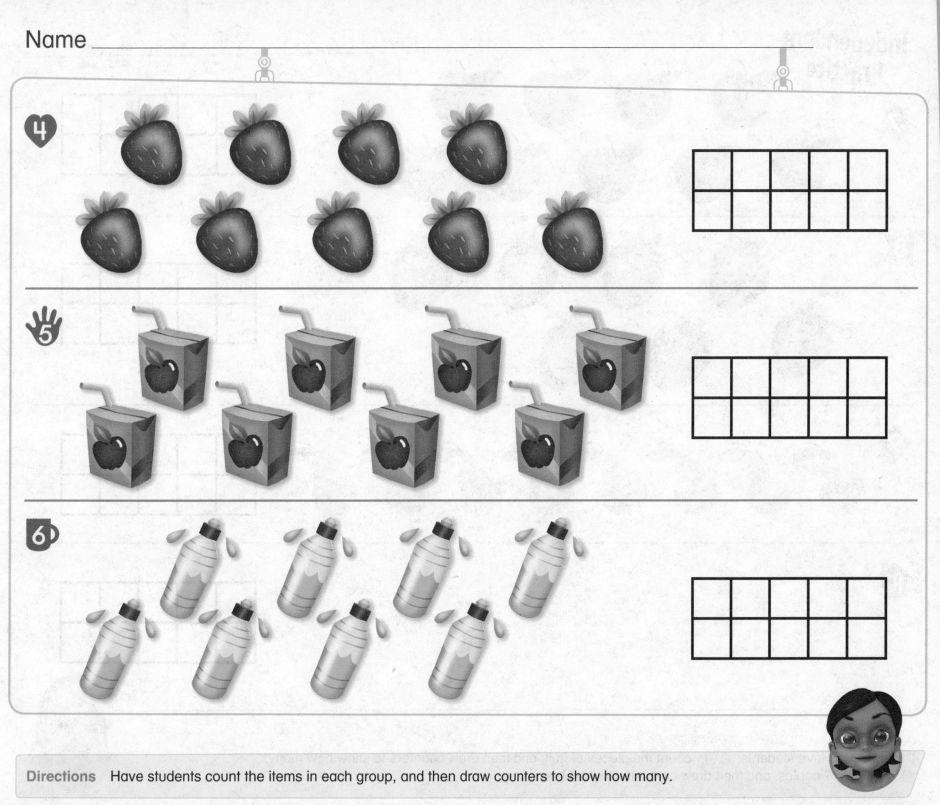

4

5

6

Directions Have students count the items in each group, and then draw counters to show how many.

Topic 3 | **Lesson 4**　　　　　　　　　　　　　　　one hundred forty-one　**141**

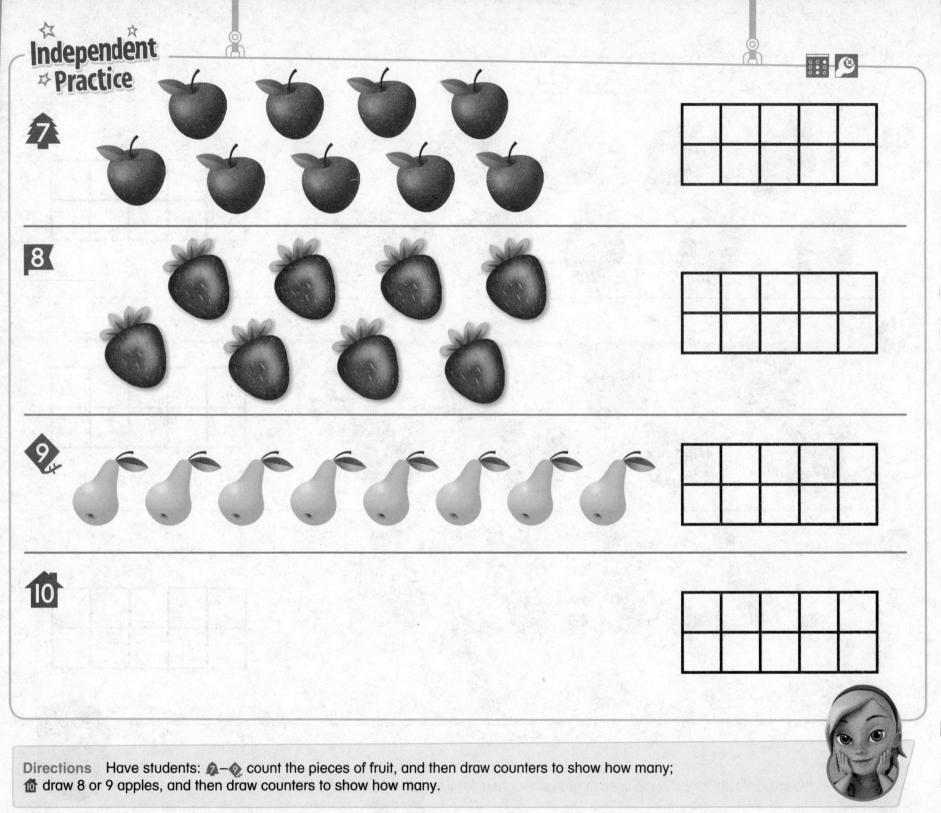

7

8

9

10

Directions Have students: **7**–**9** count the pieces of fruit, and then draw counters to show how many; **10** draw 8 or 9 apples, and then draw counters to show how many.

© Pearson Education, Inc. K

Another Look

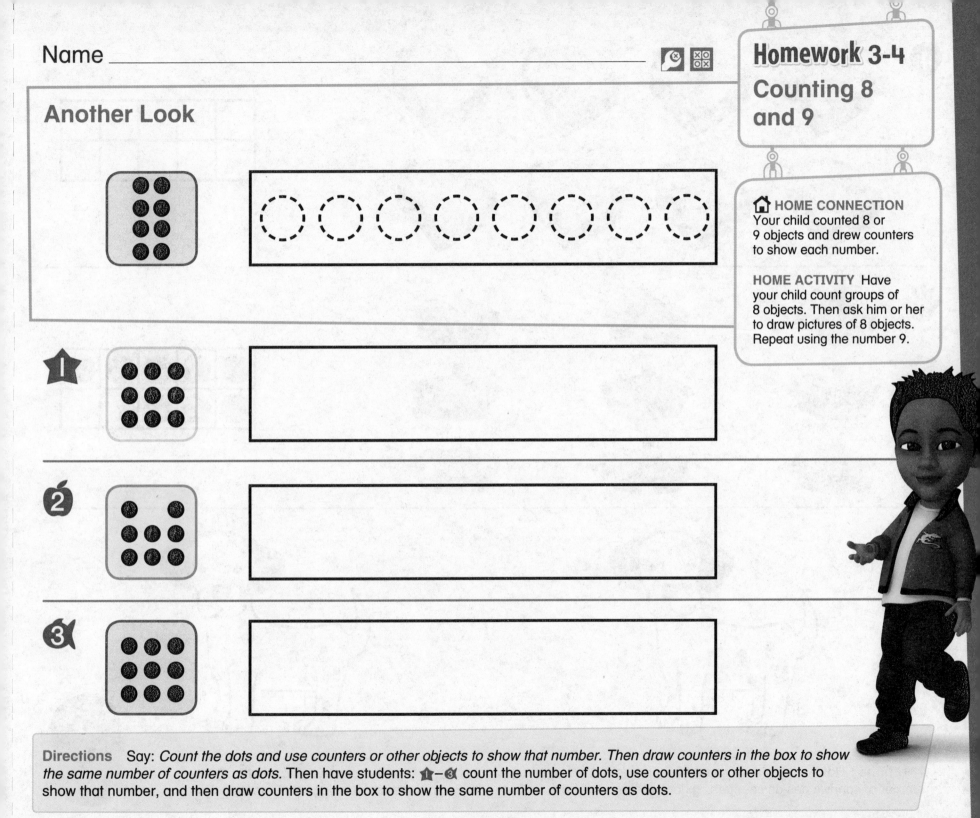

1

2

3

Directions Say: *Count the dots and use counters or other objects to show that number. Then draw counters in the box to show the same number of counters as dots.* Then have students: **1**—**3** count the number of dots, use counters or other objects to show that number, and then draw counters in the box to show the same number of counters as dots.

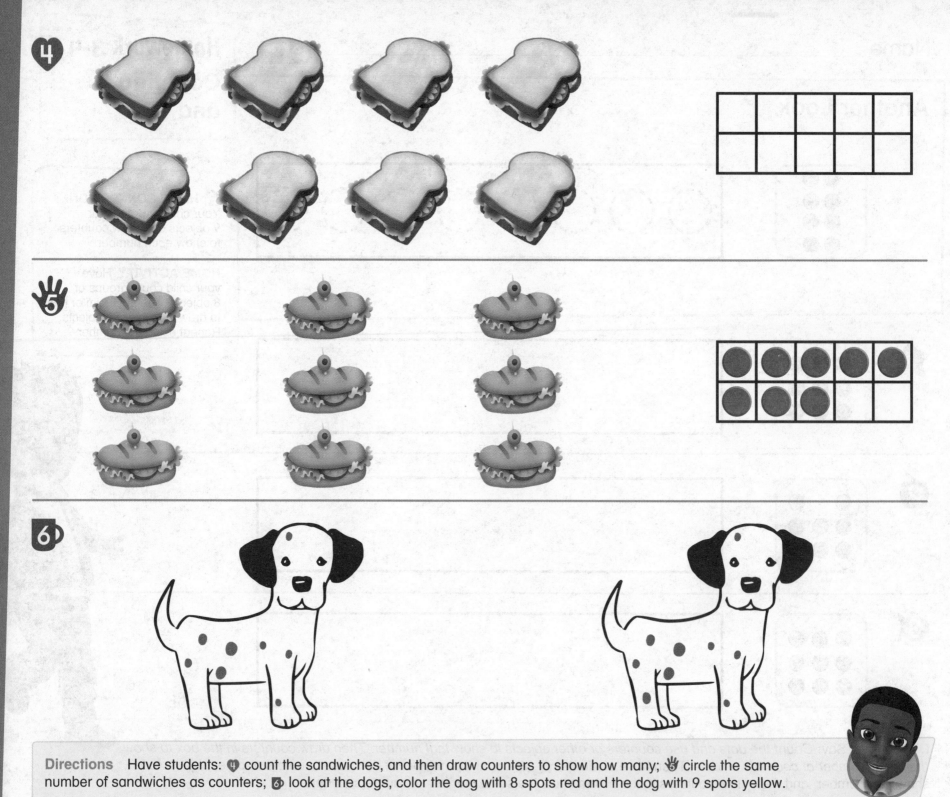

Directions Have students: ❹ count the sandwiches, and then draw counters to show how many; ✋ circle the same number of sandwiches as counters; ❻ look at the dogs, color the dog with 8 spots red and the dog with 9 spots yellow.

© Pearson Education, Inc. K

Topic 3 | Lesson 4

Solve & Share   Name _____

Directions Say: *Jackson brought 8 apples for his friends to eat at the picnic. How can you use counters to show 8 in different ways? Color the counters red and yellow to show your work. Has the total number of counters changed? Why or why not?*

⭐ **TEKS K.2I** Compose and decompose numbers up to 10 with objects and pictures. Also, K.2. **Mathematical Process Standards** K.1C, K.1D, K.1F.

Digital Resources at PearsonTexas.com
Solve Learn Glossary Check Tools Games

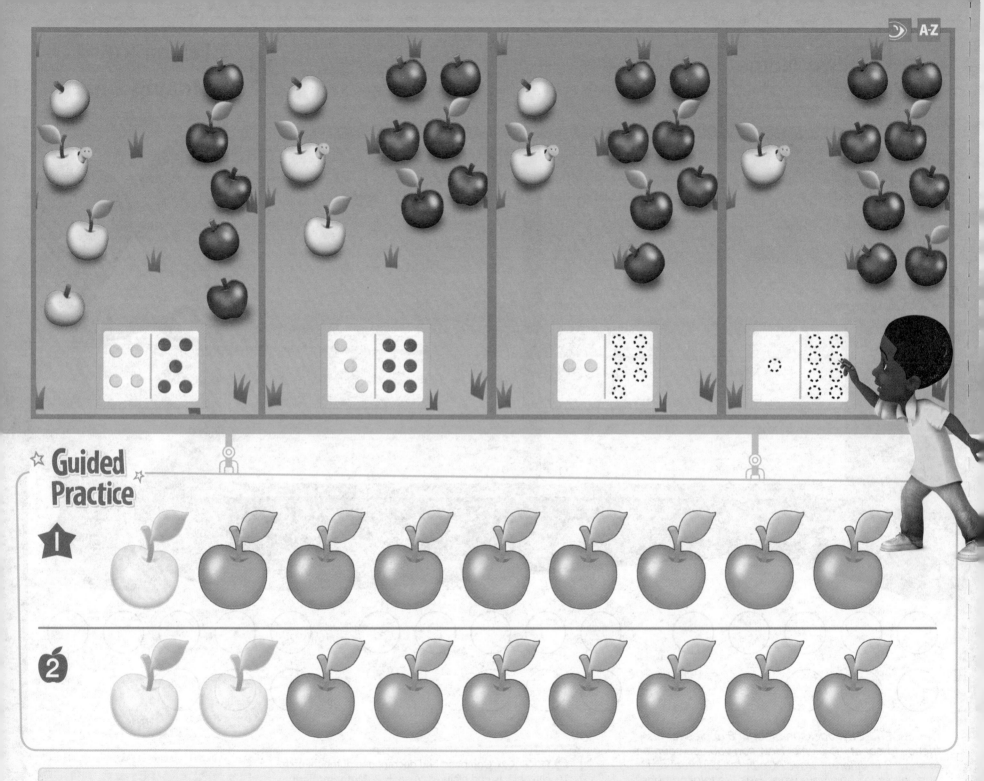

Guided Practice

1

2

Directions Have students use counters to find these two ways to make 9, and then color the apples to show these ways.

© Pearson Education, Inc. K

Topic 3 | Lesson 5

Name _____

3

4

5

6

Directions Have students: **3** and **4** use counters to find two more ways to make 9, and then color the fruit red and yellow to show the ways; **5** and **6** use counters to find two different ways to make 8, and then color the fruit red and yellow to show the ways.

Topic 3 | Lesson 5   one hundred forty-seven   **147**

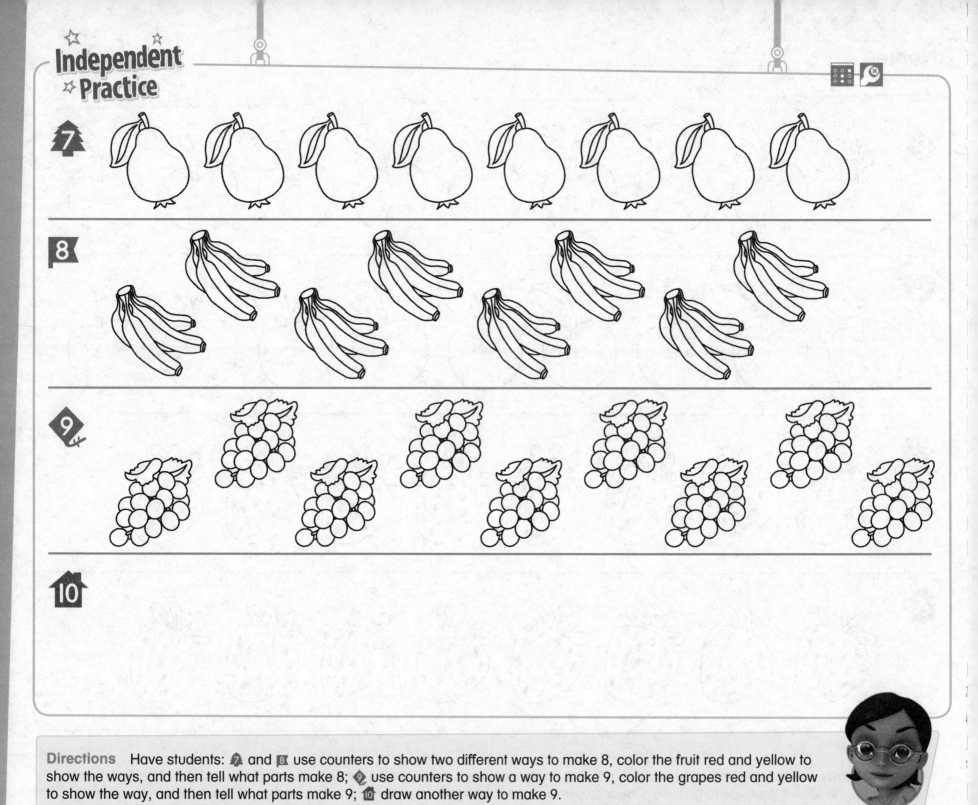

7

8

9

10

Directions Have students: **7** and **8** use counters to show two different ways to make 8, color the fruit red and yellow to show the ways, and then tell what parts make 8; **9** use counters to show a way to make 9, color the grapes red and yellow to show the way, and then tell what parts make 9; **10** draw another way to make 9.

Name _____

Another Look

⭐ 1

② 2

③ 3

Directions Say: *Use red and blue cubes or pieces of paper to model this way to make 8, and then color the cubes to show the way.* Then have students: ⭐ use red and blue cubes or pieces of paper to find a different way to make 8, and then color the cubes to show the way; ② and ③ use red and blue cubes or pieces of paper to find two different ways to make 9, and then color the cubes to show the ways.

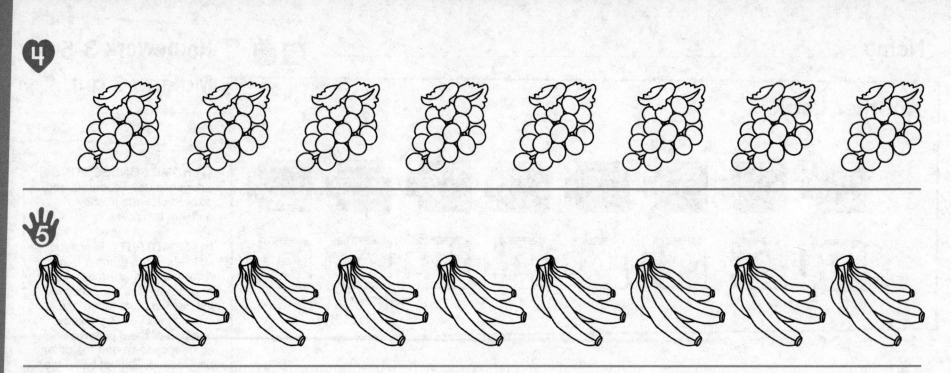

4

5

6

7

Directions Have students: **4** color the grapes red and blue to show a way to make 8; **5** color the bananas green and yellow to show a way to make 9; **6** draw yellow counters to complete this way to make 8; **7** draw red and yellow counters to show two different ways to make 9.

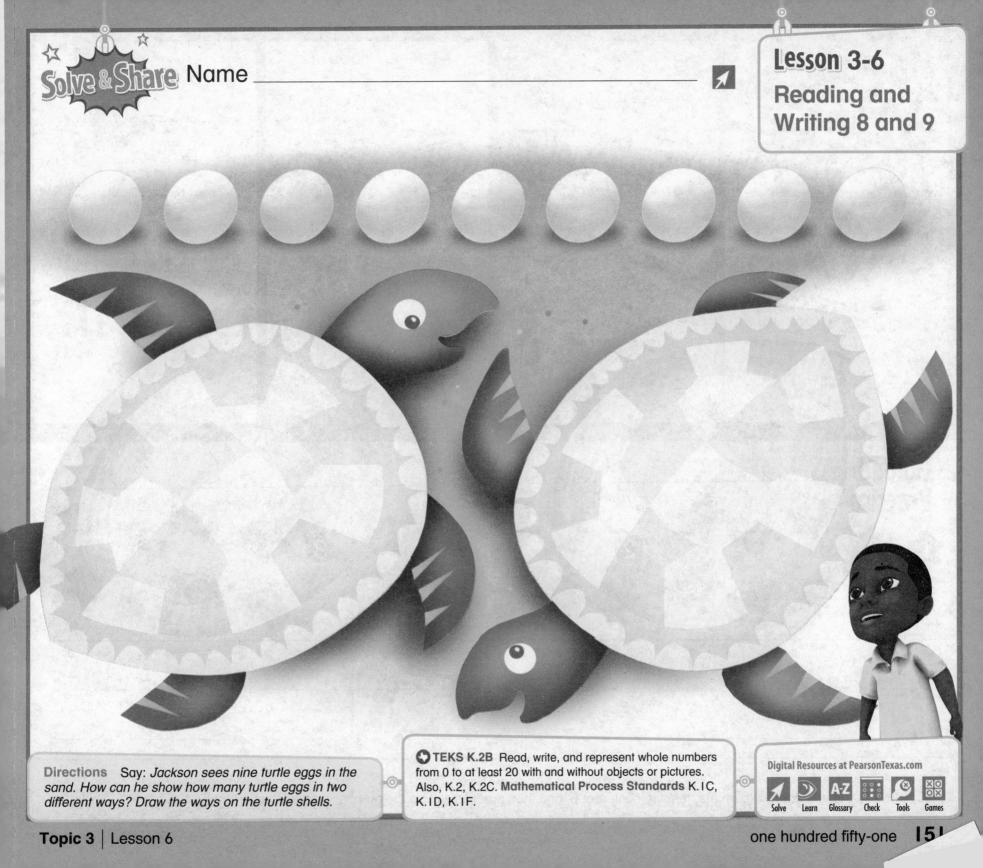

Solve & Share Name _____

Directions Say: *Jackson sees nine turtle eggs in the sand. How can he show how many turtle eggs in two different ways? Draw the ways on the turtle shells.*

⭐ **TEKS K.2B** Read, write, and represent whole numbers from 0 to at least 20 with and without objects or pictures. Also, K.2, K.2C. **Mathematical Process Standards** K.1C, K.1D, K.1F.

Digital Resources at PearsonTexas.com

Solve Learn Glossary Check Tools Games

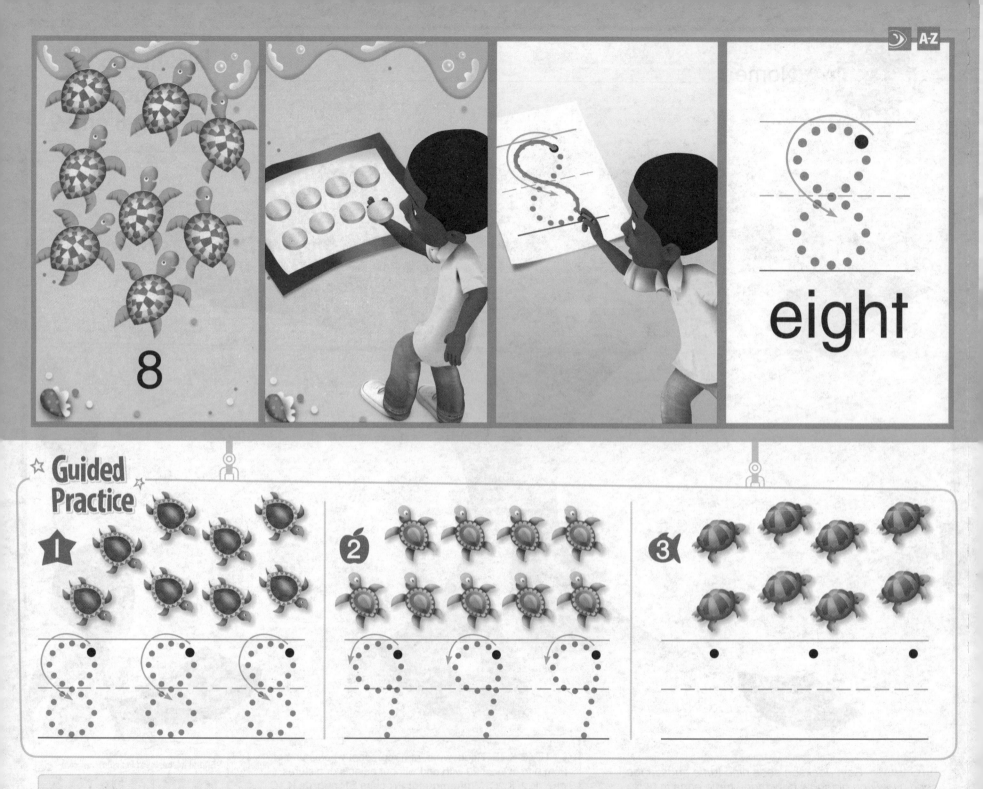

8

eight

☆ Guided Practice ☆

1

2

3

Directions Have students count the items in each group, and then practice writing the number that tells how many.

© Pearson Education, Inc. K

Topic 3 | Lesson 6

Name _____

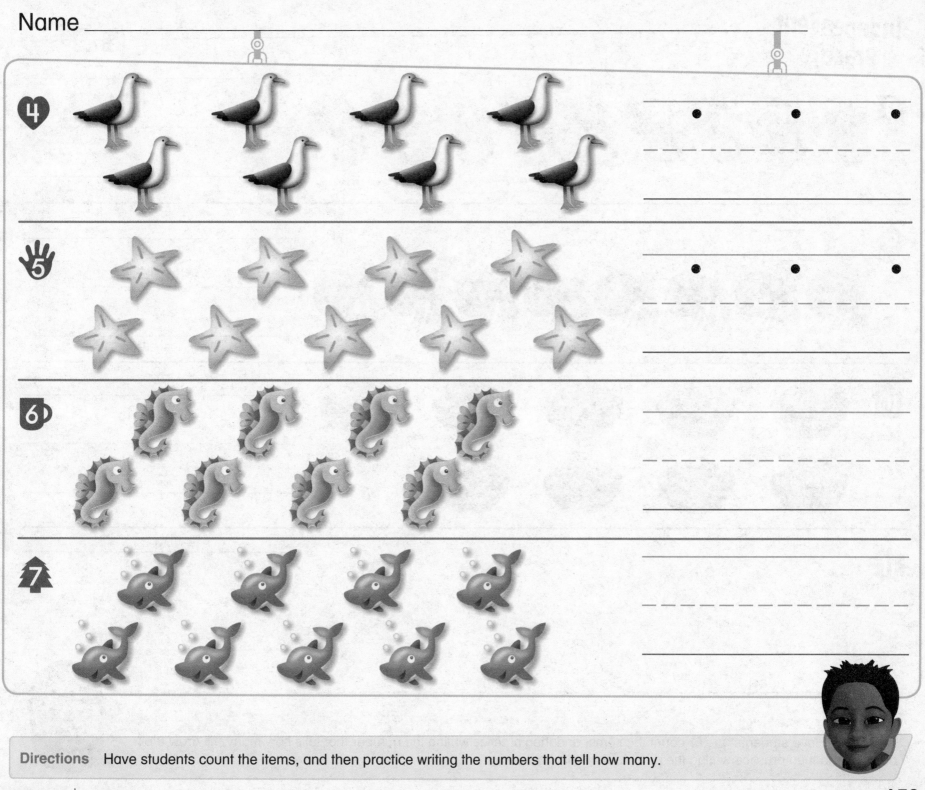

♥ 4

🖐 5

☕ 6

🌲 7

Directions Have students count the items, and then practice writing the numbers that tell how many.

Independent Practice

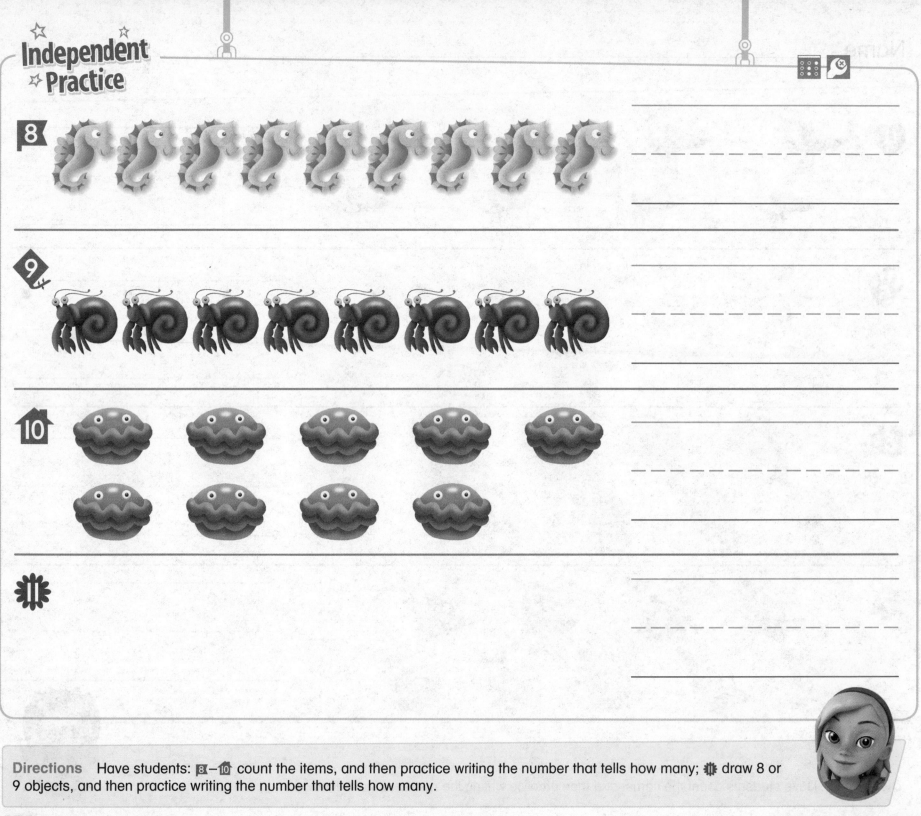

8

9

10

⁂

Directions Have students: **8**–**10** count the items, and then practice writing the number that tells how many; **⁂** draw 8 or 9 objects, and then practice writing the number that tells how many.

© Pearson Education, Inc. K

Name _____

Another Look

HOME CONNECTION Your child counted, read, and wrote the numbers 8 and 9.

HOME ACTIVITY Draw groups of 8 and 9 circles on two index cards. Have your child write the correct number on the back of each card. Then use the cards to practice counting and reading the numbers 8 and 9.

Directions Say: *Count the counters, and then practice writing the numbers that tell how many.* Then have students:
★–③ count the dots, and then practice writing the number that tells how many.

4 ♥

_____

_ _ _ _ _ _ _ _ _ _

_____

5 ✋

_____

_ _ _ _ _ _ _ _ _ _

_____

6 ☕

_____   _ _ _ _ _ _ _ _ _ _   _____

_ _ _ _ _ _ _ _ _ _   _____

Directions Have students: **4** count the items, and then practice writing the number that tells how many; **5** draw more beach balls to show 9, and then practice writing the number 9; **6** count each group of objects, and then write the numbers that tell how many.

© Pearson Education, Inc. K

Solve & Share Name _____

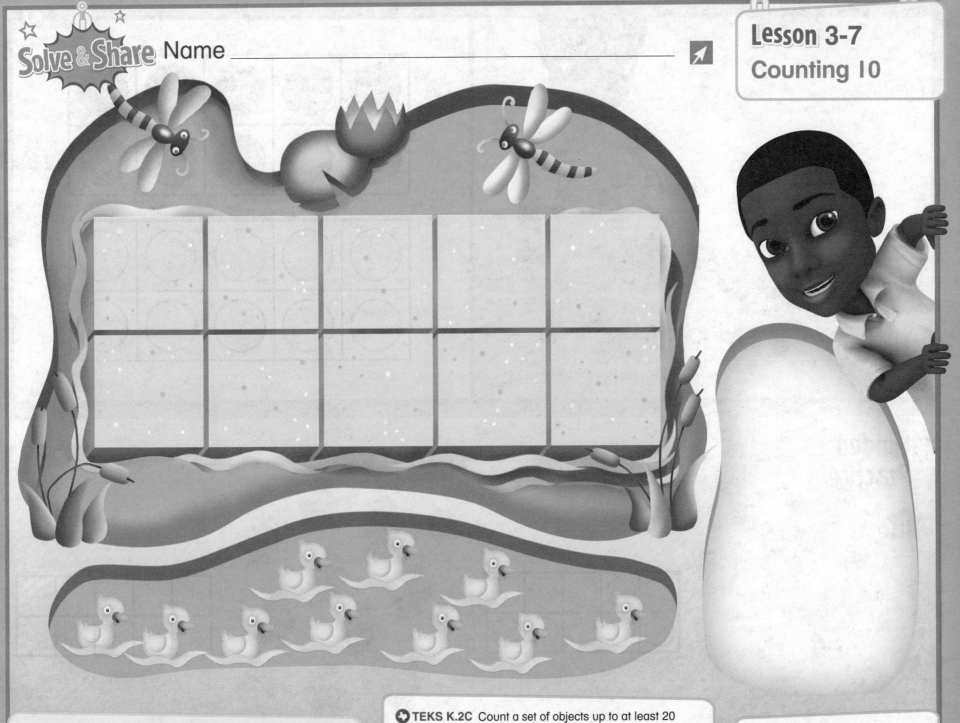

Directions Say: *Jackson sees some ducks swimming in a pond. Use counters and draw a picture in the empty pond to show how many ducks Jackson sees. Tell how you know you are correct.*

⭐ **TEKS K.2C** Count a set of objects up to at least 20 and demonstrate that the last number said tells the number of objects in the set regardless of their arrangement or order. Also, K.2, K.2A, K.2B. **Mathematical Process Standards** K.1C, K.1D, K.1E.

Digital Resources at PearsonTexas.com

Solve Learn Glossary Check Tools Games

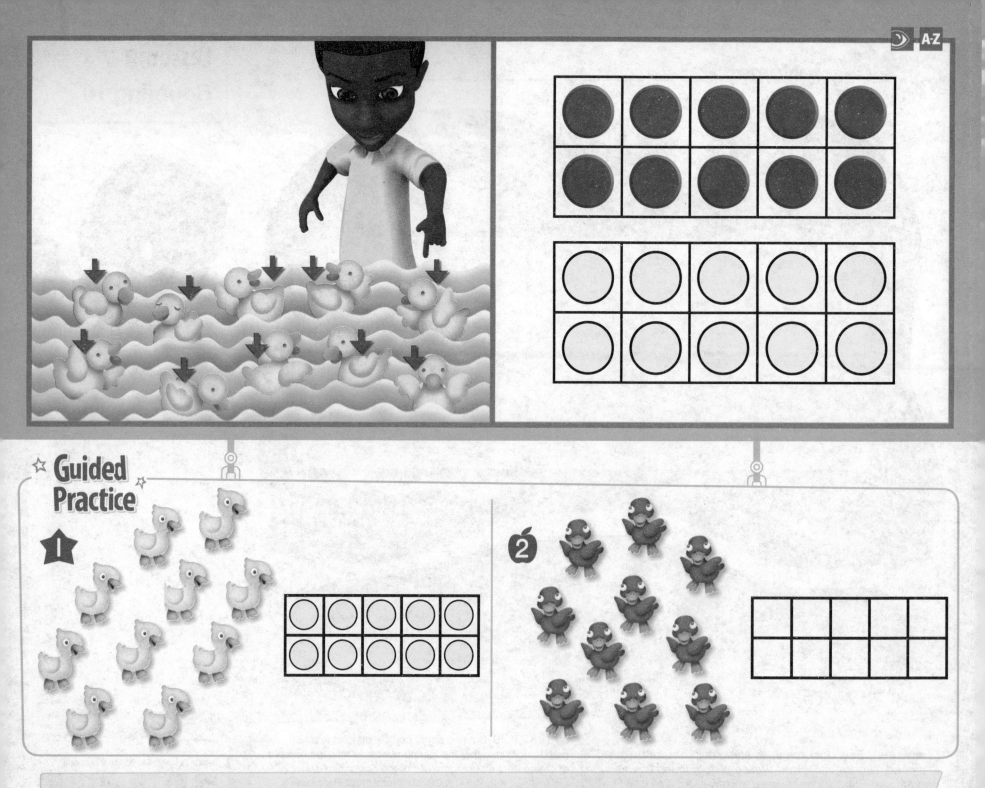

Guided Practice

1

2

Directions Have students count the birds in each group, and then draw counters to show how many.

© Pearson Education, Inc. K

Name _____

Directions Have students count the birds in each group, and then draw counters to show how many.

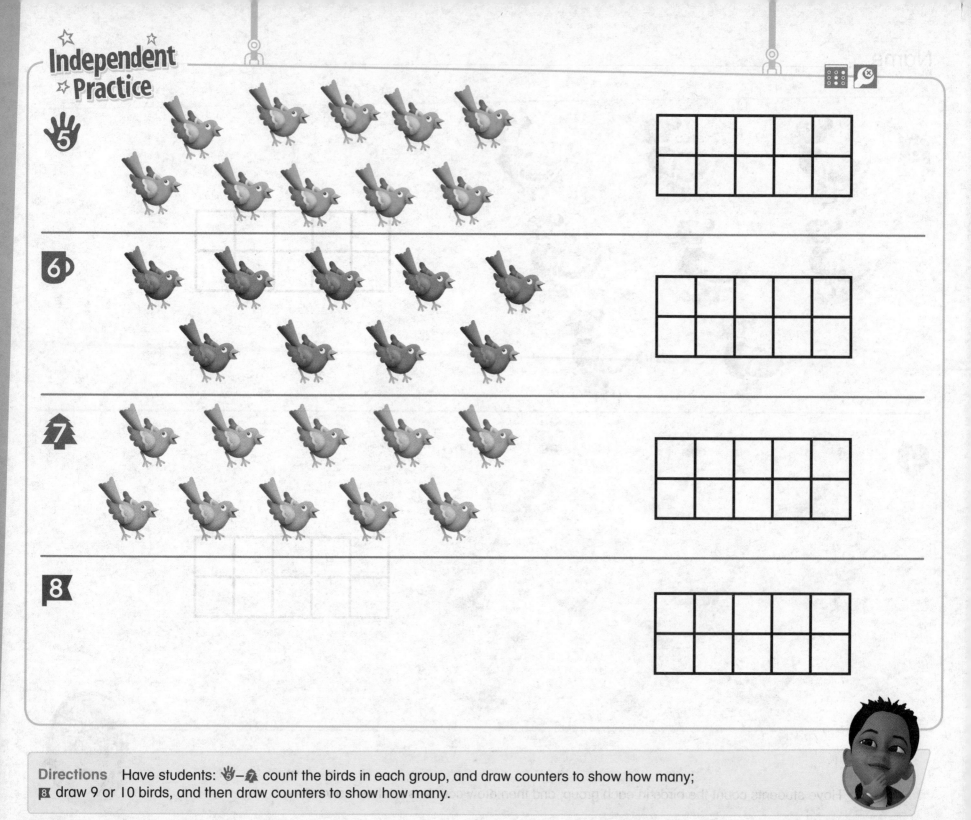

✋5

6

7

8

Directions Have students: ✋5–7 count the birds in each group, and draw counters to show how many; 8 draw 9 or 10 birds, and then draw counters to show how many.

© Pearson Education, Inc. K

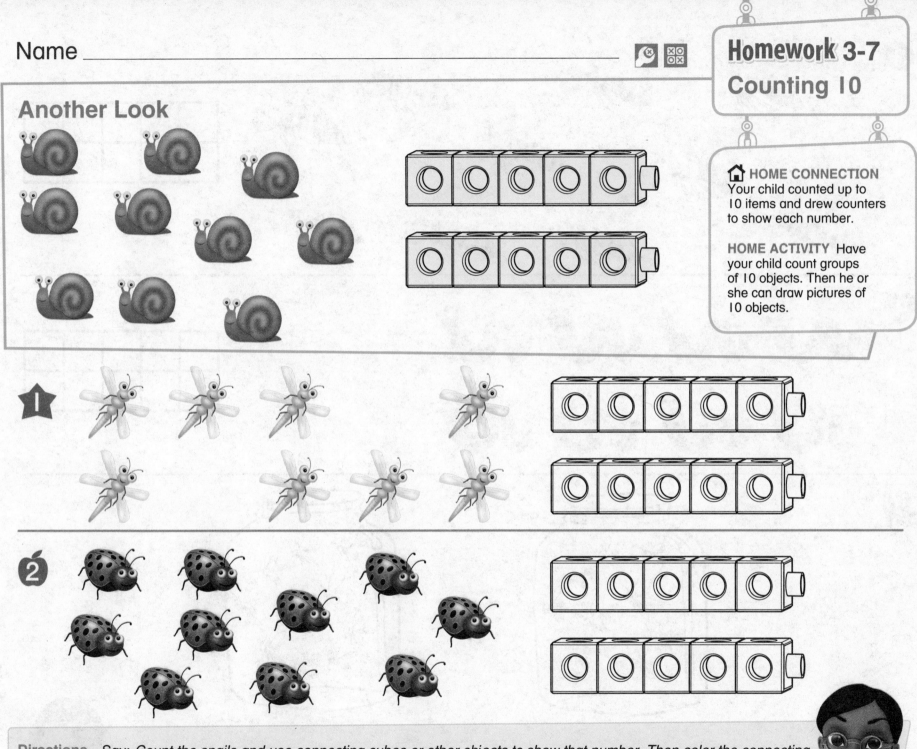

Another Look

🏠 **HOME CONNECTION** Your child counted up to 10 items and drew counters to show each number.

HOME ACTIVITY Have your child count groups of 10 objects. Then he or she can draw pictures of 10 objects.

⭐ 1

2

Directions Say: *Count the snails and use connecting cubes or other objects to show that number. Then color the connecting cubes to show the same number of cubes as snails.* Then have students: ⭐ and ❷ count the bugs and use connecting cubes or other objects to show that number, and then color the connecting cubes to show the same number of cubes as bugs.

3

4

5

© Pearson Education, Inc. K

Solve & Share

Name _____

Directions Say: *Jackson puts 10 watering cans on a shelf in the garden store. How can you use counters to show the 10 watering cans in different ways? Color the counters red and yellow to show your work.*

⭐ **TEKS K.2I** Compose and decompose numbers up to 10 with objects and pictures. Also, K.2. **Mathematical Process Standards** K.1C, K.1D, K.1E, K.1F.

Digital Resources at PearsonTexas.com

Solve Learn Glossary Check Tools Games

Guided Practice

1

2

Directions Have students use counters to find these two ways to make 10, and then color the bugs to show these ways.

© Pearson Education, Inc. K

Topic 3 | Lesson 8

Name _____

3

4

5

Directions Have students use counters to find three more ways to make 10, and then color the bugs red and yellow to show the ways.

Topic 3 | Lesson 8

one hundred sixty-five **165**

Directions Have students: 🔟–🔟 use counters to show three different ways to make 10, color the bugs red and yellow to show the ways, and then tell what parts make 10; 🔟 draw a way to make 10.

Another Look

🏠 **HOME CONNECTION**
Your child used counters to show 10 in two parts. Your child colored in pictures to show 10 in two parts.

HOME ACTIVITY Have your child show the number 10 in different ways using 10 cards or pictures. Ask your child to tell the two parts that make the 10. Have your child show one part of the 10 pictures or cards facedown and the other part faceup.

⭐ 1

🍎 2

🐟 3

Directions Say: *Use red and blue cubes or pieces of paper to model this way to make 10, and then color the cubes to show the way.* Then have students: ⭐–🐟 *use red and blue cubes or pieces of paper to find three different ways to make 10, and then color the cubes to show the ways.*

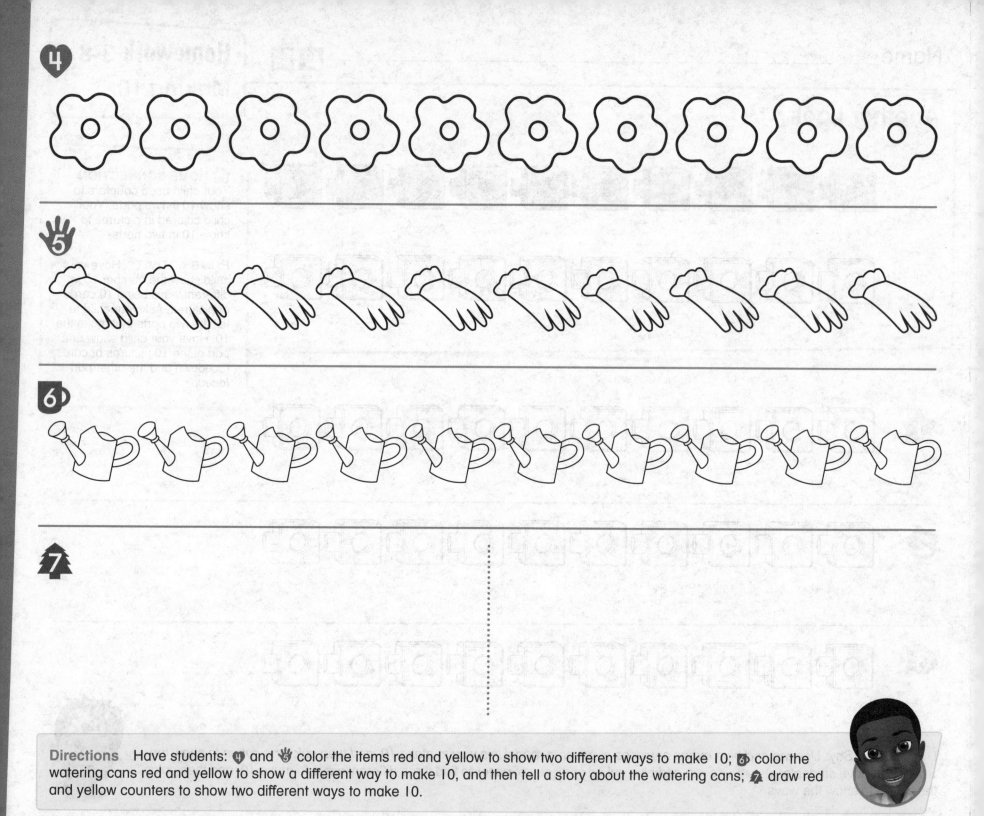

4

5

6

7

© Pearson Education, Inc. K

Solve & Share Name _____

Directions Say: *Jackson sees 10 fish in the water. How can he show how many fish he sees? Show or draw one way on the boat.*

⭐**TEKS K.2B** Read, write, and represent whole numbers from 0 to at least 20 with and without objects or pictures. Also, K.2, K.2C. **Mathematical Process Standards** K.1C, K.1D, K.1F.

Digital Resources at PearsonTexas.com

Solve Learn Glossary Check Tools Games

Topic 3 | Lesson 9

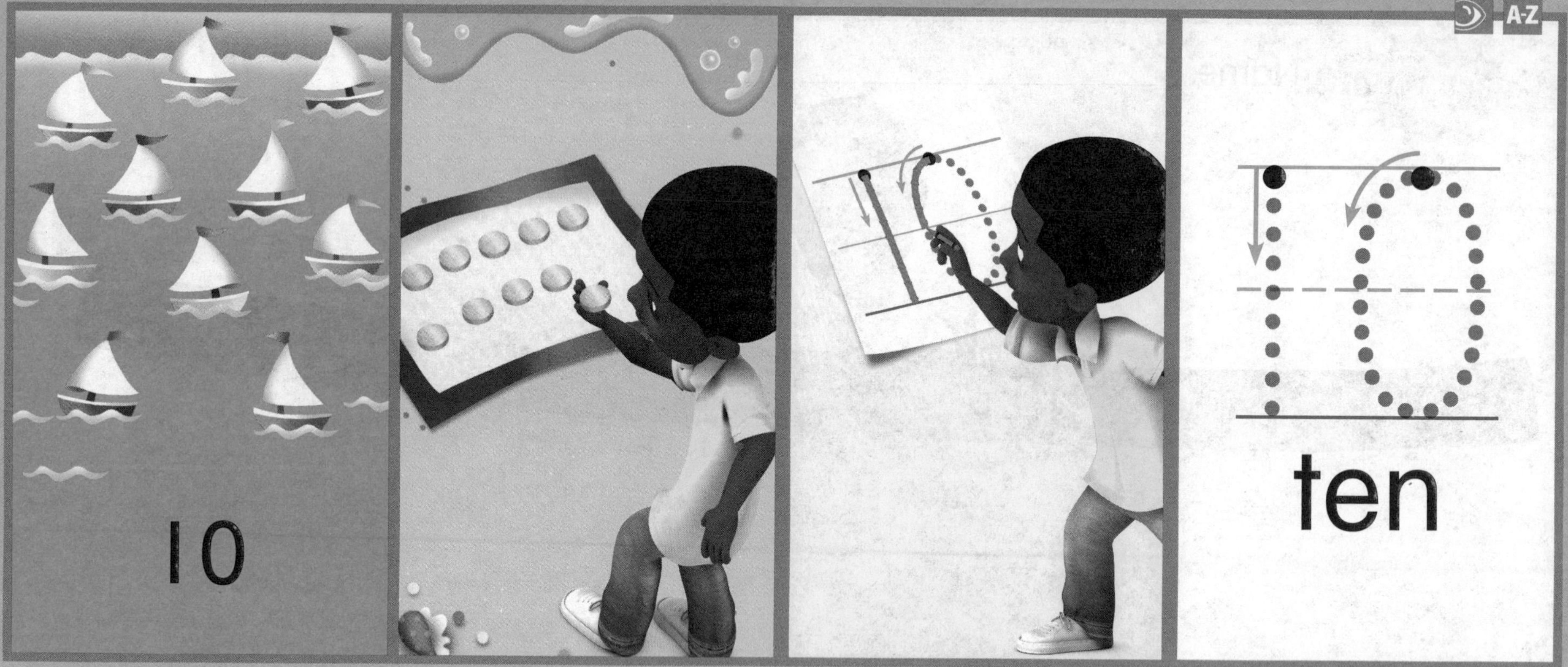

10

ten

☆ **Guided Practice** ☆

1

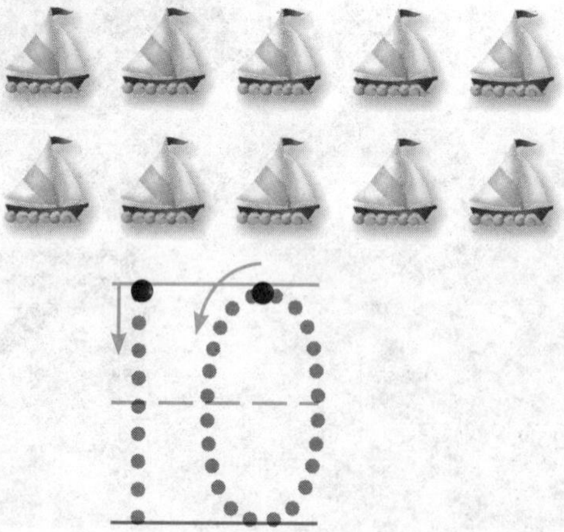

2

3

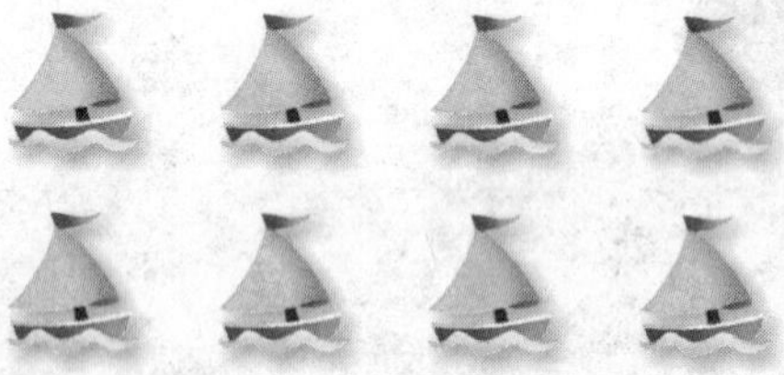

Directions Have students count the items in each group, and then write the number that tells how many.

170 one hundred seventy

© Pearson Education, Inc. K

Topic 3 | Lesson 9

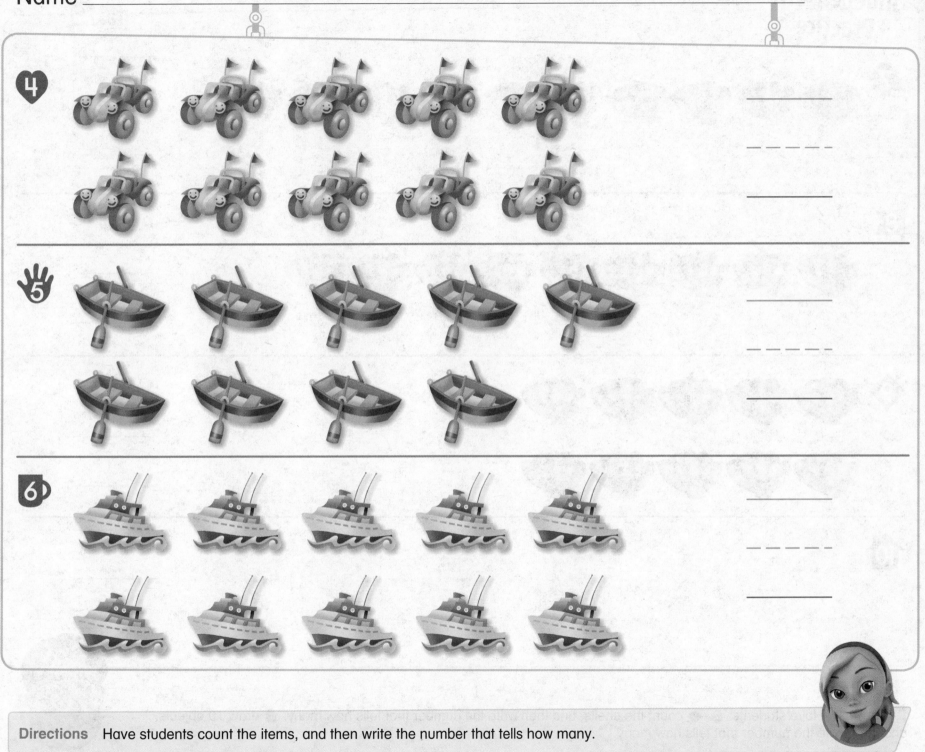

4

5

6

Directions Have students count the items, and then write the number that tells how many.

7
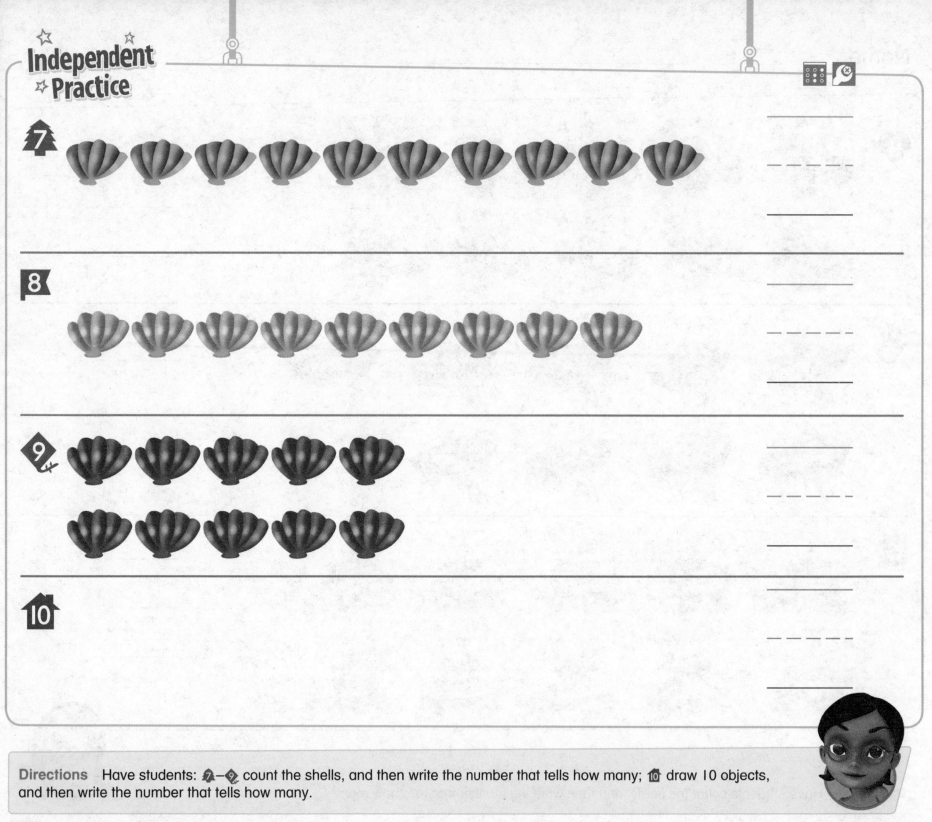

8

9

10

Directions Have students: **7**–**9** count the shells, and then write the number that tells how many; **10** draw 10 objects, and then write the number that tells how many.

172 one hundred seventy-two   © Pearson Education, Inc. K   **Topic 3** | **Lesson 9**

Another Look

🏠 **HOME CONNECTION**
Your child counted, read, and
wrote the number 10.

HOME ACTIVITY Draw
groups of 9 and 10 circles on
two index cards. Have your
child write the correct number
on the back of each card.
Then use the cards to practice
counting and reading the
numbers 9 and 10.

Directions Say: *Count the sea stars, and then write the number that tells how many.* Then have students:
⭐ count each group of sea stars, and then write the number that tells how many.

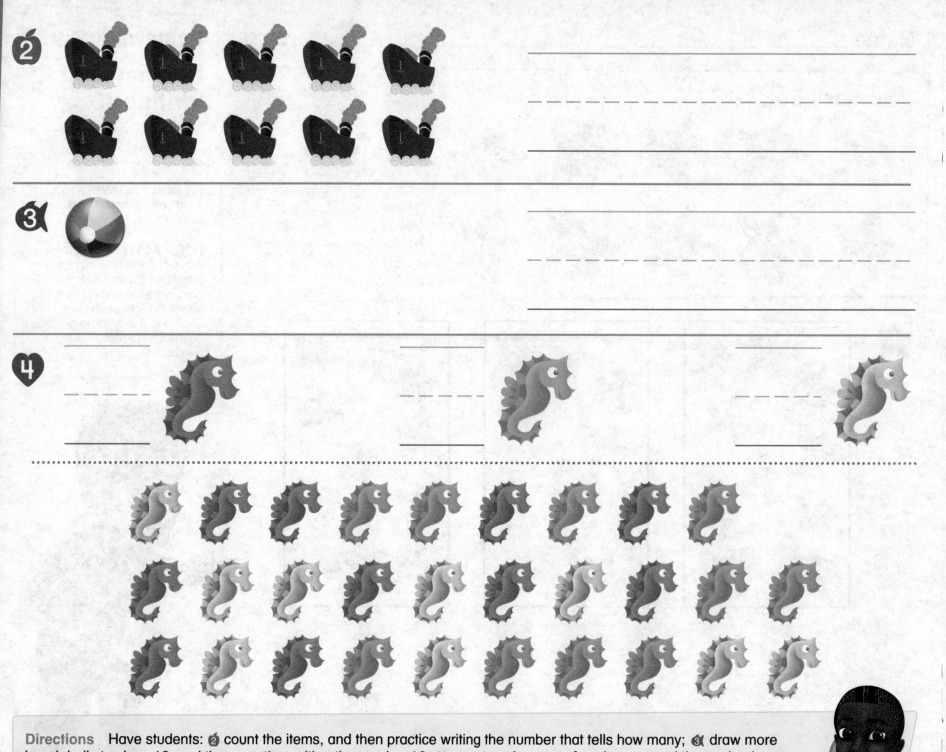

© Pearson Education, Inc. K

Solve & Share Name _____

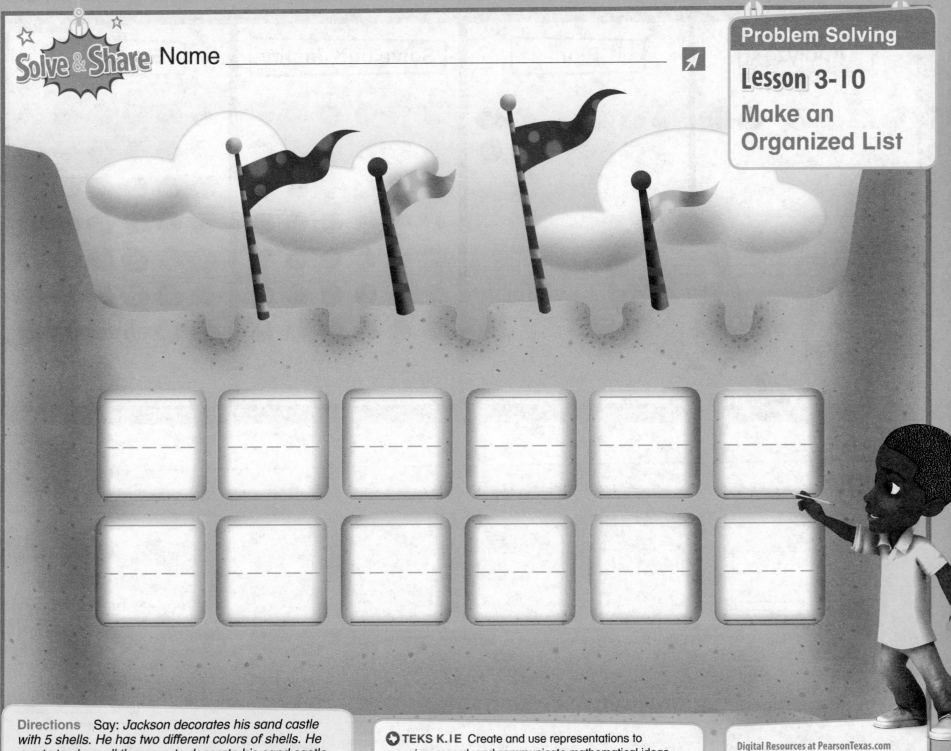

Directions Say: *Jackson decorates his sand castle with 5 shells. He has two different colors of shells. He wants to show all the ways to decorate his sand castle with 5 shells. How can he use a list to help himself keep track of all the ways to make 5?*

⭐ **TEKS K.1E** Create and use representations to organize, record, and communicate mathematical ideas. Also, **K.2, K.2I. Mathematical Process Standards K.1B, K.1C, K.1G.**

Digital Resources at PearsonTexas.com

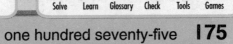

Solve Learn Glossary Check Tools Games

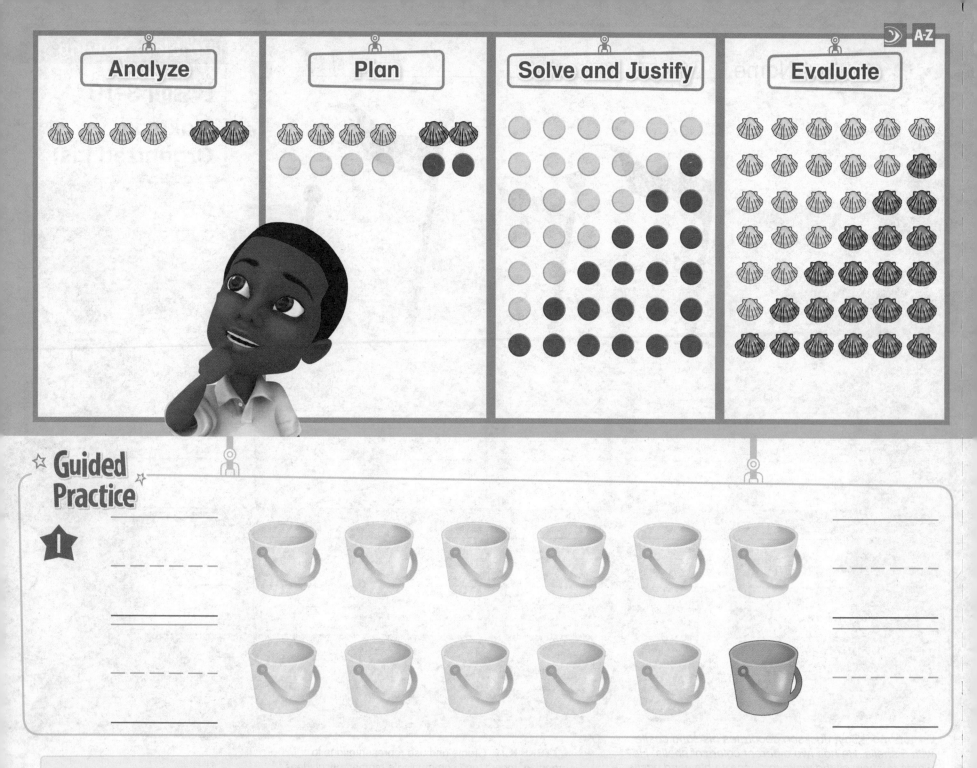

Analyze	Plan	Solve and Justify	Evaluate

☆ Guided Practice ☆

1

Directions Say: *How can you color the pails to show all of the different ways to make 6?* Have students use red and yellow crayons to make an organized list showing these two ways to make 6, and then write the numbers.

© Pearson Education, Inc. K

Topic 3 | Lesson 10

Name _____

2

Directions Say: *How can you color the pails to show all of the different ways to make 6?* Have students use red and yellow crayons to complete the organized list showing the other five ways to make 6, and then write the numbers.

Topic 3 | Lesson 10

one hundred seventy-seven **177**

3

4

Directions Have students: **3** color the shells red and yellow to make an organized list showing all the ways to make 2, and then write the numbers; **4** show two different ways to make 7, and then write the numbers.

178 one hundred seventy-eight   © Pearson Education, Inc. K   **Topic 3** | Lesson 10

Another Look

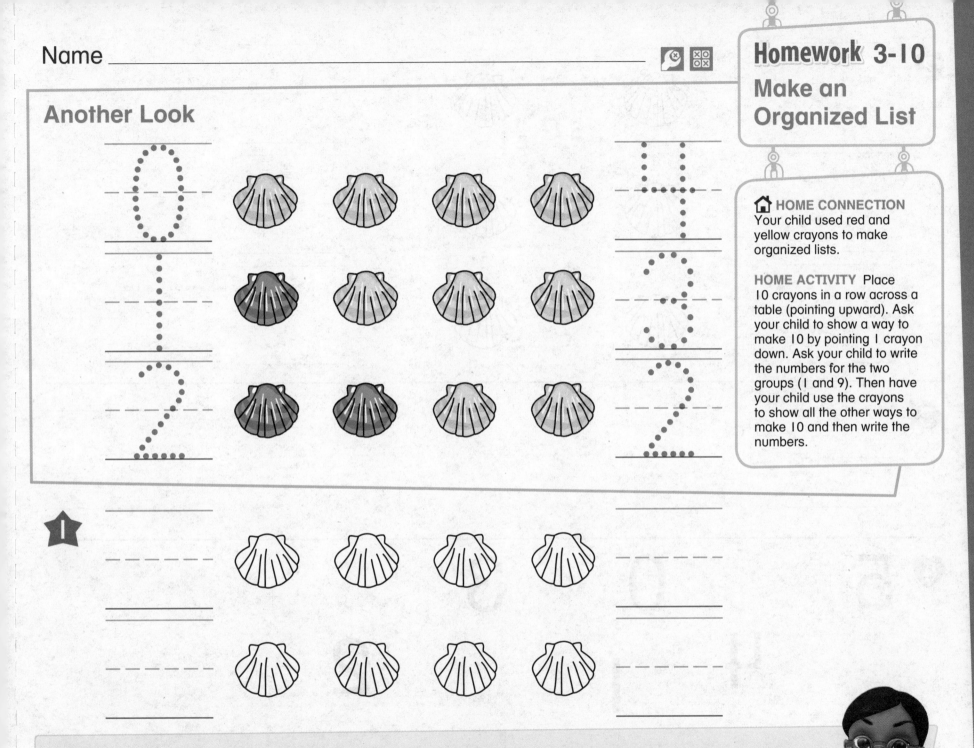

🏠 **HOME CONNECTION**
Your child used red and yellow crayons to make organized lists.

HOME ACTIVITY Place 10 crayons in a row across a table (pointing upward). Ask your child to show a way to make 10 by pointing 1 crayon down. Ask your child to write the numbers for the two groups (1 and 9). Then have your child use the crayons to show all the other ways to make 10 and then write the numbers.

Directions Say: *You can make an organized list to show all of the different ways to make 4. First, you can show 0 red shells and 4 yellow shells. Next, you can show 1 red shell and 3 yellow shells. Show the next way to make 4.* Then have students: ⭐ color the shells red and yellow to complete the organized list showing all the ways to make 4, and then write the numbers.

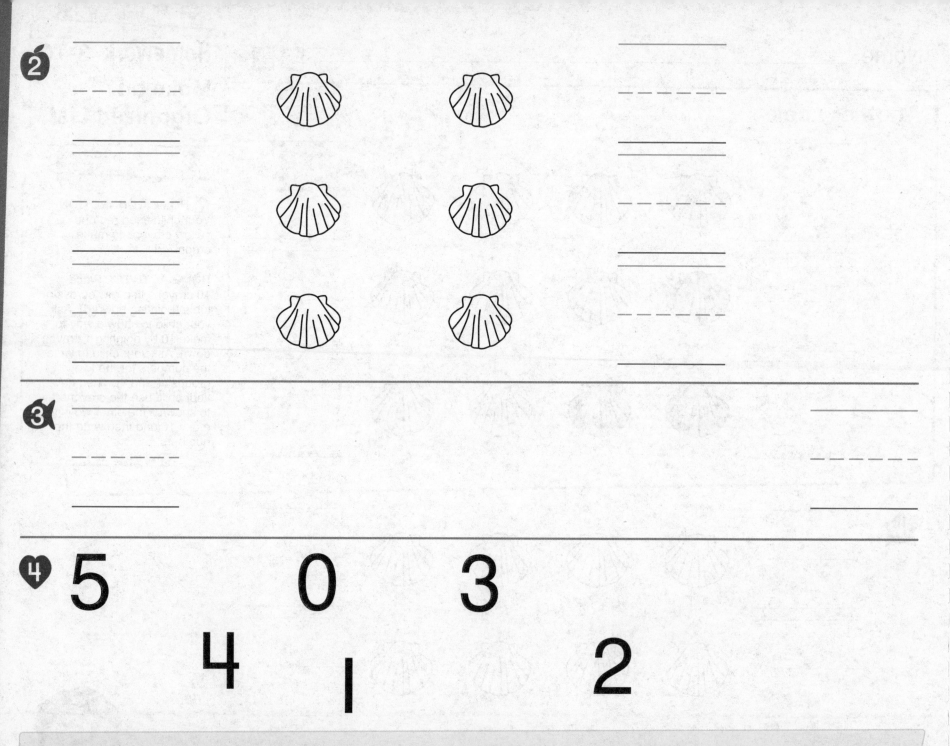

2

3

4 5   0   3

4   1   2

Name _____

Set A _____

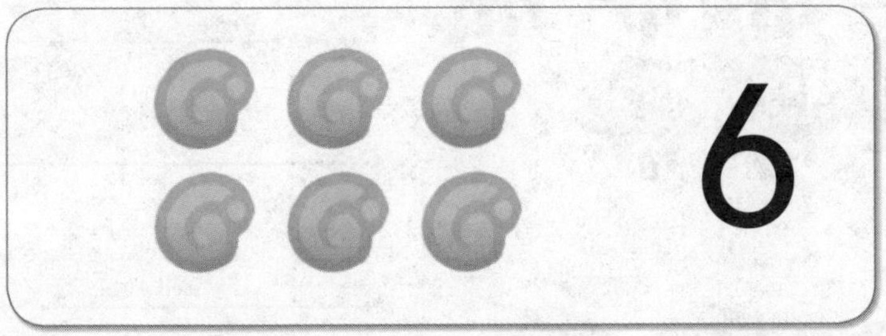

6

7

⭐1

🍎2

Set B _____

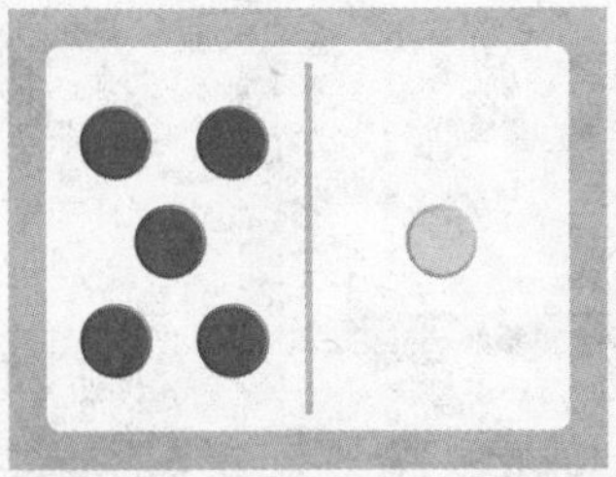

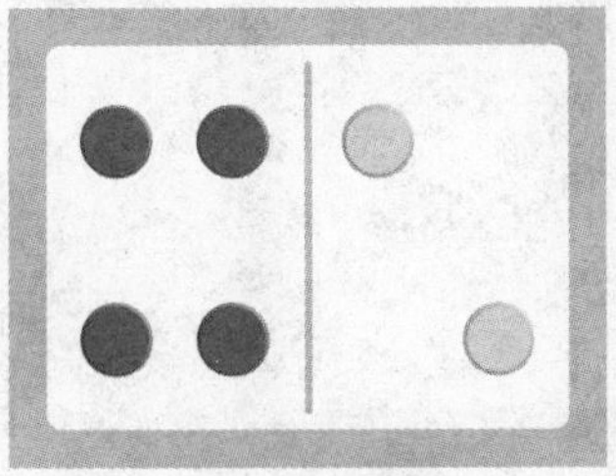

❸

❤4

Directions   Have students: ⭐ and 🍎 count the items, and then practice writing the numbers that tell how many; ❸ and ❤ use counters and a part-part mat to show two more ways to make 6, and then draw counters to show the ways.

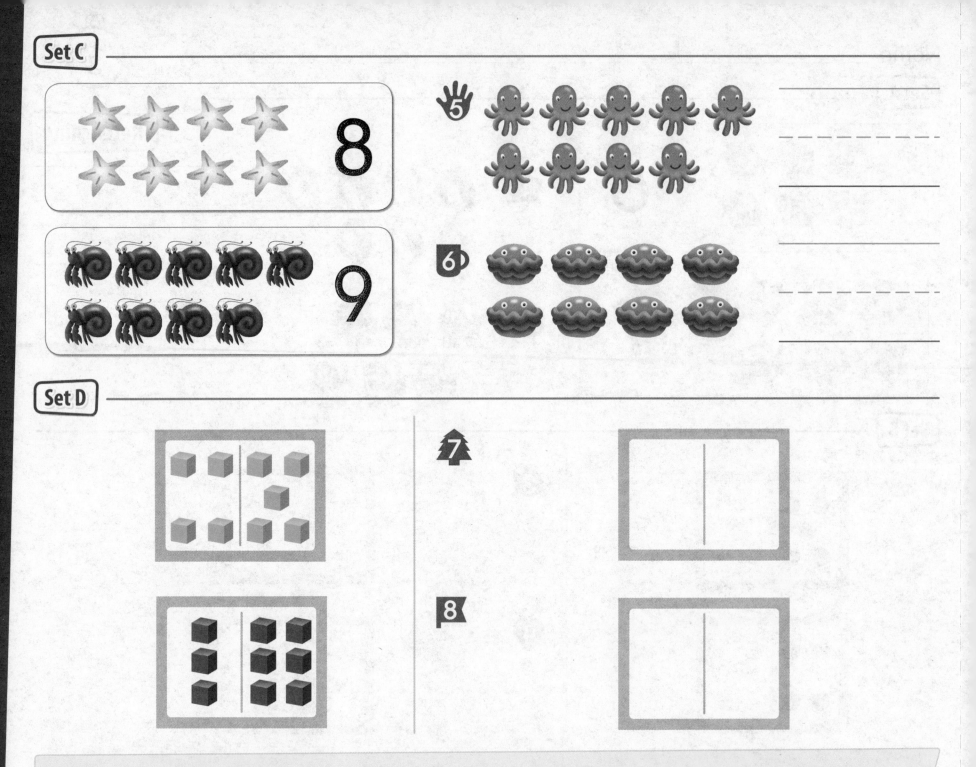

Directions Have students: 👋 and 🐚 count the items, and then practice writing the numbers that tell how many; 🌲 and 🚩 draw boxes to show two more ways to make 9.

182 one hundred eighty-two   © Pearson Education, Inc. K   Topic 3

Name _____

10

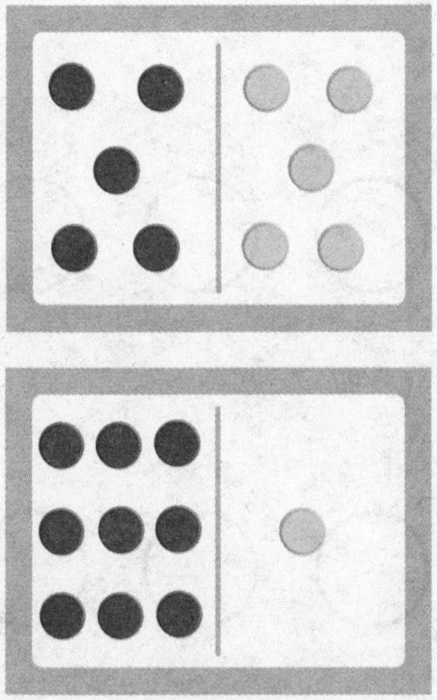

🏠10

Directions Have students: 9️⃣ count the items, and then practice writing the number that tells how many; 🔟 and ⏸ use counters and a part-part mat to show two more ways to make 10, and then draw counters to show the ways.

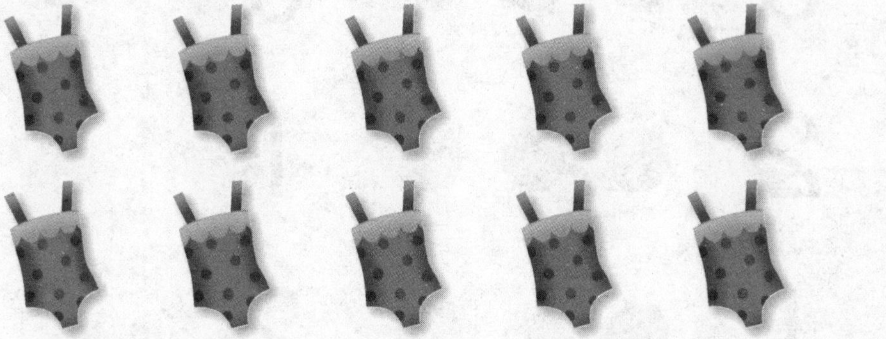

Topic 3

one hundred eighty-three **183**

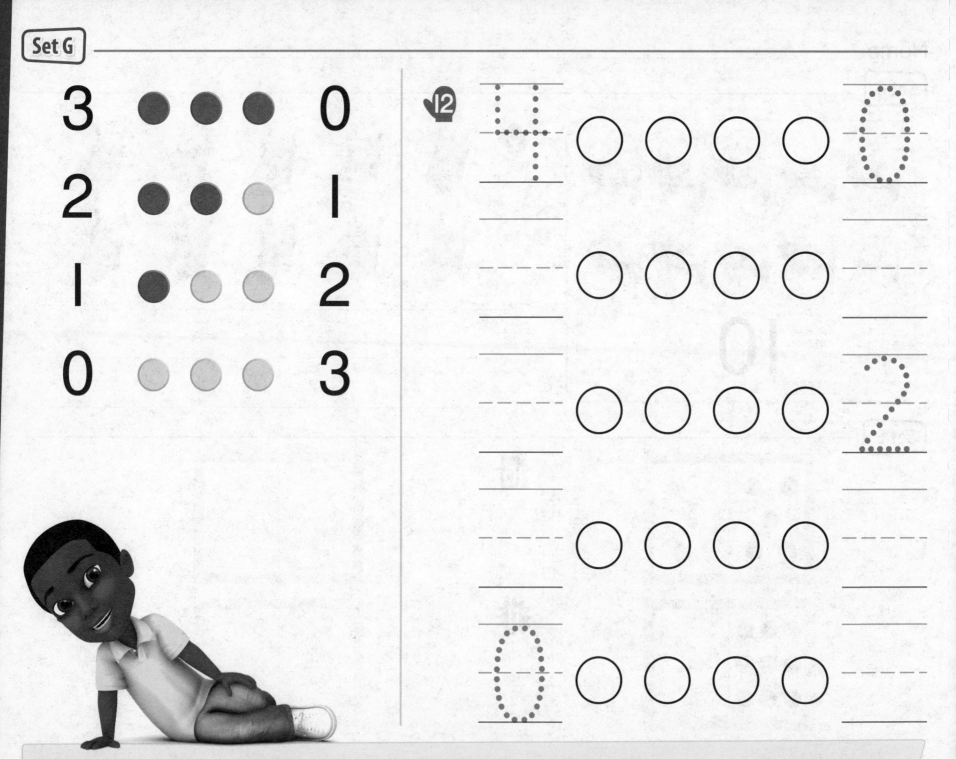

Directions Have students use two different colored crayons to complete the organized list showing all of the ways to make 4, and then write the numbers.

© Pearson Education, Inc. K

Name _____

⭐ 1

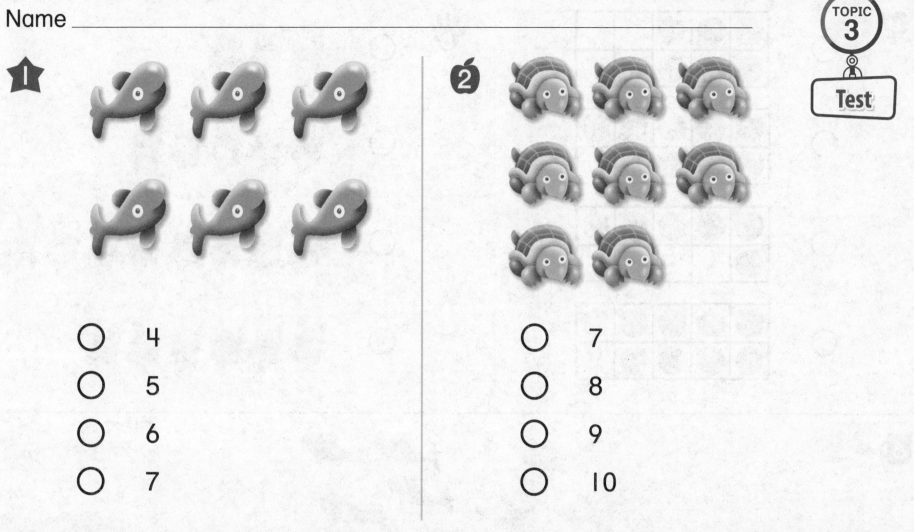

○ 4

○ 5

○ 6

○ 7

🍎 2

○ 7

○ 8

○ 9

○ 10

3

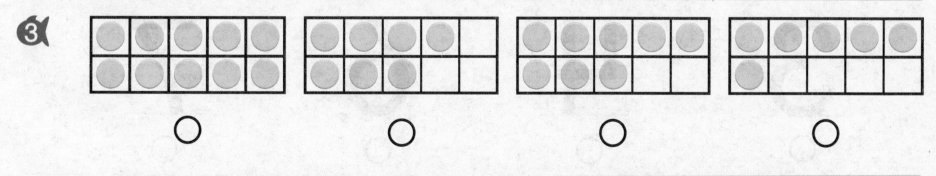

○   ○   ○   ○

Directions Have students mark the best answer. ⭐ How many fish are there? 🍎 How many turtles are there? 3 Which shows the number 8?

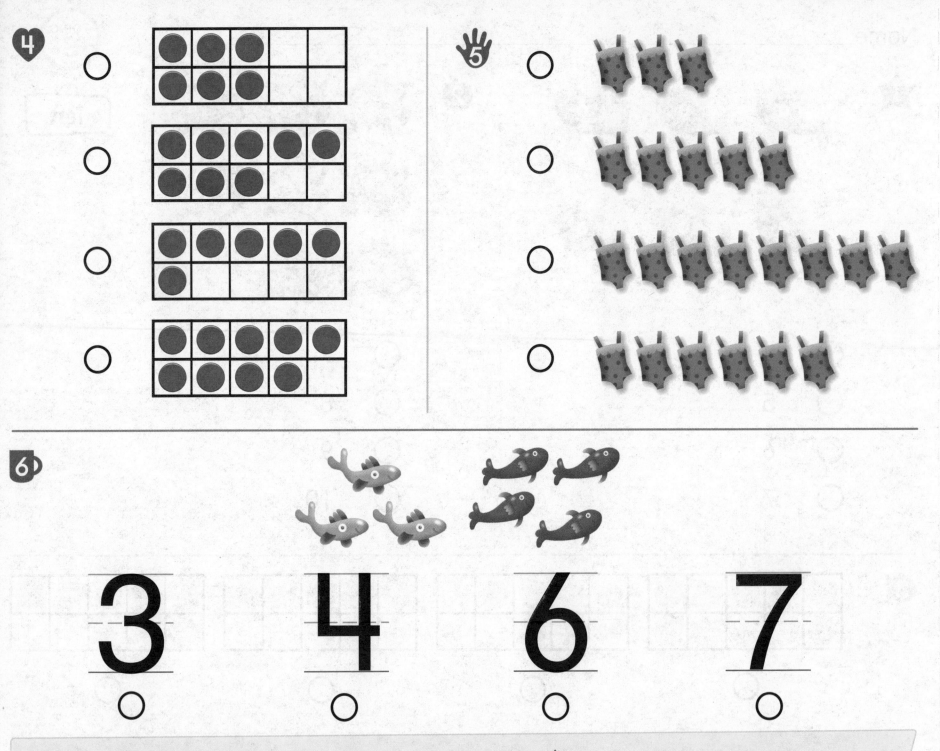

4 ○

○

○

○

5 ○

○

○

○

6

3   4   6   7

○   ○   ○   ○

Directions   Have students mark the best answer. **4** Which shows the number 9? **5** Which shows 8 swimsuits? **6** Which number tells how many fish?

© Pearson Education, Inc. K   **Topic 3**

Name _____

○

○

○

○

8

7   8   9   10

○   ○   ○   ○

9

_____

- - - - - -

_____

Directions Have students: 🌲 mark the best answer. Which shows a way to make 8? 🏴 mark the best answer. The ten-frame shows a way to make which number? 🔶 count the pails, and then write the number that tells how many.

Topic 3   one hundred eighty-seven **187**

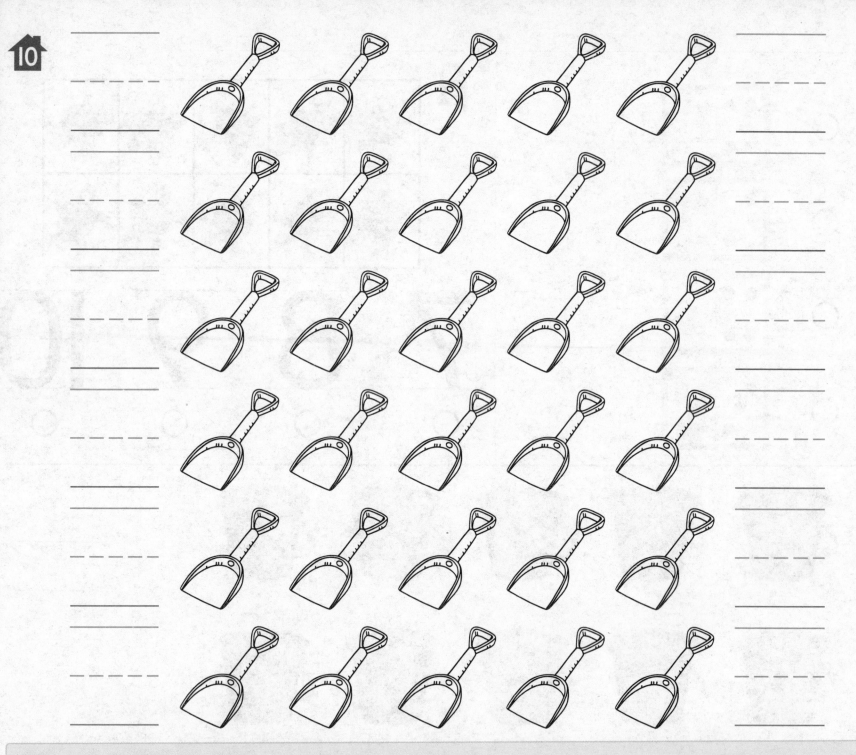

Directions Have students: 10 color the shovels red and yellow and write the numbers to make an organized list that shows all the ways to make 5.

© Pearson Education, Inc. K

TOPIC 4 · Comparing Numbers 0 to 10

Essential Question: How can numbers from 0 to 10 be compared and ordered?

Rain!

It rains on some days. It is sunny on other days.

Math and Science Project: Weather Changes

Directions Read the character speech bubbles to students. **Find Out!** Have students find out about weather changes. Say: *The weather changes from day to day. Talk to friends and relatives about the weather. Ask them to help you record the number of sunny days and rainy days during the week.* **Journal: Make a Poster** Then have students make a poster for the weather information they collected. Have them draw suns for the number of sunny days and clouds for the number of rainy days. Have them write the numbers that tell how many, and then circle the number that is greater.

Name _____

1

2

3

4

5

6

_____

_____

_____

Directions Have students: **1** circle the group that shows 4 birds; **2** circle the group of dogs that has more; **3** circle the 2 groups with the same number of marbles; **4** and **5** count the number of objects, and then write the number that tells how many; **6** count the ladybugs, cross out 1 ladybug, and then write the number that is 1 less.

© Pearson Education, Inc. K

My Word Cards

Directions Have students cut out the vocabulary cards. Read the front of the card, and then ask them to explain what the word or phrase means.

A-Z

greater (than)

less (than)

Directions Review the definitions and have students study the cards. Extend learning by having students draw pictures for each word on a separate piece of paper.

Point to the 3.
Say: *3 is **less than** 4.*

Point to the 9.
Say: *9 is **greater than** 6.*

© Pearson Education, Inc. K

Topic 4 | My Word Cards

Solve & Share   Name _____

Directions Say: *Emily visits a chicken farm. She sees a group of black chicks and a group of yellow chicks. Does Emily see more black or yellow chicks? How do you know?*

⊕ **TEKS K.2G** Compare sets of objects up to at least 20 in each set using comparative language. Also, K.2. **Mathematical Process Standards** K.1C, K.1F, K.1G.

Digital Resources at PearsonTexas.com

Solve   Learn   Glossary   Check   Tools   Games

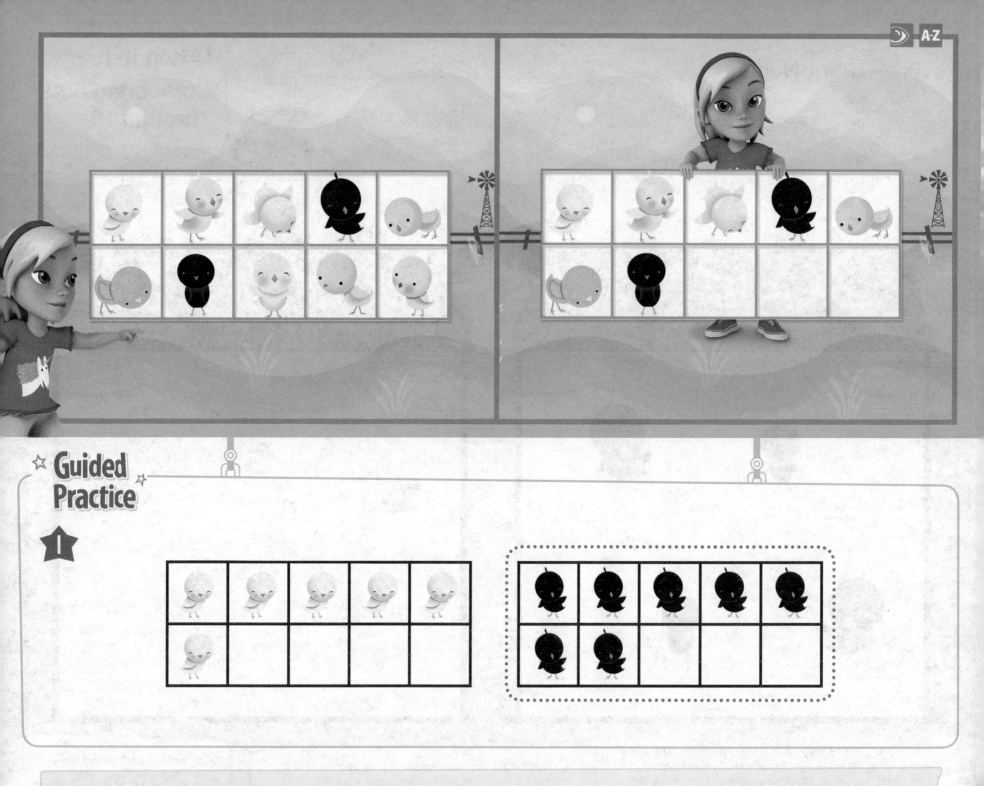

Guided Practice

1

Directions Have students compare the sets and circle the set that has more.

© Pearson Education, Inc. K

Topic 4 | Lesson 1

Name _____

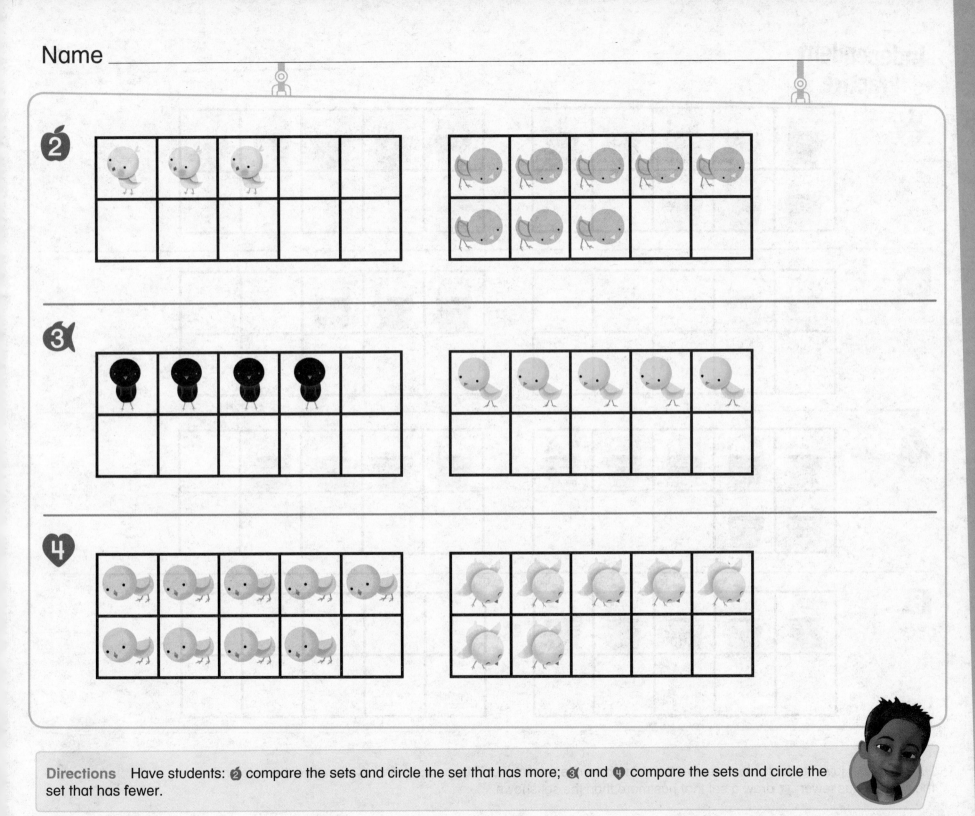

Directions Have students: ② compare the sets and circle the set that has more; ③ and ④ compare the sets and circle the set that has fewer.

Topic 4 | Lesson 1   one hundred ninety-five **195**

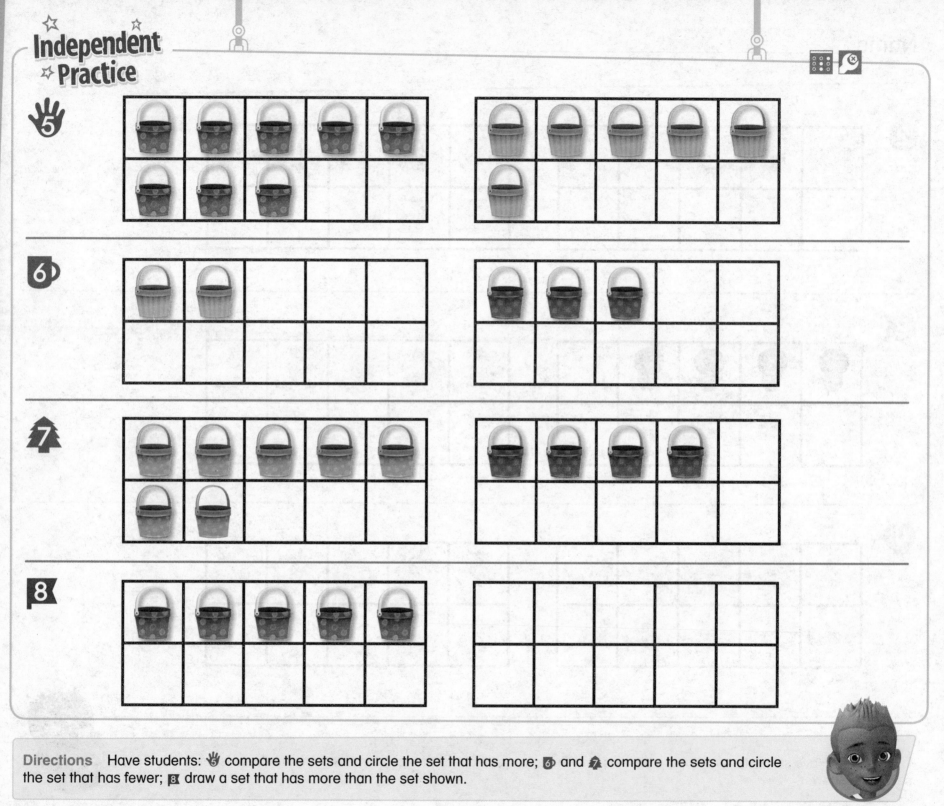

5

6

7

8

Directions Have students: ✋ compare the sets and circle the set that has more; 🍵 and 🌲 compare the sets and circle the set that has fewer; 🚩 draw a set that has more than the set shown.

Topic 4 | **Lesson 1**

Name _____

Another Look

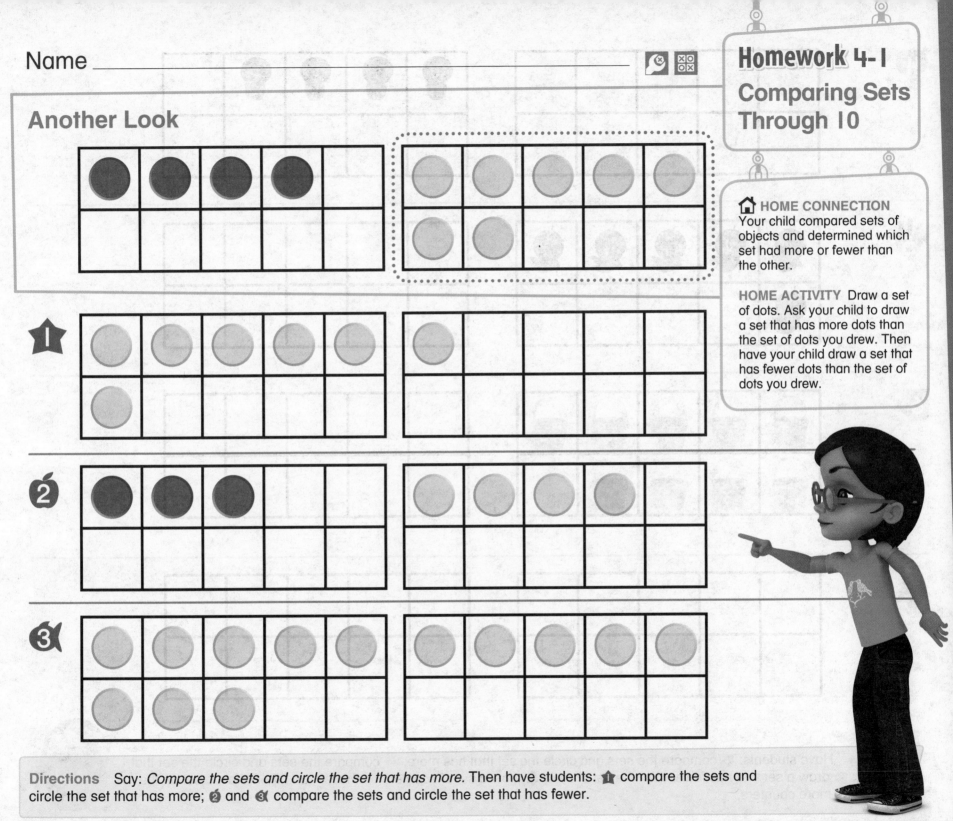

🏠 **HOME CONNECTION**
Your child compared sets of objects and determined which set had more or fewer than the other.

HOME ACTIVITY Draw a set of dots. Ask your child to draw a set that has more dots than the set of dots you drew. Then have your child draw a set that has fewer dots than the set of dots you drew.

Directions Say: *Compare the sets and circle the set that has more.* Then have students: ⭐ compare the sets and circle the set that has more; ② and ③ compare the sets and circle the set that has fewer.

4

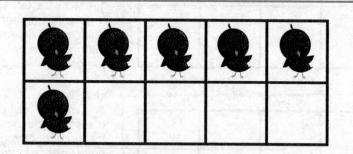

 5

6

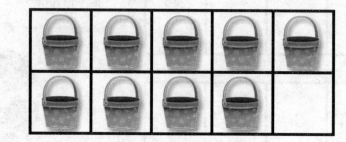

7

Directions Have students: **4** compare the sets and circle the set that has more; **5** compare the sets and circle the set that has fewer; **6** draw a set that has fewer than the set shown; **7** draw a set of counters on the left, and then draw a set on the right that has more counters.

198 one hundred ninety-eight   © Pearson Education, Inc. K   **Topic 4** | Lesson 1

Solve & Share Name _____

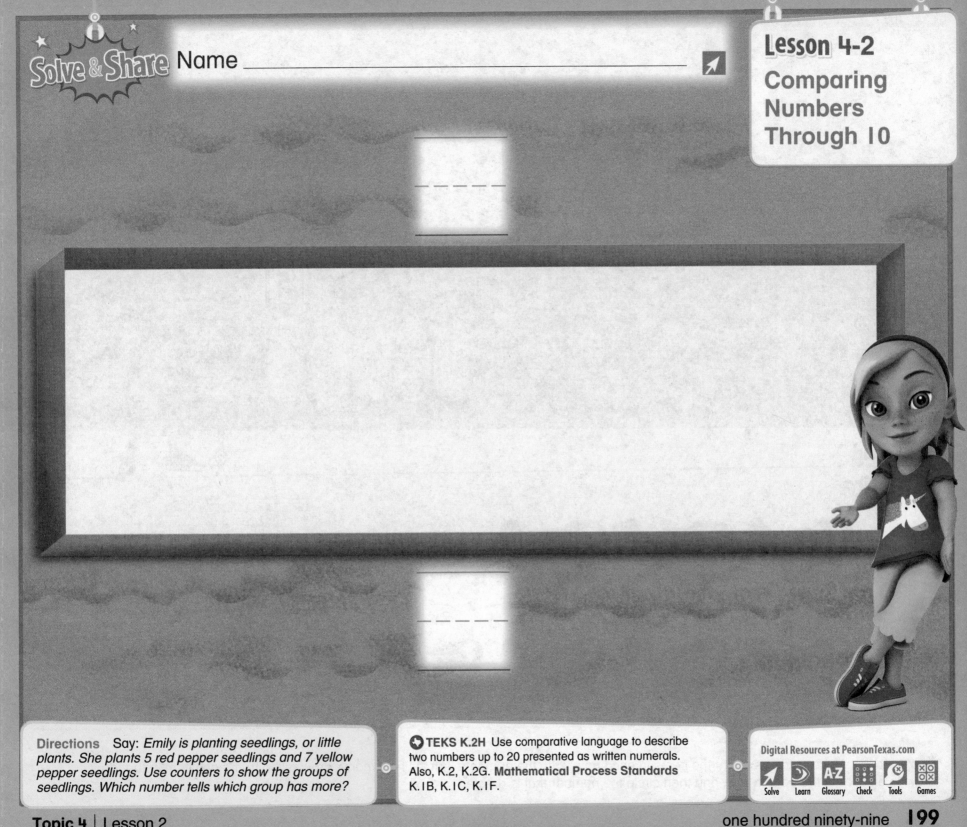

Directions Say: *Emily is planting seedlings, or little plants. She plants 5 red pepper seedlings and 7 yellow pepper seedlings. Use counters to show the groups of seedlings. Which number tells which group has more?*

⭐ **TEKS K.2H** Use comparative language to describe two numbers up to 20 presented as written numerals. Also, K.2, K.2G. **Mathematical Process Standards** K.1B, K.1C, K.1F.

Digital Resources at PearsonTexas.com
Solve Learn Glossary Check Tools Games

Guided Practice

⭐ 1

Directions Have students count the items in each row, write the numbers that tell how many, draw a line from each item in the top row to an item in the bottom row, and then circle the number that is greater.

© Pearson Education, Inc. K

Name _____

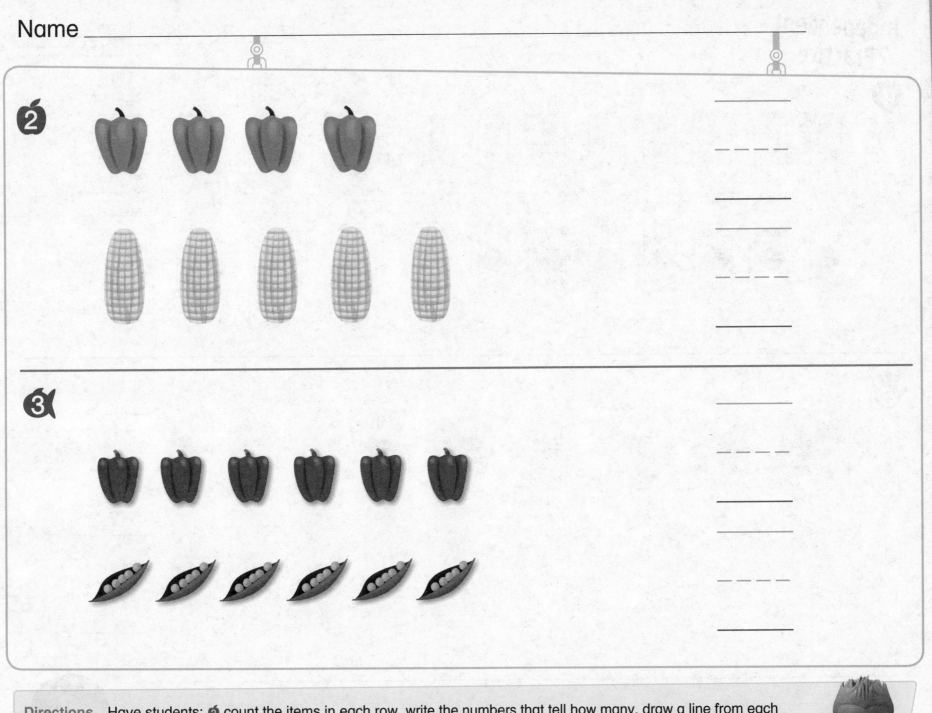

2

_____

_ _ _ _ _ _ _ _

_____

_ _ _ _ _ _ _ _

_____

3

_____

_ _ _ _ _ _ _ _

_____

_ _ _ _ _ _ _ _

_____

Directions Have students: **2** count the items in each row, write the numbers that tell how many, draw a line from each item in the top row to an item in the bottom row, and then circle the number that is less; **3** count the items in each row, write the numbers that tell how many, draw a line from each item in the top row to an item in the bottom row, and then circle the numbers that are the same.

Topic 4 | Lesson 2

two hundred one **201**

Independent Practice

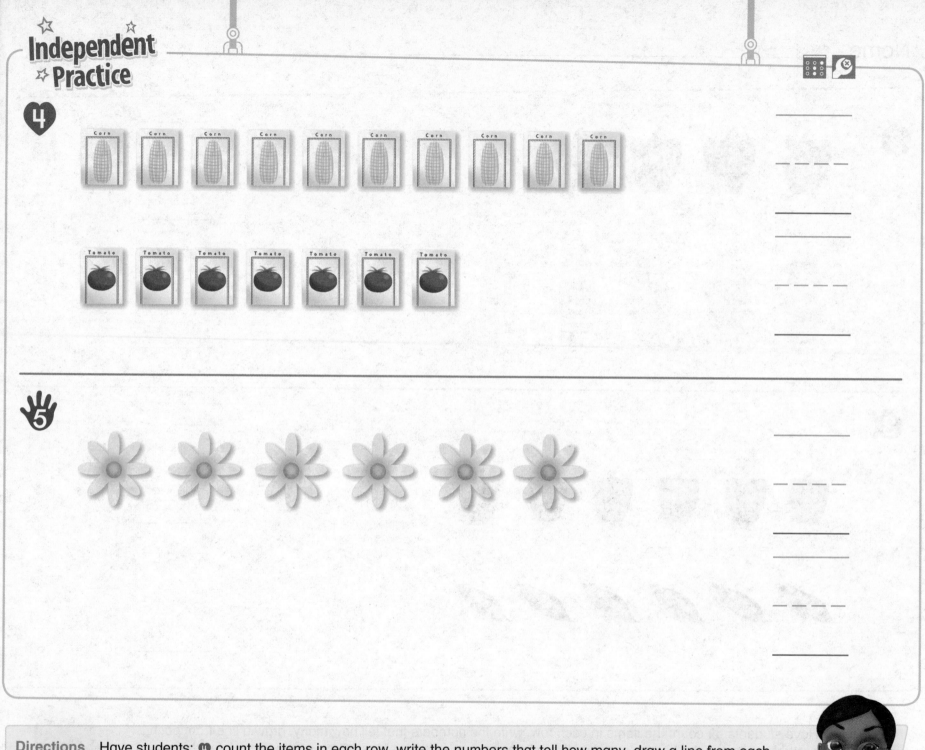

© Pearson Education, Inc. K

Directions Have students: ❤ count the items in each row, write the numbers that tell how many, draw a line from each item in the top row to an item in the bottom row, and then circle the number that is less; ✋ count the flowers in the row, draw a new row with fewer flowers, and then write the numbers that tell how many.

Topic 4 | **Lesson 2**

Name _____

Another Look

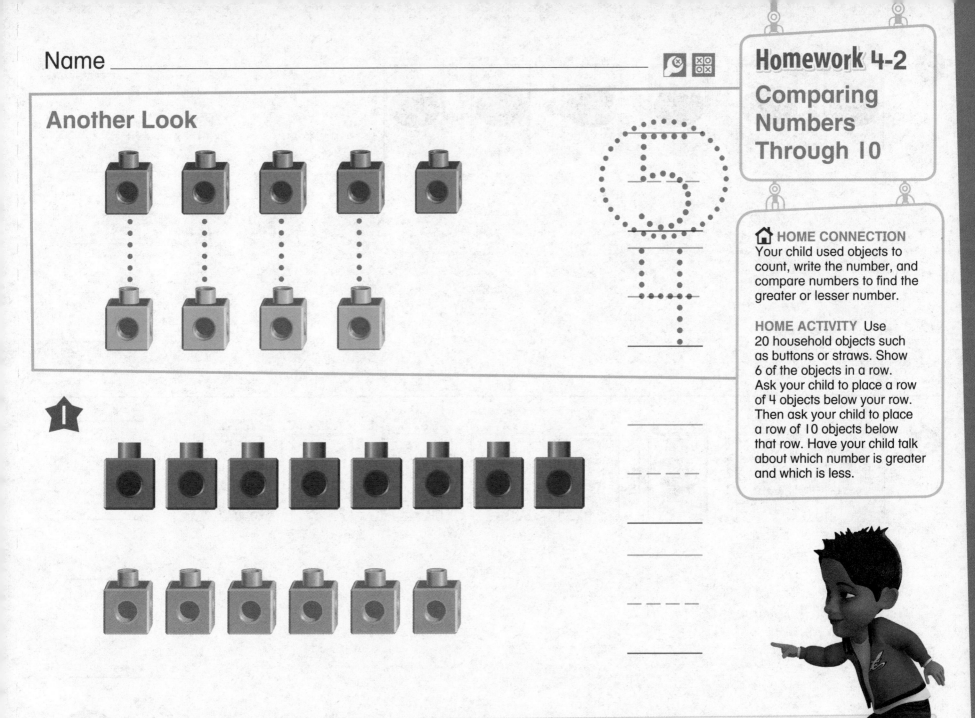

🏠 **HOME CONNECTION**
Your child used objects to count, write the number, and compare numbers to find the greater or lesser number.

HOME ACTIVITY Use 20 household objects such as buttons or straws. Show 6 of the objects in a row. Ask your child to place a row of 4 objects below your row. Then ask your child to place a row of 10 objects below that row. Have your child talk about which number is greater and which is less.

★ 1

Directions Say: *You can draw lines to help you decide which group has a greater number of items. Count the items in each row, write the numbers that tell how many, draw a line from each item in the top row to an item in the bottom row, and then circle the number that is greater.* Have students: ★ count the items in each row, write the numbers that tell how many, draw a line from each item in the top row to an item in the bottom row, and then circle the number that is less.

2

_____

‒ ‒ ‒ ‒ ‒ ‒ ‒

_____

‒ ‒ ‒ ‒ ‒ ‒ ‒

_____

‒ ‒ ‒ ‒ ‒ ‒ ‒

_____

3

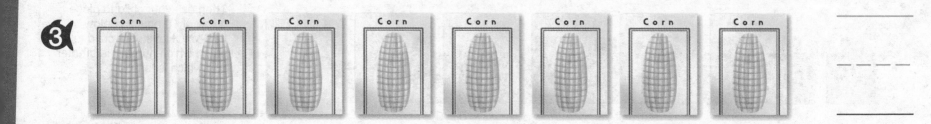

_____

‒ ‒ ‒ ‒ ‒ ‒ ‒

_____

‒ ‒ ‒ ‒ ‒ ‒ ‒

_____

‒ ‒ ‒ ‒ ‒ ‒ ‒

_____

Directions Have students: **2** count how many tomato seed packets are in the row, draw a row with more tomatoes, and then write the numbers that tell how many; **3** count how many corn seed packets are in the row, draw a row with the same number of corn cobs, and then write the numbers that tell how many.

Solve & Share   Name _____

_____

_ _ _ _ _ _

_____

Directions   Say: *Emily has 6 sandwiches. Another friend comes for lunch. She needs 1 more sandwich. Use counters to show how many sandwiches Emily needs. Write the number that tells how many.*

⭐ **TEKS K.2E** Generate a set using concrete and pictorial models that represents a number that is more than, less than, and equal to a given number up to 20. Also, **K.2, K.2F. Mathematical Process Standards** K.1A, K.1C, K.1F, K.1G

Digital Resources at PearsonTexas.com

Solve   Learn   Glossary   Check   Tools   Games

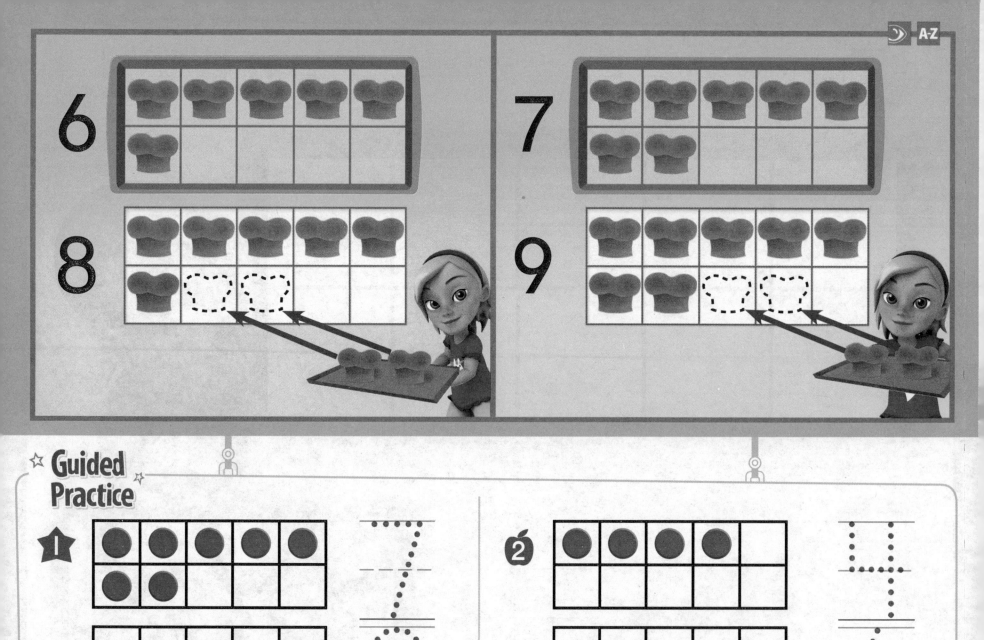

☆ Guided Practice ☆

Directions Have students: ❶ count the counters, draw a group that has 1 more counter, and then write the numbers that tell how many; ❷ count the counters, draw a group that has 2 more counters, and then write the numbers that tell how many.

© Pearson Education, Inc. K

Topic 4 | Lesson 3

Name _____

3

4

5

6

Directions Have students: **3** and **4** count the counters, draw a group that has 1 more counter, and then write the numbers that tell how many; **5** and **6** count the counters, draw a group that has 2 more counters, and then write the numbers that tell how many.

Topic 4 | Lesson 3   two hundred seven **207**

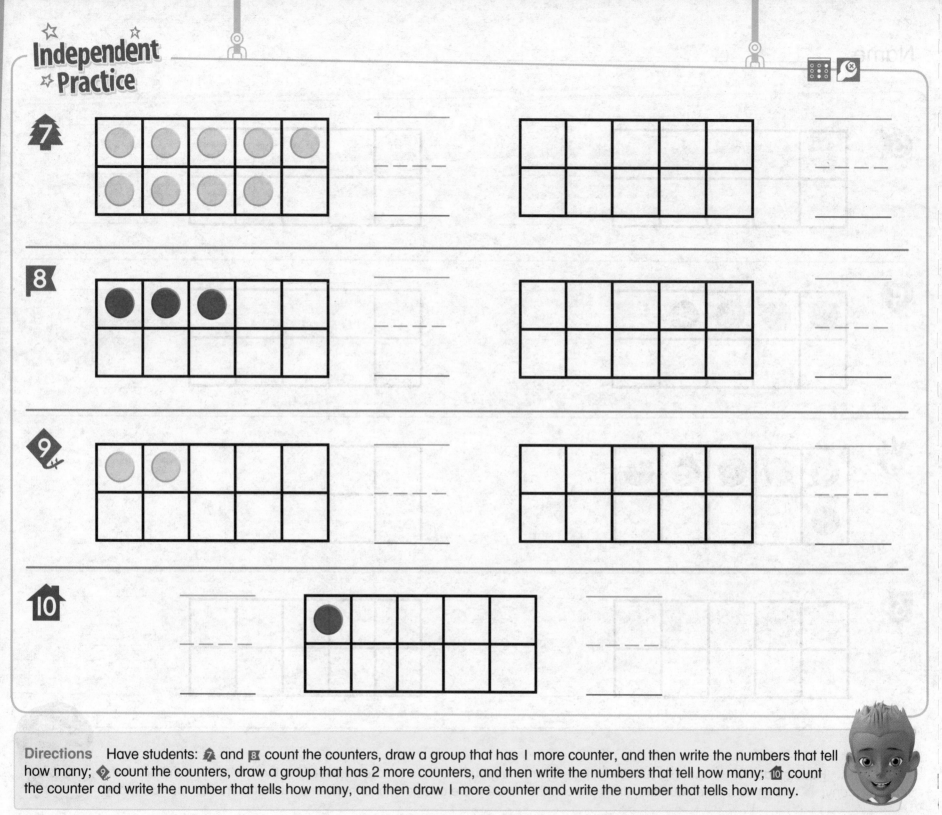

7

8

9

10

Directions Have students: **7** and **8** count the counters, draw a group that has 1 more counter, and then write the numbers that tell how many; **9** count the counters, draw a group that has 2 more counters, and then write the numbers that tell how many; **10** count the counter and write the number that tells how many, and then draw 1 more counter and write the number that tells how many.

© Pearson Education, Inc. K

Topic 4 | Lesson 3

Another Look

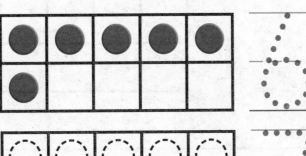

🏠 **HOME CONNECTION**
Your child drew counters to show 1 more and 2 more.

HOME ACTIVITY Draw a row of 6 dots. Ask your child to draw a row with 1 more below your row. Then ask your child to draw a row with 2 more below the second row. Have your child explain how he or she knows his or her rows show 1 more and 2 more than 6.

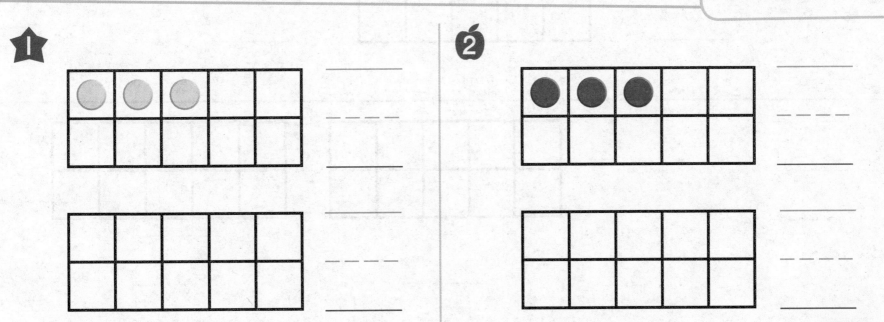

Directions Say: *Count the counters. How many did you count? Write that number. Draw a group that has 1 more counter. How many counters did you draw? Write the number that tells how many.* Then have students: ⭐ count the counters, draw a group that has 2 more counters, and then write the numbers that tell how many; 🍎 count the counters, draw a group that has 1 more counter, and then write the numbers that tell how many.

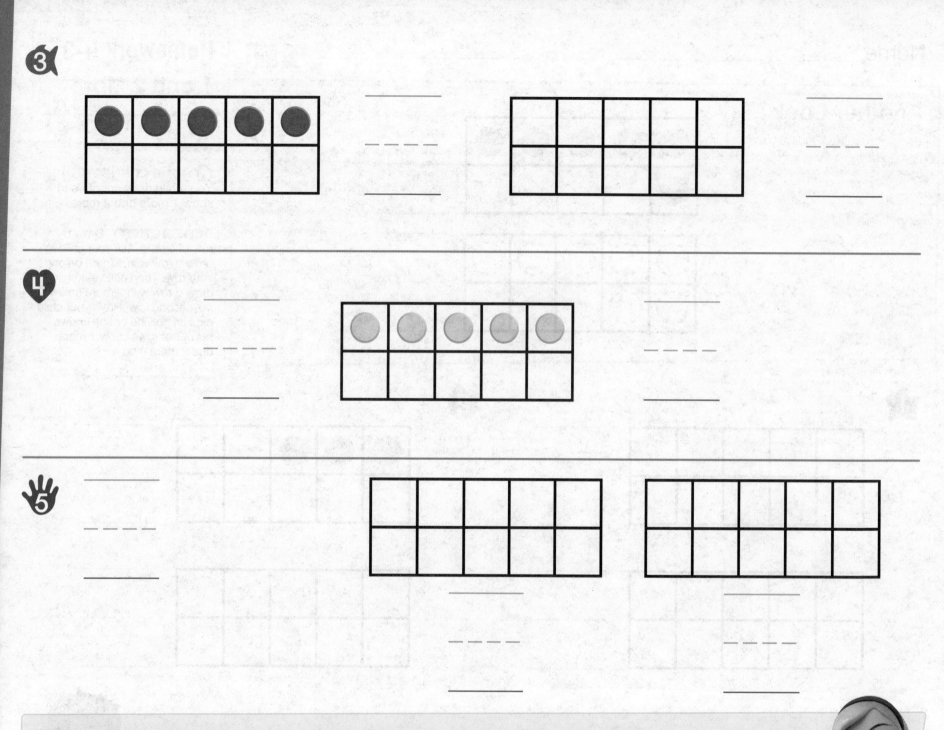

3

4

5

© Pearson Education, Inc. K

Solve & Share Name _____

★ **TEKS K.2E** Generate a set using concrete and pictorial models that represents a number that is more than, less than, and equal to a given number up to 20. Also, K.2, K.2F. **Mathematical Process Standards** K.1A, K.1B, K.1C, K.1F, K.1G.

Directions Say: *Emily has 6 stuffed dinosaurs. She gives 1 dinosaur to a friend. Use counters to show how many dinosaurs Emily has left. Write the number that tells how many.*

Digital Resources at PearsonTexas.com

Solve   Learn   Glossary   Check   Tools   Games

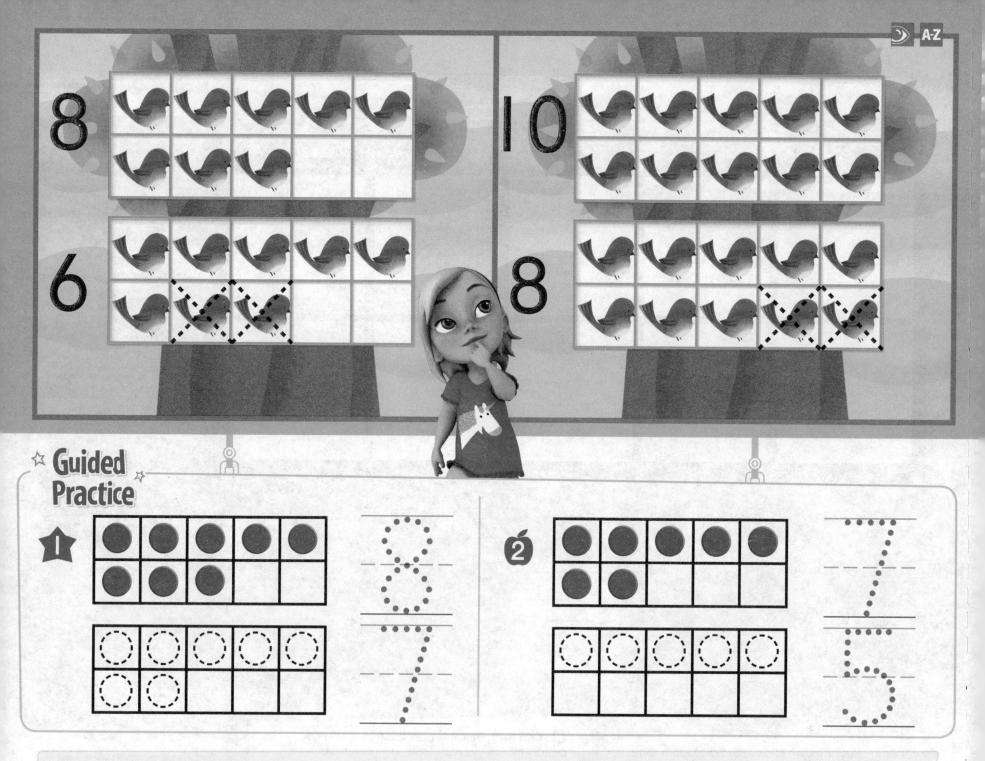

☆ **Guided Practice**

1

2

Directions Have students: ⭐ count the counters, draw a group that has 1 fewer counter, and then write the numbers that tell how many; 🍎 count the counters, draw a group that has 2 fewer counters, and then write the numbers that tell how many.

© Pearson Education, Inc. K

Topic 4 | Lesson 4

Name _____

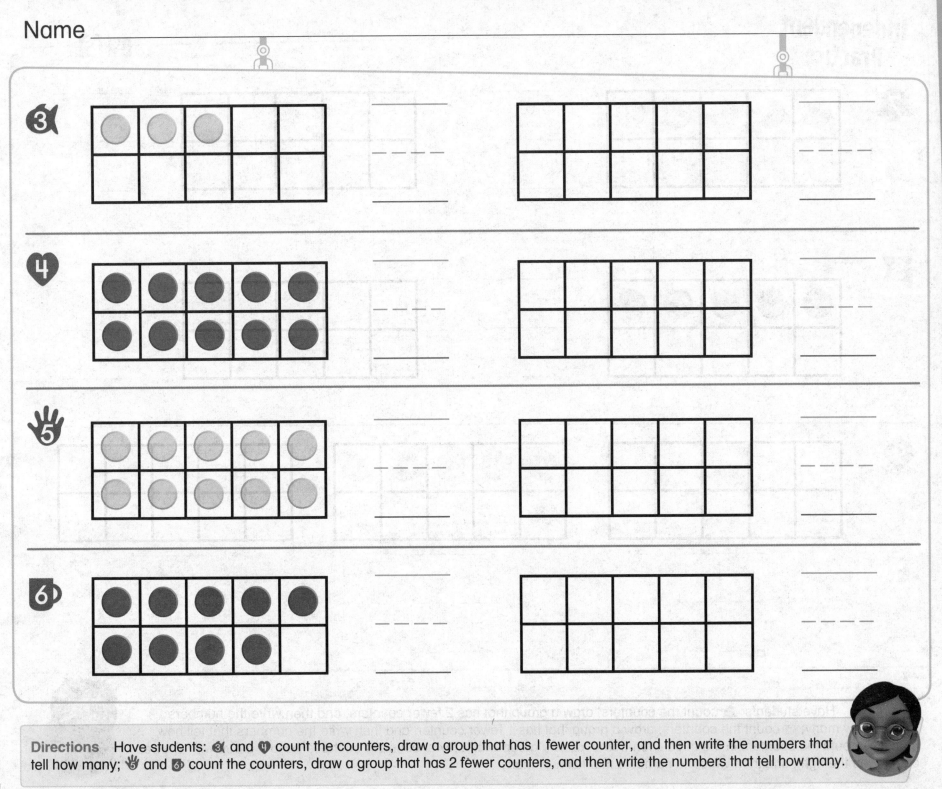

Directions Have students: ❸ and ❹ count the counters, draw a group that has 1 fewer counter, and then write the numbers that tell how many; ✋ and ☕ count the counters, draw a group that has 2 fewer counters, and then write the numbers that tell how many.

Topic 4 | **Lesson 4**

two hundred thirteen **213**

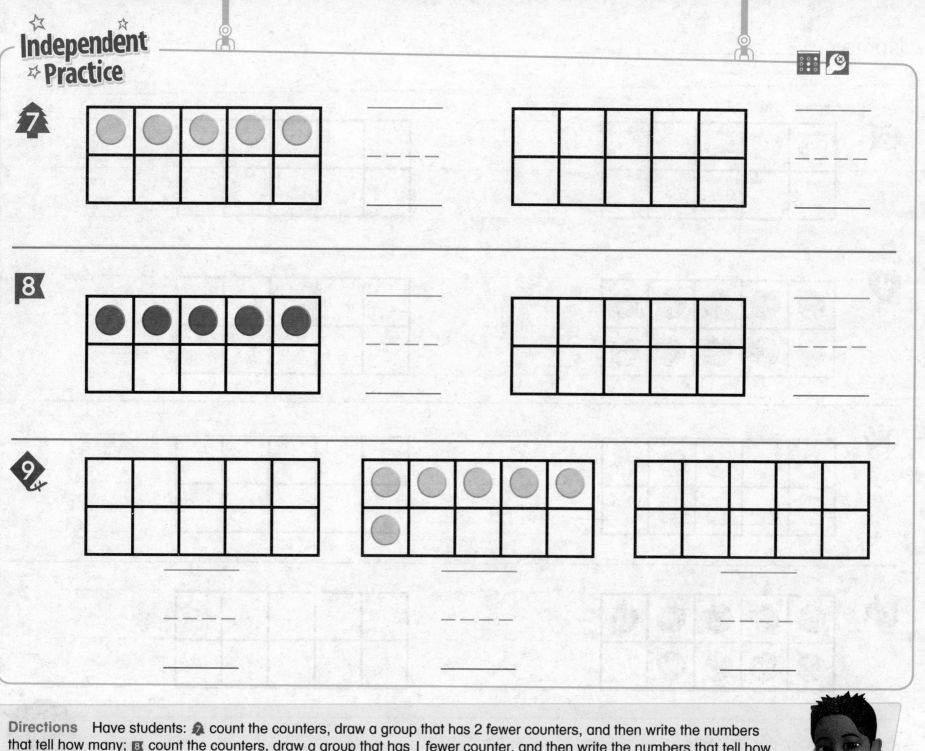

7

8

9

Directions Have students: **7** count the counters, draw a group that has 2 fewer counters, and then write the numbers that tell how many; **8** count the counters, draw a group that has 1 fewer counter, and then write the numbers that tell how many; **9** count the counters in the middle ten-frame, draw a group with 2 fewer counters on the left and a group with 1 fewer counter on the right, and then write the numbers that tell how many.

© Pearson Education, Inc. K

Topic 4 | Lesson 4

Another Look

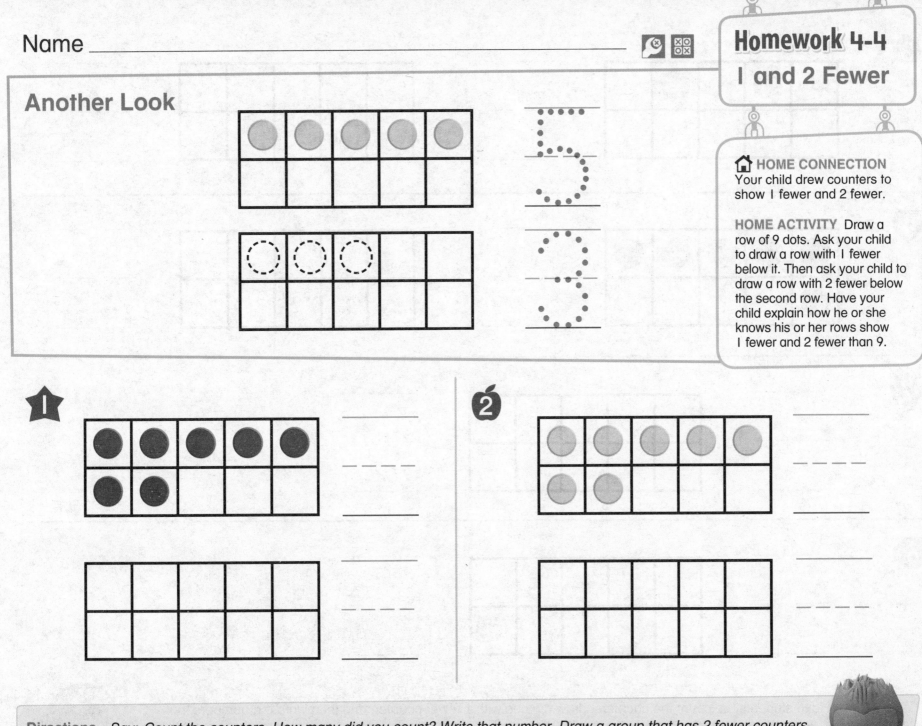

🏠 **HOME CONNECTION**
Your child drew counters to show 1 fewer and 2 fewer.

HOME ACTIVITY Draw a row of 9 dots. Ask your child to draw a row with 1 fewer below it. Then ask your child to draw a row with 2 fewer below the second row. Have your child explain how he or she knows his or her rows show 1 fewer and 2 fewer than 9.

Directions Say: *Count the counters. How many did you count? Write that number. Draw a group that has 2 fewer counters. How many counters did you draw? Write the number that tells how many.* Then have students: ⭐ count the counters, draw a group that has 1 fewer counter, and then write the numbers that tell how many; ❷ count the counters, draw a group that has 2 fewer counters, and then write the numbers that tell how many.

3

[ten-frame with 4 gray counters in top row]   _ _ _   [empty ten-frame]   _ _ _

4

[ten-frame with 5 dark counters in top row and 1 in bottom row]   _ _ _   [empty ten-frame]   _ _ _

5

_ _ _   [empty ten-frame]   _ _ _

6

_ _ _   [empty ten-frame]   _ _ _

Directions Have students: **3** count the counters, draw a group with 1 fewer counter, and then write the numbers that tell how many; **4** count the counters, draw a group with 2 fewer counters, and then write the numbers that tell how many; **5** write a number between 1 and 10, draw a group with that number of counters, draw Xs on the counters to show 1 fewer, and then write the number that tells how many; **6** write a number between 2 and 10, draw a group with that number of counters, draw Xs on the counters to show 2 fewer, and then write the number that tells how many.

© Pearson Education, Inc. K

Topic 4 | Lesson 4

Name _____

_____ 8 _____

Directions Say: *Emily thinks of two numbers, one that is 1 less than 8 and another that is 1 more than 8. Write the two numbers Emily is thinking of. Show how you know you are correct.*

⭐ **TEKS K.2F** Generate a number that is one more than or one less than another number up to at least 20. Also, K.2, K.2A. **Mathematical Process Standards** K.1C, K.1E, K.1F, K.1G.

Digital Resources at PearsonTexas.com

Solve Learn Glossary Check Tools Games

0 1 2 3 4 5 6 7 8 9 10

☆ **Guided Practice** ☆

⭐1

2

Directions Have students: ⭐ write the number that is 1 less than 2 and the number that is 1 more than 2, and then continue writing the numbers in order.

Name _____

2

_ _ _ _ _

7

_ _ _ _ _

3

| 6 | 9 |
| 8 | 7 |

_ _ _ _ _   _ _ _ _ _

_____   _____

4

| 3 | 6 |
| 5 | 4 |

_ _ _ _ _   _ _ _ _ _

_____   _____

Directions Have students: **2** write the number that is 1 less than 7 and the number that is 1 more than 7; **3** and **4** write the numbers in order.

✋ **5** [ ] _ _ _ _ _ 　 [•] _ _ _ _ | 1 _ _ _ _ 　 [••] _ _ _ _

☕ **6** [dots] _ _ _ _ 　 [dots] 9 　 [dots] _ _ _ _

🌲 **7** | 10 | 8 | 7 | 9 |

8 | 9 | 6 | 7 |

Directions Have students: ✋ write the number that is 1 less than 1 and the number that is 1 more than 1; ☕ write the number that is 1 less than 9 and the number that is 1 more than 9; 🌲 write the numbers in order; **8** find the missing number, and then write the numbers in order.

Topic 4 | Lesson 5

Another Look

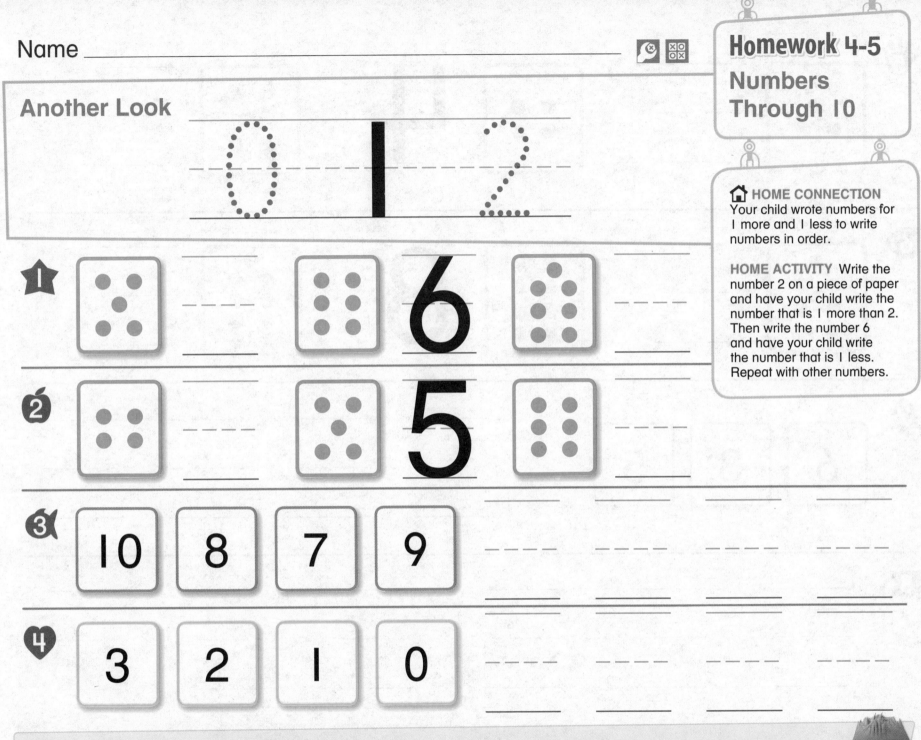

0 1 2

⭐ 1   6

❷   5

❸ 10 8 7 9

❹ 3 2 1 0

Directions Say: *Write the number that is 1 less than 1 and the number that is 1 more than 1. Now say the numbers in order.*
Then have students: ⭐ write the number that is 1 less than 6 and the number that is 1 more than 6; ❷ write the number that is 1 less than 5 and the number that is 1 more than 5; ❸ and ❹ write the numbers in order.

🖐 **5**

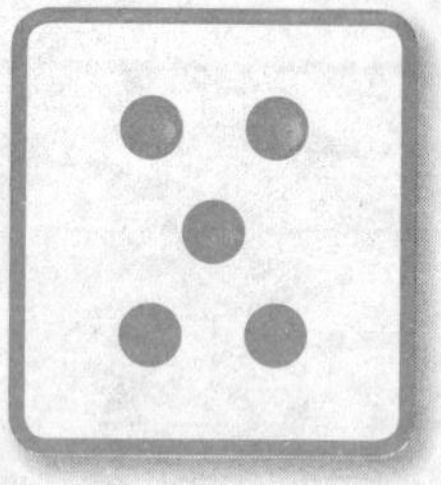

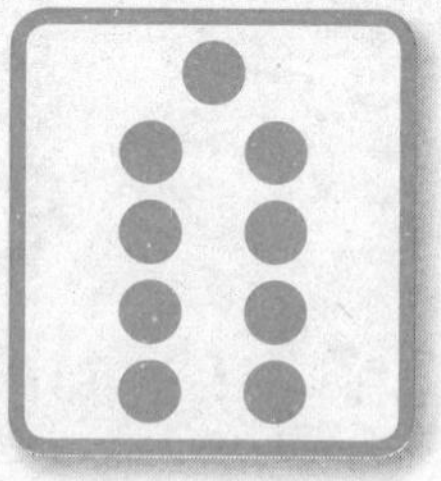

3 _____ 4 _____ 5 _____

🍵 **6**

7 _____ 8 _____ 9 _____

🌲 **7**

| 6 | 3 | 5 |

_____ _____ _____

_____ _____ _____

▸ **8**

_____ _____ _____

_____ _____ _____

TEKS K.1C Select tools, including real objects, manipulatives, ... as appropriate, and techniques, including ... number sense as appropriate, to solve problems. Also, K.2, K.2E. Mathematical Process Standards K.1B, K.1D, K.1F.

Directions Say: *There are 7 fish in a bowl. Emily puts 1 more fish in the bowl. How many fish are in the bowl now? How can you solve this problem?*

Digital Resources at PearsonTexas.com
Solve Learn Glossary Check Tools Games

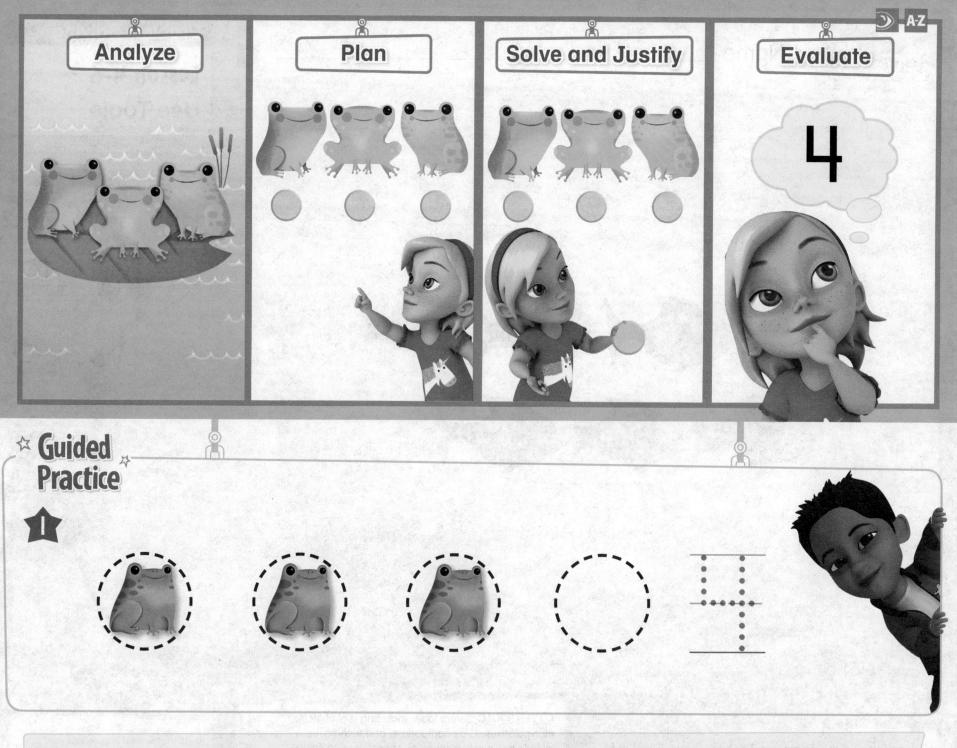

Analyze	Plan	Solve and Justify	Evaluate

☆ Guided Practice

1

Directions Say: *Carlos sees 3 frogs at the pond. Then he sees 1 more frog. How many frogs are there now?* Have students place a counter on each picture of a frog, show 1 more counter, trace the counters, and then write the number that tells how many.

224 two hundred twenty-four   © Pearson Education, Inc. K   **Topic 4** | Lesson 6

Name _____

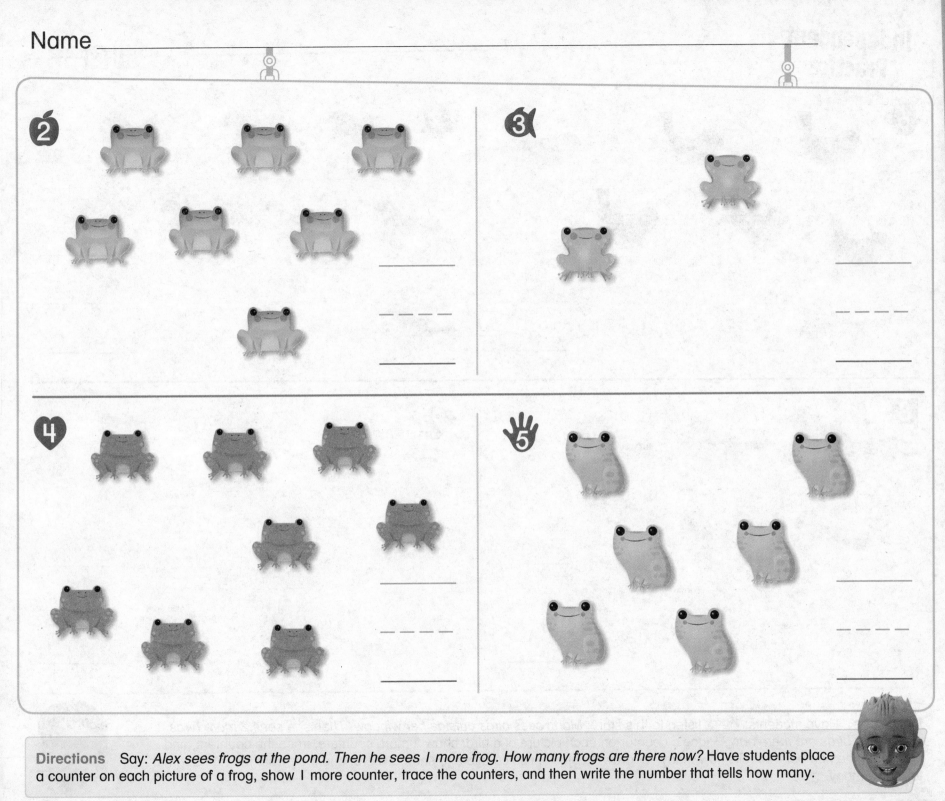

Directions Say: *Alex sees frogs at the pond. Then he sees 1 more frog. How many frogs are there now?* Have students place a counter on each picture of a frog, show 1 more counter, trace the counters, and then write the number that tells how many.

Topic 4 | Lesson 6   two hundred twenty-five   225

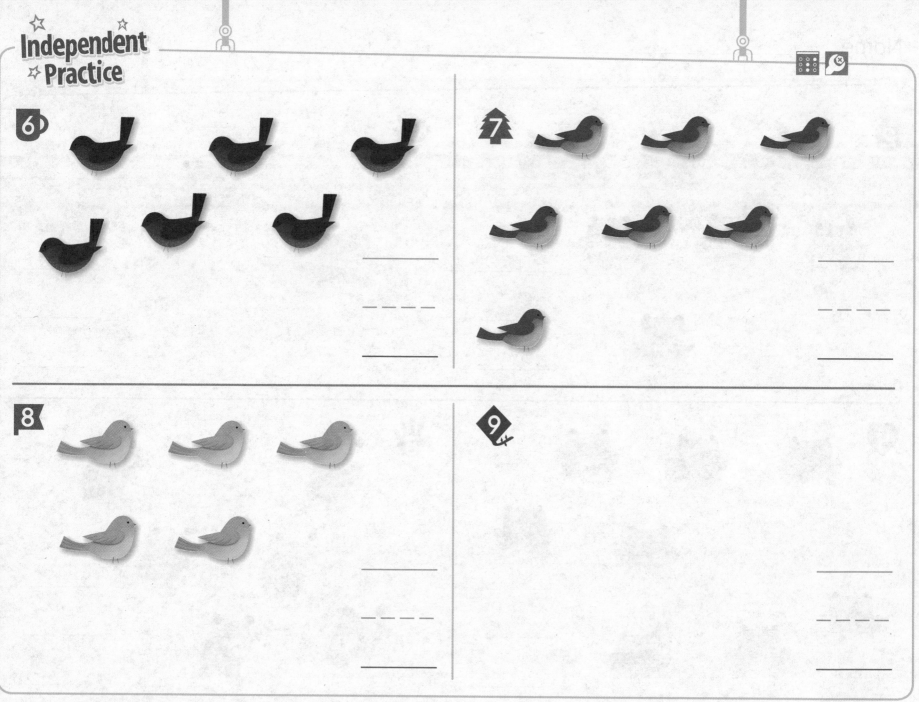

6

7

8

9

Directions Have students: **6**–**8** listen to this story: *Marta sees birds outside her window. Then she sees 2 more birds. How many birds are there now?* Place a counter on each picture of a bird, show 2 more counters, trace the counters, and then write the number that tells how many; **9** draw 4 objects, use counters to show 2 more, and then write the number that tells how many.

226 two hundred twenty-six
© Pearson Education, Inc. K
Topic 4 | Lesson 6

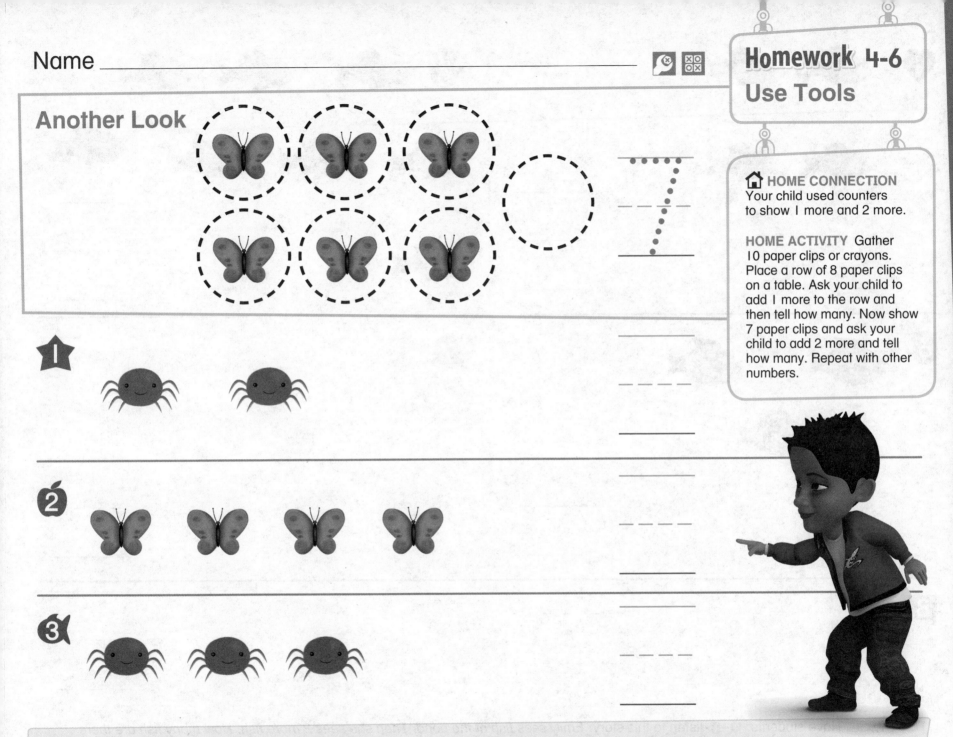

Another Look

7

HOME CONNECTION
Your child used counters to show 1 more and 2 more.

HOME ACTIVITY Gather 10 paper clips or crayons. Place a row of 8 paper clips on a table. Ask your child to add 1 more to the row and then tell how many. Now show 7 paper clips and ask your child to add 2 more and tell how many. Repeat with other numbers.

1

2

3

Directions Say: *You can show 1 more than the group of butterflies using counters. Place 1 counter on each butterfly, trace the counters, show 1 more counter, and then write the number that tells how many.* Then have students: ⭐ and ❷ place counters or small objects on each picture of a spider or butterfly, show 1 more counter or small object, and then write the number that tells how many; ❸ place a counter or small object on each picture of a spider, show 2 more counters, and then write the number that tells how many.

Digital Resources at PearsonTexas.com

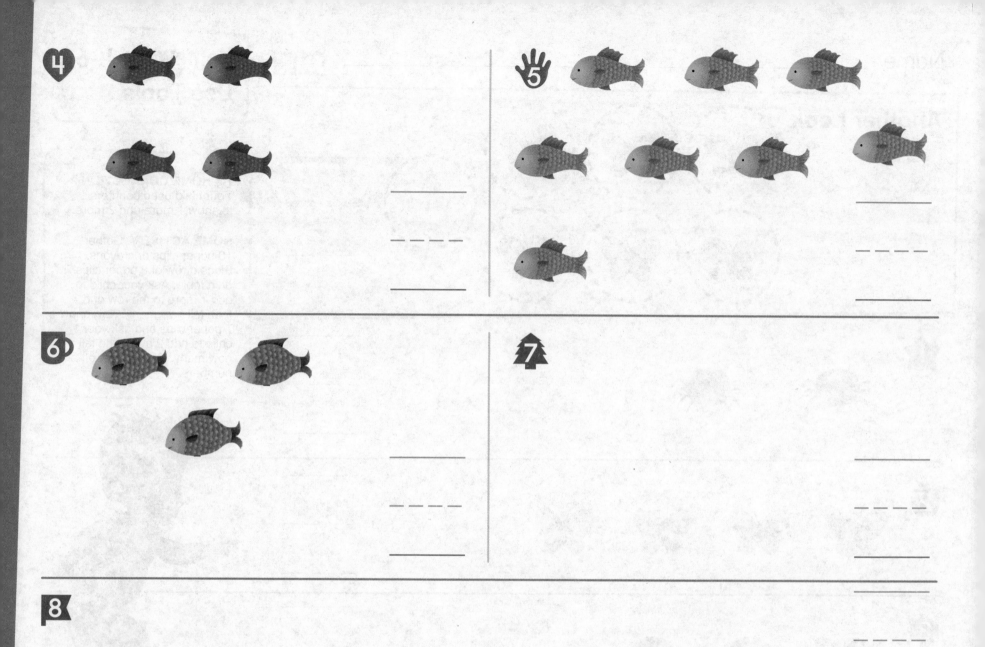

4 _____

_ _ _ _ _ _

_____

5 _____

_ _ _ _ _ _

_____

6 _____

_ _ _ _ _ _

_____

7 _____

_ _ _ _ _ _

_____

8 _____

_ _ _ _ _ _

_____

Directions Have students: **4–6** listen to this story: *Emily sees fish at the pond. Then she sees 2 more fish. How many fish are there now?* Place a counter or small object on each picture of a fish, show 2 more counters, and then write the number that tells how many; **7** draw a group of 1 to 3 objects, place a counter or small object on each picture, show 1 more counter, and then write the number that tells how many; **8** draw a group of 1 to 3 objects, place a counter or small object on each picture, show 2 more counters, and then write the number that tells how many.

© Pearson Education, Inc. K

Topic 4 | Lesson 6

Set A

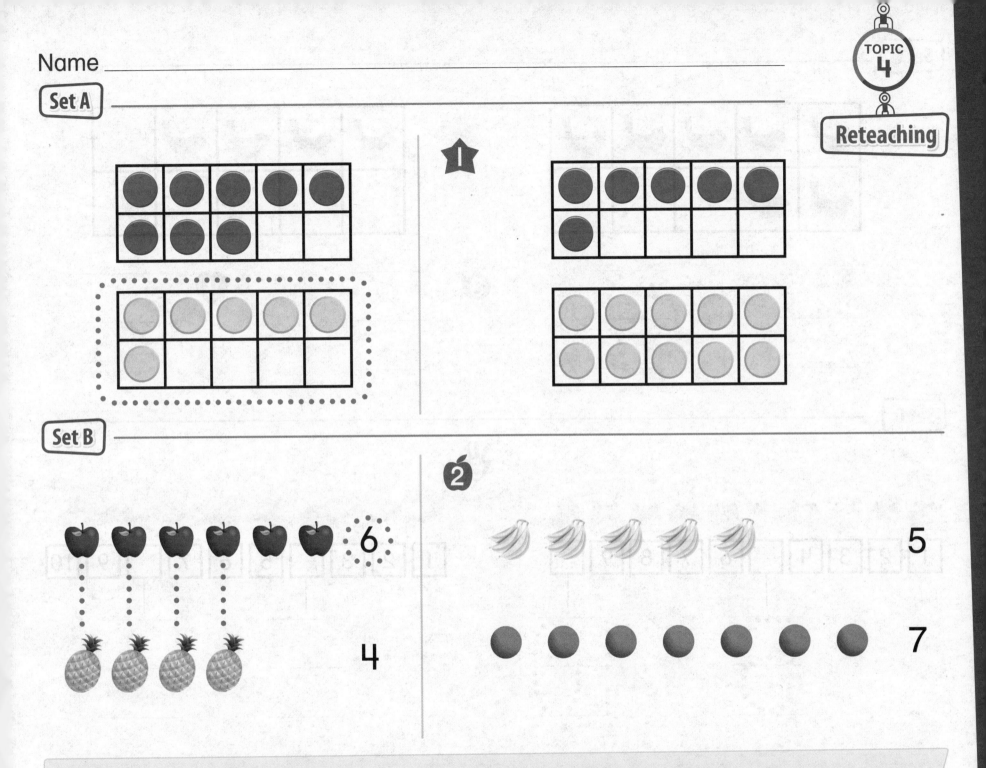

Set B

6

4

5

7

Directions Have students: ⭐ compare the sets and circle the set that has fewer; ② count the fruit in each row, draw a line from each piece of fruit in the top row to a piece of fruit in the bottom row, and then circle the number that is greater.

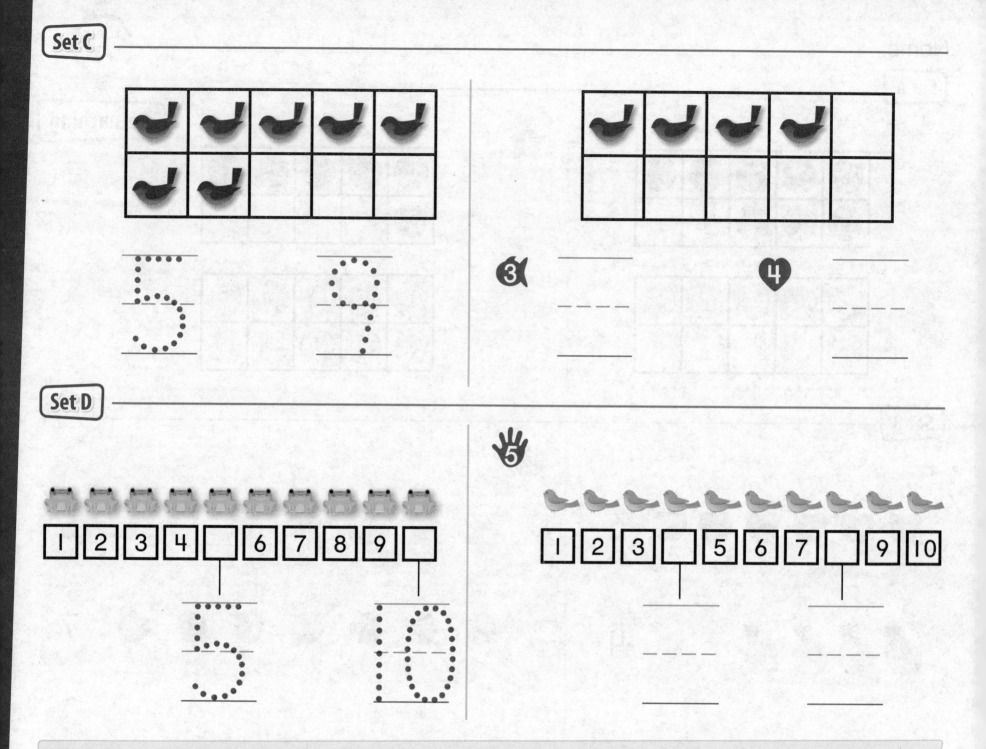

Directions Have students: ❸ count the number of birds in the ten-frame, and then write the number that is 2 less; ❹ count the number of birds in the ten-frame, and then write the number that is 2 more; ✋ write the missing numbers to write the numbers in order from 1 to 10.

Name _____

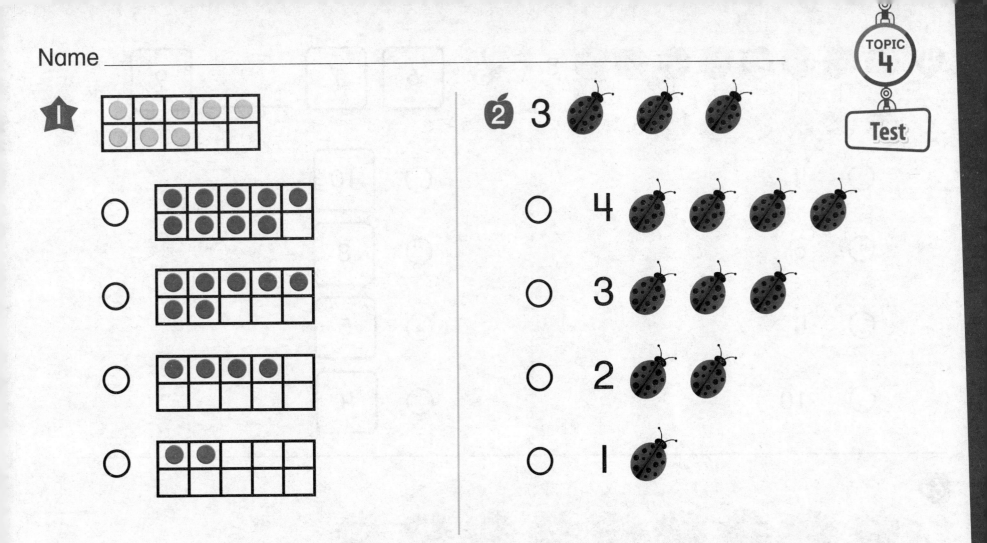

1

2 3

○ 4

○ 3

○ 2

○ 1

3 4   ○ 5   ○ 3

○ 4   ○ 2

Directions Have students mark the best answer. **1** Which shows a group of red counters that has more than the group of yellow counters? **2** Which shows 2 fewer than 3? **3** Which shows 1 more than 4?

Topic 4   two hundred thirty-one **231**

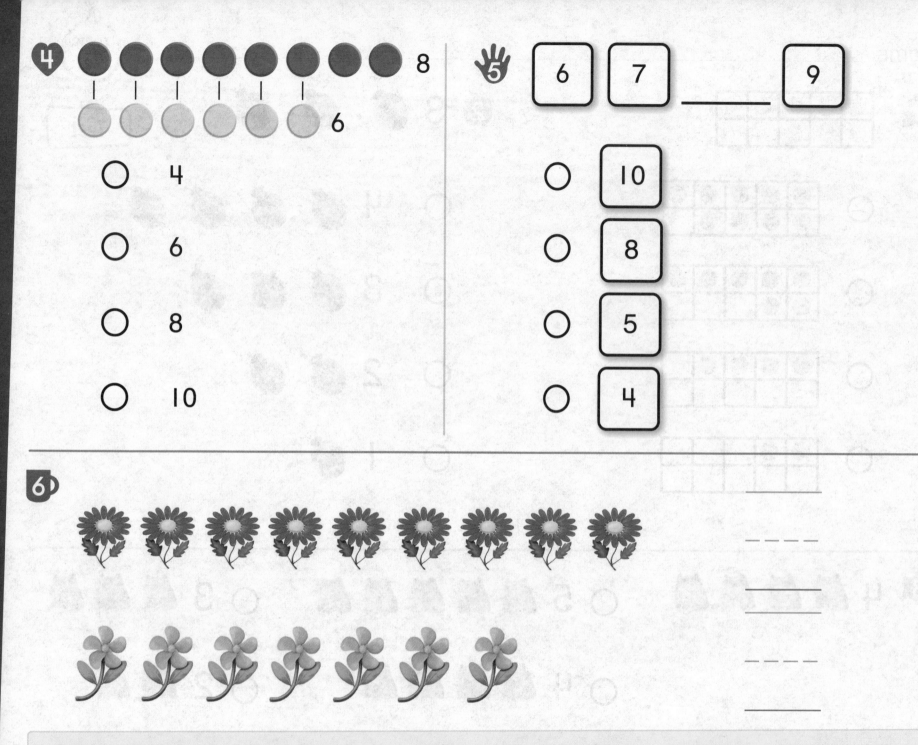

4 8

6

○ 4

○ 6

○ 8

○ 10

5 6 7 ____ 9

○ 10

○ 8

○ 5

○ 4

6

_____

_ _ _ _

_____

_ _ _ _

_____

Directions Have students: **4** mark the best answer. Look at the rows of counters. Which of these two numbers is greater? **5** mark the best answer. Which shows the number that is 1 more than 7? **6** draw lines from each purple flower in the top row to an orange flower in the bottom row, write the numbers that tell how many, and then circle the number that is greater.

Topic 4

Numbers to 20

Essential Question: How can numbers to 20 be counted, read, written, pictured, and compared?

Animals!

All living things are called organisms.

Math and Science Project: Organisms

Directions Read the character speech bubbles to students. **Find Out!** Have students find out about large and small organisms. Say: *All living things are organisms. Non-living objects like rocks are not organisms. Talk to friends and relatives about organisms.* **Journal: Make a Poster** Then have students make a poster. Have them choose one large and one small organism they learned about. Ask them to draw a group with 10 large organisms and a group with 20 small organisms and color them using two different colors. Then have them write the numbers that tell how many organisms are in each group.

Review What You Know

1

2

3

4

5

6

_____

_____

- - - - - - - - - -

- - - - - - - - - -

- - - - - - - - - -

_____

Directions Have students: **1** circle the group with 10 bugs; **2** circle the group that has a number of birds that is less than 5; **3** circle the group that has a number of birds that is greater than 5; **4**–**6** count the frogs or bugs in each group, and then write the number that tells how many.

My Word Cards

Directions Have students cut out the vocabulary cards. Read the front of the card, and then ask them to explain what the word or phrase means.

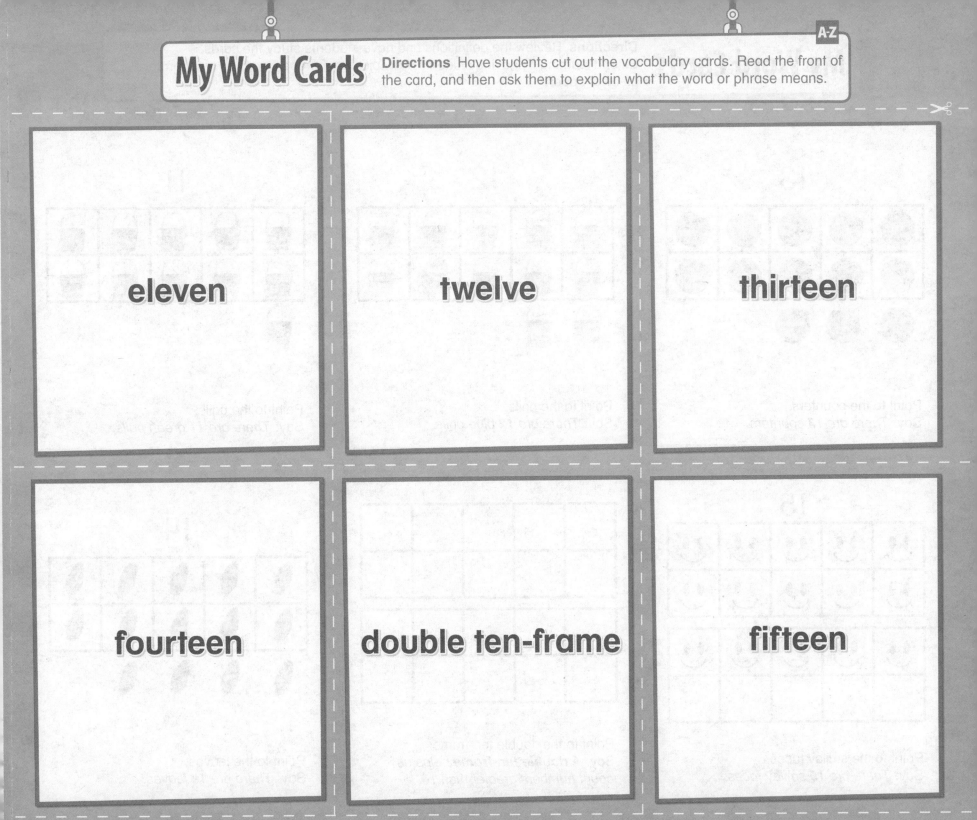

eleven

twelve

thirteen

fourteen

double ten-frame

fifteen

My Word Cards

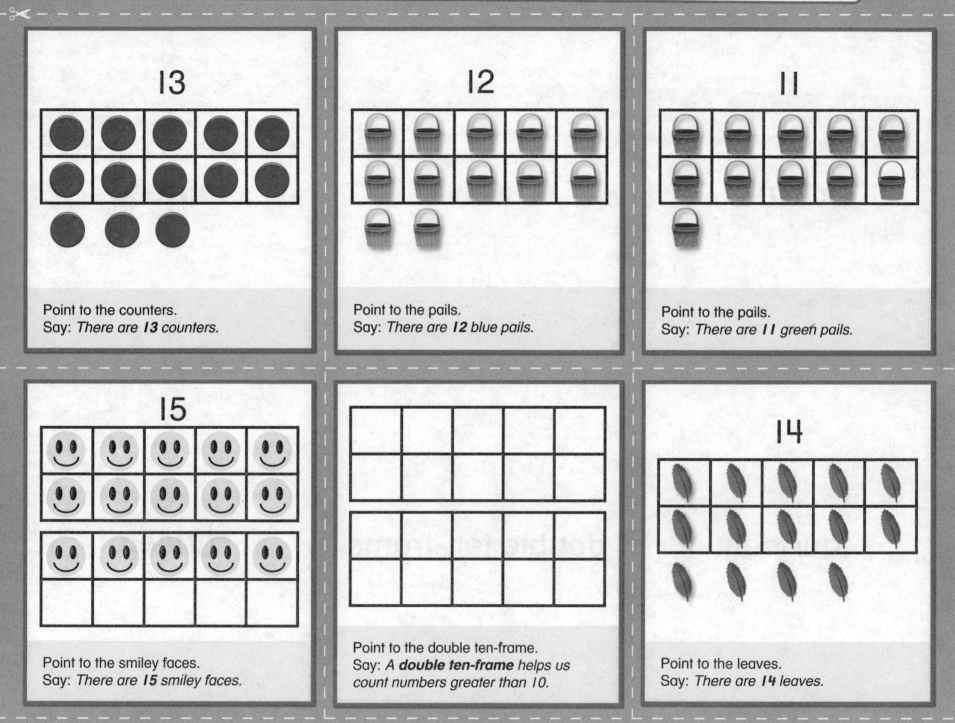

13

Point to the counters.
Say: *There are 13 counters.*

12

Point to the pails.
Say: *There are 12 blue pails.*

11

Point to the pails.
Say: *There are 11 green pails.*

15

Point to the smiley faces.
Say: *There are 15 smiley faces.*

Point to the double ten-frame.
Say: *A **double ten-frame** helps us count numbers greater than 10.*

14

Point to the leaves.
Say: *There are 14 leaves.*

© Pearson Education, Inc. K

My Word Cards

Directions Have students cut out the vocabulary cards. Read the front of the card, and then ask them to explain what the word or phrase means.

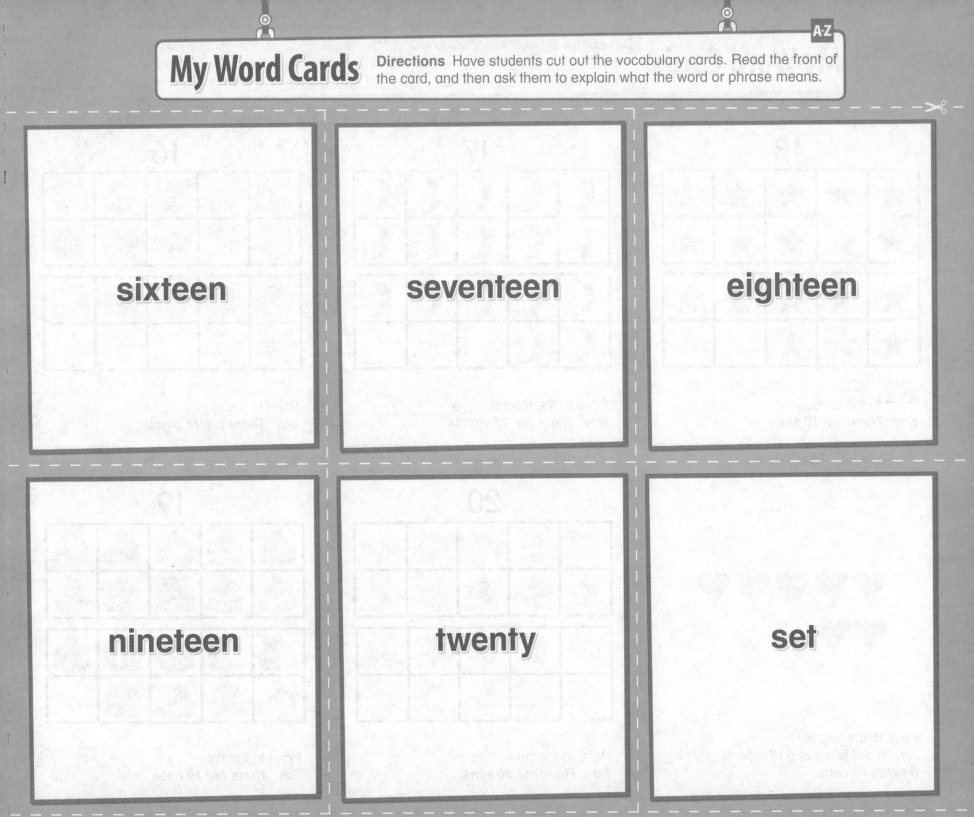

sixteen

seventeen

eighteen

nineteen

twenty

set

My Word Cards

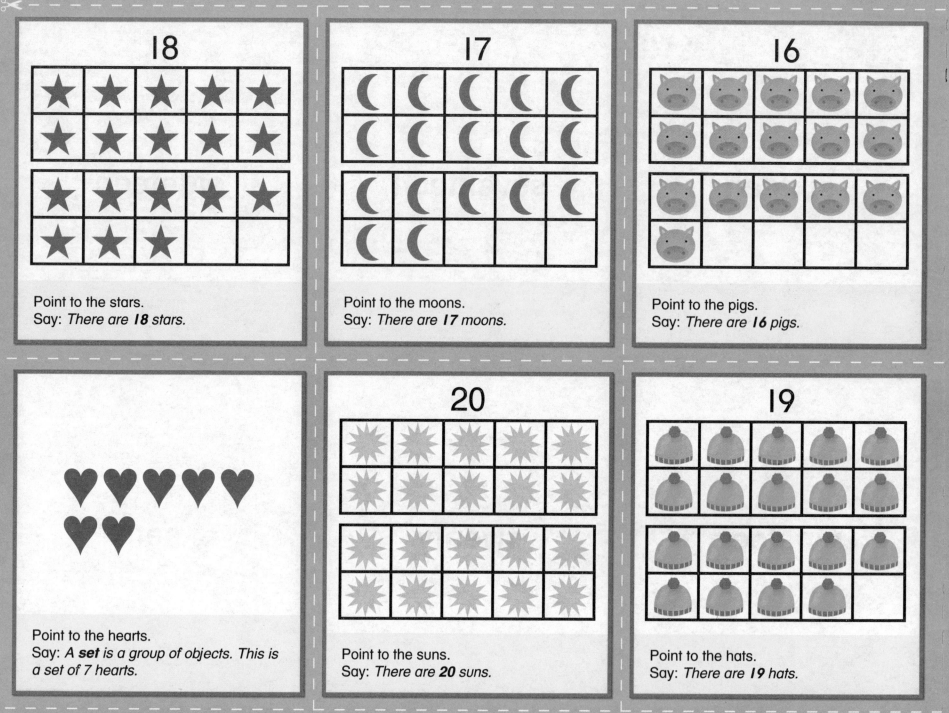

18

Point to the stars.
Say: *There are 18 stars.*

17

Point to the moons.
Say: *There are 17 moons.*

16

Point to the pigs.
Say: *There are 16 pigs.*

Point to the hearts.
Say: *A set is a group of objects. This is a set of 7 hearts.*

20

Point to the suns.
Say: *There are 20 suns.*

19

Point to the hats.
Say: *There are 19 hats.*

Solve & Share   Name _____

Directions Say: *Carlos has twelve toy cars. What other ways can Carlos use to show the number of cars he has? Use counters or a number to show one other way.*

⭐ **TEKS K.2B** Read, write, and represent whole numbers from 0 to at least 20 with and without objects or pictures. Also, K.2, K.2A, K.2C. **Mathematical Process Standards** K.1D, K.1F, K.1G.

Digital Resources at PearsonTexas.com

Solve   Learn   Glossary   Check   Tools   Games

eleven

☆ **Guided** ☆
Practice

1

2

Directions Have students count the cars in each group, and then practice writing the number that tells how many.

© Pearson Education, Inc. K

Topic 5 | Lesson 1

Name _____

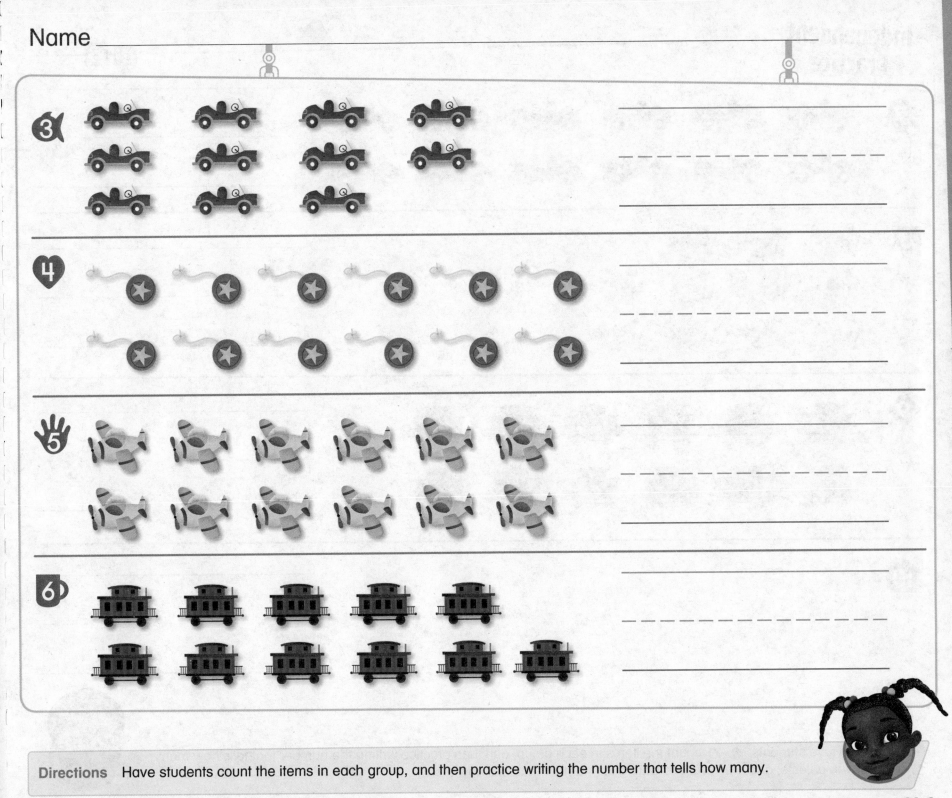

3

_____

4

_____

5

_____

6

_____

Directions Have students count the items in each group, and then practice writing the number that tells how many.

Topic 5 | Lesson 1

two hundred forty-one 241

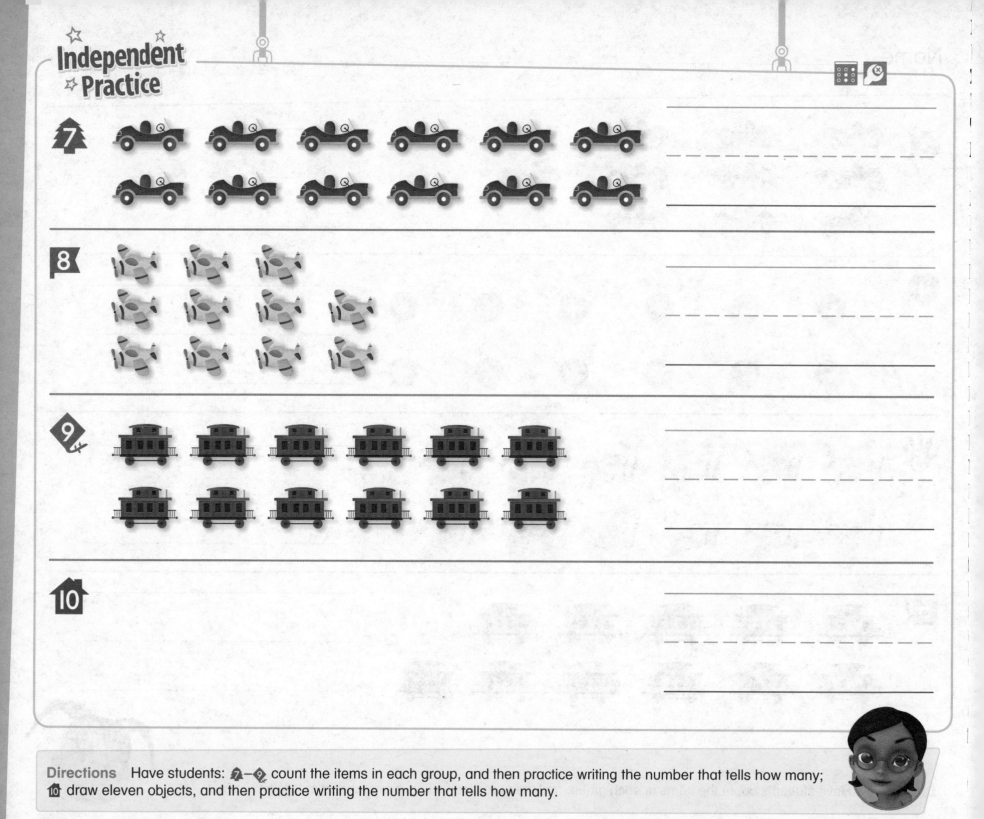

7

8

9

10

Directions Have students: **7–9** count the items in each group, and then practice writing the number that tells how many; **10** draw eleven objects, and then practice writing the number that tells how many.

© Pearson Education, Inc. K

Name _____

Another Look

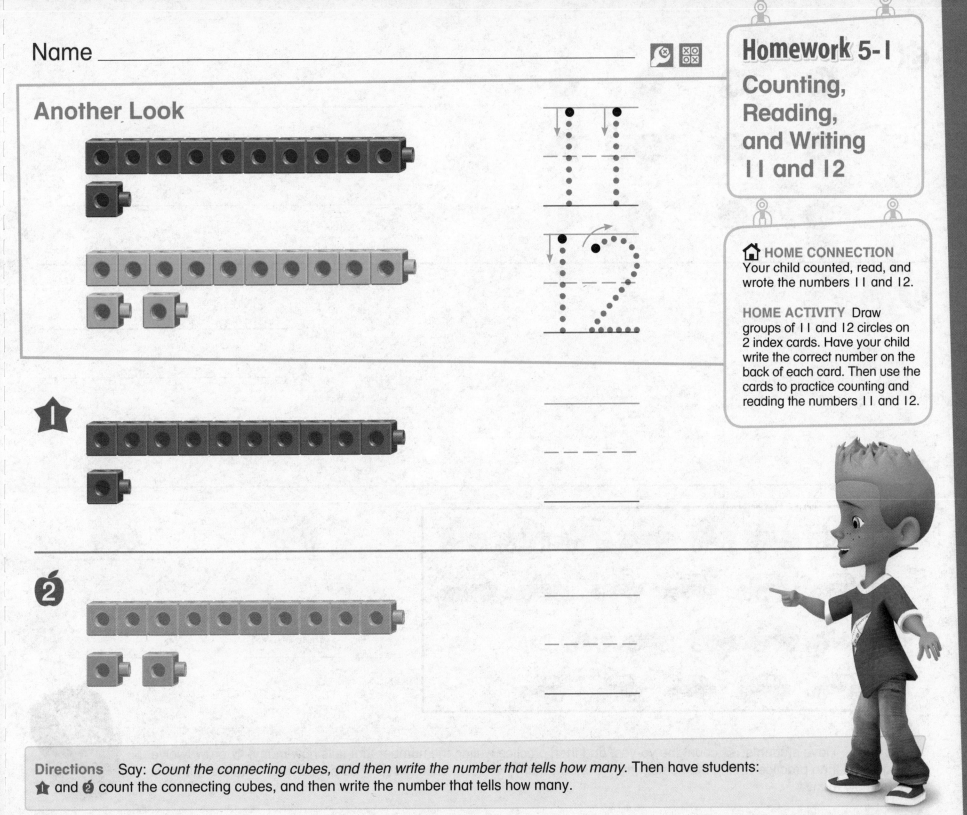

Directions Say: *Count the connecting cubes, and then write the number that tells how many.* Then have students:
⭐ and ② count the connecting cubes, and then write the number that tells how many.

3

_____

- - - - - - - - - - - - - - - - -

_____

4

_____

- - - - - - - - - - - - - - - - -

_____

5

_____   _____

- - - - -   - - - - -

_____   _____

Directions Have students: **3** count the yo-yos, and then practice writing the number that tells how many; **4** draw twelve objects, and then practice writing the number that tells how many; **5** count each group of cars, and then write the numbers that tell how many.

244 two hundred forty-four   © Pearson Education, Inc. K   **Topic 5** | Lesson I

Solve & Share   Name _____

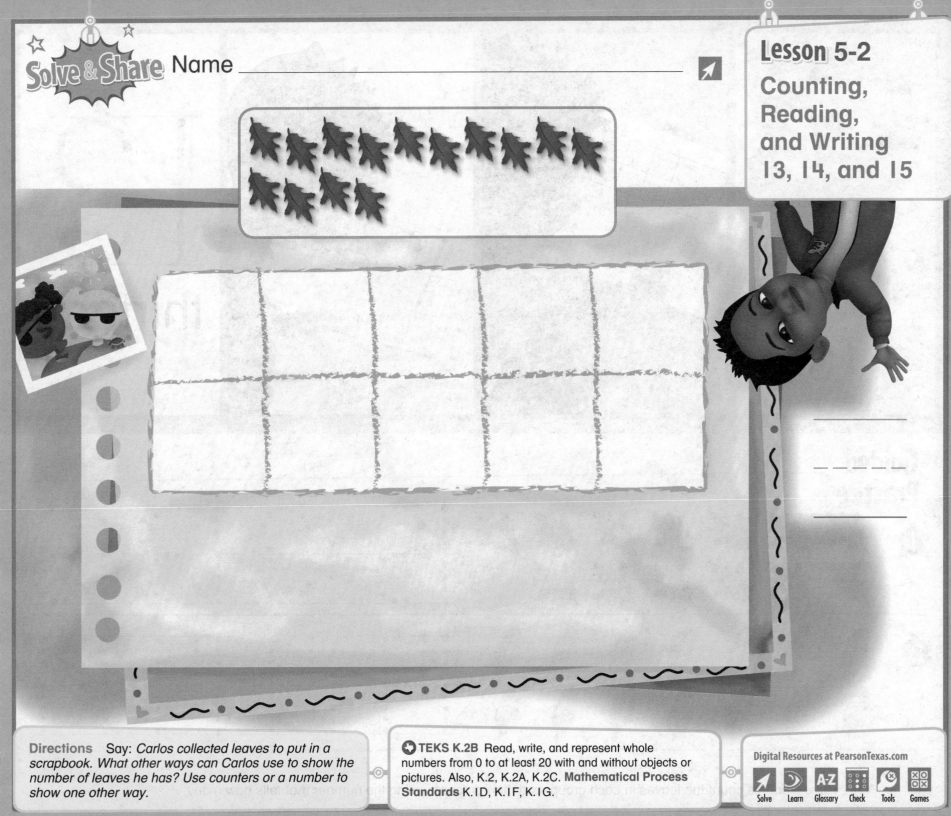

Directions Say: *Carlos collected leaves to put in a scrapbook. What other ways can Carlos use to show the number of leaves he has? Use counters or a number to show one other way.*

★ **TEKS K.2B** Read, write, and represent whole numbers from 0 to at least 20 with and without objects or pictures. Also, K.2, K.2A, K.2C. **Mathematical Process Standards** K.1D, K.1F, K.1G.

Digital Resources at PearsonTexas.com

Solve   Learn   A-Z Glossary   Check   Tools   Games

13

thirteen

☆ **Guided Practice** ☆

1

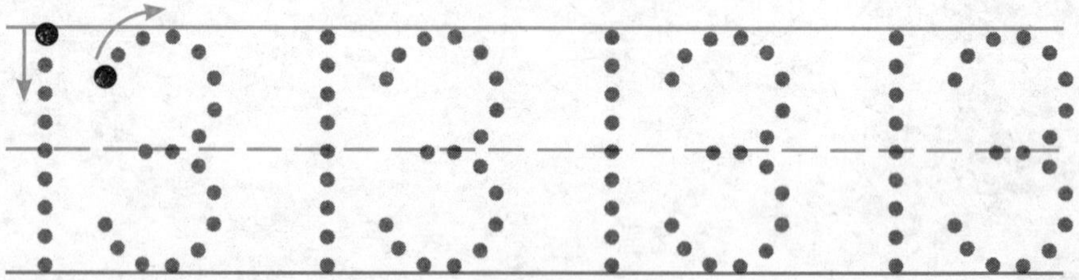

2

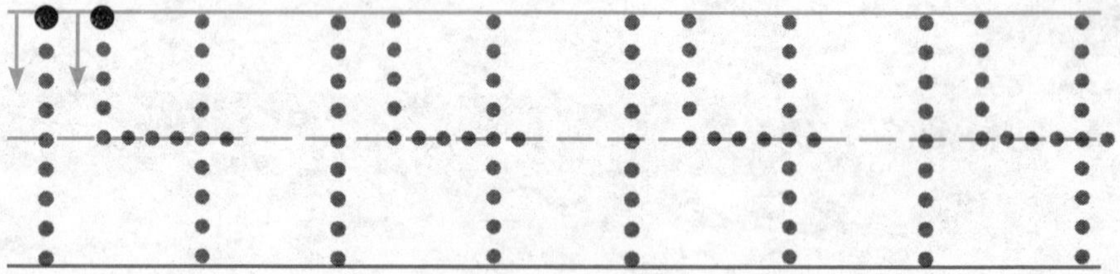

Directions Have students count the leaves in each group, and then practice writing the number that tells how many.

© Pearson Education, Inc. K

Name _____

3 15 15 15 15

4

5

6

Directions Have students count the leaves in each group, and then practice writing the number that tells how many.

Topic 5 | Lesson 2   two hundred forty-seven **247**

7

8

9

10

Directions Have students: 🌲–✏️ count the leaves in each group, and then practice writing the number that tells how many; 🏠 draw fourteen objects, and then practice writing the number that tells how many.

248 two hundred forty-eight   © Pearson Education, Inc. K   **Topic 5** | Lesson 2

Another Look

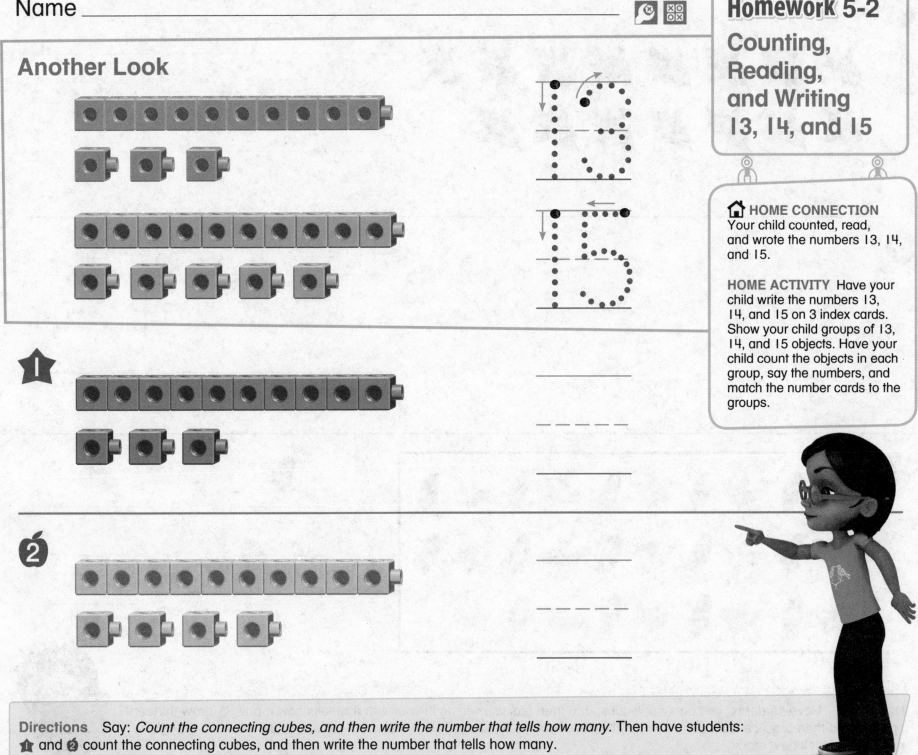

🏠 **HOME CONNECTION**
Your child counted, read, and wrote the numbers 13, 14, and 15.

HOME ACTIVITY Have your child write the numbers 13, 14, and 15 on 3 index cards. Show your child groups of 13, 14, and 15 objects. Have your child count the objects in each group, say the numbers, and match the number cards to the groups.

⭐ 1

🍎 2

Directions Say: *Count the connecting cubes, and then write the number that tells how many.* Then have students:
⭐ and 🍎 count the connecting cubes, and then write the number that tells how many.

④

🖐 5

© Pearson Education, Inc. K

Solve & Share Name _____

Directions Say: *Jada has a collection of toy pigs in her room. What other ways can Carlos use to show the number of toy pigs Jada has? Use counters or a number to show one other way.*

⭐ **TEKS K.2B** Read, write, and represent whole numbers from 0 to at least 20 with and without objects or pictures. Also, K.2, K.2A, K.2C. **Mathematical Process Standards** K.1A, K.1D, K.1F.

Digital Resources at PearsonTexas.com

Solve   Learn   Glossary   Check   Tools   Games

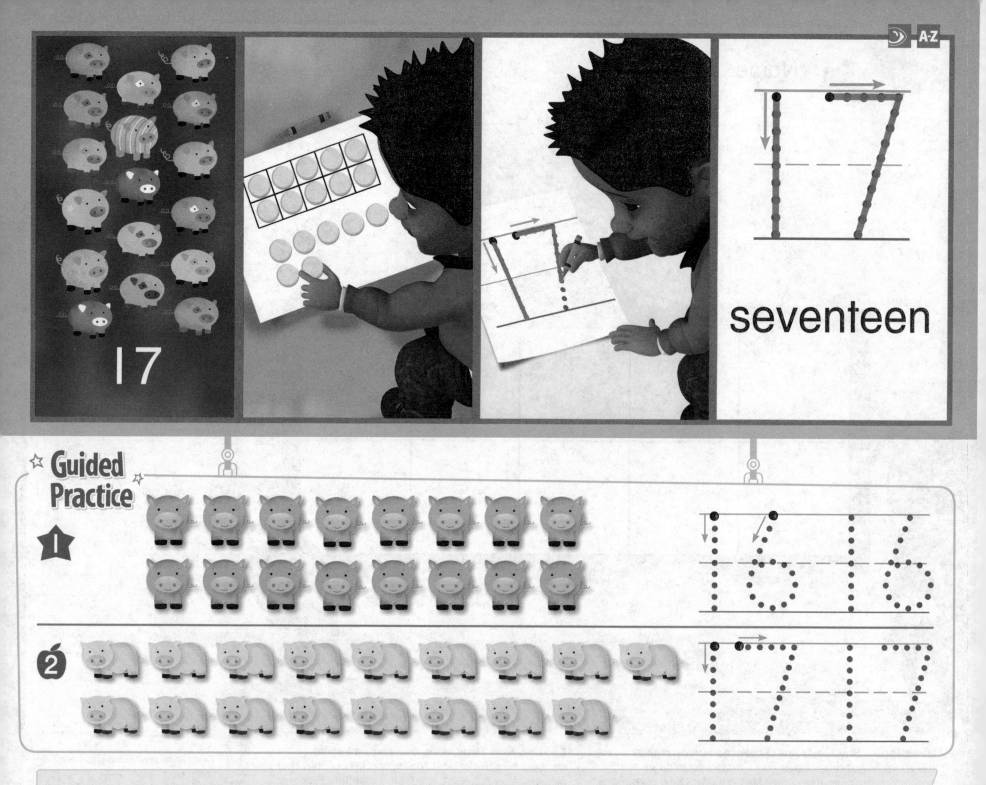

17

seventeen

☆ **Guided Practice** ☆

1

2

Directions Have students count the toy pigs in each group, and then practice writing the number that tells how many.

© Pearson Education, Inc. K

Name ______________________________

3 

4 

5 

6 

7 

Directions Have students count the toys in each group, and then practice writing the number that tells how many.

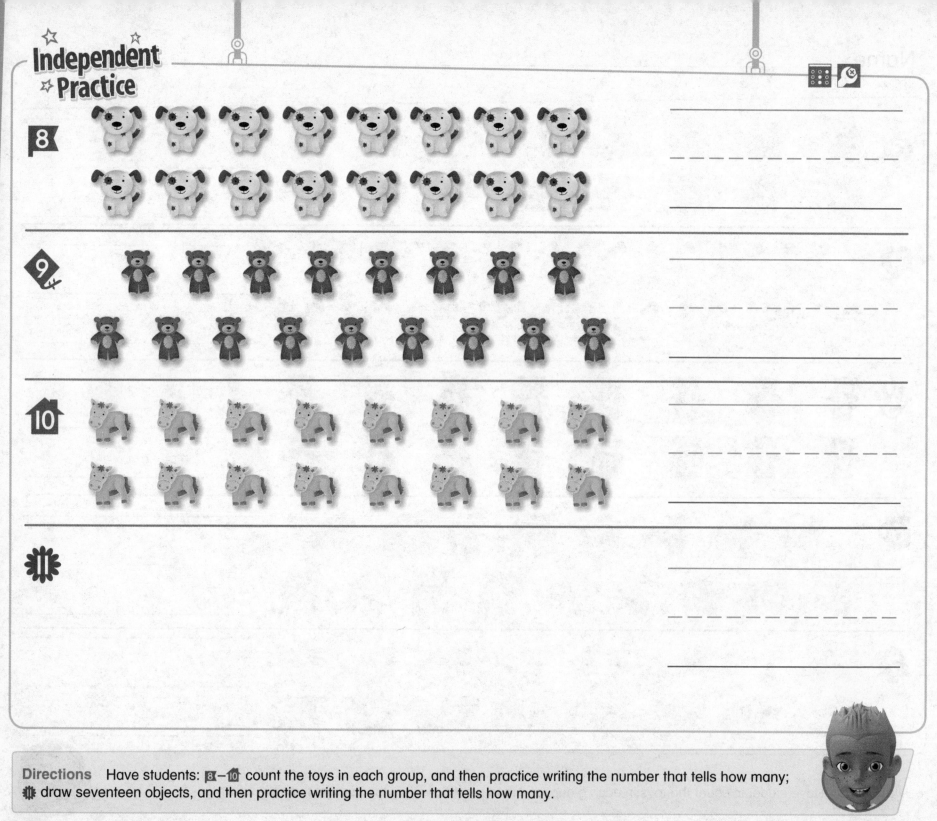

8

9

10

⁕

Directions Have students: **8**—**10** count the toys in each group, and then practice writing the number that tells how many; **⁕** draw seventeen objects, and then practice writing the number that tells how many.

254 two hundred fifty-four   © Pearson Education, Inc. K   **Topic 5** | Lesson 3

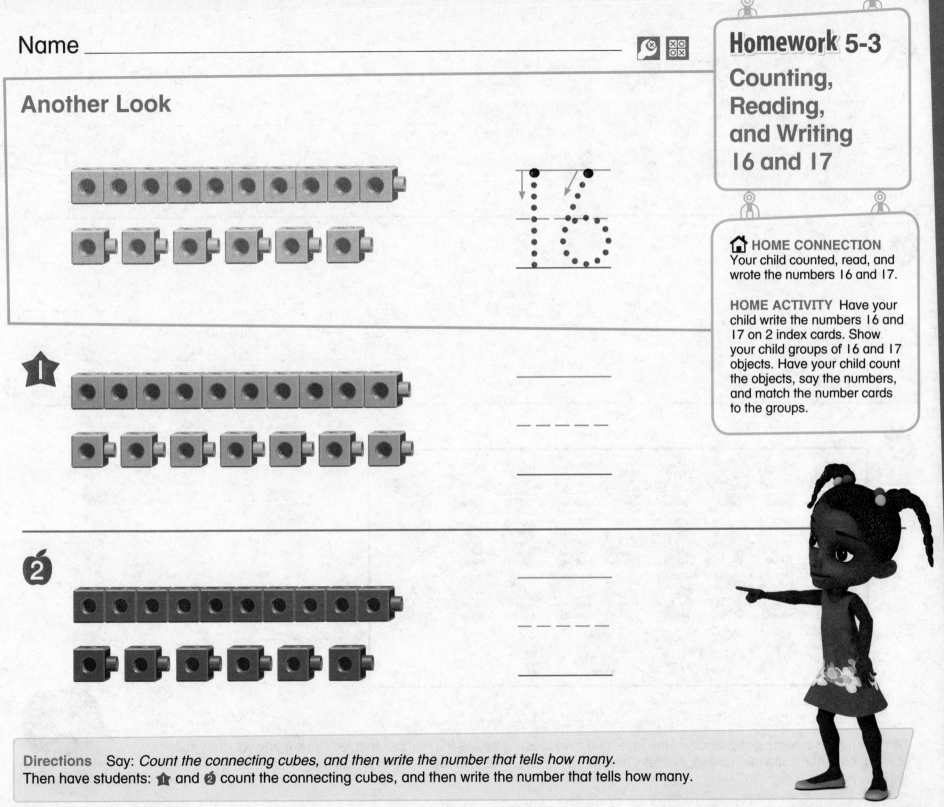

Another Look

🏠 **HOME CONNECTION**
Your child counted, read, and wrote the numbers 16 and 17.

HOME ACTIVITY Have your child write the numbers 16 and 17 on 2 index cards. Show your child groups of 16 and 17 objects. Have your child count the objects, say the numbers, and match the number cards to the groups.

1

2

Directions Say: *Count the connecting cubes, and then write the number that tells how many.*
Then have students: **1** and **2** count the connecting cubes, and then write the number that tells how many.

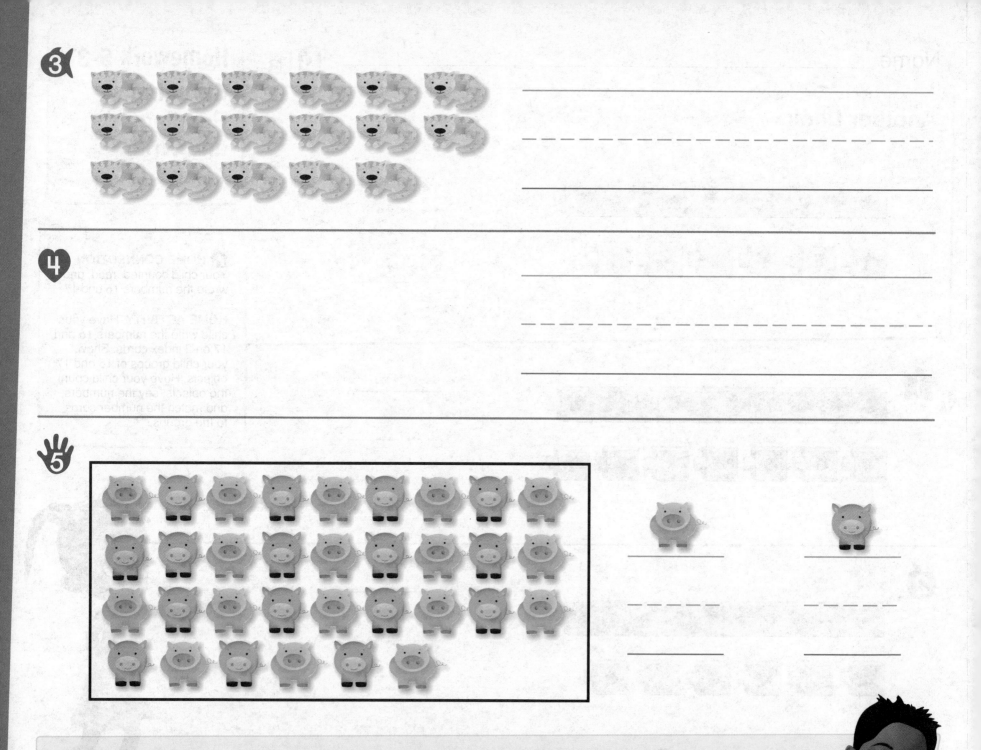

3

4

5

Directions Have students: **3** count the toys, and then practice writing the number that tells how many; **4** draw sixteen objects, and then write the number that tells how many; **5** count each group of toy pigs, and then write the numbers that tell how many.

Solve & Share

Name _____

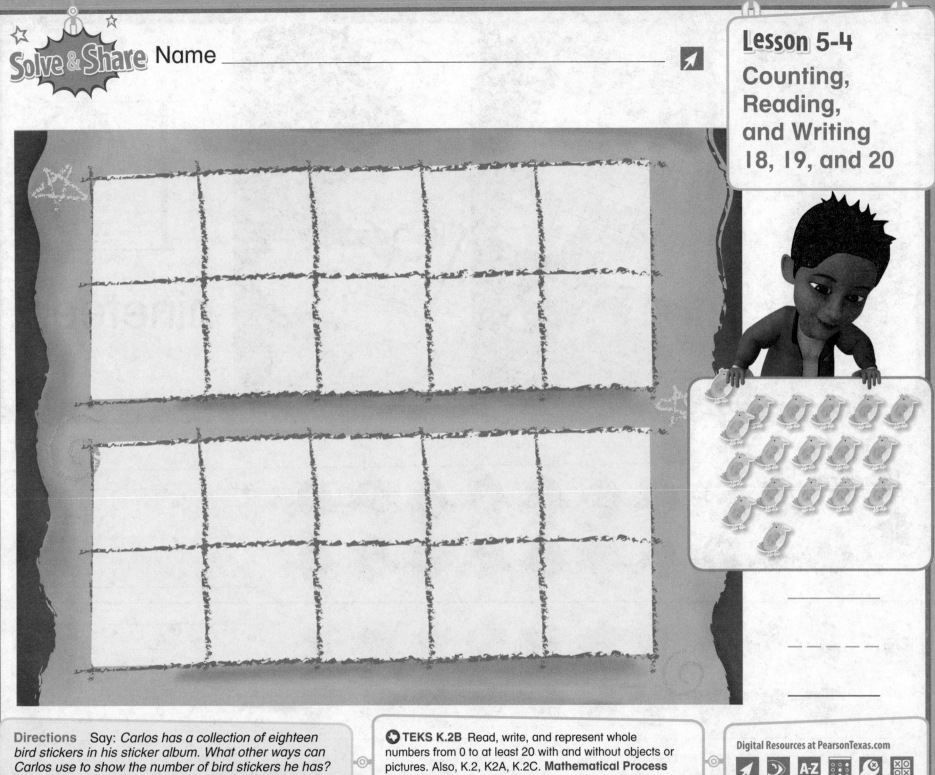

Directions Say: *Carlos has a collection of eighteen bird stickers in his sticker album. What other ways can Carlos use to show the number of bird stickers he has? Use counters or a number to show one other way.*

★ **TEKS K.2B** Read, write, and represent whole numbers from 0 to at least 20 with and without objects or pictures. Also, K.2, K2A, K.2C. **Mathematical Process Standards** K.1D, K.1E, K.1F, K.1G.

Digital Resources at PearsonTexas.com

Solve · Learn · Glossary · Check · Tools · Games

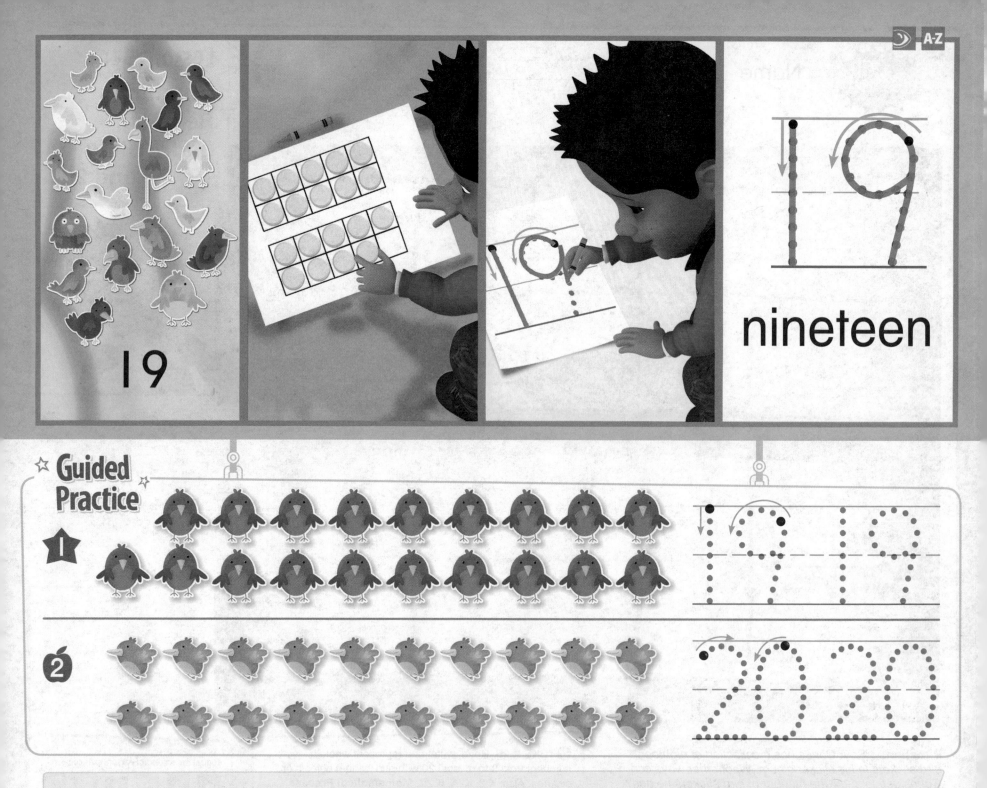

19

nineteen

☆ Guided Practice ☆

1

19 19

2

20 20

Directions Have students count the bird stickers in each group, and then practice writing the number that tells how many.

© Pearson Education, Inc. K

Name _____

3

4

5

6

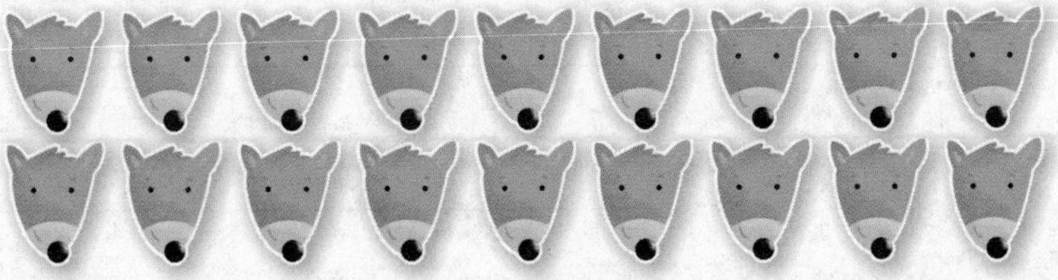

7

Directions Have students count the stickers in each group, and then practice writing the number that tells how many.

Topic 5 | Lesson 4

two hundred fifty-nine **259**

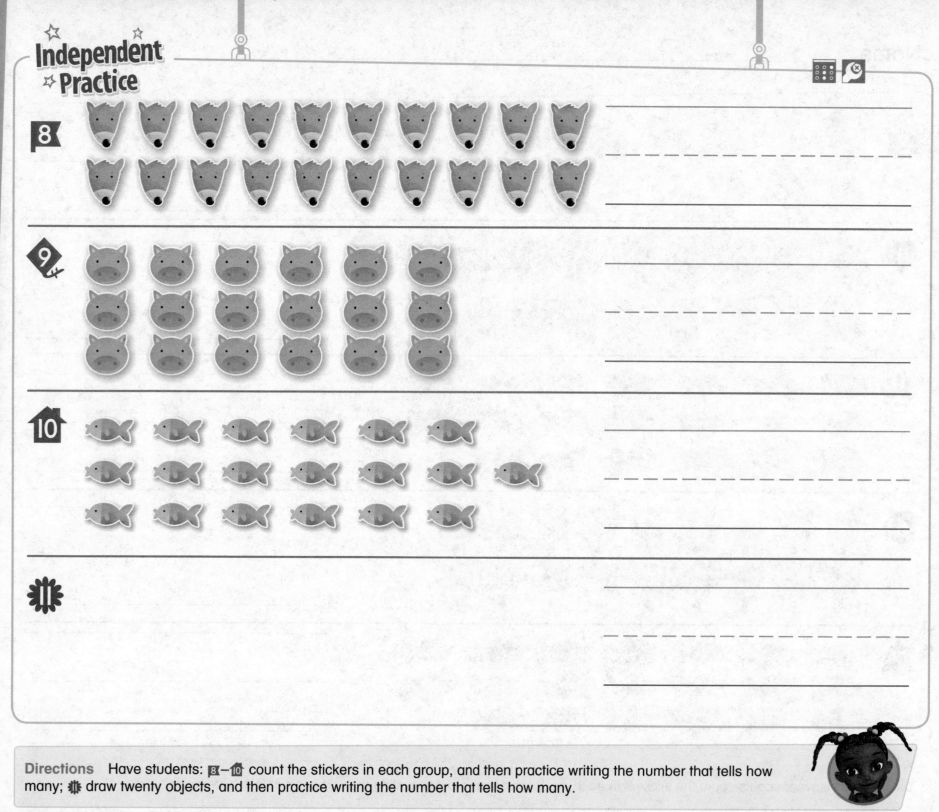

8

9

10

⁂

Directions Have students: **8**–**10** count the stickers in each group, and then practice writing the number that tells how many; ⁂ draw twenty objects, and then practice writing the number that tells how many.

260 two hundred sixty   © Pearson Education, Inc. K   **Topic 5** | Lesson 4

Name _____

Another Look

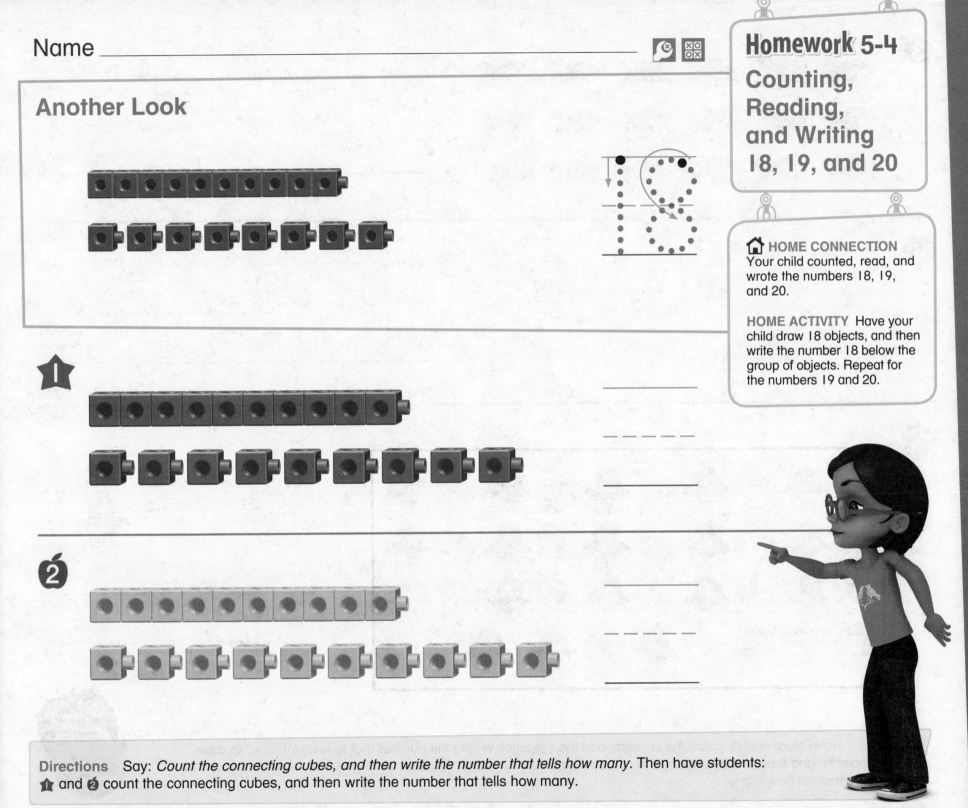

🏠 **HOME CONNECTION** Your child counted, read, and wrote the numbers 18, 19, and 20.

HOME ACTIVITY Have your child draw 18 objects, and then write the number 18 below the group of objects. Repeat for the numbers 19 and 20.

⭐ 1

🍎 2

Directions Say: *Count the connecting cubes, and then write the number that tells how many*. Then have students:
⭐ and 🍎 count the connecting cubes, and then write the number that tells how many.

3

_____

- - - - - - - - - - - - - - - -

_____

4

_____

- - - - - - - - - - - - - - - -

_____

5

_____   _____

- - - - -   - - - - -

_____   _____

Directions Have students: **3** count the stickers, and then practice writing the number that tells how many; **4** draw nineteen objects, and then practice writing the number that tells how many; **5** count each group of stickers, and then write the numbers that tell how many.

© Pearson Education, Inc. K **Topic 5 | Lesson 4**

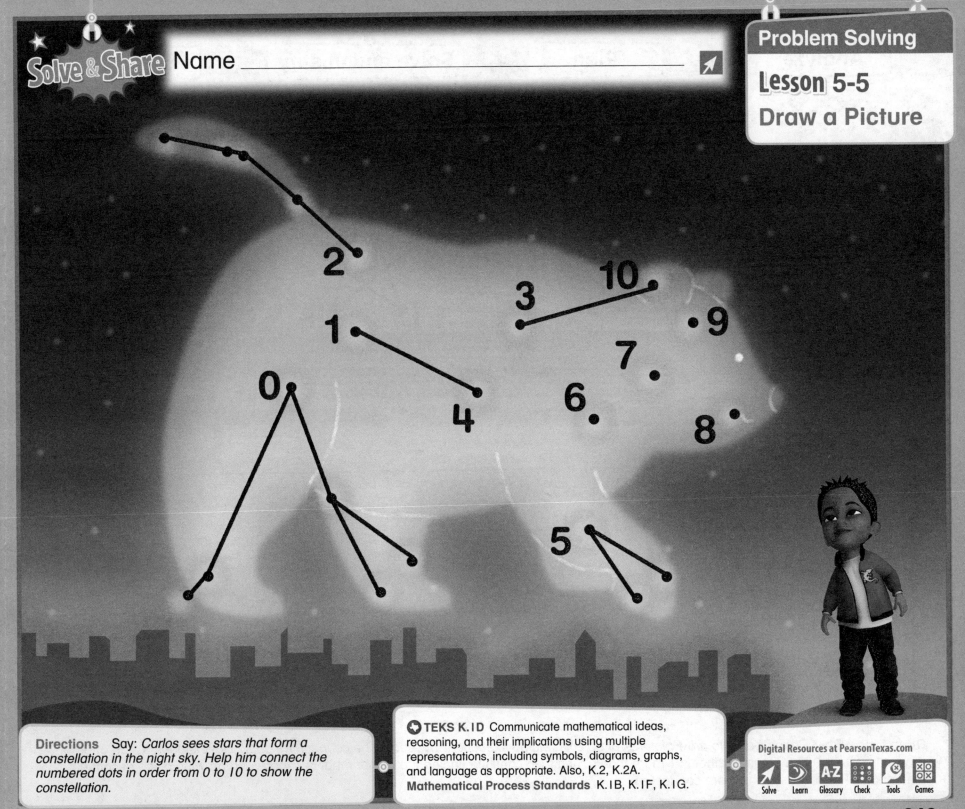

Solve & Share Name _____

2

10

3

1

9

7

0

4

6

8

5

Directions Say: *Carlos sees stars that form a constellation in the night sky. Help him connect the numbered dots in order from 0 to 10 to show the constellation.*

✪**TEKS K.1D** Communicate mathematical ideas, reasoning, and their implications using multiple representations, including symbols, diagrams, graphs, and language as appropriate. Also, **K.2, K.2A. Mathematical Process Standards** K.1B, K.1F, K.1G.

Digital Resources at PearsonTexas.com

Solve Learn Glossary Check Tools Games

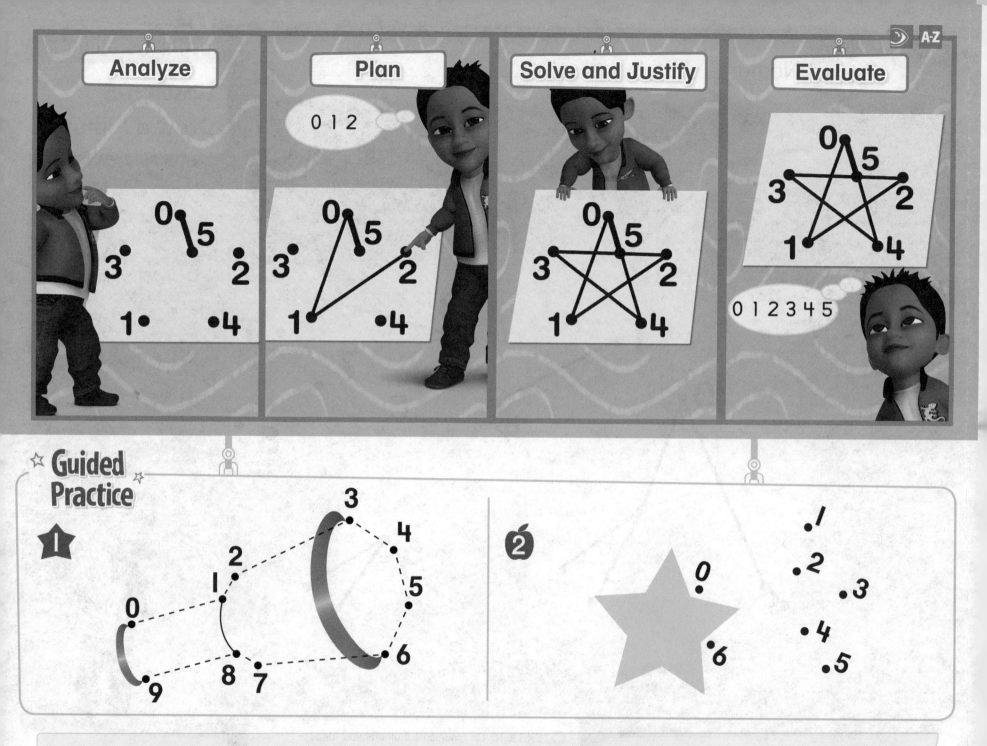

Analyze

Plan

0 1 2

Solve and Justify

Evaluate

0 1 2 3 4 5

☆ **Guided Practice**

1

2

Directions Say: *Carlos wants to draw pictures of objects related to space. How should he connect the dots?* Have students start at 0, draw a line from 0 to the number that is 1 more than 0, and then continue finding the number that is 1 more and drawing a line to connect the dots until all of the numbers are connected.

© Pearson Education, Inc. K

Name _____

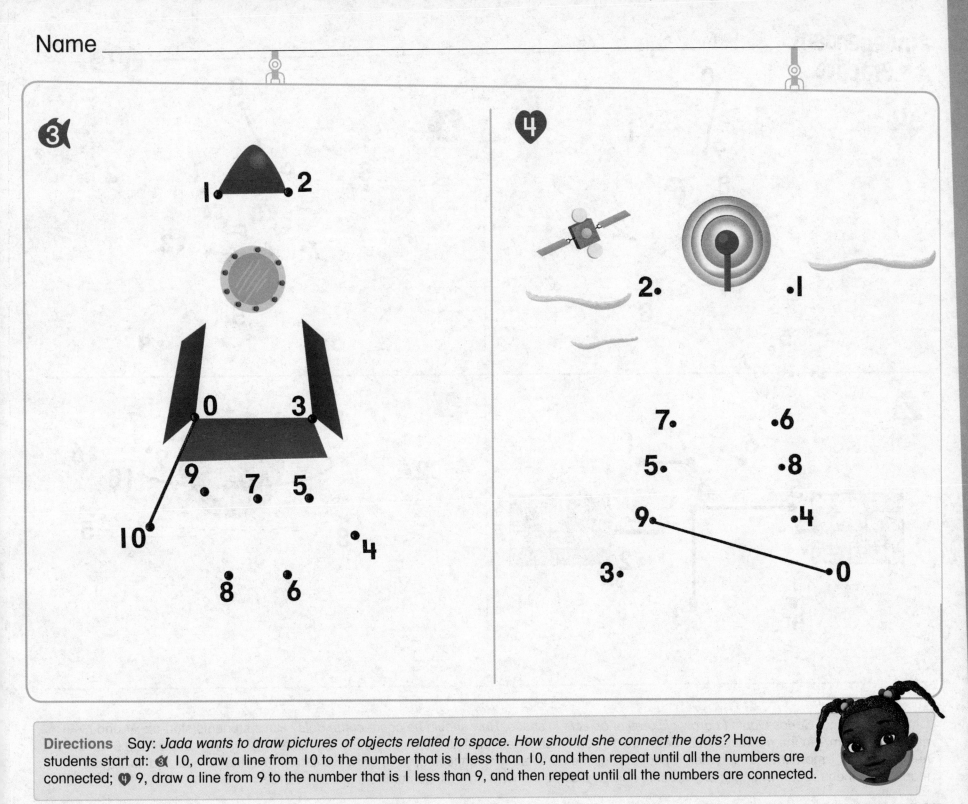

1 • 2

0   3

9   7   5

10

8   6   4

④

2 •   • 1

7 •   • 6

5 •   • 8

9   • 4

3 •   0

Directions Say: *Jada wants to draw pictures of objects related to space. How should she connect the dots?* Have students start at: ③ 10, draw a line from 10 to the number that is 1 less than 10, and then repeat until all the numbers are connected; ④ 9, draw a line from 9 to the number that is 1 less than 9, and then repeat until all the numbers are connected.

Topic 5 | Lesson 5

two hundred sixty-five **265**

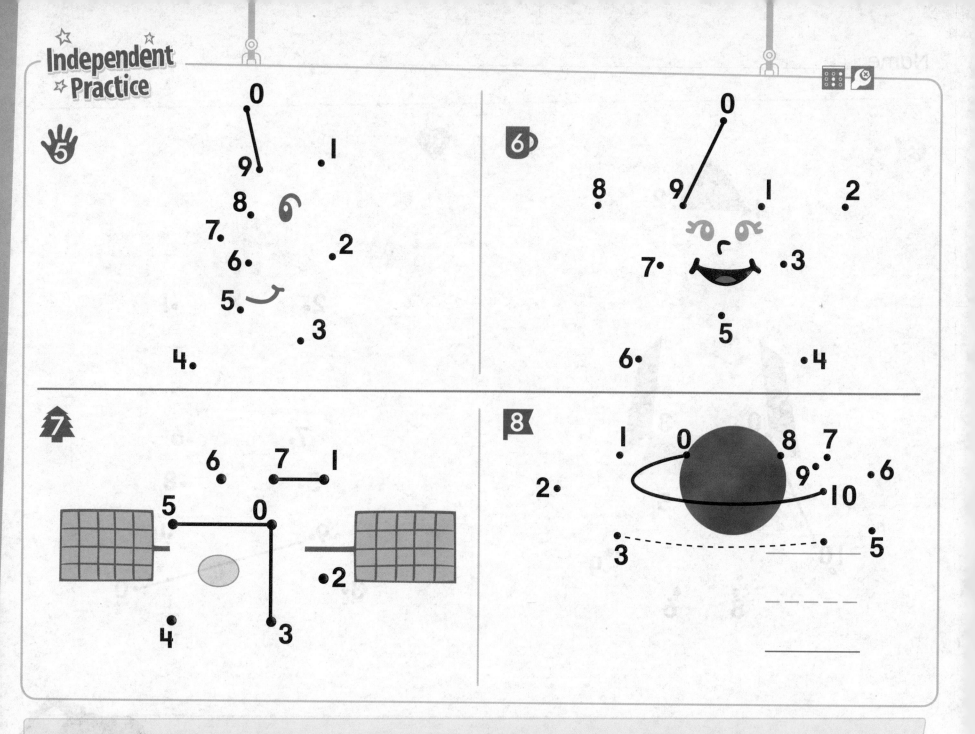

Directions Say: *Carlos wants to draw pictures of objects in space. How should he connect the dots?* Have students start at: ✋ and ☕ 9, draw a line from 9 to the number that is 1 less than 9, and then repeat until all the numbers are connected; 🌲 0, draw a line from 0 to the number that is 1 more than 0, and then repeat until all the numbers are connected; 🚩 0, draw a line from 0 to the number that is 1 more than 0, and then repeat, writing in any missing numbers along the way, until all the numbers are connected.

Topic 5 | Lesson 5

Name _____

Another Look

0 1 2 3 4 5 6 7 8 9 10

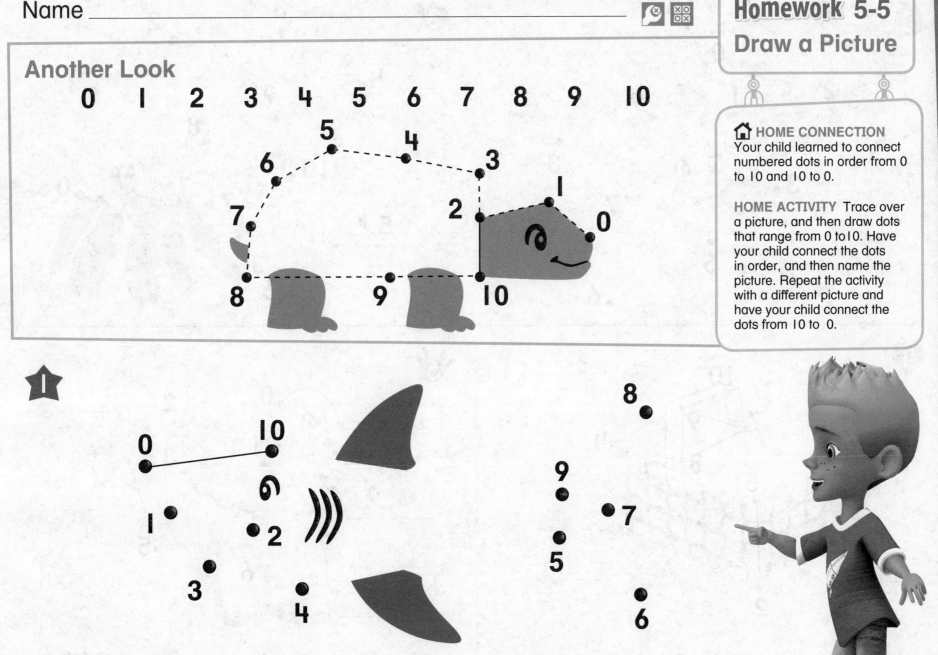

Directions Say: *Let's say the numbers from 0 to 10 in order. Point to each number as you say it. Now, let's count back from 10 to 0. Alex wants to draw pictures of animals in the ocean. You can find the number that is 1 more each time to connect the dots in order. Start with 0. Now, draw a line to the number that is 1 more.* Then have students: ⭐ start at 0, draw a line from 0 to the number that is 1 more than 0, and then repeat until all the numbers are connected.

2

10
0
2   1   9
3   8
7
5
4   6

3

3   2
4   9   1
8
10
7   0
5   6

4

10
7   9   4
6   8
0   5
1   2

5

0
10   2
6   1   3
9   8
5
6

© Pearson Education, Inc. K

Topic 5 | Lesson 5

Solve & Share Name _____

Directions Say: *Look at the trays of pineapples and oranges. Circle the tray that has more pieces of fruit. Draw an X on the tray that has fewer pieces of fruit. Show how you know you are correct.*

⭐ **TEKS K.2G** Compare sets of objects up to at least 20 in each set using comparative language. Also, K.2, K.2E. **Mathematical Process Standards** K.1A, K.1C, K.1F, K.1G.

Digital Resources at PearsonTexas.com

Solve Learn Glossary Check Tools Games

Topic 5 | Lesson 6

Same as!

☆ Guided Practice ☆

1

2

Directions Have students compare the 2 sets and circle the set that has more, or circle the exercise number if both sets have the same number of pieces of fruit. Allow students to use counters as needed.

© Pearson Education, Inc. K

Name _____

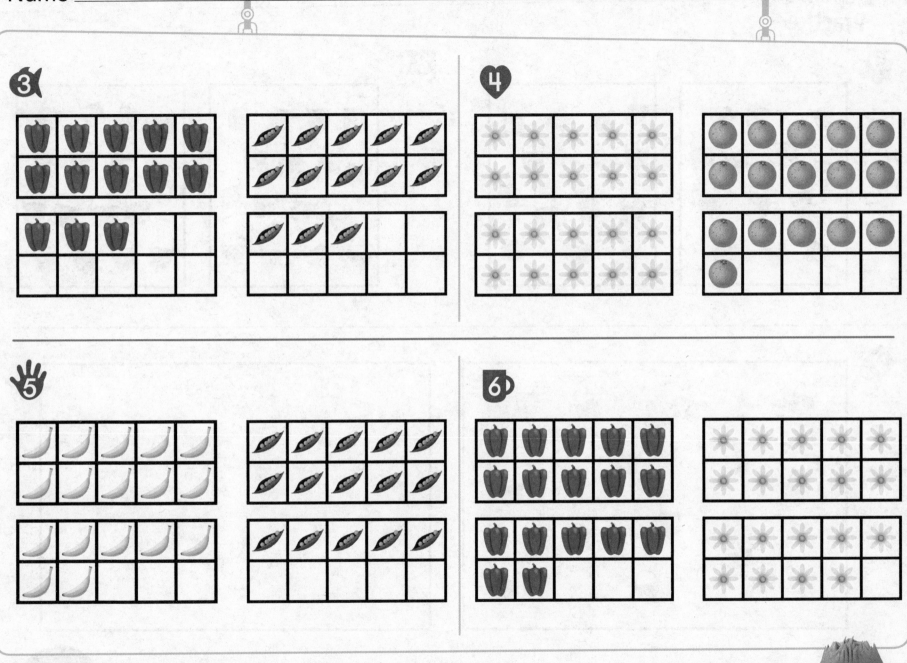

Directions Have students compare the 2 sets and: ❸ and ❹ circle the set that has more, or circle the exercise number if both sets have the same number of objects; ✋ and ☕ circle the set that has fewer, or circle the exercise number if both sets have the same number of objects.

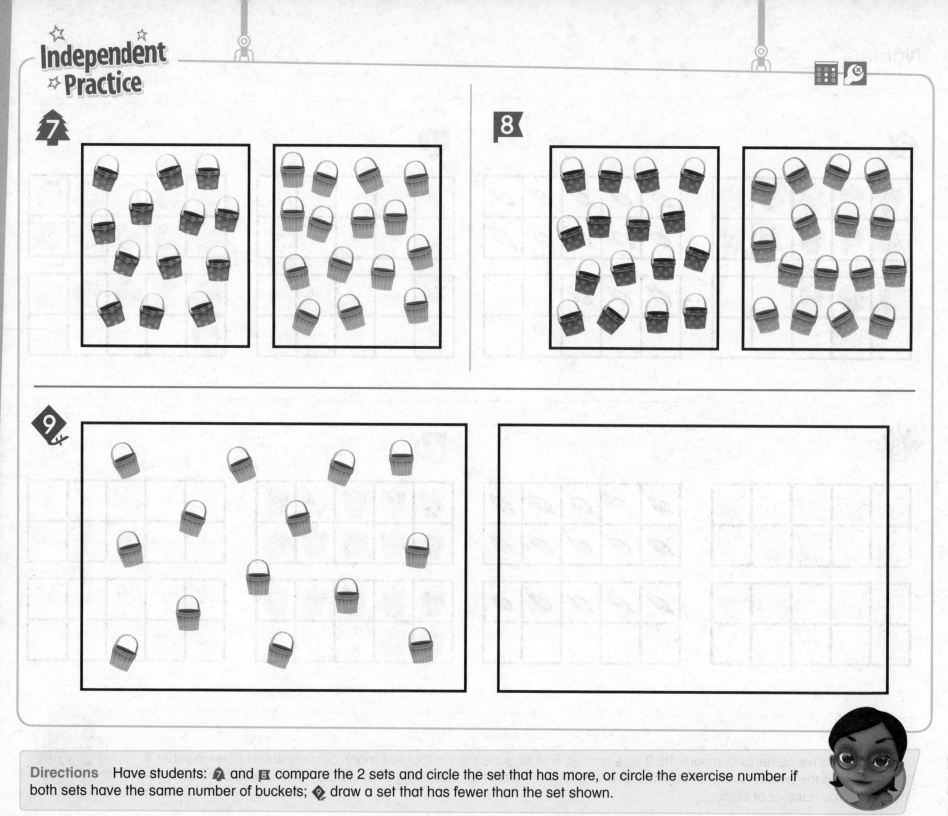

7

8

9

© Pearson Education, Inc. K

Topic 5 | Lesson 6

Directions Have students: **7** and **8** compare the 2 sets and circle the set that has more, or circle the exercise number if both sets have the same number of buckets; **9** draw a set that has fewer than the set shown.

Another Look

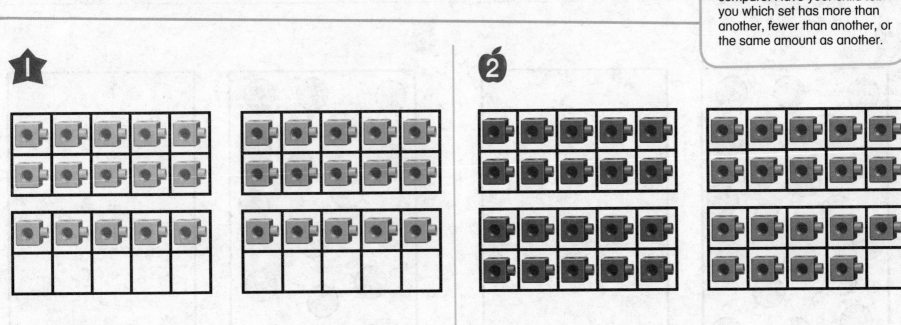

🏠 HOME CONNECTION
Your child compared sets and determined which set had more or fewer than the other. He or she also identified sets with the same amount.

HOME ACTIVITY Create different sets of up to 20 small objects for your child to compare. Have your child tell you which set has more than another, fewer than another, or the same amount as another.

Directions Say: *Compare the 2 sets of connecting cubes. Which set has more cubes? Circle that set. The set with yellow cubes has fewer.* Then have students: ★ and ② compare the 2 sets and circle the set that has more, or circle the exercise number if both sets have the same number of cubes.

Topic 5 | Lesson 6   Digital Resources at PearsonTexas.com   two hundred seventy-three **273**

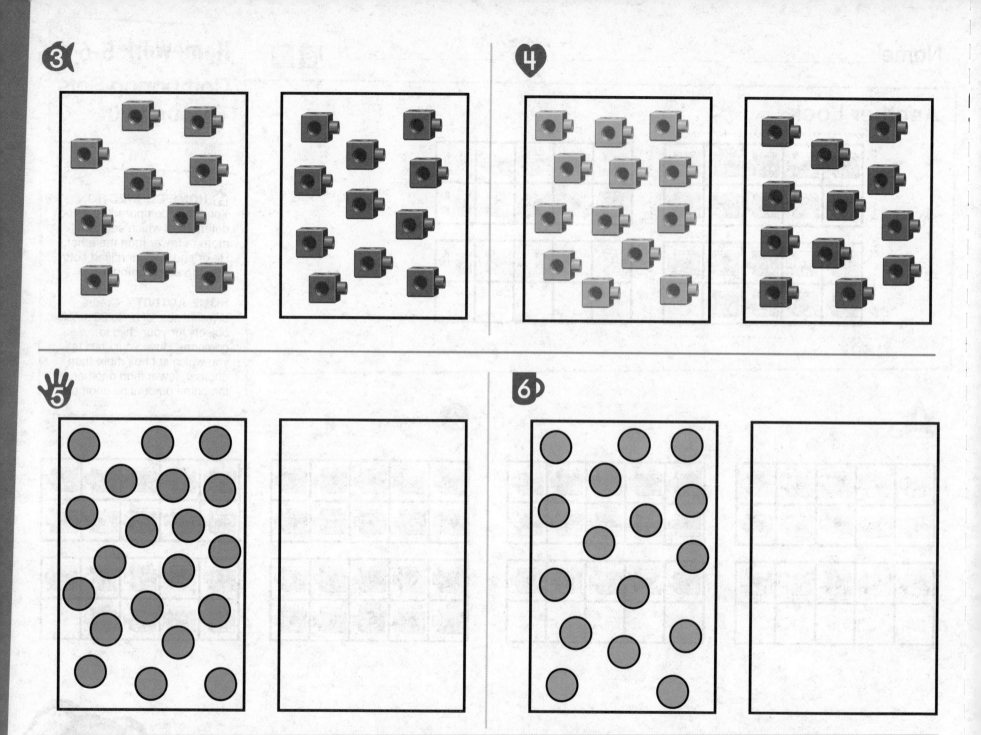

Solve & Share Name _____

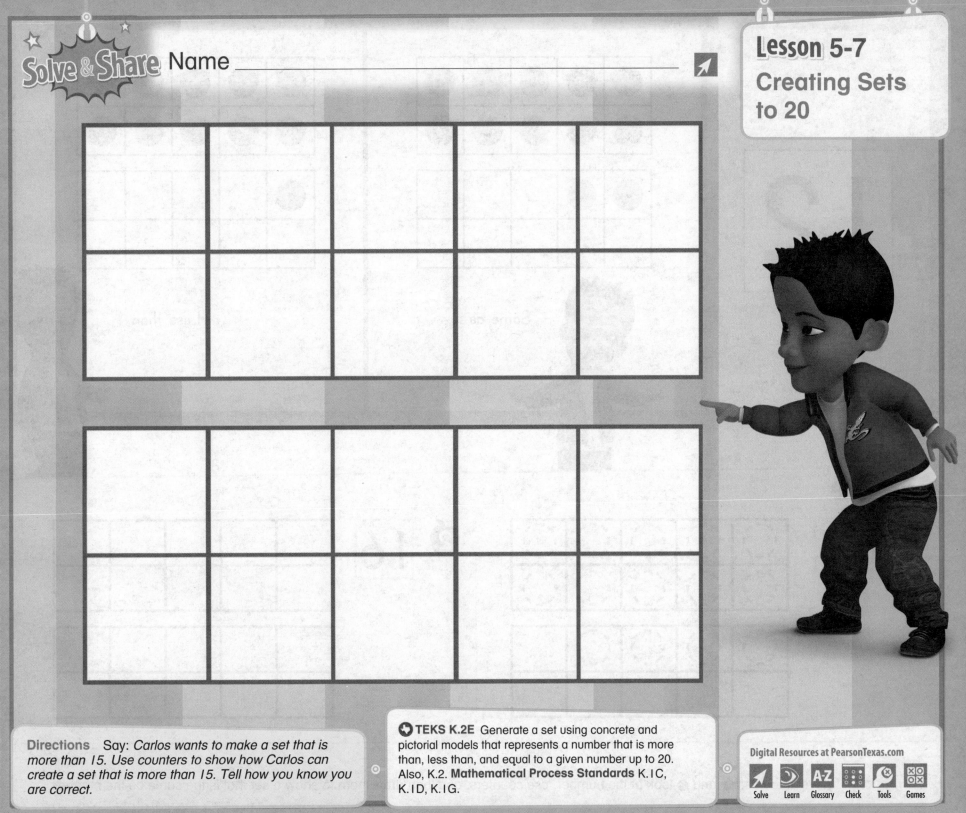

Directions Say: *Carlos wants to make a set that is more than 15. Use counters to show how Carlos can create a set that is more than 15. Tell how you know you are correct.*

⭐ **TEKS K.2E** Generate a set using concrete and pictorial models that represents a number that is more than, less than, and equal to a given number up to 20. Also, K.2. **Mathematical Process Standards** K.1C, K.1D, K.1G.

Digital Resources at PearsonTexas.com

Solve   Learn   Glossary   Check   Tools   Games

Same as

Less than

☆ **Guided Practice** ☆

1 14

2 16

Directions Have students: **1** and **2** look at the number, use counters, and then draw them to show a set that is the same as the number.

© Pearson Education, Inc. K **Topic 5 | Lesson 7**

Name _____

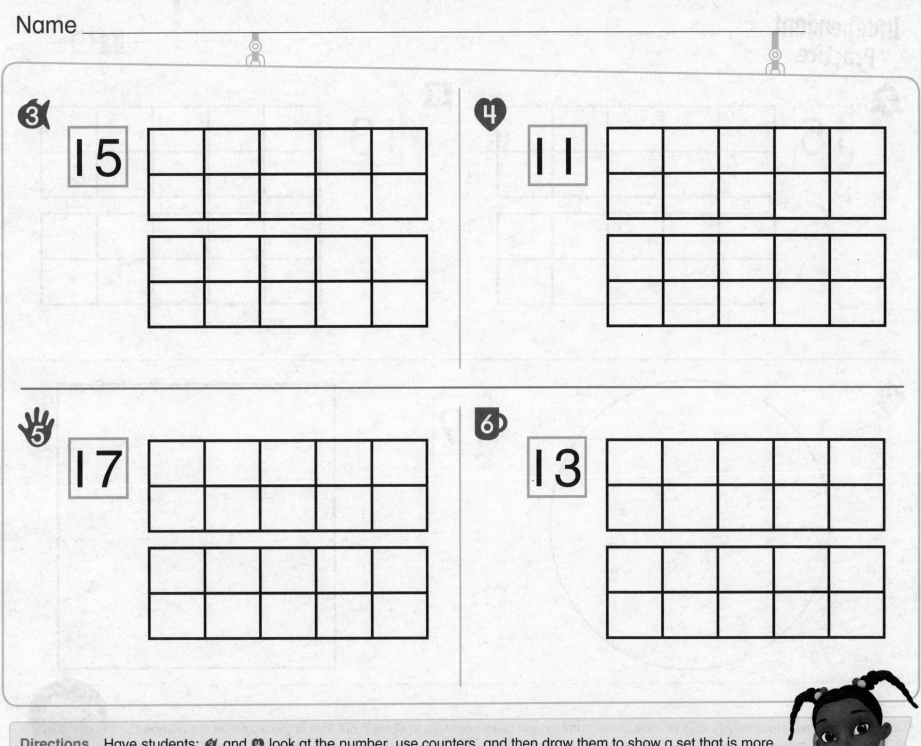

3 15

4 11

5 17

6 13

Directions Have students: **3** and **4** look at the number, use counters, and then draw them to show a set that is more than the number; **5** and **6** look at the number, use counters, and then draw them to show a set that is less than the number.

Topic 5 | Lesson 7

two hundred seventy-seven **277**

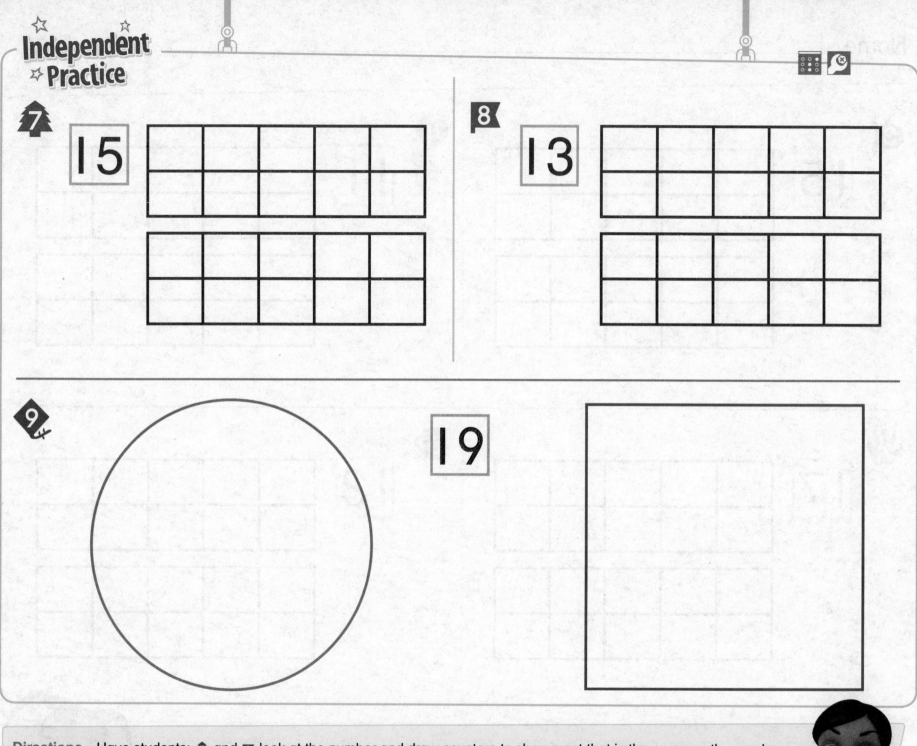

Independent Practice

7 15

8 13

9 19

Directions Have students: **7** and **8** look at the number and draw counters to show a set that is the same as the number; **9** look at the number, draw in the blue shape a set of objects that is less than the number, and draw in the red shape a set of objects that is more than the number.

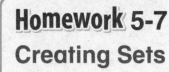

Another Look

18

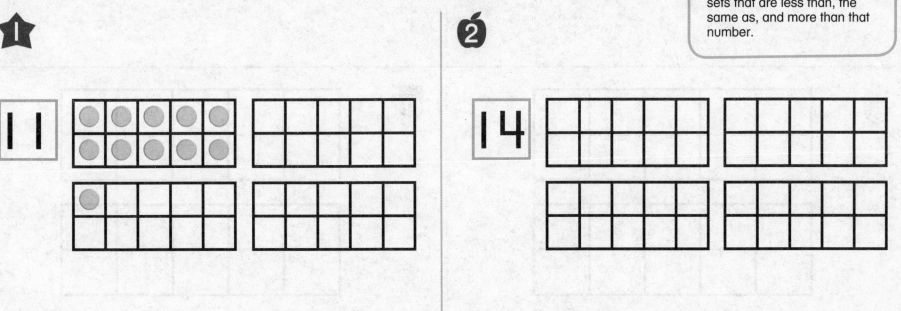

⌂ HOME CONNECTION
Your child used objects and pictures to make sets less than, the same as, and more than a number.

HOME ACTIVITY Say or show a number up to 20. Then have your child use blocks or small objects to make sets that are less than, the same as, and more than that number.

★ 1

11

🍎 2

14

Directions Say: *Count the counters. There are the same number of counters as the number in the box. Now draw a set of counters that is less than 18.* Then have students: ★ count to see that there are the same number of counters as the number in the box, and then draw a set that is more than 11; 🍎 draw a set that is the same number as the number in the box, and then draw a set that is less than 14.

Homework 5-7
Creating Sets
to 20

3 13

4 16

5

6

Directions Have students: **3** draw a set of objects that is less than 13; **4** draw a set of objects that is more than 16; **5** draw a set of objects that is more than 17 but less than 20; **6** draw a set of objects that is more than 11 but less than 13.

© Pearson Education, Inc. K **Topic 5** | Lesson 7

Name _____

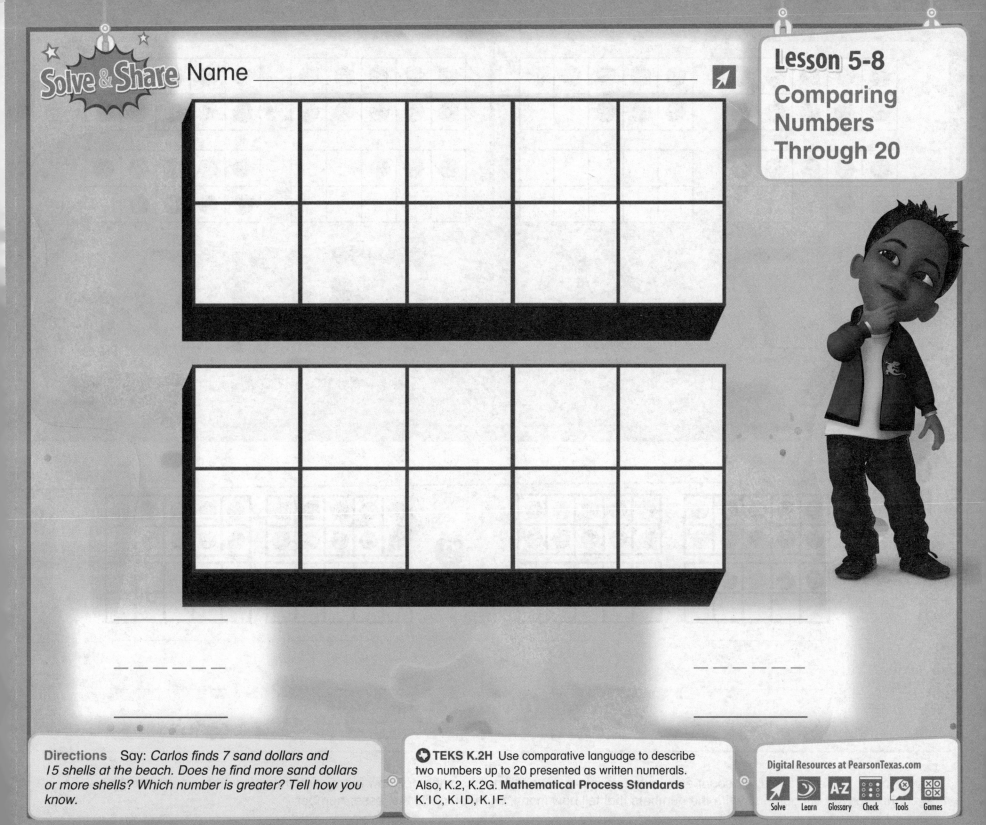

_____   _____

_ _ _ _ _ _ _   _ _ _ _ _ _ _

_____   _____

Directions Say: *Carlos finds 7 sand dollars and 15 shells at the beach. Does he find more sand dollars or more shells? Which number is greater? Tell how you know.*

⬆ **TEKS K.2H** Use comparative language to describe two numbers up to 20 presented as written numerals. Also, K.2, K.2G. **Mathematical Process Standards** K.1C, K.1D, K.1F.

Digital Resources at PearsonTexas.com

Solve Learn Glossary Check Tools Games

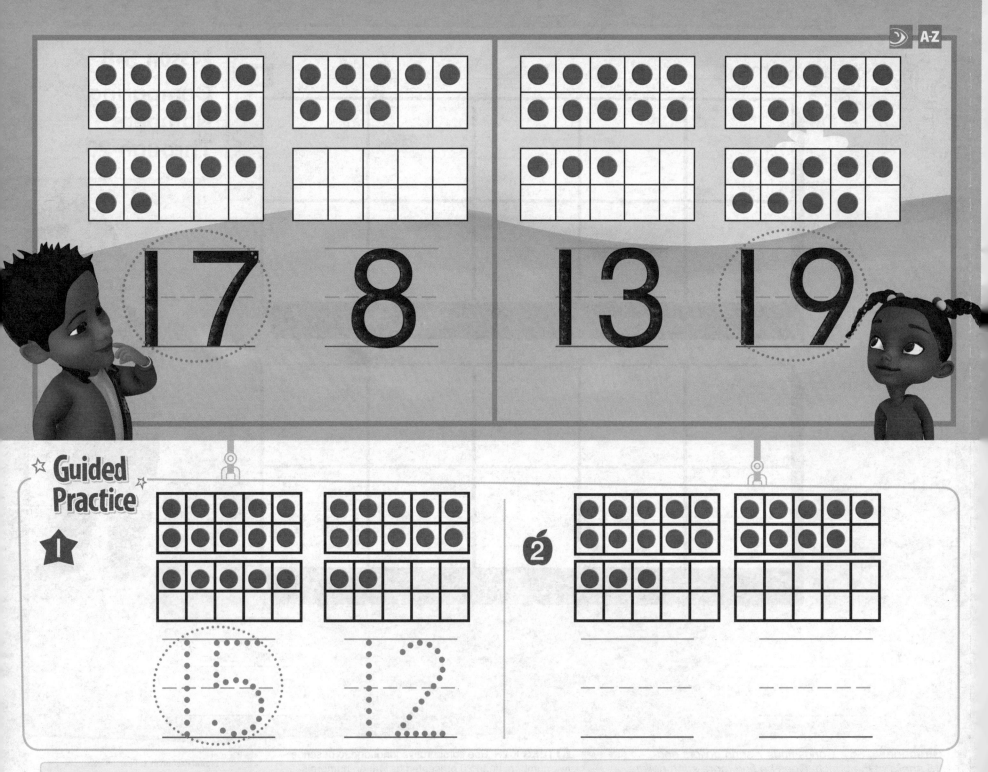

17   8   13   19

Guided Practice

1   15   12

2

Directions Have students: ⭐ count each set of counters, write the numbers that tell how many, and then circle the greater number; ❷ count each set of counters, write the numbers that tell how many, and then circle the lesser number.

© Pearson Education, Inc. K   **Topic 5** | Lesson 8

Name _____

3

4

_____ _____   _____ _____

- - - - - - - - - - - - - -   - - - - - - - - - - - - - -

_____ _____   _____ _____

5

6

_____ _____   _____ _____

- - - - - - - - - - - - - -   - - - - - - - - - - - - - -

_____ _____   _____ _____

Directions Have students: **3** and **4** count each set of counters, write the numbers that tell how many, and then circle the greater number; **5** and **6** count each set of counters, write the numbers that tell how many, and then circle the number that is less.

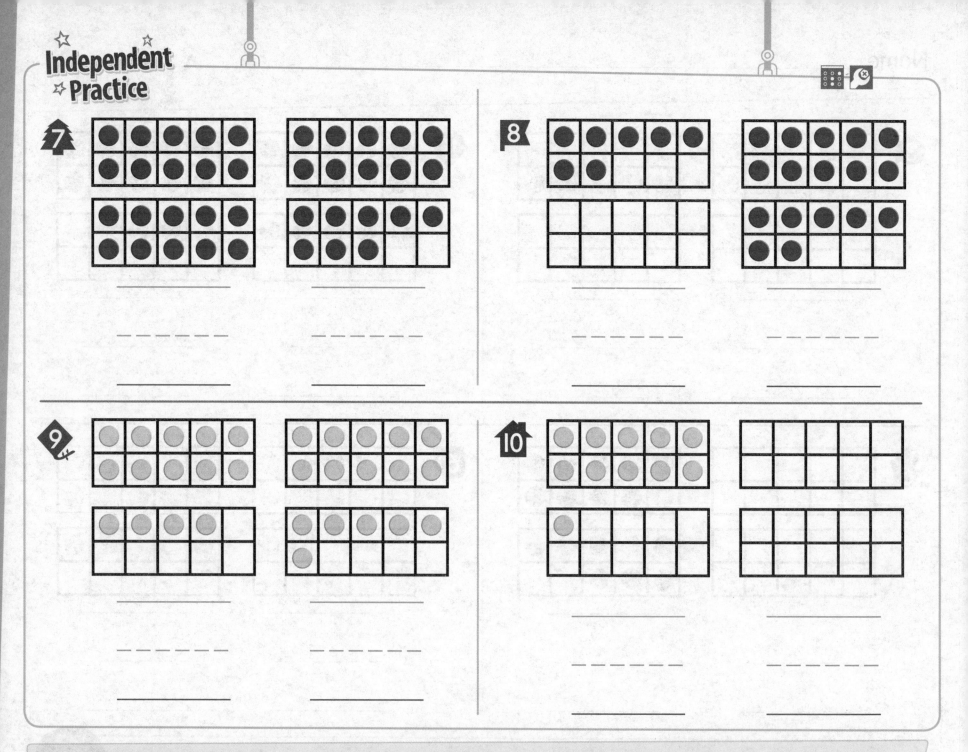

🎄 7

8

9

🏠 10

Directions Have students: 🎄 and 8 count each set of counters, write the numbers that tell how many, and then circle the greater number; 🖉 count each set of counters, write the numbers that tell how many, and then circle the number that is less; 🏠 count the counters and write the number that tells how many, draw a set that has fewer counters, write the number that tells how many, and then circle the number that is less.

284 two hundred eighty-four   © Pearson Education, Inc. K   **Topic 5** | Lesson 8

Another Look

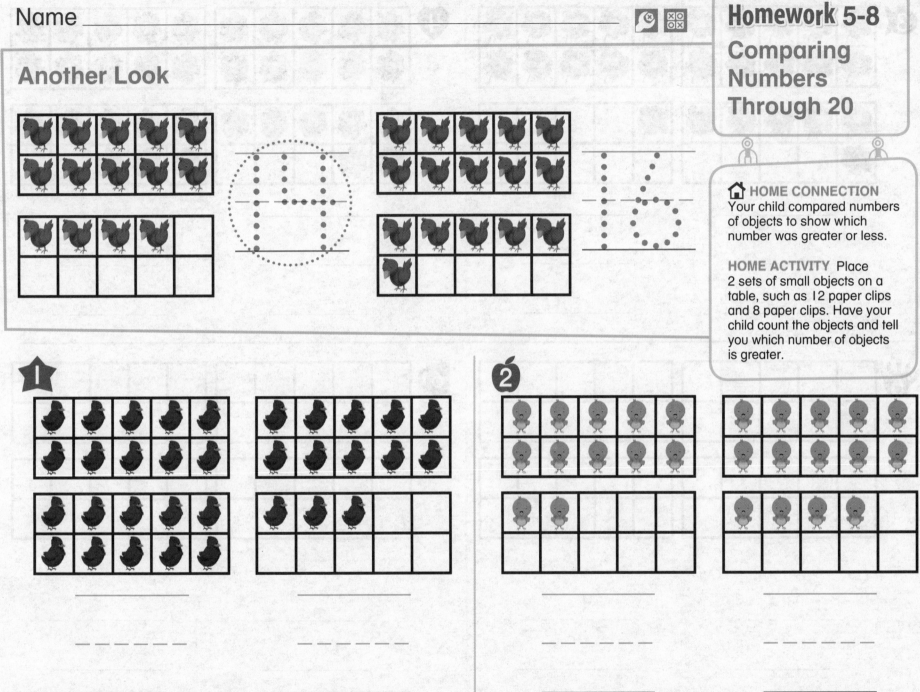

🏠 **HOME CONNECTION**
Your child compared numbers
of objects to show which
number was greater or less.

HOME ACTIVITY Place
2 sets of small objects on a
table, such as 12 paper clips
and 8 paper clips. Have your
child count the objects and tell
you which number of objects
is greater.

Directions Say: *Count the number of birds in each set of ten-frames, write the numbers that tell how many, and then circle the number that is less.* Have students: ⭐ and ② count each set, write the numbers that tell how many, and then circle the number that is less.

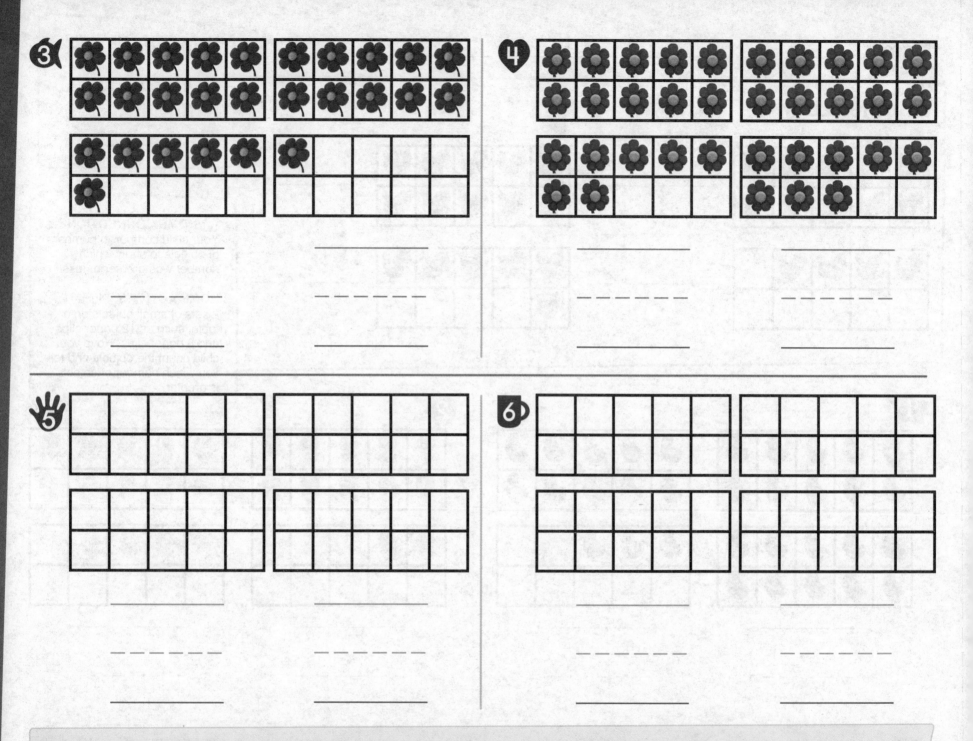

3

_____   _____

- - - - - - -   - - - - - - -

_____   _____

4

_____   _____

- - - - - - -   - - - - - - -

_____   _____

5

_____   _____

- - - - - - -   - - - - - - -

_____   _____

6

_____   _____

- - - - - - -   - - - - - - -

_____   _____

Directions Have students: **3** and **4** count each set, write the numbers that tell how many, and then circle the greater number; **5** draw a set of counters, draw a set that has a greater number of counters, and then write the numbers that tell how many; **6** draw a set of counters, draw a set that has fewer counters, and then write the numbers that tell how many.

© Pearson Education, Inc. K

Topic 5 | Lesson 8

Solve & Share Name _____

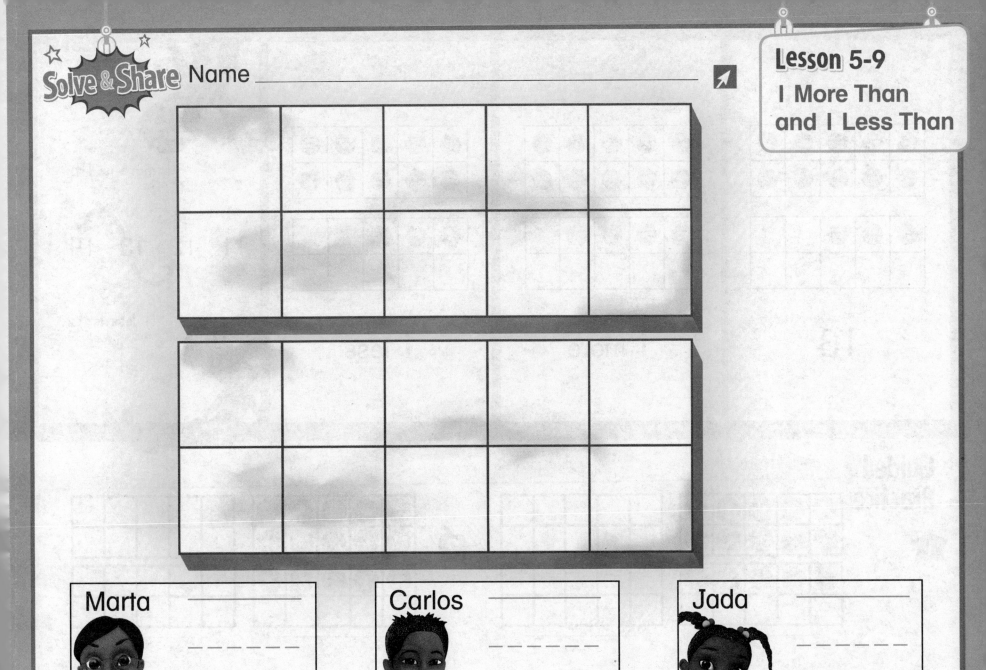

Marta _____

Carlos _____

Jada _____

Directions Say: *Carlos collects 12 tokens to use at the amusement park. Jada says she has I more token than Carlos. Marta says she has I token less than Carlos. How many tokens does Jada have? How many tokens does Marta have?*

⭐ **TEKS K.2F** Generate a number that is one more than or one less than another number up to at least 20. Also, K.2, K.2B. **Mathematical Process Standards K.1C, K.1D, K.1F.**

Digital Resources at PearsonTexas.com

Solve Learn Glossary Check Tools Games

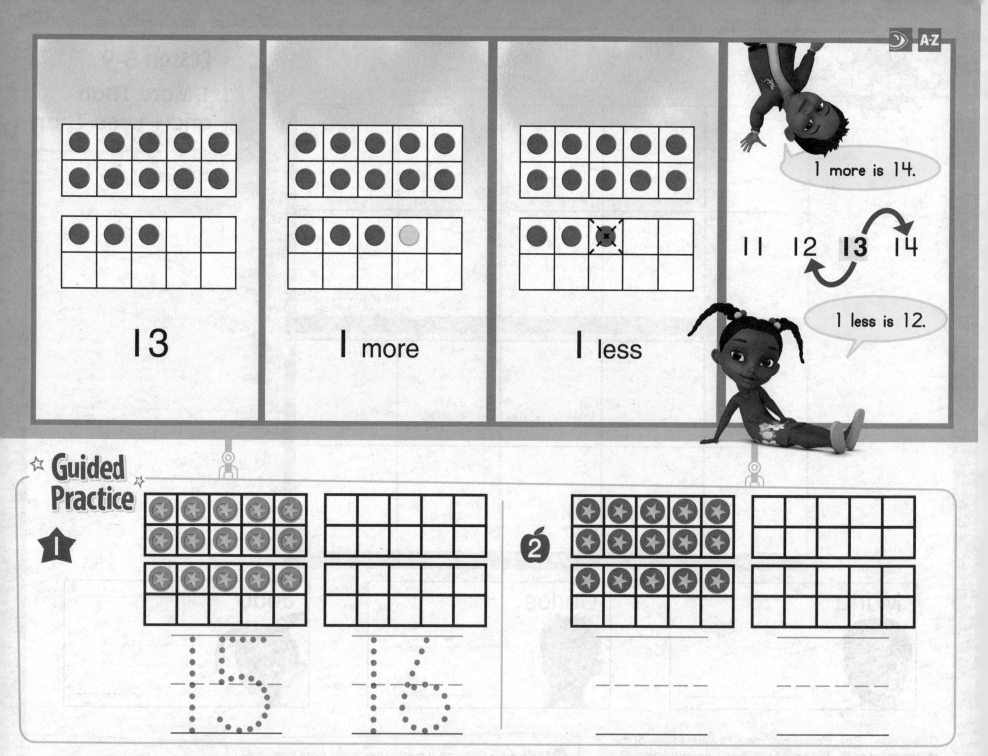

13

1 more

1 less

1 more is 14.

11   12   13   14

1 less is 12.

☆ Guided Practice ☆

1

15

2

16

Directions Have students: **1** count the tokens, draw a set that has 1 token more, and then write the numbers that tell how many; **2** count the tokens, draw a set that has 1 token less, and then write the numbers that tell how many.

Topic 5 | Lesson 9

Name _____

Directions Have students: ③ and ④ count the tokens, draw a set that has I token more, and then write the numbers that tell how many; ⑤ and ⑥ count the tokens, draw a set that has I token less, and then write the numbers that tell how many.

Topic 5 | Lesson 9

two hundred eighty-nine **289**

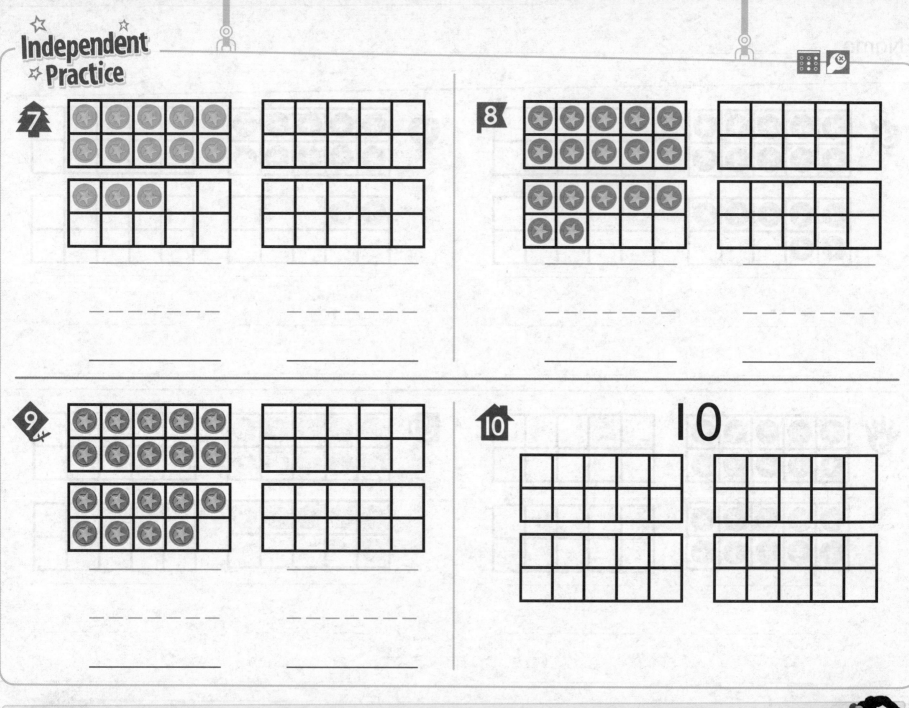

7

8

9

10   10

Name _____

Another Look

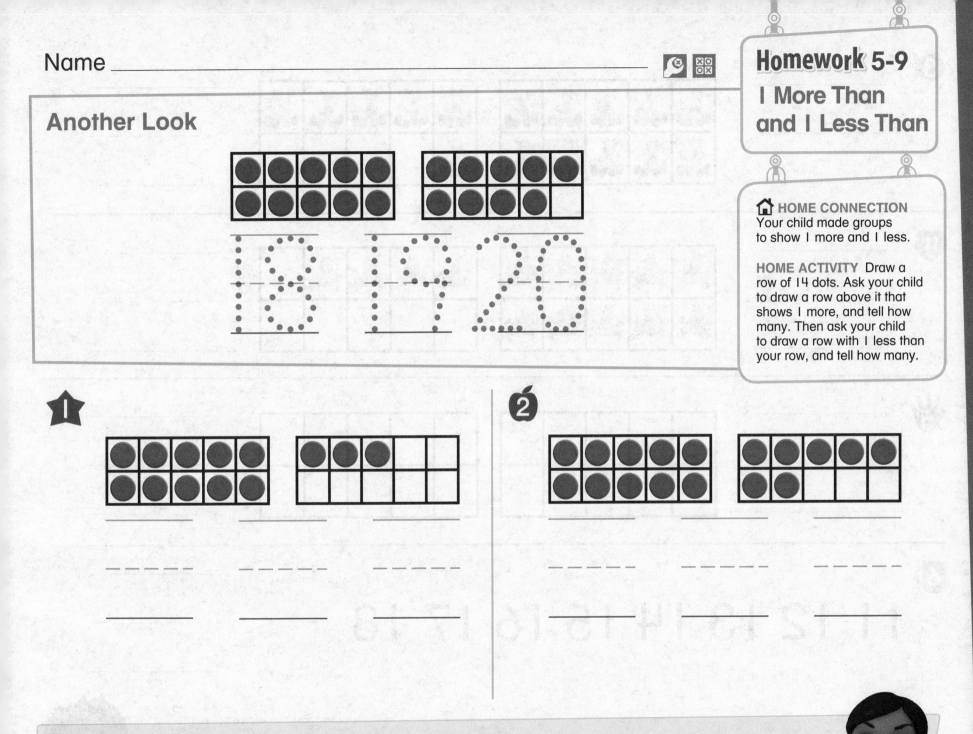

13 14 20

🏠 **HOME CONNECTION**
Your child made groups
to show I more and I less.

HOME ACTIVITY Draw a
row of 14 dots. Ask your child
to draw a row above it that
shows I more, and tell how
many. Then ask your child
to draw a row with I less than
your row, and tell how many.

⭐ 1

🍎 2

Directions Say: *Count the number of counters in the set, and then write the number in the middle that tells how many.*
Then write the number on the left that is I less than that number of counters and the number on the right that is I more.
Then have students: ⭐ *and* 🍎 *count the number of counters, write the number in the middle, and then write the number*
that is I less than that number of counters on the left and the number that is I more on the right.

Topic 5 | Lesson 9   Digital Resources at PearsonTexas.com   two hundred ninety-one **291**

3

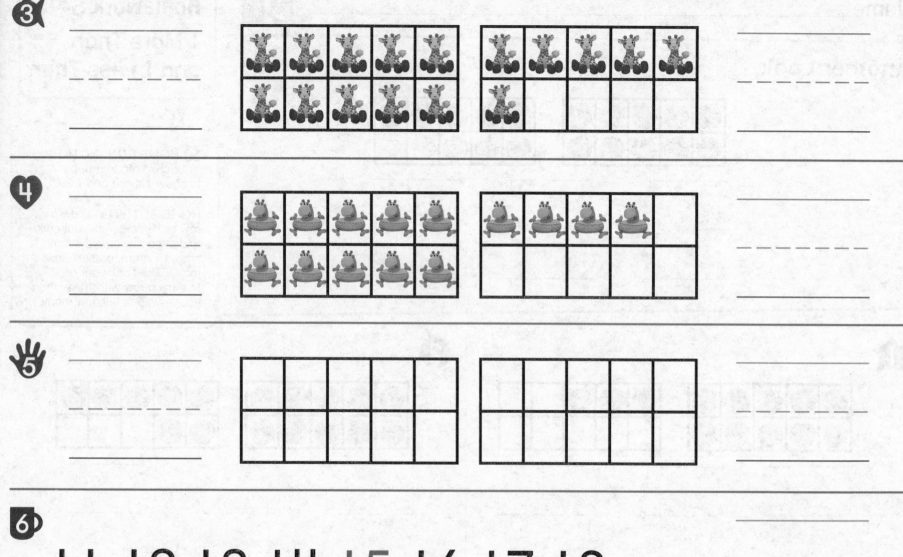

4

5

6

11 12 13 14 15 16 17 18

© Pearson Education, Inc. K

Topic 5 | Lesson 9

Solve & Share Name _____

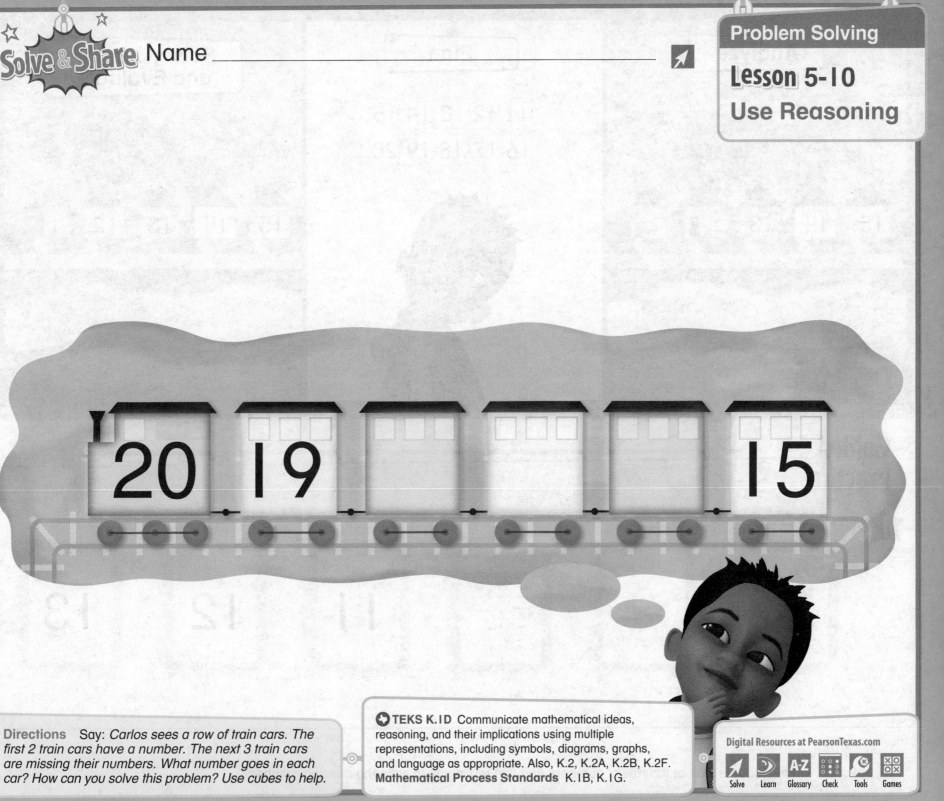

Directions Say: *Carlos sees a row of train cars. The first 2 train cars have a number. The next 3 train cars are missing their numbers. What number goes in each car? How can you solve this problem? Use cubes to help.*

⭐**TEKS K.1D** Communicate mathematical ideas, reasoning, and their implications using multiple representations, including symbols, diagrams, graphs, and language as appropriate. Also, K.2, K.2A, K.2B, K.2F. **Mathematical Process Standards** K.1B, K.1G.

Digital Resources at PearsonTexas.com

Solve Learn Glossary Check Tools Games

Topic 5 | Lesson 10

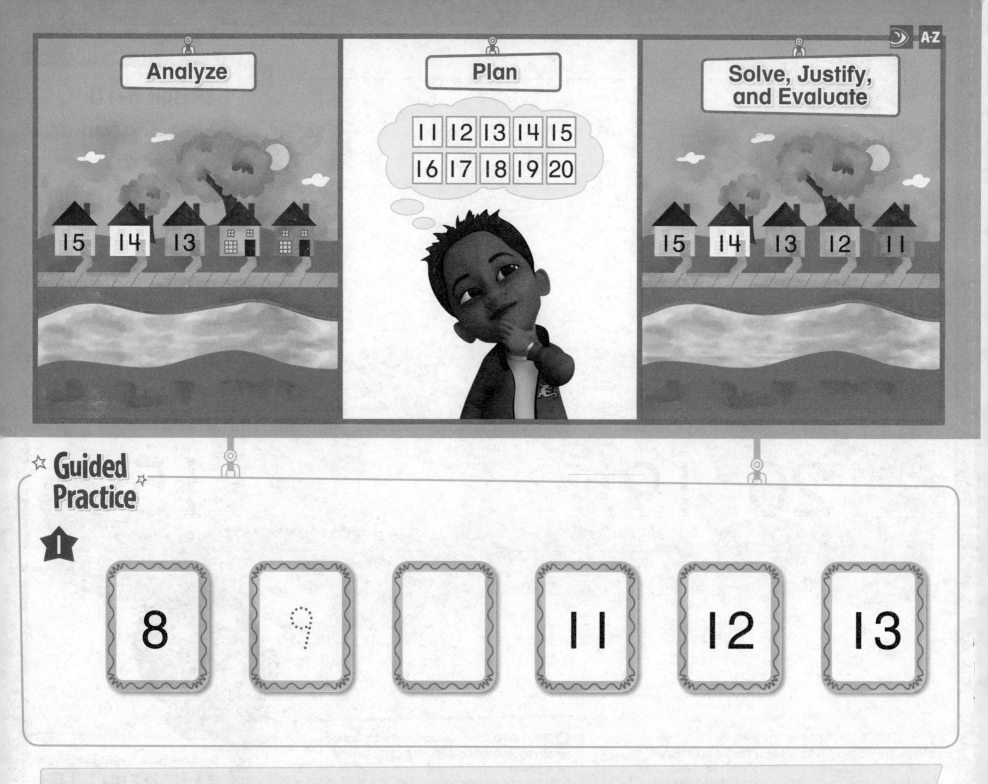

Analyze

15 14 13

Plan

11	12	13	14	15
16	17	18	19	20

Solve, Justify, and Evaluate

15 14 13 12 11

☆ **Guided Practice** ☆

⭐ 1

| 8 | 9 | | 11 | 12 | 13 |

Directions Have students look at the row of numbers and use reasoning to write the missing numbers.

© Pearson Education, Inc. K

Name _____

🍎 **2** 19 | | 17 | 16 | 15 |

🐟 **3** 17 | 16 | 15 | 14 | | 12

❤️ **4** 20 | 19 | 18 | | | 15

✋ **5** 12 | | 14 | 15 | 16 | 17

Directions Have students look at each row of numbers and use reasoning to write the missing numbers.

6 | 20 | 19 | | 17 | 16 | |

7 | | 9 | 10 | 11 | 12 | 13 |

8 | 15 | 14 | | | 12 | 11 | 10 |

9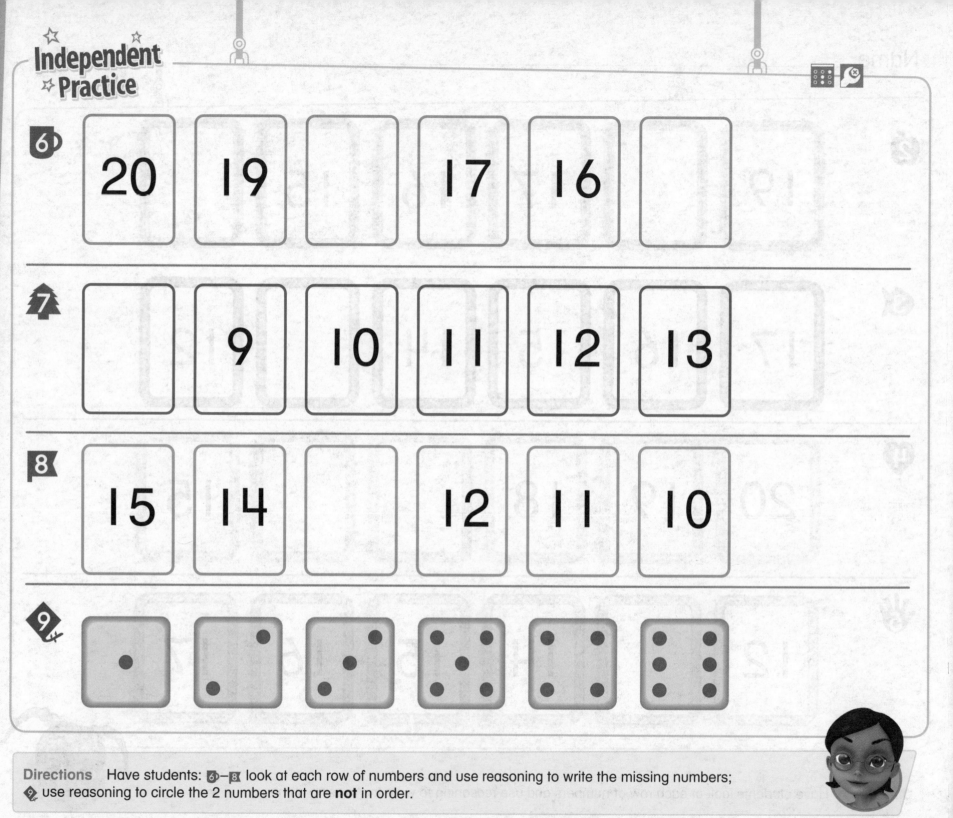

Directions Have students: **6–8** look at each row of numbers and use reasoning to write the missing numbers; **9** use reasoning to circle the 2 numbers that are **not** in order.

Topic 5 | Lesson 10

Name _____

Another Look

1 2 3 4 5 6

🏠 **HOME CONNECTION**
Your child used logical reasoning to order numbers and find missing numbers.

HOME ACTIVITY Use cards numbered from 1 to 10. Shuffle the cards and ask your child to put them in order. Repeat with a set of cards numbered from 11 to 20. Then remove a number card from a set of cards. Place the cards on a table faceup. Have your child identify the missing number.

⭐ 1

11 12 ___ ___ 15

🍎 2

20 19 ___ ___ 16 15

Directions Say: *Read the numbers in order from 1 to 6 and write the numbers that are missing.* Then have students:
⭐ and 🍎 *read the numbers and use reasoning to find and write the missing numbers.*

3 | 17 | 16 | | 14 | | 12 | 11 |

4 | 13 | 12 | | | 10 | 9 | 8 | |

5

6 16 13 15
12 14

Directions Have students: **3** and **4** look at each row of numbers and use reasoning to write the missing numbers; **5** circle the 2 numbers that are **not** in order, and then write them in order; **6** write the numbers in backward order starting with 16.

298 two hundred ninety-eight   © Pearson Education, Inc. K   **Topic 5** | Lesson 10

Name _____

Set A

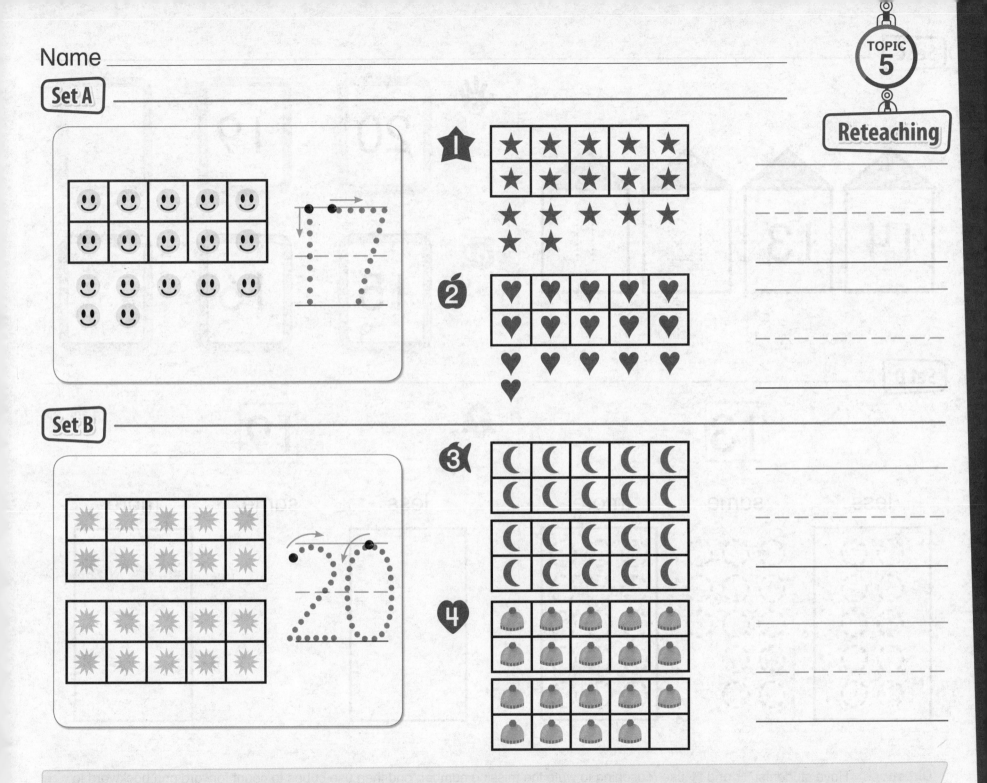

Directions Have students: ★–♥ count the items in each group, and then practice writing the number that tells how many.

14   13   12   11

✋ **5**   20   19   [ ]

☕ **6**   15   16   [ ]

13

less   same   more

🌲 **7**   19

less   same   more

Directions Have students: ✋ and ☕ use reasoning to write the missing number, and then use cubes to count forward and backward to and from 20; 🌲 use counters to make sets less than, the same as, and more than 19, and then draw their sets.

© Pearson Education, Inc. K

Name _____

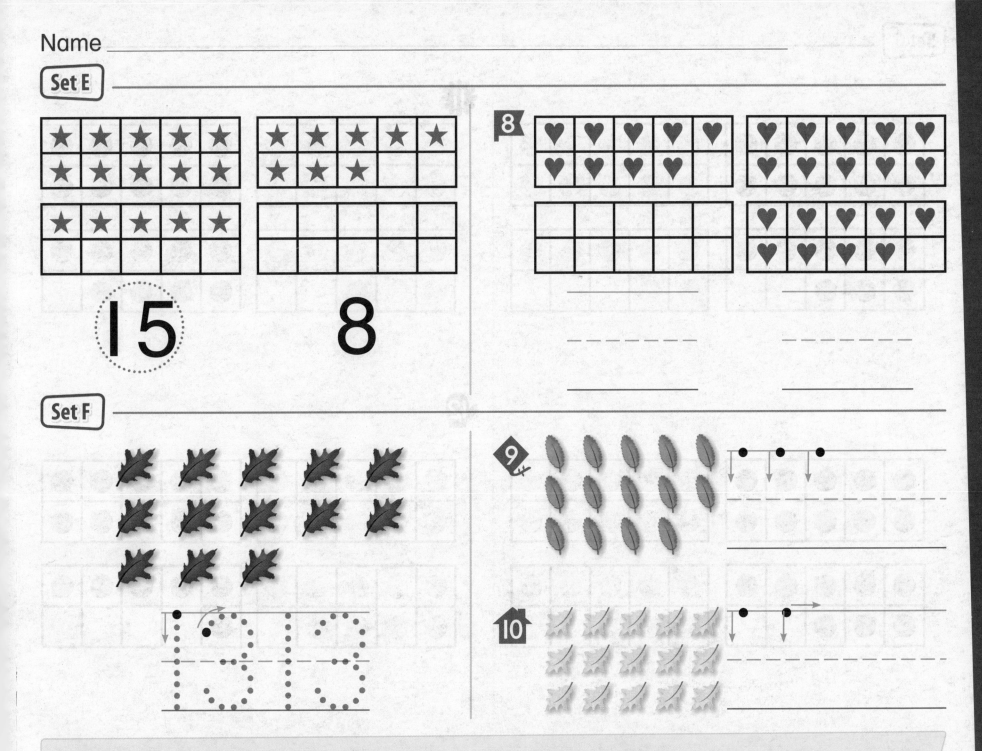

15

8

8

Set F

9

10

Directions Have students: 8 count each set, write the numbers that tell how many, and then circle the greater number; 9 and 10 count the leaves in each group, and then practice writing the numbers that tell how many.

Topic 5   three hundred one **301**

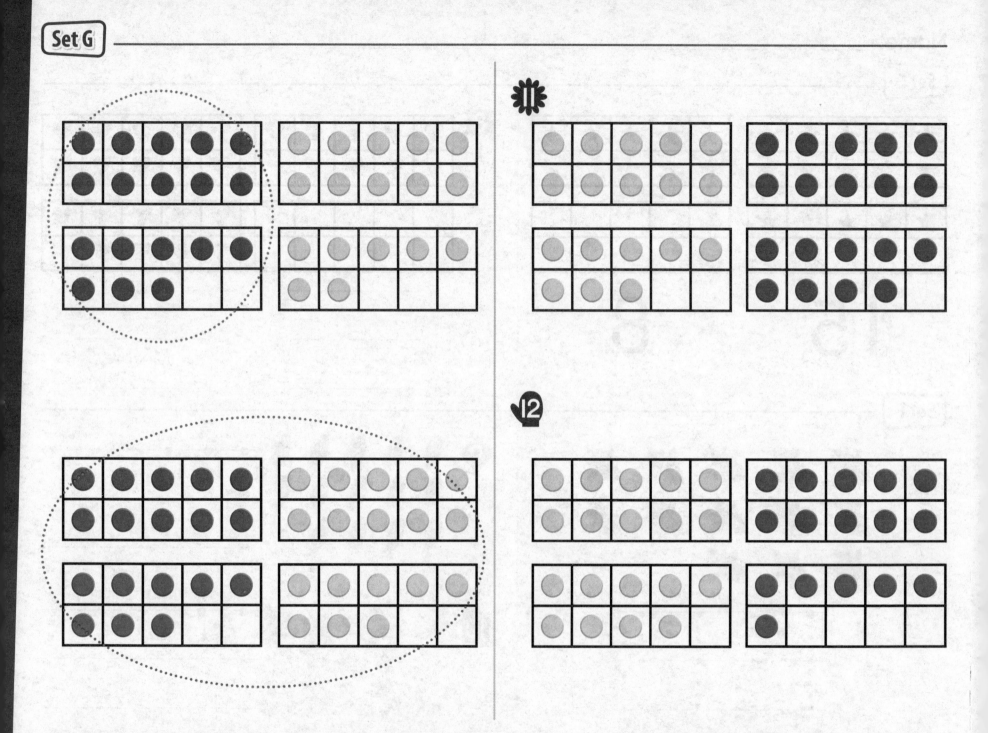

Directions Have students: ✿ and ✿ compare the 2 sets and circle the set that has more, or circle both sets if they have the same number of counters.

© Pearson Education, Inc. K

Name _____

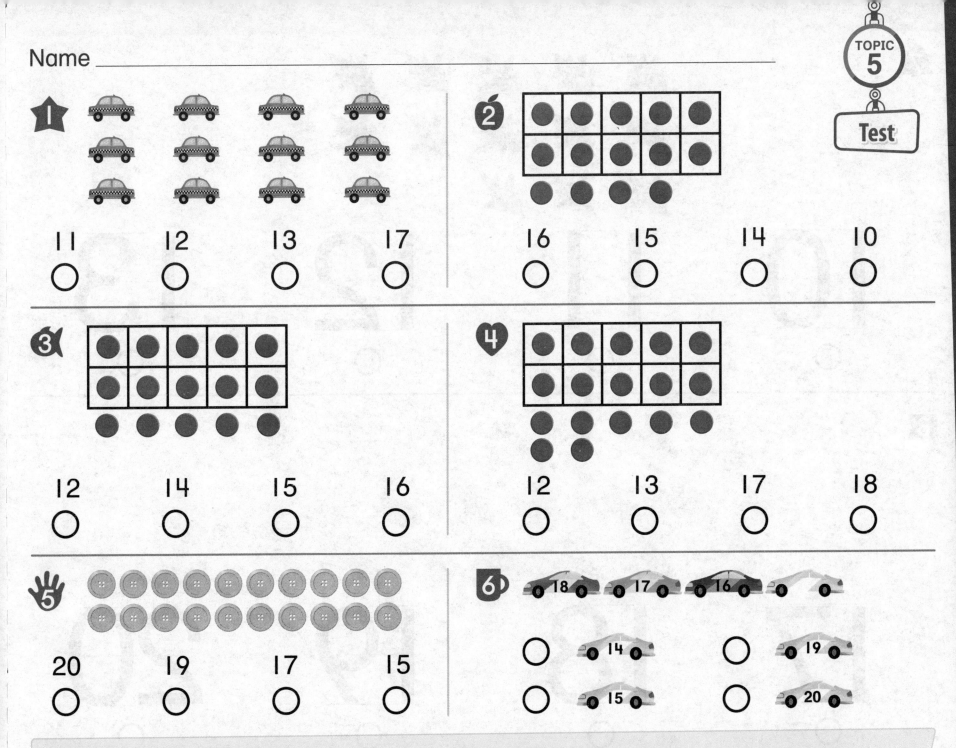

1

11   12   13   17
○   ○   ○   ○

2

16   15   14   10
○   ○   ○   ○

3

12   14   15   16
○   ○   ○   ○

4

12   13   17   18
○   ○   ○   ○

5

20   19   17   15
○   ○   ○   ○

6

18   17   16

○   14   ○   19

○   15   ○   20

Directions   Have students mark the best answer. ⭐ How many toy cars are there? 🍎 Which number is 1 more than the number of counters shown? 🐟 Which number is 1 less than the number of counters shown? 💜 Which number tells how many counters? ✋ Which number tells how many buttons? ☕ Which car shows the missing number?

Topic 5   three hundred three **303**

7

10 ○ 11 ○ 12 ○ 13 ○

8

17 ○ 18 ○ 19 ○ 20 ○

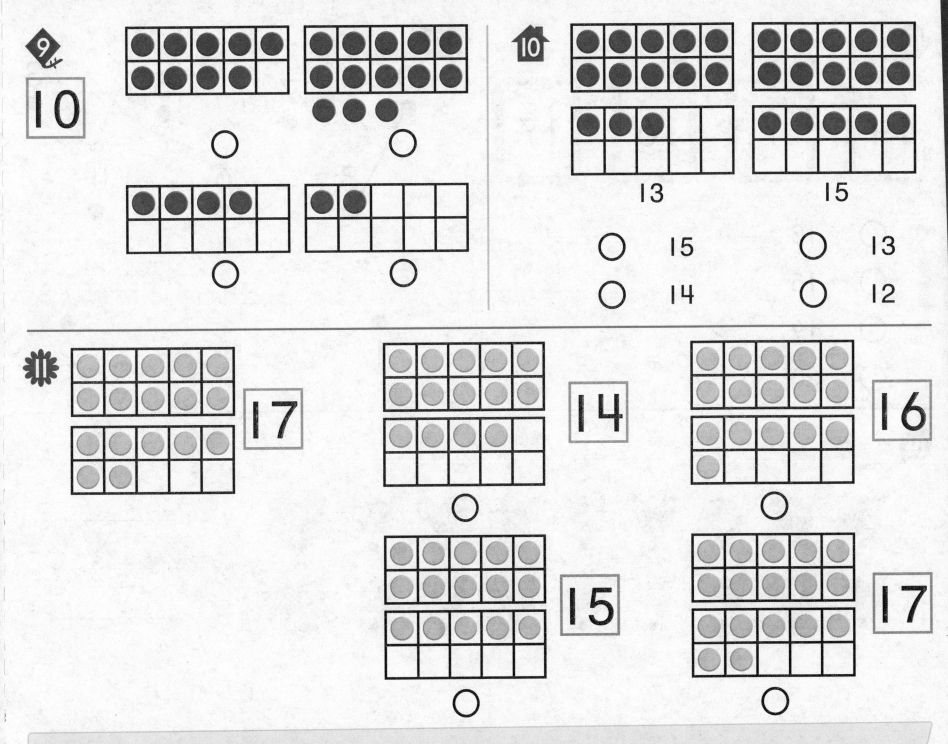

9

10

10

15   13

14   12

17

14

16

15

17

Directions Have students mark the best answer. 9 Which shows a set that has more than 10 counters? 10 Which number tells how many counters are in the greater set? Which shows 1 less than the set shown?

Topic 5

three hundred five   **305**

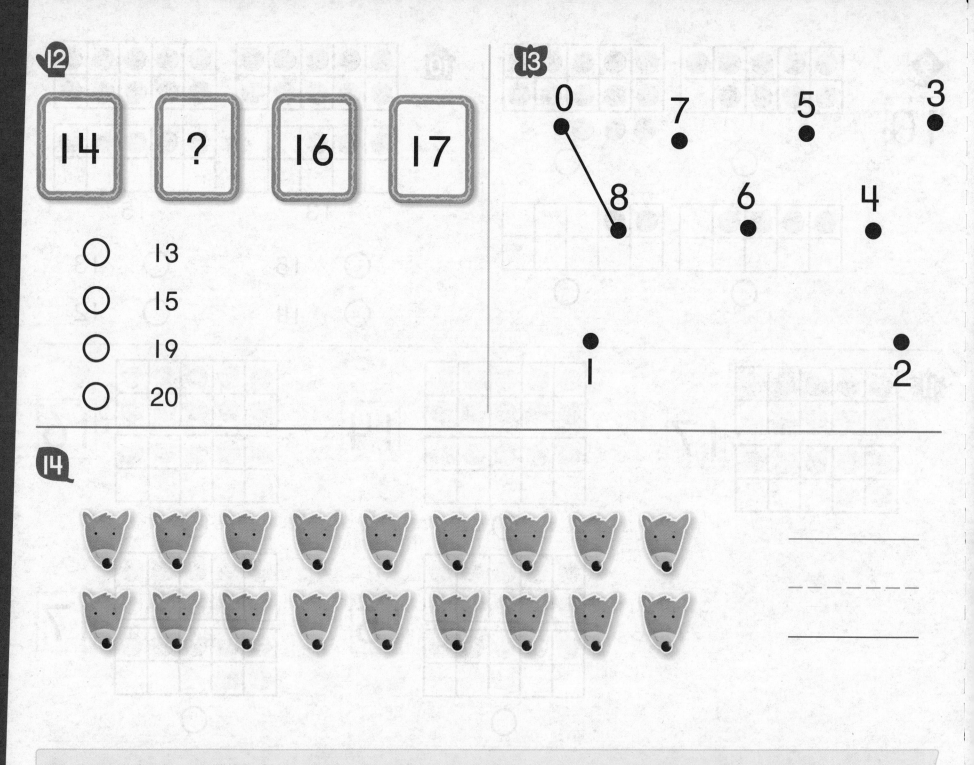

12

| 14 | ? | 16 | 17 |

○ 13

○ 15

○ 19

○ 20

13

0   7   5   3

8   6   4

1   2

14

_____

_ _ _ _ _ _

_____

Directions Have students: **12** mark the best answer. The numbers are in order from 14 to 17. Which number is missing?
13 connect the dots in order from 0 to 8 to reveal the picture; **14** count the stickers, and then write the number that tells how many.

306 three hundred six   © Pearson Education, Inc. K   **Topic 5**

Numbers to 30

Essential Question: How can numbers to 30 be counted, written, ordered, pictured, and compared?

Math and Science Project: Location

Directions Read the character speech bubbles to students. Explain that the white train car is also before the blue one. **Find Out!** Have students find out about the location of objects in relation to one another using the words *above* and *below*, and the location of numbers using the terms *before* and *after*. Say: *Talk to your friends and relatives about the location of objects and numbers in your classroom and home.* **Journal: Make a Poster** Then have students make a poster. Have them draw an object, and then draw an X above the object and a counter below the object. Then have them write a number between 20 and 29, and write the numbers that come before and after the number they chose.

Name ________________________

Review What You Know

1

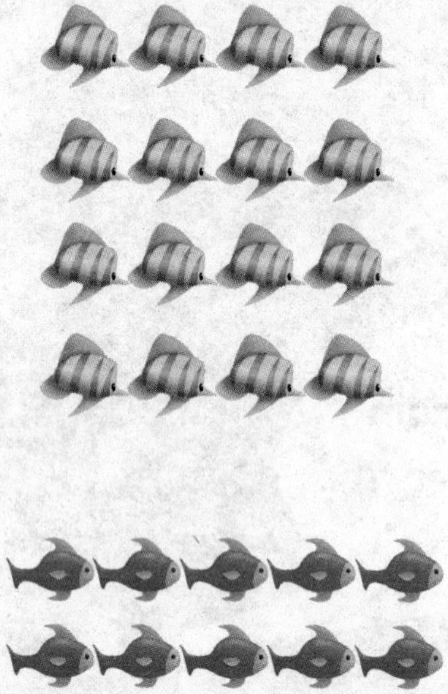

2

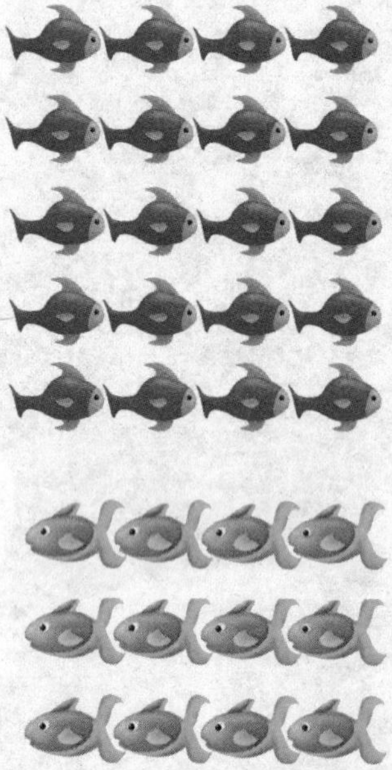

3

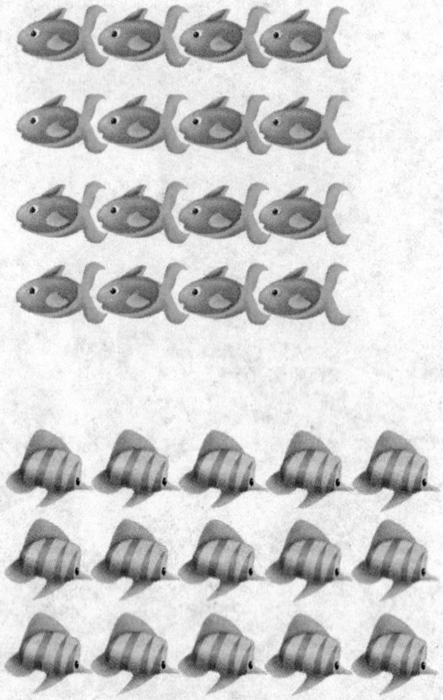

4

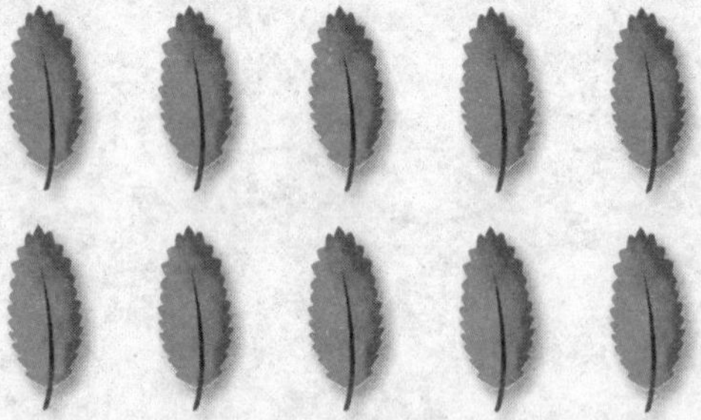

5

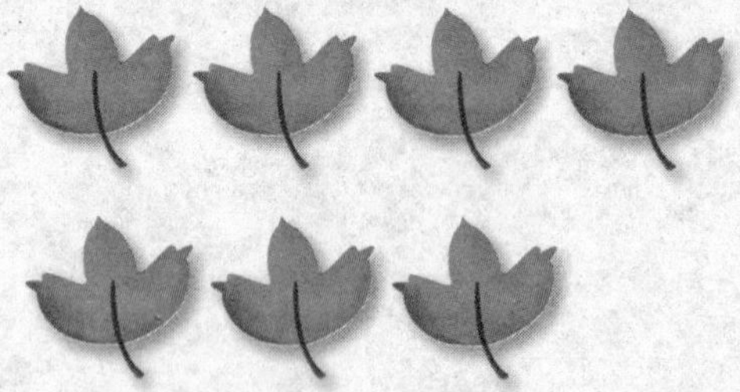

6

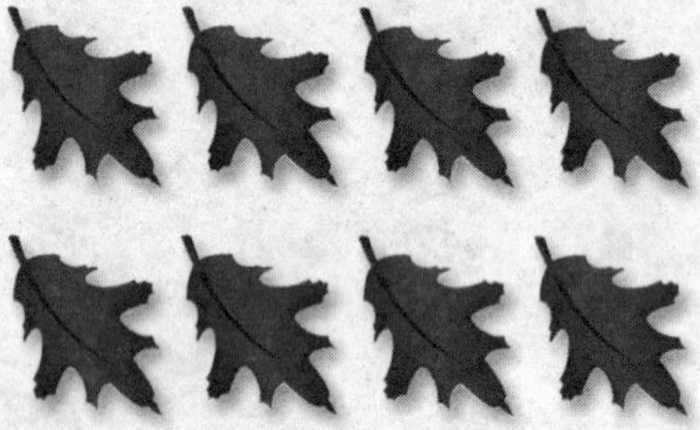

Directions Have students: 1 circle the set with 16; 2 circle the set with 20; 3 circle the set that has fewer; 4–6 count the leaves, and then write the number that tells how many.

Directions Have students cut out the vocabulary cards. Read the front of the card, and then ask them to explain what the word or phrase means.

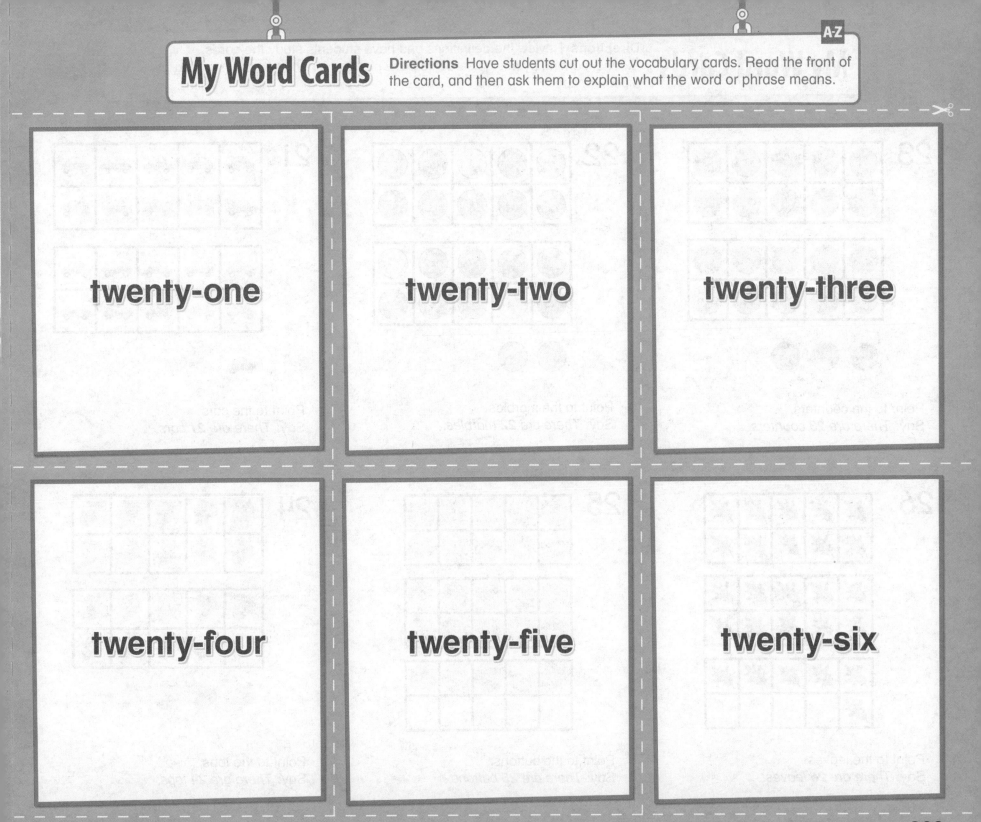

twenty-one

twenty-two

twenty-three

twenty-four

twenty-five

twenty-six

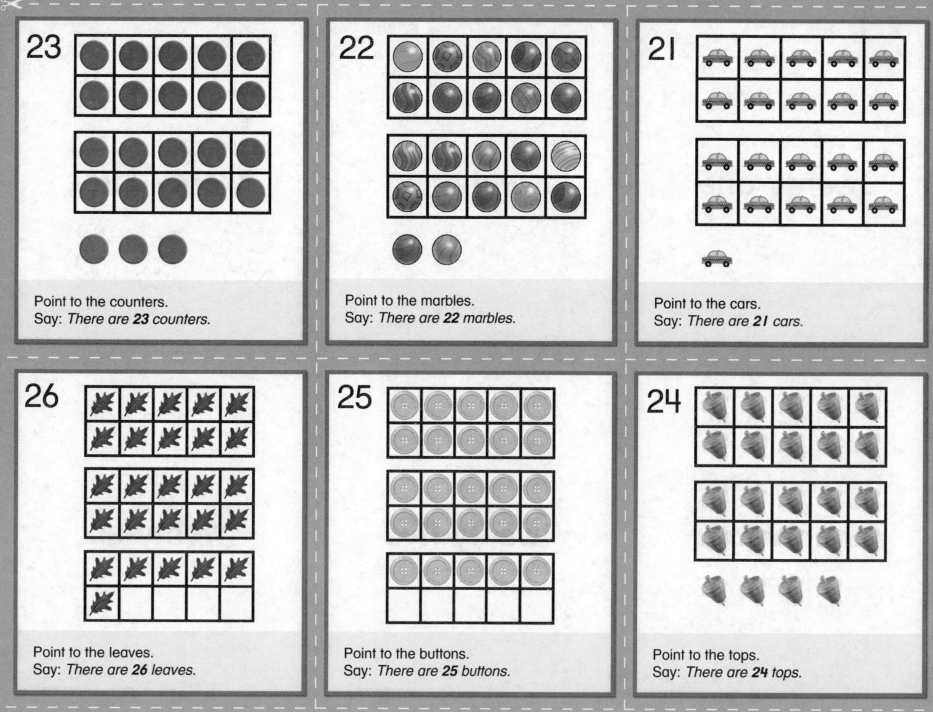

23

Point to the counters.
Say: *There are 23 counters.*

22

Point to the marbles.
Say: *There are 22 marbles.*

21

Point to the cars.
Say: *There are 21 cars.*

26

Point to the leaves.
Say: *There are 26 leaves.*

25

Point to the buttons.
Say: *There are 25 buttons.*

24

Point to the tops.
Say: *There are 24 tops.*

My Word Cards

Directions Have students cut out the vocabulary cards. Read the front of the card, and then ask them to explain what the word or phrase means.

A-Z

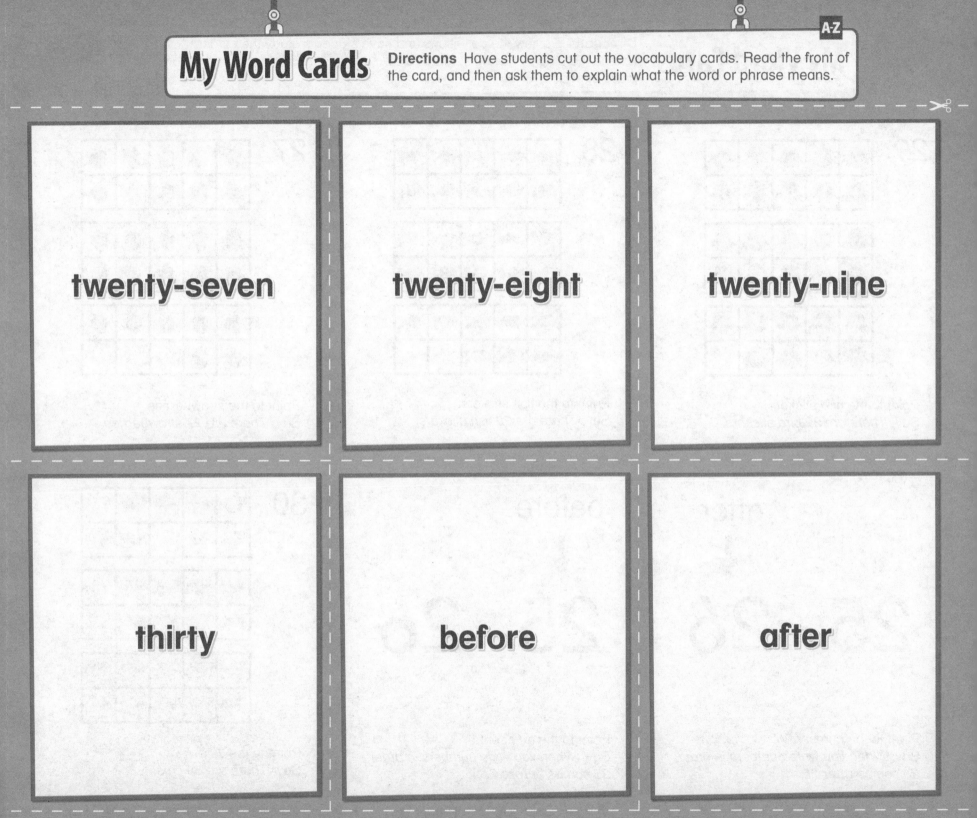

twenty-seven

twenty-eight

twenty-nine

thirty

before

after

My Word Cards

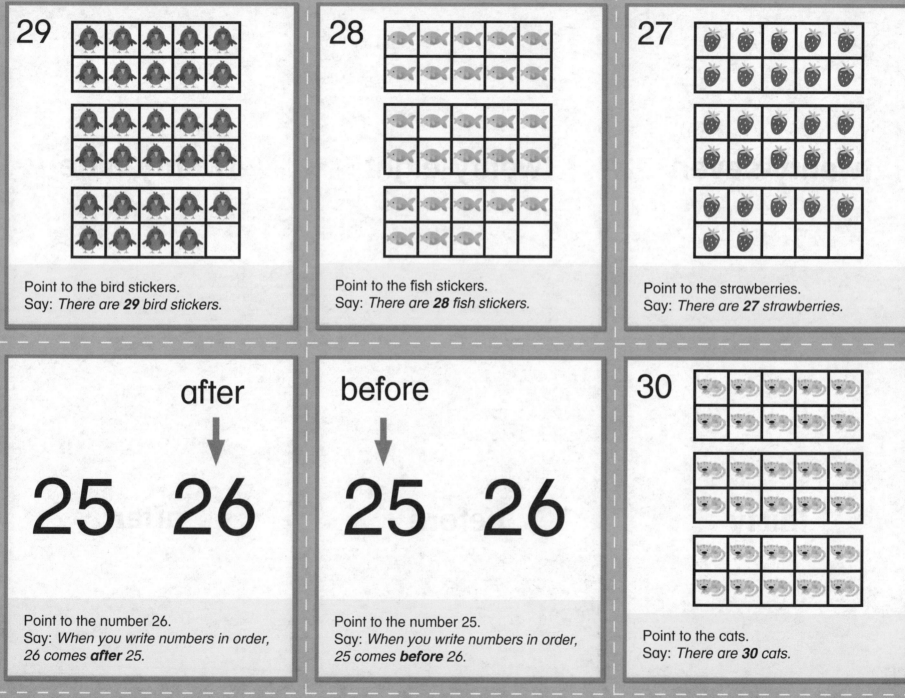

29

Point to the bird stickers.
Say: *There are **29** bird stickers.*

28

Point to the fish stickers.
Say: *There are **28** fish stickers.*

27

Point to the strawberries.
Say: *There are **27** strawberries.*

after
↓
25   26

Point to the number 26.
Say: *When you write numbers in order, 26 comes **after** 25.*

before
↓
25   26

Point to the number 25.
Say: *When you write numbers in order, 25 comes **before** 26.*

30

Point to the cats.
Say: *There are **30** cats.*

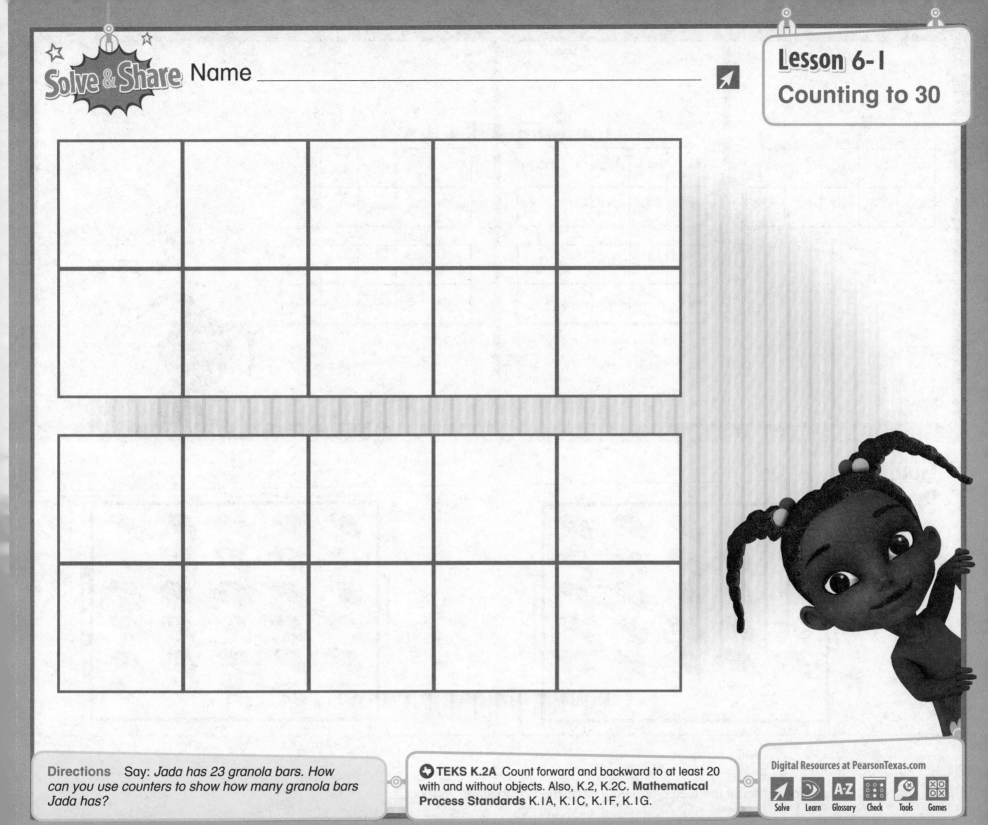

Directions Say: *Jada has 23 granola bars. How can you use counters to show how many granola bars Jada has?*

✪ **TEKS K.2A** Count forward and backward to at least 20 with and without objects. Also, K.2, K.2C. **Mathematical Process Standards** K.1A, K.1C, K.1F, K.1G.

Digital Resources at PearsonTexas.com

Solve Learn Glossary Check Tools Games

Topic 6 | Lesson 1

three hundred thirteen **313**

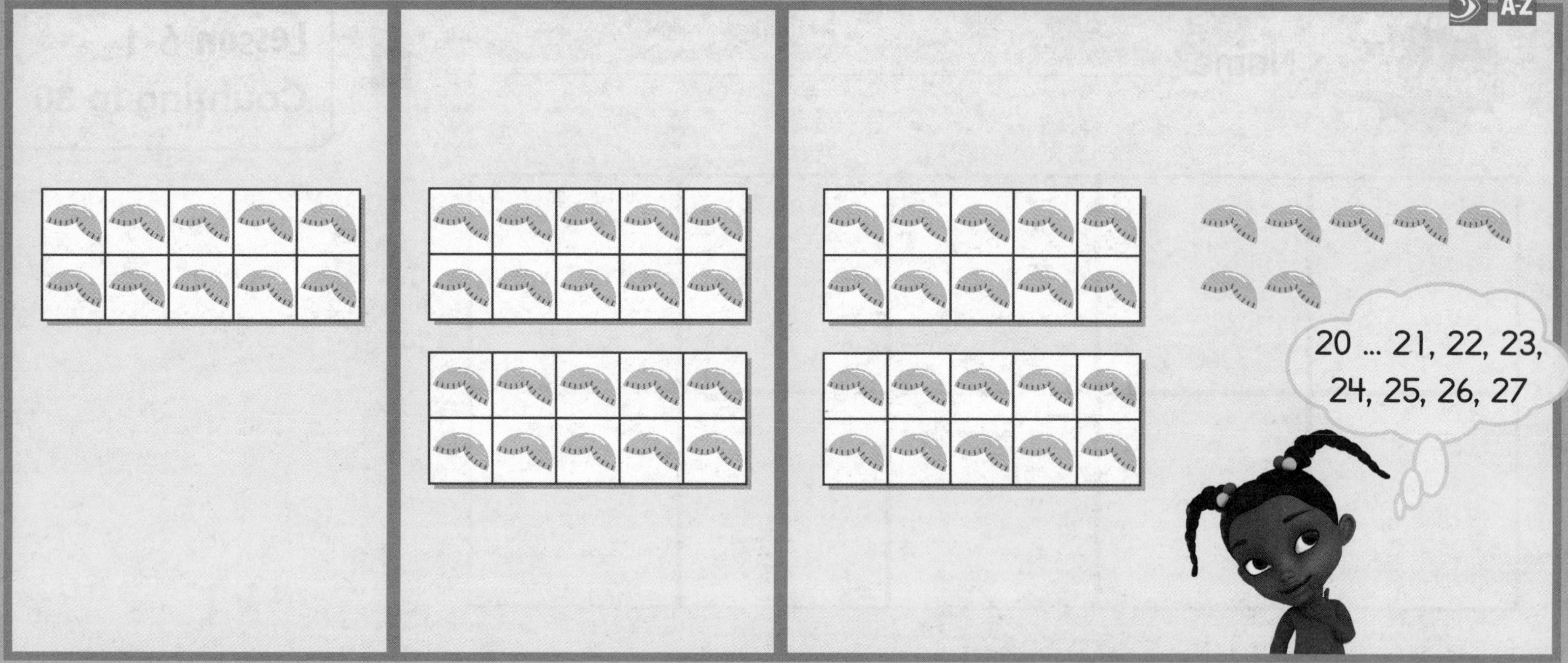

20 ... 21, 22, 23, 24, 25, 26, 27

☆ **Guided Practice** ☆

1

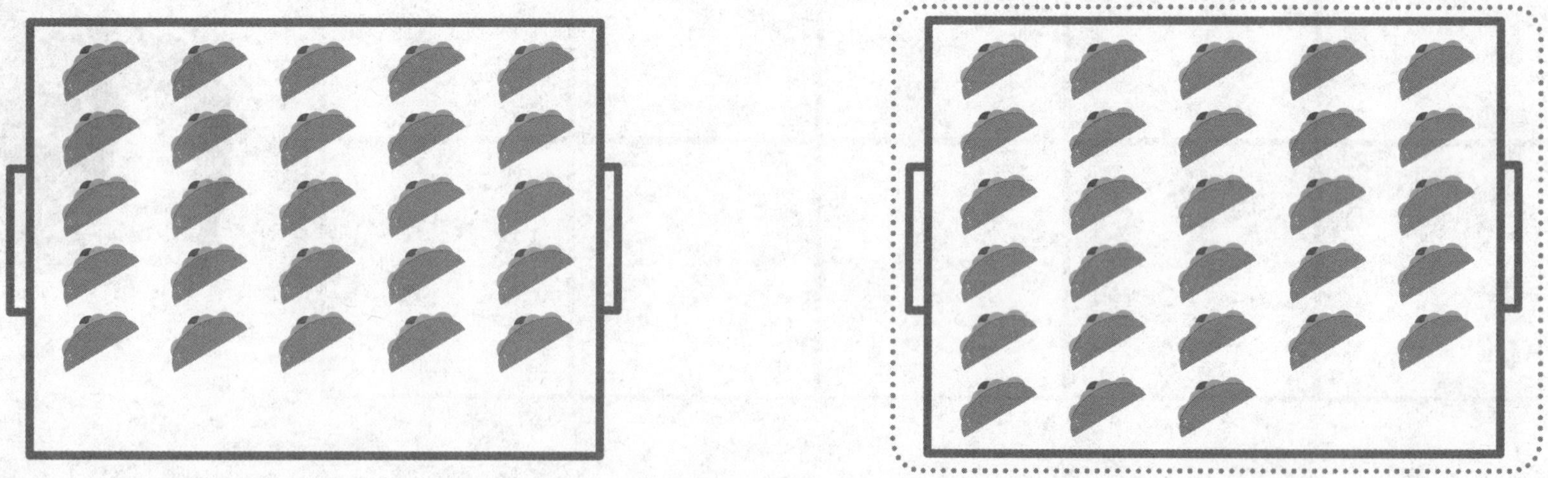

Directions Have students count the tacos, and then circle the tray that has 28 tacos.

© Pearson Education, Inc. K

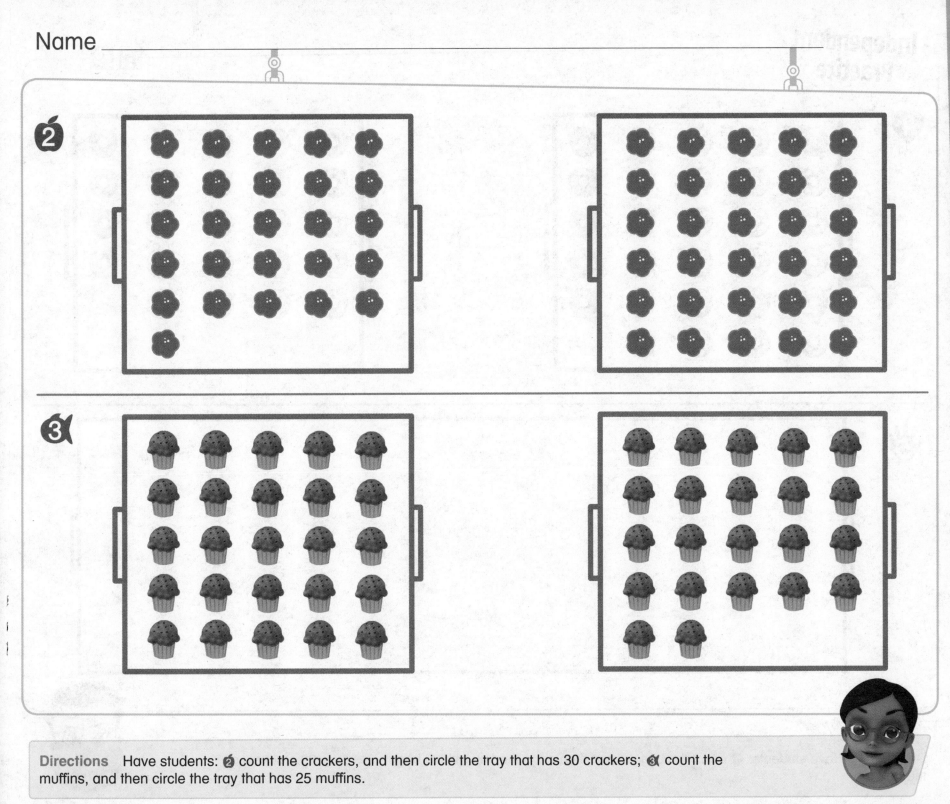

2

3

Directions Have students: **2** count the crackers, and then circle the tray that has 30 crackers; **3** count the muffins, and then circle the tray that has 25 muffins.

Topic 6 | Lesson 1

three hundred fifteen **315**

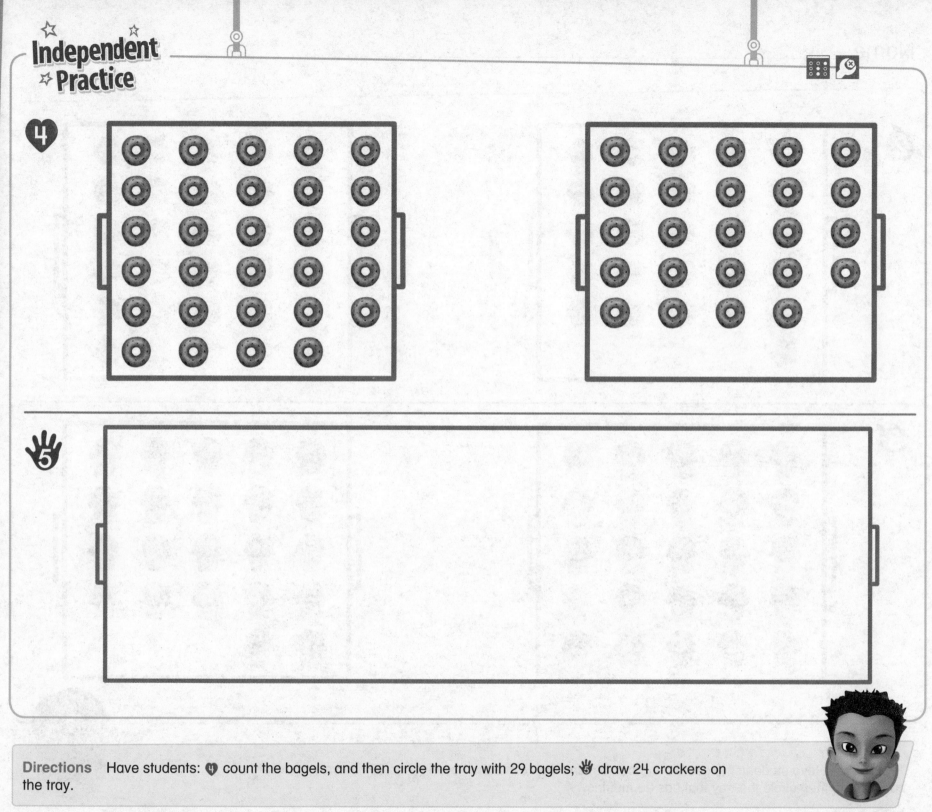

❤ 4

✋ 5

Directions Have students: ❤ count the bagels, and then circle the tray with 29 bagels; ✋ draw 24 crackers on the tray.

Another Look

🏠 **HOME CONNECTION**
Your child counted numbers to 30.

HOME ACTIVITY Choose 2 numbers between 1 and 30. Have your child count from the first number you say to the second number. For example, say the numbers 15 and 20. Your child can count 15, 16, 17, 18, 19, 20.

Directions Say: *Count the connecting cubes with me. How many cubes are there? Now draw cubes to show 23 cubes in all.*
Then have students: ⭐ draw cubes to show 21 cubes in all; 🍎 draw cubes to show 26 cubes in all.

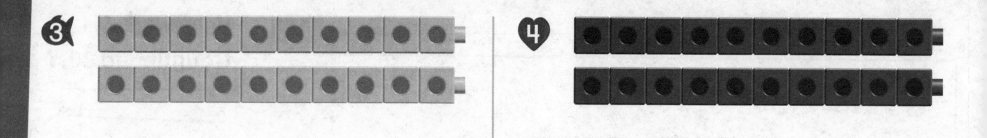

3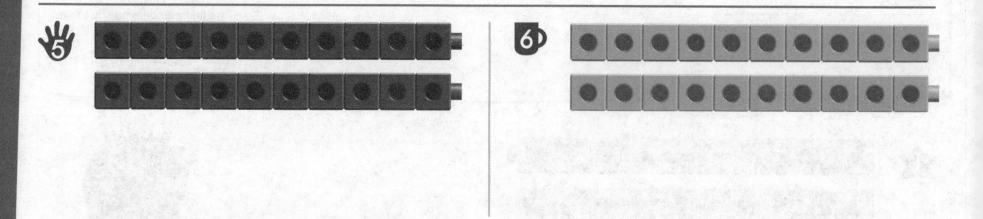

4

5

6

7

8

Directions Have students: **3** draw cubes to show 22 cubes in all; **4** draw cubes to show 28 cubes in all; **5** draw cubes to show 25 cubes in all; **6** draw cubes to show 24 cubes in all; **7** draw cubes to show 27 cubes in all; **8** choose a number between 20 and 30, say the number, and then draw cubes to show that number.

© Pearson Education, Inc. K

Solve & Share   Name _____

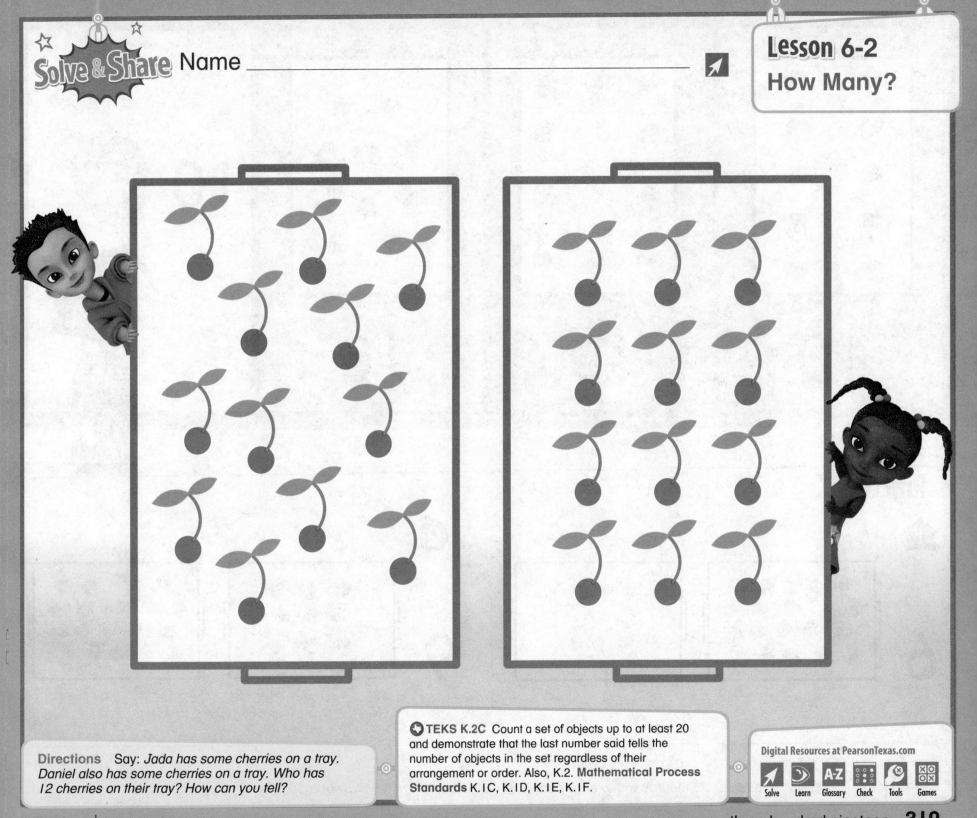

Directions Say: *Jada has some cherries on a tray. Daniel also has some cherries on a tray. Who has 12 cherries on their tray? How can you tell?*

⭐ **TEKS K.2C** Count a set of objects up to at least 20 and demonstrate that the last number said tells the number of objects in the set regardless of their arrangement or order. Also, **K.2. Mathematical Process Standards** K.1C, K.1D, K.1E, K.1F.

Digital Resources at PearsonTexas.com

Solve   Learn   Glossary   Check   Tools   Games

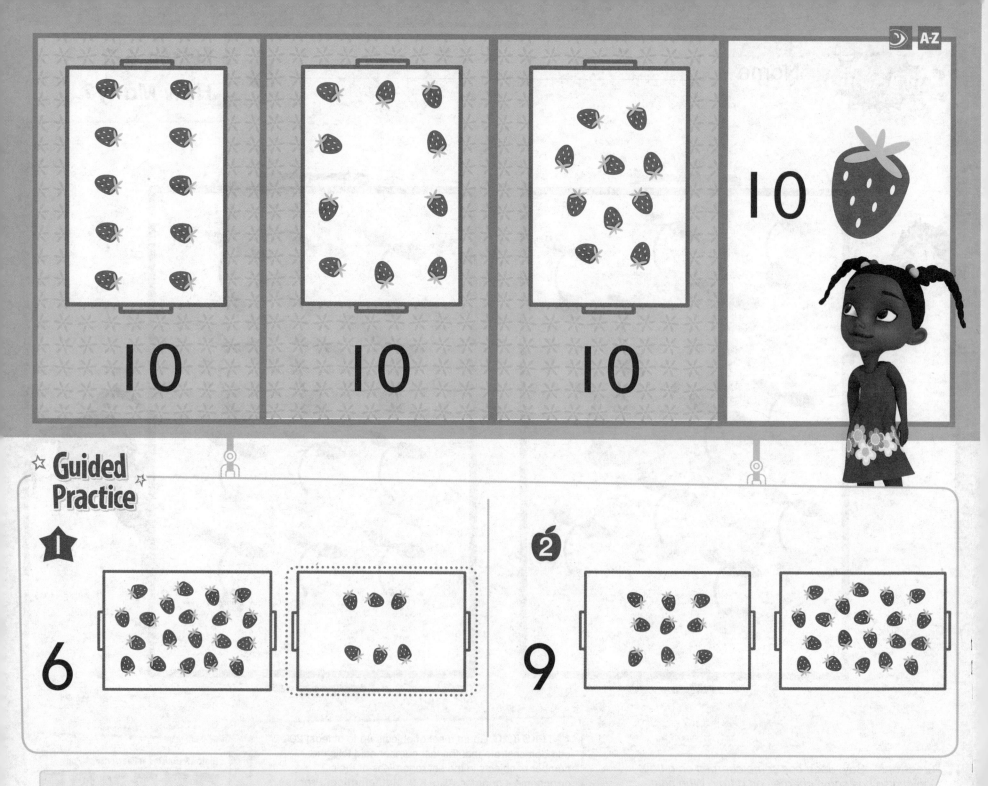

Guided Practice

⭐ 1

6

2

9

Directions Have students: ⭐ circle the tray with 6 strawberries; 2 circle the tray with 9 strawberries.

© Pearson Education, Inc. K

Topic 6 | Lesson 2

Name _____

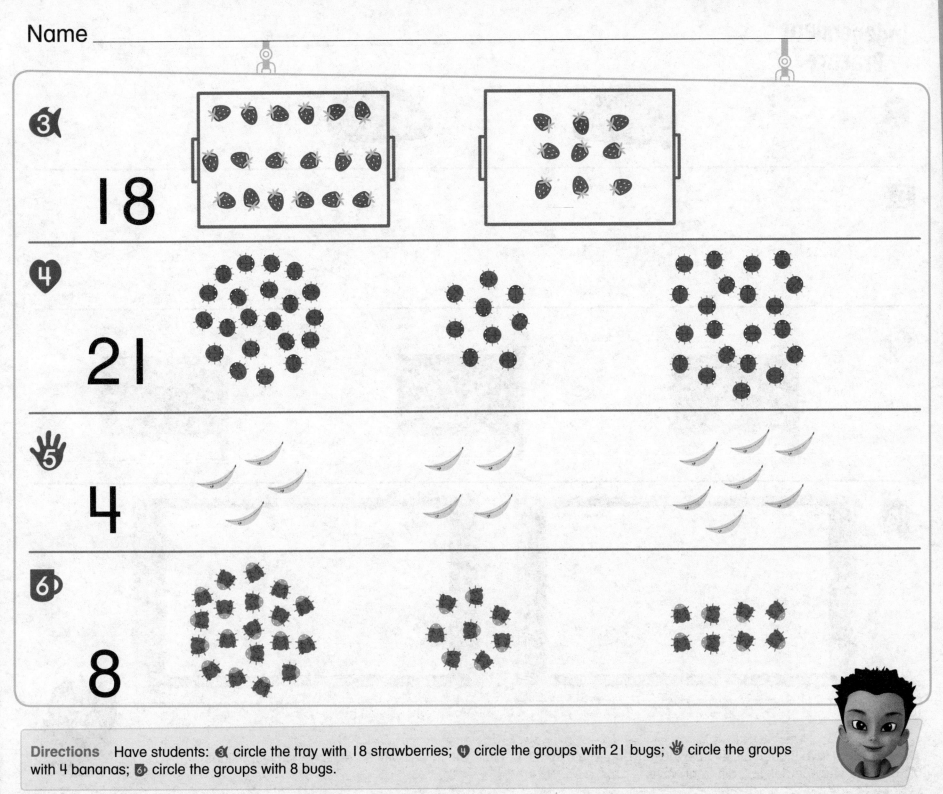

Directions Have students: ❸ circle the tray with 18 strawberries; ❹ circle the groups with 21 bugs; ❺ circle the groups with 4 bananas; ❻ circle the groups with 8 bugs.

7

8

9

10

Directions Have students: **7** circle the ladybug with 6 spots; **8** circle the flower with 8 petals; **9** circle the flags with 13 stars; **10** draw 19 strawberries in 2 different ways.

© Pearson Education, Inc. K
Topic 6 | Lesson 2

Name _____

Another Look

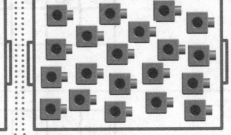

⭐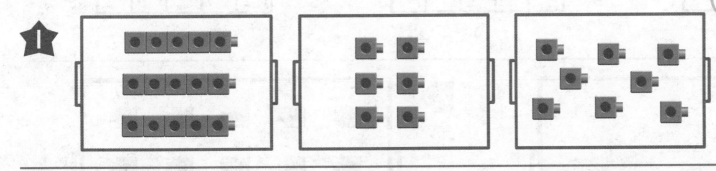

🍎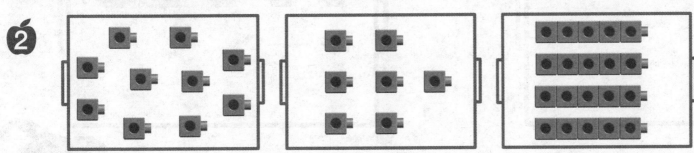

Directions Say: *Which trays have 20 connecting cubes on them? Circle the trays. How did you find how many?* Then have students: ⭐ circle the tray with 8 cubes; 🍎 circle the tray with 7 cubes.

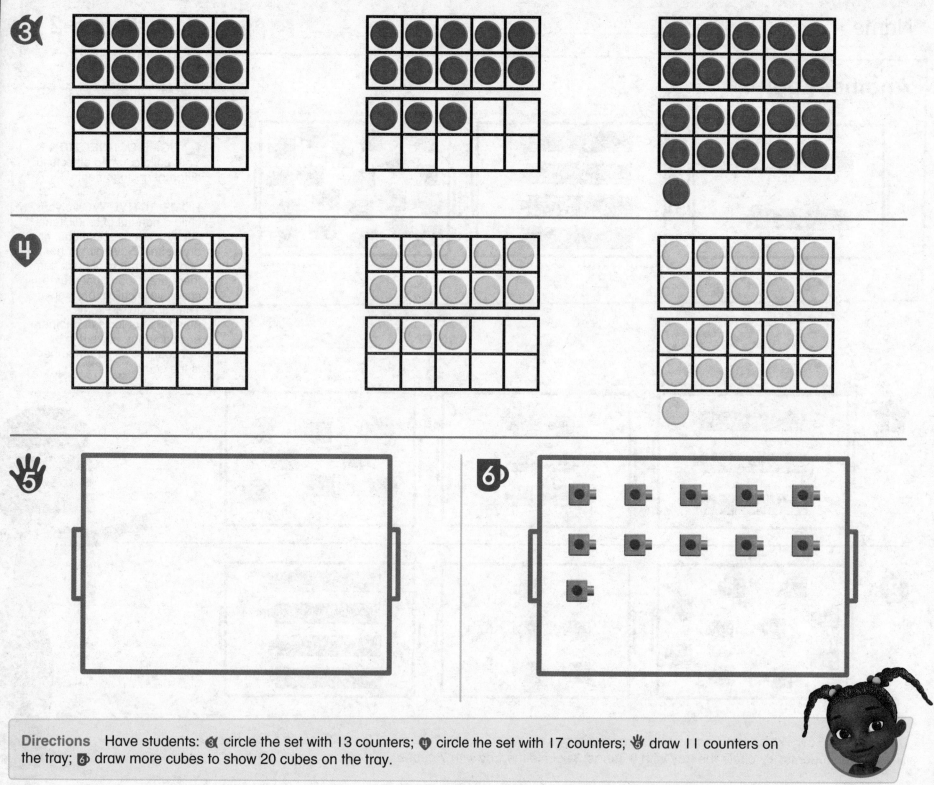

Directions Have students: ③ circle the set with 13 counters; ④ circle the set with 17 counters; ✋ draw 11 counters on the tray; ⑥ draw more cubes to show 20 cubes on the tray.

324 three hundred twenty-four © Pearson Education, Inc. K **Topic 6** | Lesson 2

Solve & Share Name _____

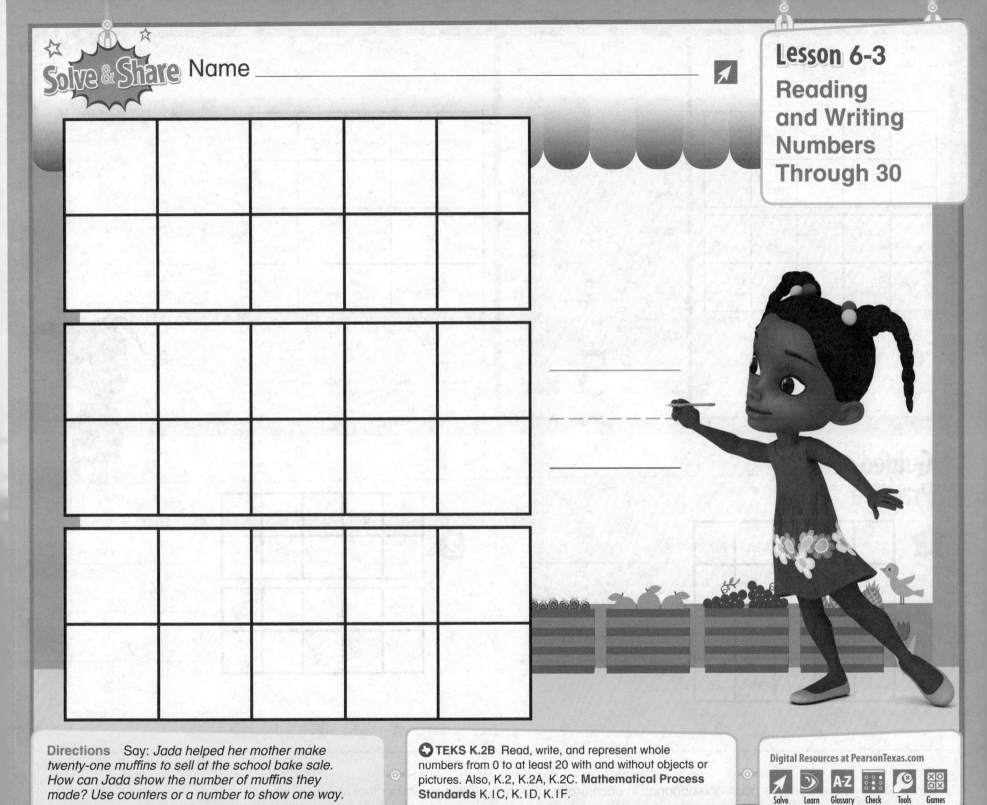

Directions Say: *Jada helped her mother make twenty-one muffins to sell at the school bake sale. How can Jada show the number of muffins they made? Use counters or a number to show one way.*

⭐ **TEKS K.2B** Read, write, and represent whole numbers from 0 to at least 20 with and without objects or pictures. Also, K.2, K.2A, K.2C. **Mathematical Process Standards** K.1C, K.1D, K.1F.

Digital Resources at PearsonTexas.com

Solve   Learn   Glossary   Check   Tools   Games

Topic 6 | Lesson 3

three hundred twenty-five **325**

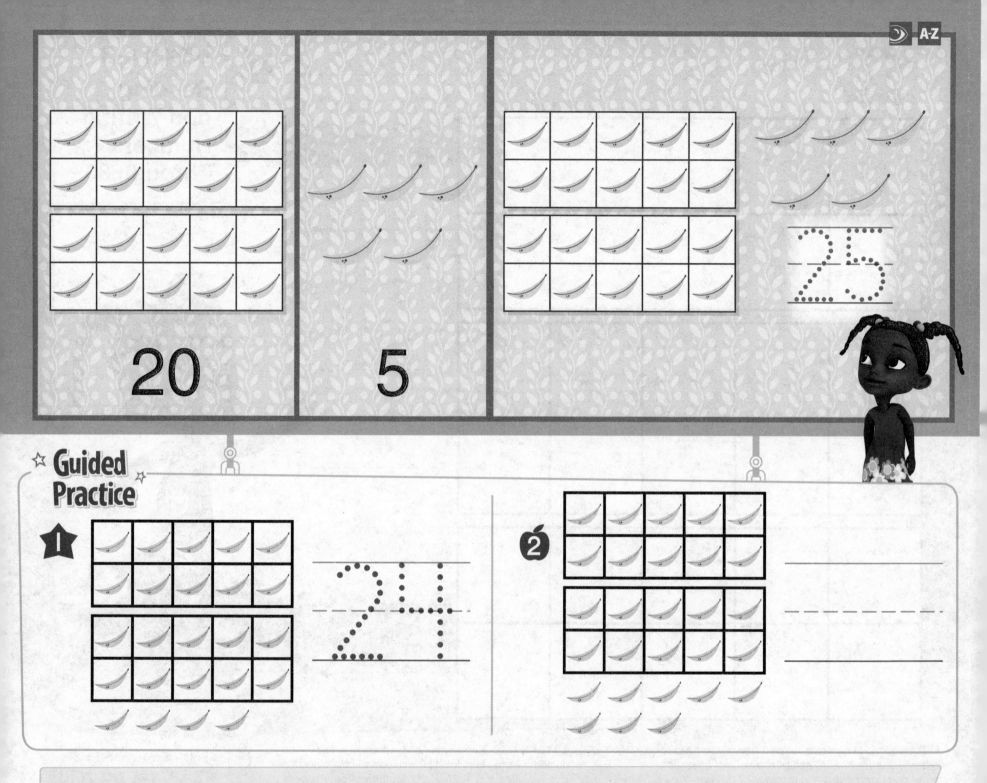

20

5

25

☆ Guided Practice ☆

1

24

2

Directions Have students count the bananas in each group, and then write the number that tells how many.

Topic 6 | Lesson 3

Name _____

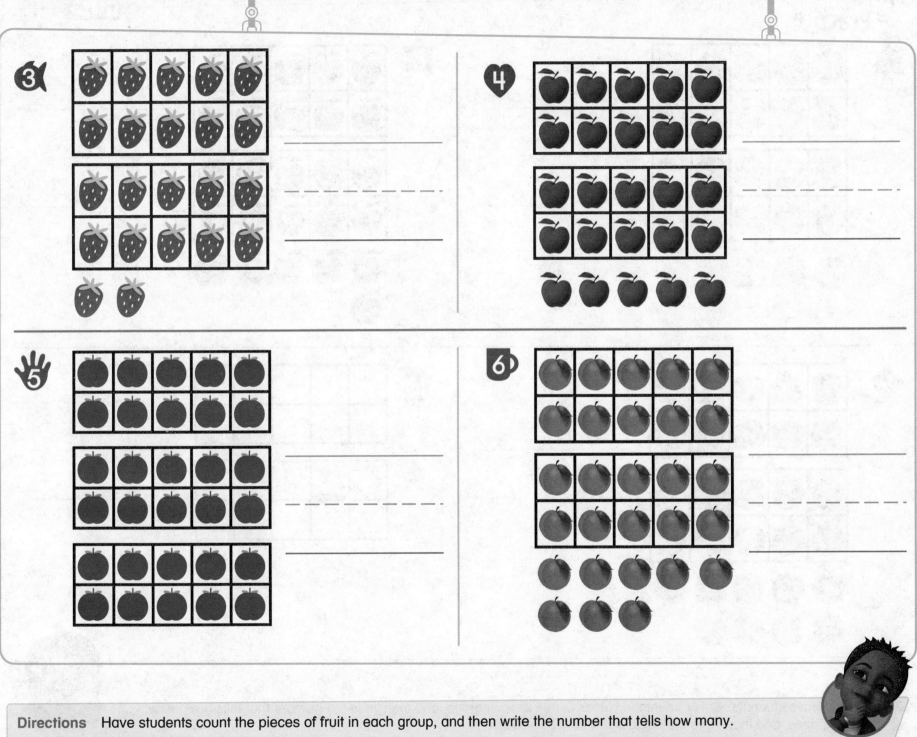

Directions Have students count the pieces of fruit in each group, and then write the number that tells how many.

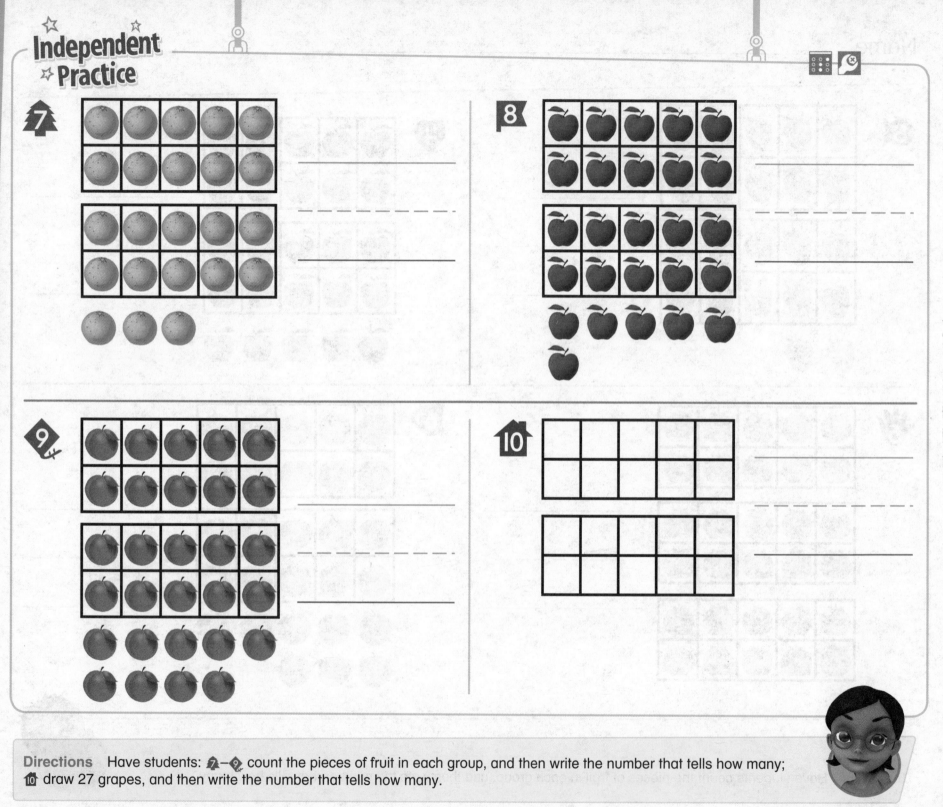

7

8

9

10

Directions Have students: 7–9 count the pieces of fruit in each group, and then write the number that tells how many; 10 draw 27 grapes, and then write the number that tells how many.

328 three hundred twenty-eight   © Pearson Education, Inc. K   **Topic 6** | Lesson 3

Name _____

Another Look

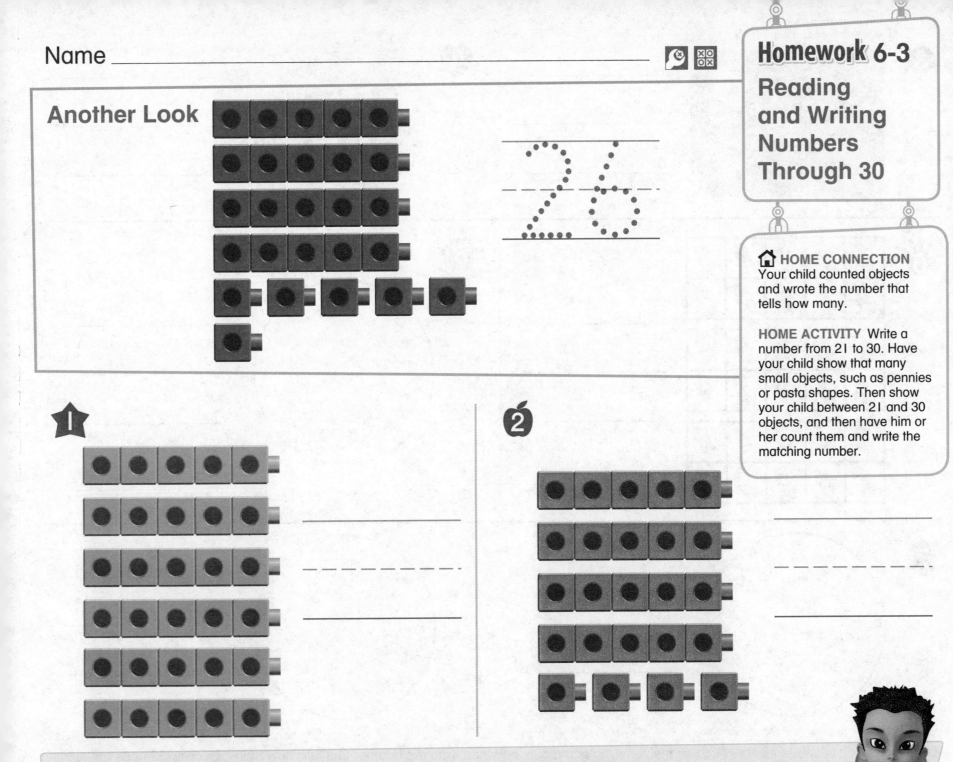

🏠 **HOME CONNECTION**
Your child counted objects and wrote the number that tells how many.

HOME ACTIVITY Write a number from 21 to 30. Have your child show that many small objects, such as pennies or pasta shapes. Then show your child between 21 and 30 objects, and then have him or her count them and write the matching number.

⭐ 1

🍎 2

Directions Say: *Count the connecting cubes. Write the number that tells how many.* Then have students: ⭐ and 🍎 count the cubes, and then write the number that tells how many.

Topic 6 | Lesson 3

Digital Resources at PearsonTexas.com

three hundred twenty-nine **329**

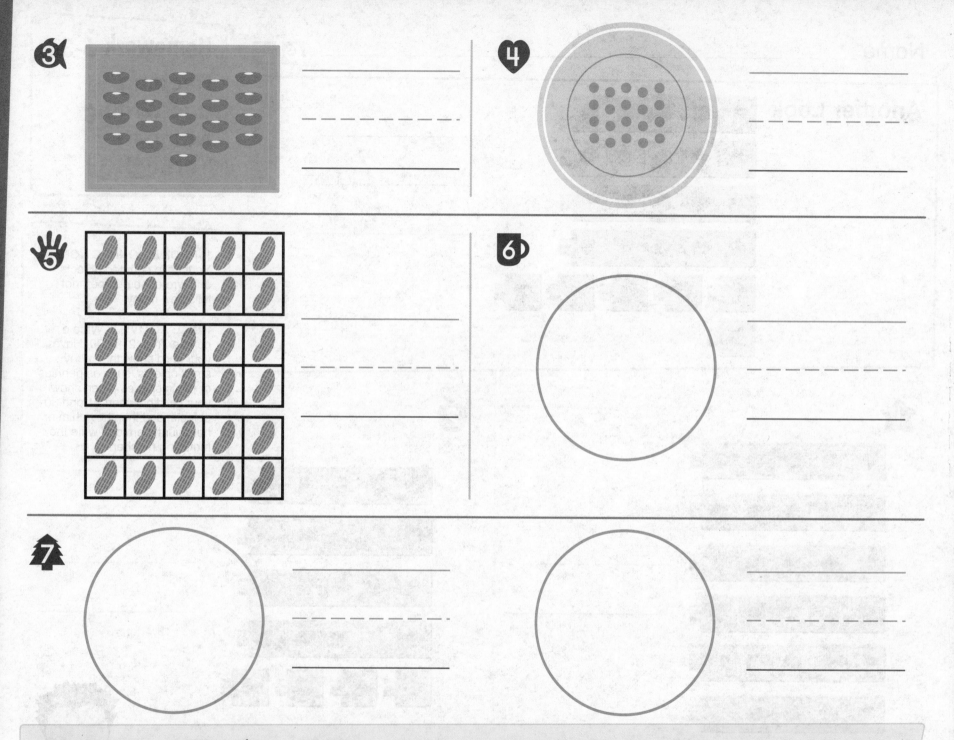

Directions **Have students:** ❸–✋ count the items in each group, and then write the number that tells how many; ☕ draw 22 peas on the plate, and then write the number that tells how many; 🌲 draw a different number of peas from 20 to 30 on each plate, and then write the numbers that tell how many.

© Pearson Education, Inc. K

Topic 6 | Lesson 3

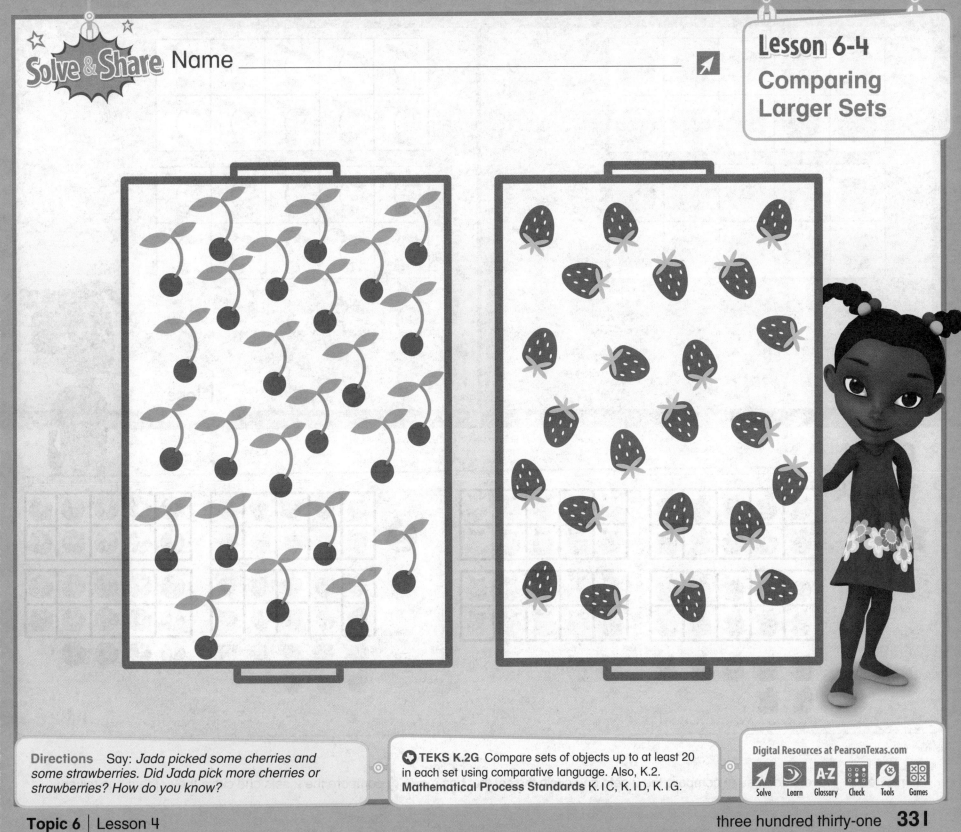

Directions Say: *Jada picked some cherries and some strawberries. Did Jada pick more cherries or strawberries? How do you know?*

⭐ **TEKS K.2G** Compare sets of objects up to at least 20 in each set using comparative language. Also, K.2. **Mathematical Process Standards** K.1C, K.1D, K.1G.

Digital Resources at PearsonTexas.com

Solve Learn Glossary Check Tools Games

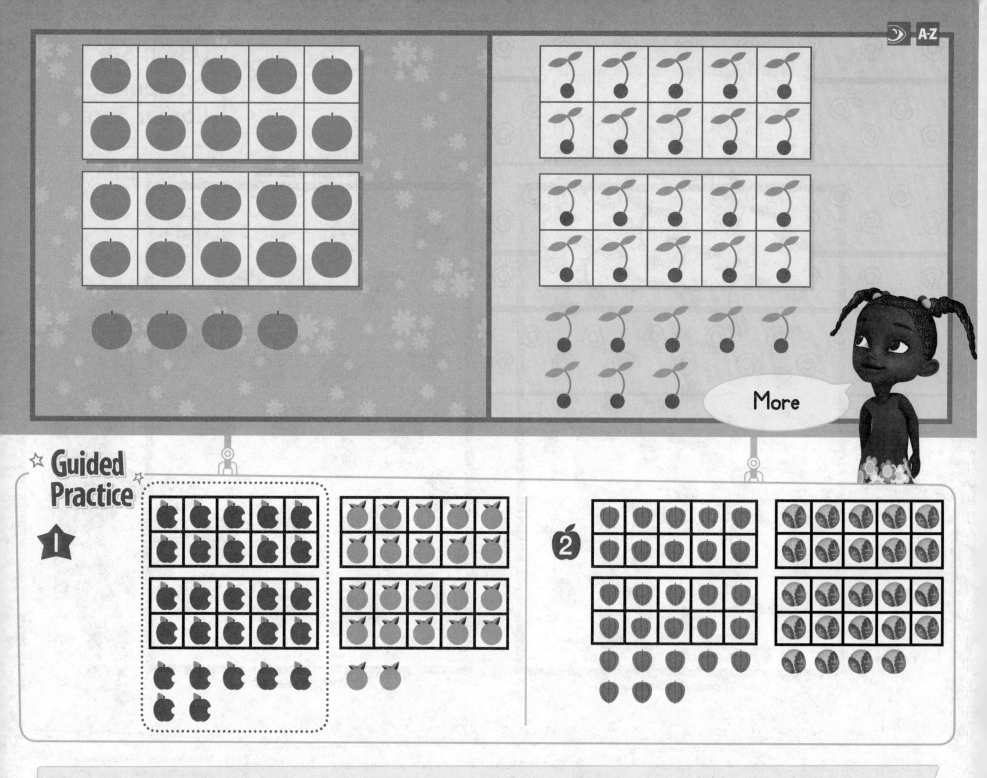

More

☆ **Guided Practice**

⭐ 1

② 2

Directions Have students: ⭐ compare the 2 sets and circle the set that has more; ② compare the 2 sets and circle the set that has fewer.

© Pearson Education, Inc. K

Topic 6 | Lesson 4

Name _____

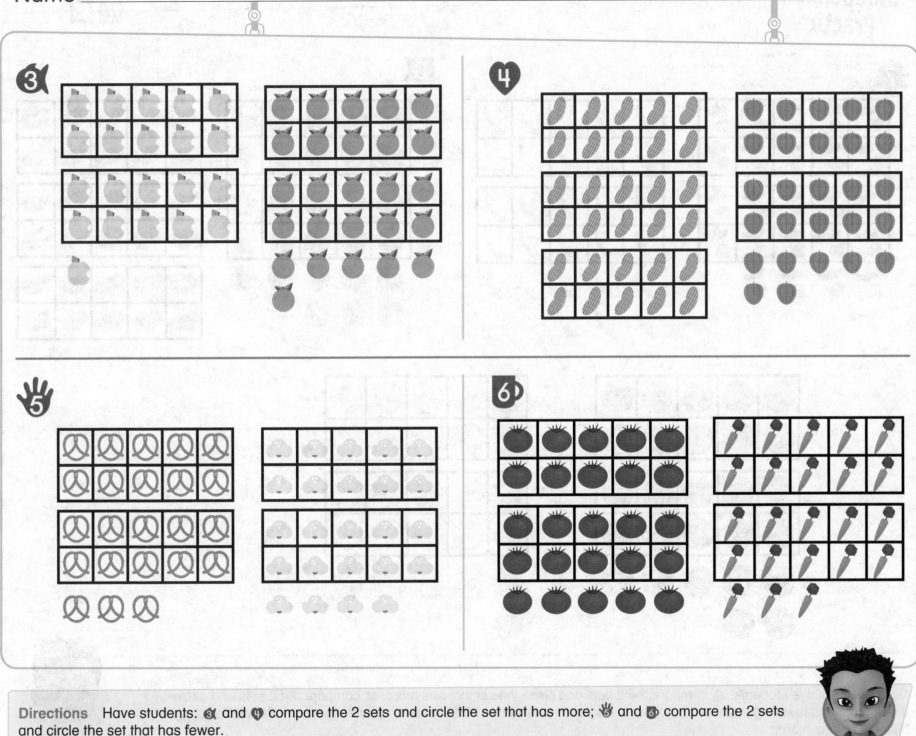

Directions Have students: ❸ and ❹ compare the 2 sets and circle the set that has more; ❺ and ❻ compare the 2 sets and circle the set that has fewer.

Topic 6 | Lesson 4

three hundred thirty-three **333**

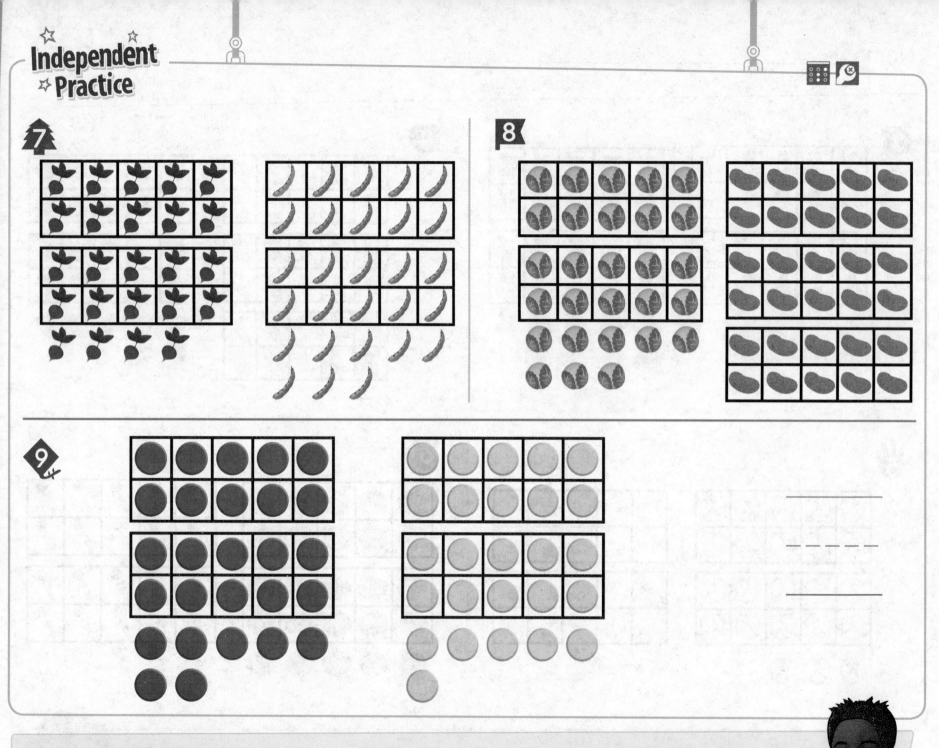

Directions Have students: **7** compare the 2 sets and circle the set that has more; **8** compare the 2 sets and circle the set that has fewer; **9** compare the 2 sets of counters, decide which set has more, and then write the number that tells how many more.

Name _____

Another Look

🏠 **HOME CONNECTION**
Your child compared sets of up to 30 objects to find which had more than or fewer than the other.

HOME ACTIVITY Prepare two different sets of 20 to 30 objects each, such as 22 nickels and 27 pennies. Have your child compare the two sets, count the objects in each, and tell which has more than the other.

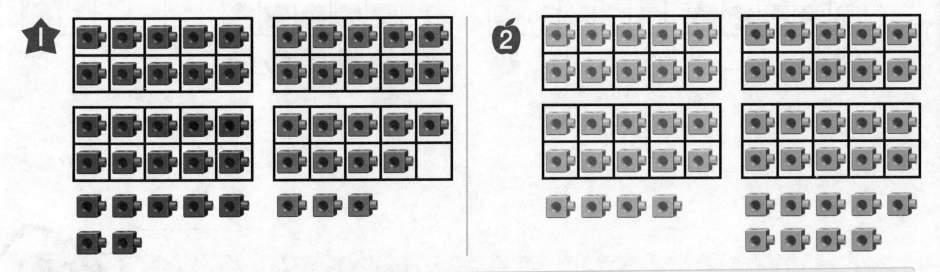

Directions Say: *Compare the 2 sets of connecting cubes. Which set has more? Circle that set.* Have students:
⭐ and 🍎 compare the 2 sets and circle the set that has more.

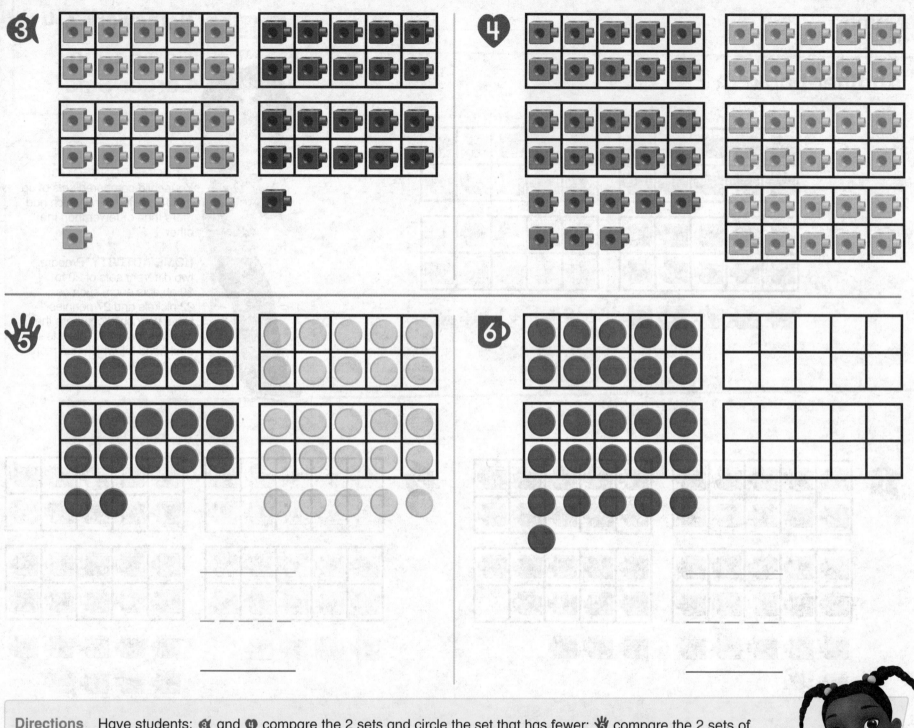

Directions Have students: ❸ and ❹ compare the 2 sets and circle the set that has fewer; ✋ compare the 2 sets of counters, decide which set has more, and then write the number that tells how many more; ❻ count the red counters, draw a set that has 2 fewer counters, and then write the number that tells how many fewer.

336 three hundred thirty-six   © Pearson Education, Inc. K   **Topic 6** | Lesson 4

Solve & Share Name _____

1 2 3 4 5 6 7 8 9 10 11 12 13 14 15 16 17 18 19 20 21 22 23 24 25 26 27 28 29 30

21   22   23   24   25

___   27   ___   29   30

Directions Say: *Jada is numbering the houses on her street in order from 21 to 30. She needs to write the numbers that are 1 less than 27 and 1 more than 27. Write the 2 numbers that Jada is missing.*

★ **TEKS K.2F** Generate a number that is one more than or one less than another number up to at least 20. Also, K.2, K.2A, K.2B. **Mathematical Process Standards** K.1C, K.1D, K.1F.

Digital Resources at PearsonTexas.com

Solve   Learn   Glossary   Check   Tools   Games

Topic 6 | Lesson 5

Guided Practice

1 25 23 24   23 24 25

2 16 18 17

Directions Have students write the numbers in order. Allow students to use number cards as needed.

© Pearson Education, Inc. K

Topic 6 | Lesson 5

Name _____

3 27 28 26

‑ ‑

4 20 19 18

‑ ‑

5 ‑ ‑ ‑ ‑ ‑ ‑ 25 ‑ ‑ ‑ ‑ ‑ ‑

6 ‑ ‑ ‑ ‑ ‑ ‑ 29 ‑ ‑ ‑ ‑ ‑ ‑

Directions Have students: **3** write the numbers in order, and then circle the number that comes after 26; **4** write the numbers in order, and then circle the number that comes before 19; **5** write the numbers that are 1 less than 25 and 1 more than 25, and then say the numbers in order; **6** write the numbers that are 1 less than 29 and 1 more than 29, and then say the numbers in order.

7 _____ **23** _____

8 15 14 13 _____ _____ _____

9 26 28 27 _____ _____ _____

10 19 20 18 _____ _____ **18**

Directions Have students: **7** write the numbers that are 1 less than 23 and 1 more than 23, and then say the numbers in order; **8** write the numbers in order, and then circle the number that comes before 15; **9** write the numbers in order, and then circle the number that comes after 26; **10** write the numbers in backward order.

Topic 6 | Lesson 5

Another Look

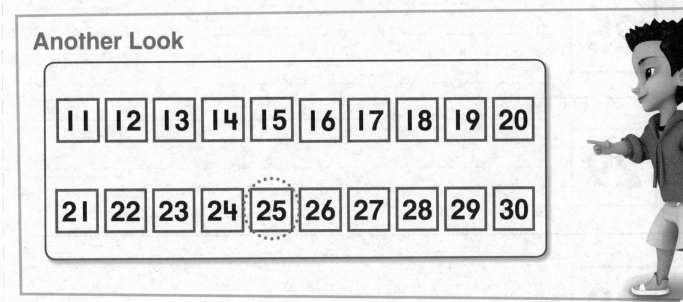

| 11 | 12 | 13 | 14 | 15 | 16 | 17 | 18 | 19 | 20 |

| 21 | 22 | 23 | 24 | (25) | 26 | 27 | 28 | 29 | 30 |

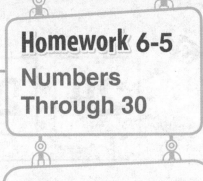

🏠 **HOME CONNECTION**
Your child ordered numbers to 30 and identified numbers that come before and after.

HOME ACTIVITY Start at any number from 11 to 20. Ask your child to count in order from that number to 30, and then count backward from 30 to 21 or from 20 to 11.

⭐ **1**

| 24 | 26 | 25 |

_ _ _ _ _ _ _ _   _ _ _ _ _ _ _ _   _ _ _ _ _ _ _ _

🍎 **2**

| 11 | 9 | 10 |

_ _ _ _ _ _ _ _   _ _ _ _ _ _ _ _   _ _ _ _ _ _ _ _

Directions Say: *Let's count the numbers 11 to 30 together. Circle the number 25. Now, name the number that comes before 25. What number comes after 25?* Then have students: ⭐ and 🍎 write the numbers in order.

3

24	23	25

4

28	27	29

5

29	28	30

6

21	19	20

7

8

Directions Have students: **3** write the numbers in the correct order; **4** write the numbers in order, and then circle the number that comes after 28; **5** write the numbers in order, and then circle the number that comes before 30; **6** write the numbers in the correct order; **7** write the number that comes after 27; **8** write the numbers that are 1 less than and 1 more than 17.

© Pearson Education, Inc. K

14   16   18

Directions Say: *Jada and Daniel are playing a game called "What Number Comes Next?" Daniel puts down the number cards 14, 16, and 18. What number cards will Jada use to complete the number pattern?*

✪ **TEKS K.1F** Analyze mathematical relationships to connect and communicate mathematical ideas. Also, K.2, K.2A, K.2F. **Mathematical Process Standards** K.1B, K.1C.

Digital Resources at PearsonTexas.com

Solve   Learn   Glossary   Check   Tools   Games

Analyze

10 8 6 4 ▢

Plan

10 8 6 4 ▢

2 less

Solve, Justify, and Evaluate

10 8 6 4 2

2 less

☆ **Guided Practice** ☆

⭐ 1

| 5 | 6 | 7 | 8 | 9 |

Directions Have students describe the pattern, and then write the number that comes next.

© Pearson Education, Inc. K

Topic 6 | **Lesson 6**

Name _____

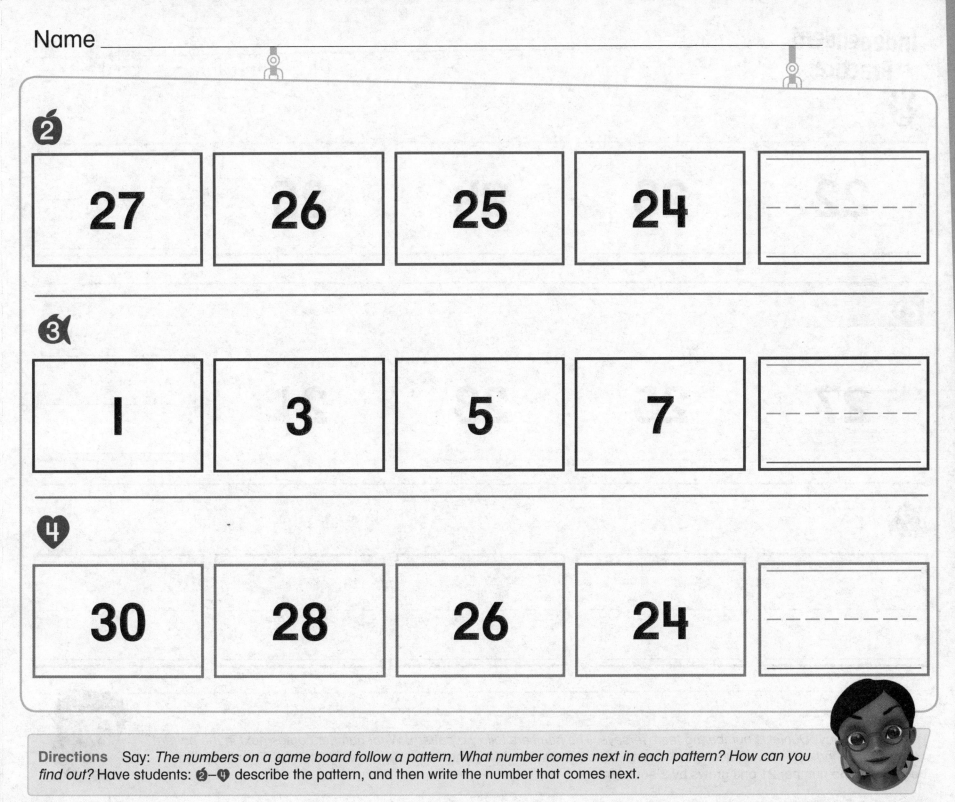

②

| 27 | 26 | 25 | 24 | - - - - - - |

③

| 1 | 3 | 5 | 7 | - - - - - - |

④

| 30 | 28 | 26 | 24 | - - - - - - |

Directions Say: *The numbers on a game board follow a pattern. What number comes next in each pattern? How can you find out?* Have students: **②–④** describe the pattern, and then write the number that comes next.

✋5

| 22 | 23 | 24 | 25 | _ _ _ _ |

🍵6

| 27 | 25 | 23 | 21 | _ _ _ _ |

🌲7

| _ _ _ _ | _ _ _ _ | _ _ _ _ | _ _ _ _ | _ _ _ _ |

Directions Say: *Daniel is numbering team jerseys. The numbers follow a pattern. What number comes next in the pattern? How can you find out?* Have students: ✋5 and 🍵6 write the number that comes next; 🌲7 show a pattern of 5 numbers that begins with the number 21 and grows by 2 each time.

© Pearson Education, Inc. K
Topic 6 | Lesson 6

Name _____

Another Look

7	**8**	**9**
10	**11**	**12**

🏠 **HOME CONNECTION**
Your child identified and completed number patterns.

HOME ACTIVITY Write the numbers 11, 13, 15, 17, 19 in a row on a sheet of paper. Have your child say the numbers in the pattern, and then write the number that comes next (21). For an added challenge, have your child write the remaining numbers up to 30 that follow the pattern (23, 25, 27, 29).

⭐**1**

21	**22**	**23**	___

🍎**2**

30	**29**	**28**	___

Directions Say: *Find the number pattern, and then write the number that comes next.* Then have students: ⭐ and 🍎 write the number that comes next in each pattern.

3

| 18 | 19 | 20 | 21 | ___ |

4

| ___ | ___ | ___ | ___ | ___ |

5

| 21 | ___ | ___ | ___ | ___ |

Directions Have students: **3** write the number that comes next in the pattern; **4** make a pattern of 5 numbers that begins with the number 23 and goes down by 2 each time; **5** make a pattern of 5 numbers that begins with 21 and grows by 2 each time.

© Pearson Education, Inc. K

Topic 6 | Lesson 6

Set A

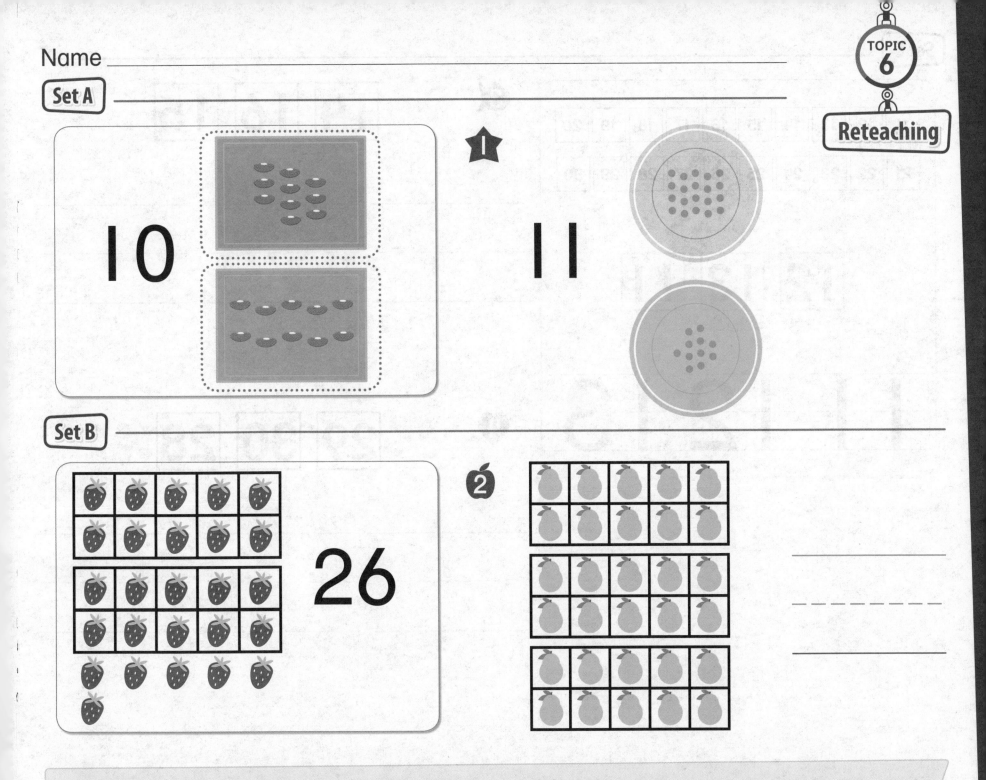

⭐ 10

1 1

Set B

26

Directions Have students: ⭐ circle the tray that has 1 1 peas; ② count the pears, and then write the number that tells how many.

11	12	13	14	15	16	17	18	19	20
21	22	23	24	25	26	27	28	29	30

12 **13** **11**

11 **12** **13**

3 **14** **16** **15**

_____

- - - - - - - - -

_____

4 **29** **30** **28**

_____

- - - - - - - - -

_____

Directions Have students: **3** and **4** write the numbers in order.

© Pearson Education, Inc. K

Name _____

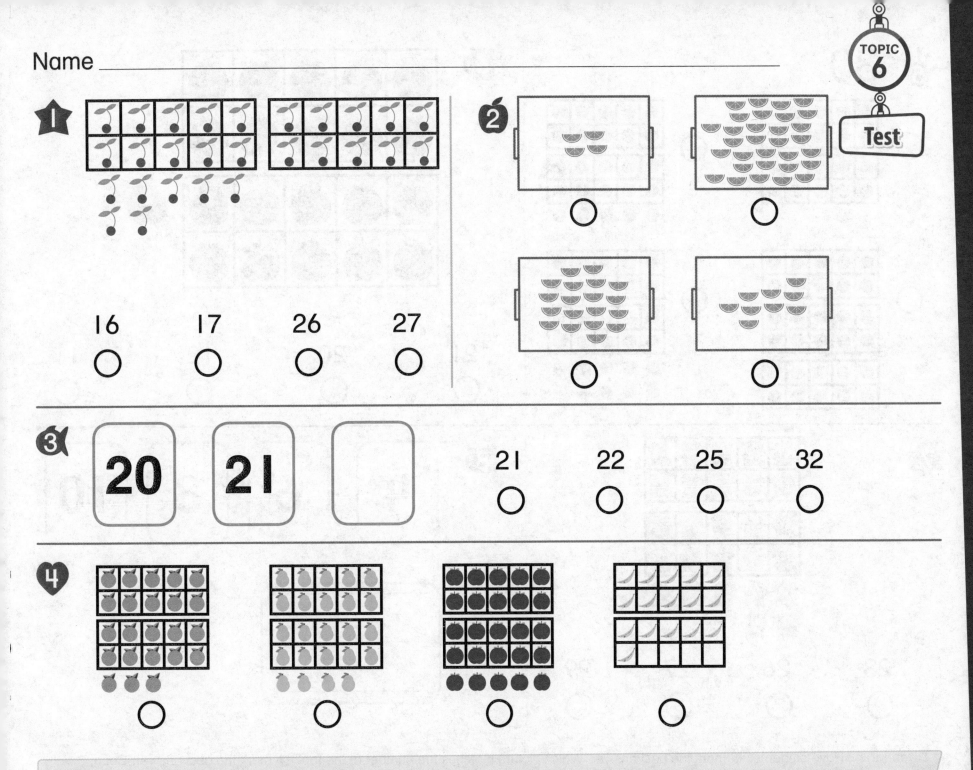

★ 1

16   17   26   27
○   ○   ○   ○

🍎 2

○   ○

○   ○

★ 3

20   **21**   [ ]

21   22   25   32
○   ○   ○   ○

♥ 4

○   ○   ○   ○

Directions   Have students mark the best answer. ★ How many cherries are there in all? 🍎 Which tray shows 19 orange slices?
★ Which number is 1 more than 21? ♥ Count the pieces of fruit in each set. Which set has the fewest?

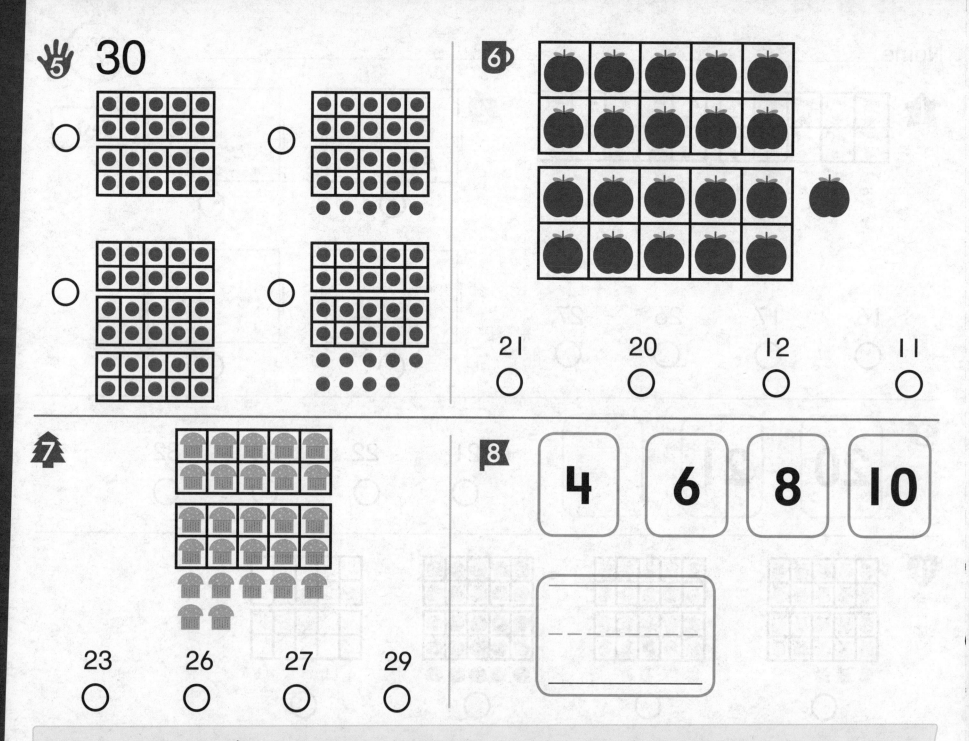

5 **30**

○ ○

○ ○

6

○ 21   ○ 20   ○ 12   ○ 11

7

23   26   27   29
○   ○   ○   ○

8

| 4 | 6 | 8 | 10 |

Directions Have students: **5** mark the best answer. Which picture matches the number at the top? **6** mark the best answer. Count the pieces of fruit. Which number tells how many? **7** mark the best answer. Which number tells how many muffins there are? **8** look at the numbers and find the pattern, and then write the number that comes next in the pattern.

© Pearson Education, Inc. K

Understanding Addition

Essential Question: What types of situations involve addition?

Math and Science Project: Baby Animals

Directions Read the character speech bubbles to students. **Find Out!** Have students explore the difference between animals and non-living things. Say: *Animals can have babies. Non-living things cannot have babies. Talk to friends and relatives about different animals and their babies.* **Journal: Make a Poster** Then have students make a poster. Have them draw a cat with 5 kittens, circle the mother cat and the kittens to join them, and tell a joining story about how many cats there are in all.

☆ Review What You Know ☆

⭐ 1

23 24 25

🍎 2

26 27 28

3

30 21 29

❤ 4

✋ 5

☕ 6

Directions Have students: ⭐ circle the number that comes before 24; 🍎 circle the number that comes after 27; 3 circle the number twenty-one; ❤–☕ count each set of objects, write the numbers that tell how many, and then circle the number that tells which group has more.

© Pearson Education, Inc. K

My Word Cards

Directions Have students cut out the vocabulary cards. Read the front of the card, and then ask them to explain what the word or phrase means.

A-Z

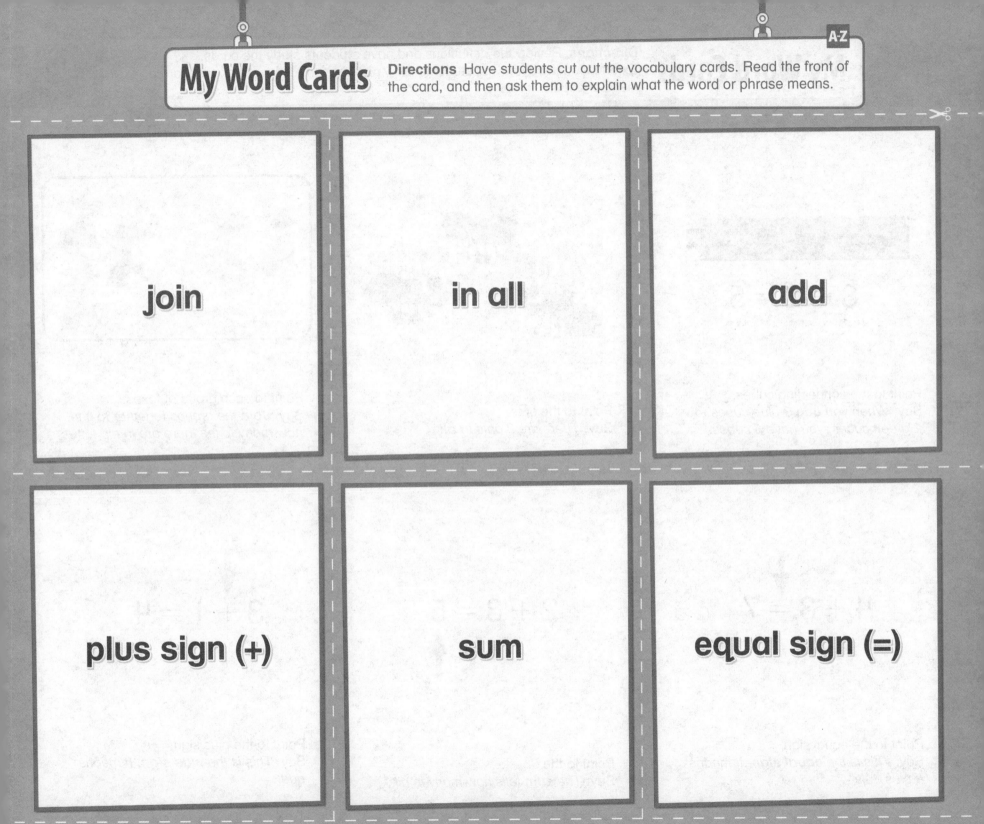

join

in all

add

plus sign (+)

sum

equal sign (=)

Directions Review the definitions and have students study the cards. Extend learning by having students draw pictures for each word on a separate piece of paper.

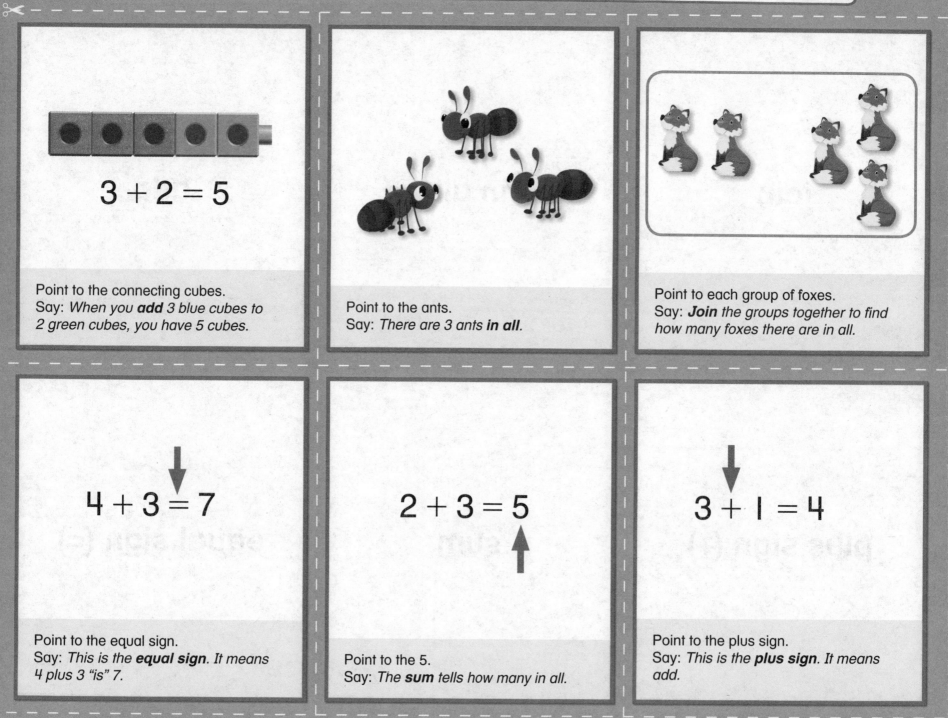

$3 + 2 = 5$

Point to the connecting cubes.
Say: *When you **add** 3 blue cubes to 2 green cubes, you have 5 cubes.*

Point to the ants.
Say: *There are 3 ants **in all**.*

Point to each group of foxes.
Say: ***Join** the groups together to find how many foxes there are in all.*

$4 + 3 = 7$

Point to the equal sign.
Say: *This is the **equal sign**. It means 4 plus 3 "is" 7.*

$2 + 3 = 5$

Point to the 5.
Say: *The **sum** tells how many in all.*

$3 + 1 = 4$

Point to the plus sign.
Say: *This is the **plus sign**. It means add.*

My Word Cards

addition sentence

$$4 + 1 = 5$$

Point to the addition sentence.
Say: *4 plus 1 equals 5 is an **addition sentence**. It tells how many there are in all.*

Solve & Share   Name _____

_____

- - - - -

____ in all

Directions Say: *Daniel is sitting on a bench in the park. 2 friends join him. How can you find out how many people are sitting on the bench in all?*

⊕ **TEKS K.3B** Solve word problems using objects and drawings to find sums up to 10 and differences within 10. Also, K.3, K.3A. **Mathematical Process Standards** K.1C, K.1D, K.1G.

Digital Resources at PearsonTexas.com

Solve Learn Glossary Check Tools Games

____ in all

☆ Guided Practice ☆

1

____ in all

2

____ in all

Directions Have students listen to each story, use counters to model the problem, circle the groups to join them, and then write the number that tells how many in all. **1** *Daniel saw 5 ducks at the park. Then he saw 3 more. How many ducks did he see in all?* **2** *Daniel saw 3 beavers. Then he saw 3 more. How many beavers did he see in all?*

360 three hundred sixty

Topic 7 | Lesson 1

Name _____

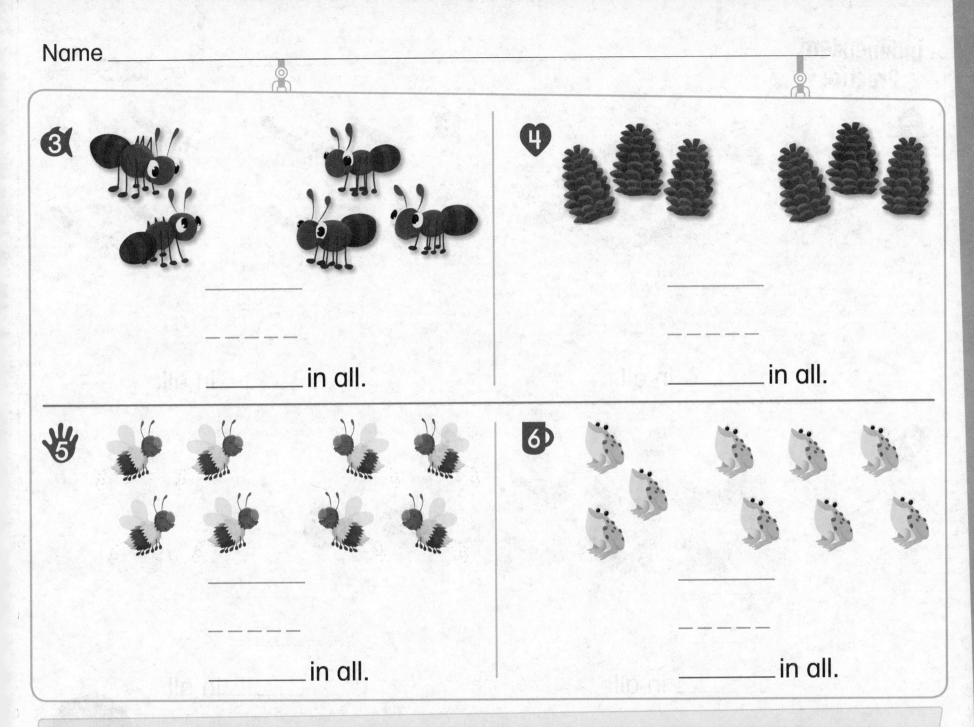

③ _____

‒ ‒ ‒ ‒ ‒

_____ in all.

❤ _____

‒ ‒ ‒ ‒ ‒

_____ in all.

✋5 _____

‒ ‒ ‒ ‒ ‒

_____ in all.

6 _____

‒ ‒ ‒ ‒ ‒

_____ in all.

Directions Have students listen to each story, use counters to model the problem, circle the groups to join them, and then write the number that tells how many in all. ③ *Daniel saw 2 ants. Then he saw 3 more. How many ants did he see in all?* ❤ *Daniel collected 3 pine cones. Then he collected 3 more. How many pine cones did he have in all?* ✋5 *Daniel saw 4 bees. Then he saw 4 more. How many bees did he see in all?* 6 *Daniel saw 3 frogs. Then he saw 6 more. How many frogs did he see in all?*

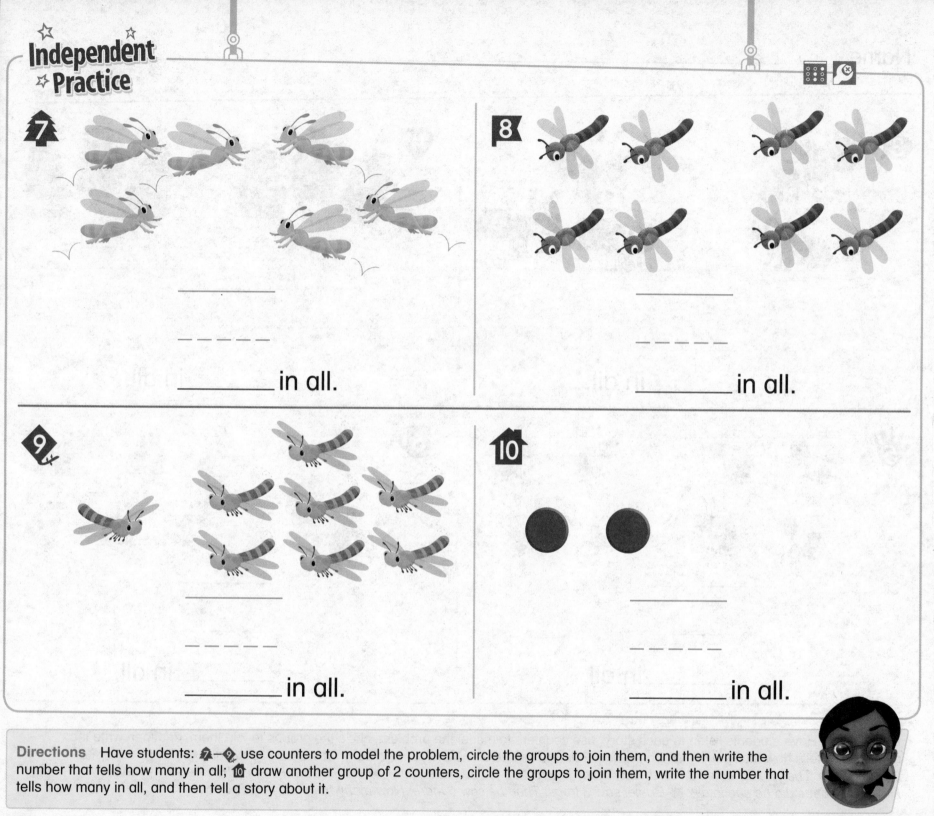

7

_____

_ _ _ _ _ _

_____ in all.

8

_____

_ _ _ _ _ _

_____ in all.

9

_____

_ _ _ _ _ _

_____ in all.

10

_____

_ _ _ _ _ _

_____ in all.

Directions Have students: **7—9** use counters to model the problem, circle the groups to join them, and then write the number that tells how many in all; **10** draw another group of 2 counters, circle the groups to join them, write the number that tells how many in all, and then tell a story about it.

Topic 7 | Lesson 1

Another Look

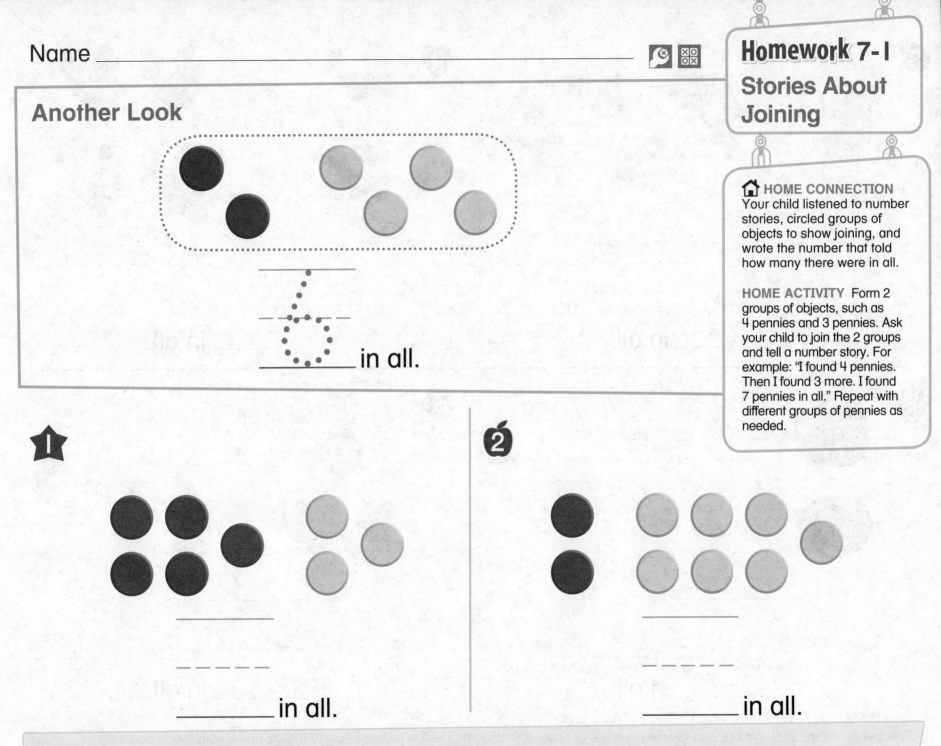

_____ in all.

🏠 **HOME CONNECTION**
Your child listened to number stories, circled groups of objects to show joining, and wrote the number that told how many there were in all.

HOME ACTIVITY Form 2 groups of objects, such as 4 pennies and 3 pennies. Ask your child to join the 2 groups and tell a number story. For example: "I found 4 pennies. Then I found 3 more. I found 7 pennies in all." Repeat with different groups of pennies as needed.

⭐ 1

_____ in all.

🍎 2

_____ in all.

Directions Say: *How many red counters are there? How many yellow counters are there? Use counters or other objects to model the problem, circle the groups to join them, and then write the number that tells how many in all.* Then have students: ⭐ and 🍎 use counters or other objects to model the problem, circle the groups to join them, and then write the number that tells how many in all.

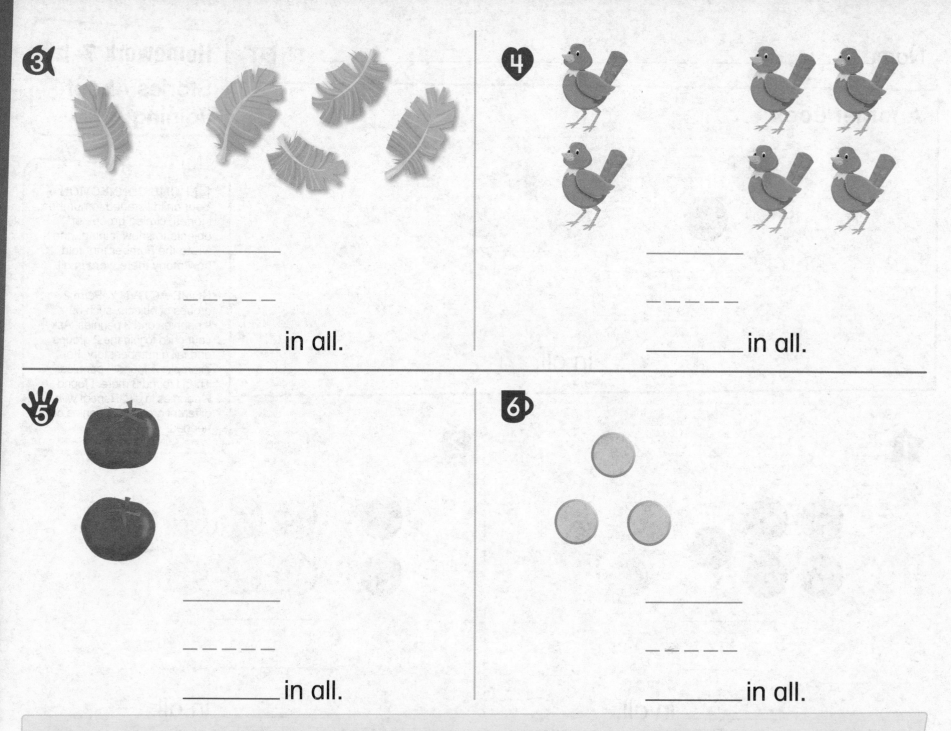

3

_____
_ _ _ _ _
_____ in all.

4

_____
_ _ _ _ _
_____ in all.

5

_____
_ _ _ _ _
_____ in all.

6

_____
_ _ _ _ _
_____ in all.

Directions Have students: **3** and **4** use counters or other objects to model the problem, circle the groups to join them, and then write the number that tells how many in all; **5** draw another group of 4 tomatoes, circle the groups to join them, write the number that tells how many in all, and then tell a story about it; **6** draw another group of 2 counters, circle the groups to join them, write the number that tells how many in all, and then tell a story about it.

© Pearson Education, Inc. K

Topic 7 | Lesson 1

Solve & Share

Name _____

_____   _____   _____

_____ and _____ is _____.

Directions Say: *Daniel sees 3 tomatoes on a plant. He sees 5 tomatoes on another plant. How many tomatoes are there in all?*

TEKS K.3A Model the action of joining to represent addition and the action of separating to represent subtraction. Also, K.3, K.3B. **Mathematical Process Standards** K.1C, K.1D, K.1F.

Digital Resources at PearsonTexas.com

Solve Learn Glossary Check Tools Games

2 and 4 is 6.

☆ **Guided Practice** ☆

1

2 and 4 is 6.

_____ ____ and _____ is _____.

2

_____ and _____ is _____.

Directions Have students use counters to model joining the groups, circle the groups to join them, and then write a sentence that tells how many in all.

© Pearson Education, Inc. K

Name _____

3

_____   _____

‎- - - - - - - -   - - - - - - - -

_____ and _____ is _____ .

4

_____   _____

‎- - - - - - - -   - - - - - - - -

_____ and _____ is _____ .

5

_____   _____

‎- - - - - - - -   - - - - - - - -

_____ and _____ is _____ .

6

_____   _____

‎- - - - - - - -   - - - - - - - -

_____ and _____ is _____ .

Directions Have students use counters to model joining the groups, circle the groups to join them, and then write a sentence that tells how many in all.

Independent Practice

7

_____ _____ _____

— — — — — — — — — — — — —

_____ and _____ is _____ .

8

_____ _____ _____

— — — — — — — — — — — — —

_____ and _____ is _____ .

9

_____ _____ _____

— — — — — — — — — — — — —

_____ and _____ is _____ .

10

_____ _____ _____

— — — — — — — — — — — — —

_____ and _____ is _____ .

8

Directions Have students: **7**—**9** use counters to model joining the groups, circle the groups to join them, and then write a sentence that tells how many in all; **10** draw the other group of counters, circle the groups to join them, and then complete the sentence.

© Pearson Education, Inc. K

Topic 7 | Lesson 2

Another Look

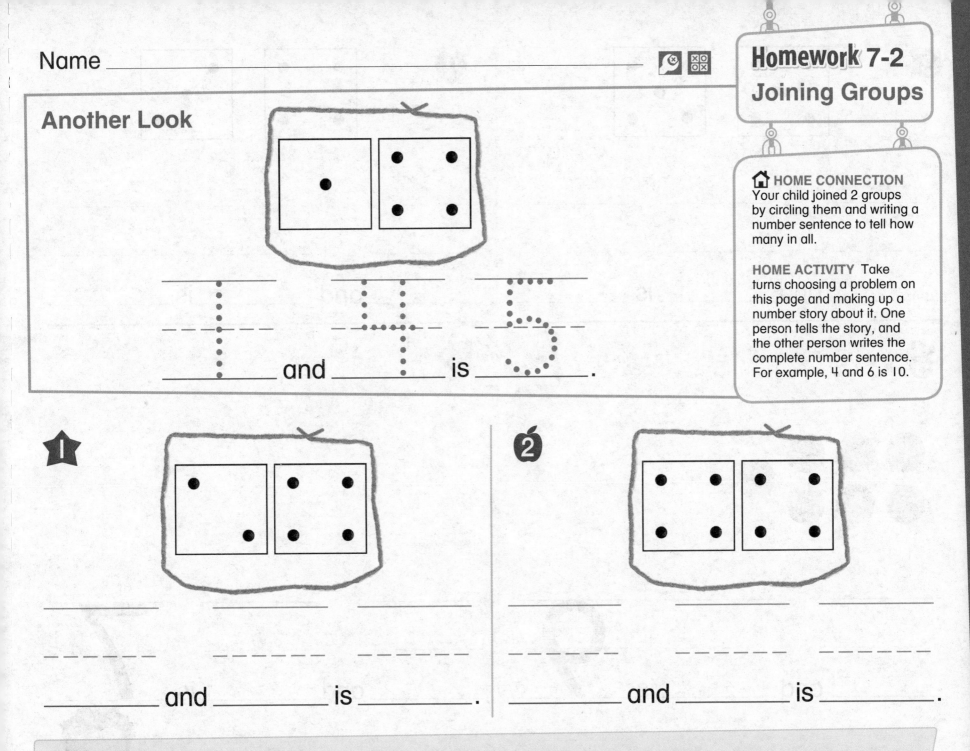

___ and ___ is ___.

🏠 **HOME CONNECTION**
Your child joined 2 groups by circling them and writing a number sentence to tell how many in all.

HOME ACTIVITY Take turns choosing a problem on this page and making up a number story about it. One person tells the story, and the other person writes the complete number sentence. For example, 4 and 6 is 10.

⭐ 1

___ and ___ is ___.

2

___ and ___ is ___.

Directions Say: *What numbers are shown by the dot cards? When you join the cards with yarn, you can count the dots to find how many in all. Write the number of dots on each card, and then write a sentence that tells how many in all.* Then have students:
⭐ and 2 write the number that tells how many dots are on each card, and then write a sentence that tells how many in all.

3

_____ _____

- - - - - - - -

_____ and _____ is _____ .

4

_____ _____

- - - - - - - -

_____ and _____ is _____ .

5

_____ _____

- - - - - - - -

_____ and _____ is _9_ .

6

_____ _____

- - - - - - - -

_____ and _____ is _7_ .

Directions Have students: **3–4** circle the groups to join them, and then write a sentence that tells how many in all; **5** draw the other group, circle the groups to join them, and then complete the sentence; **6** draw counters to show 2 groups that equal 7 when joined together, and then complete the sentence.

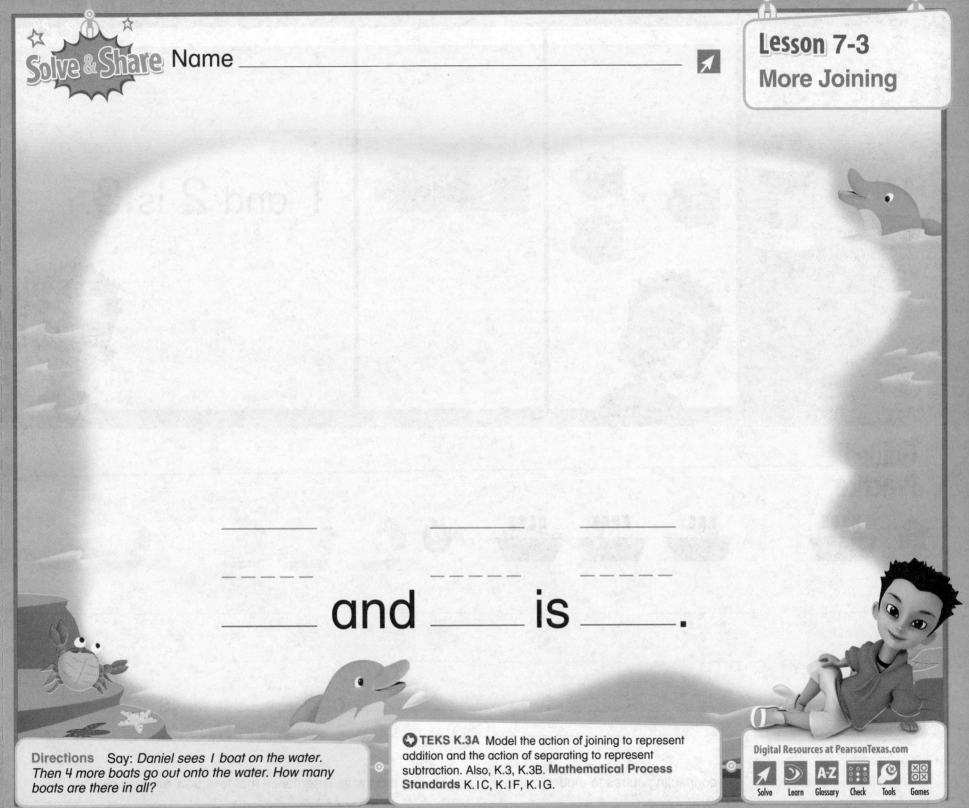

_____ and _____ is _____.

TEKS K.3A Model the action of joining to represent addition and the action of separating to represent subtraction. Also, K.3, K.3B. **Mathematical Process Standards** K.1C, K.1F, K.1G.

Directions Say: *Daniel sees 1 boat on the water. Then 4 more boats go out onto the water. How many boats are there in all?*

Digital Resources at PearsonTexas.com

Solve Learn Glossary Check Tools Games

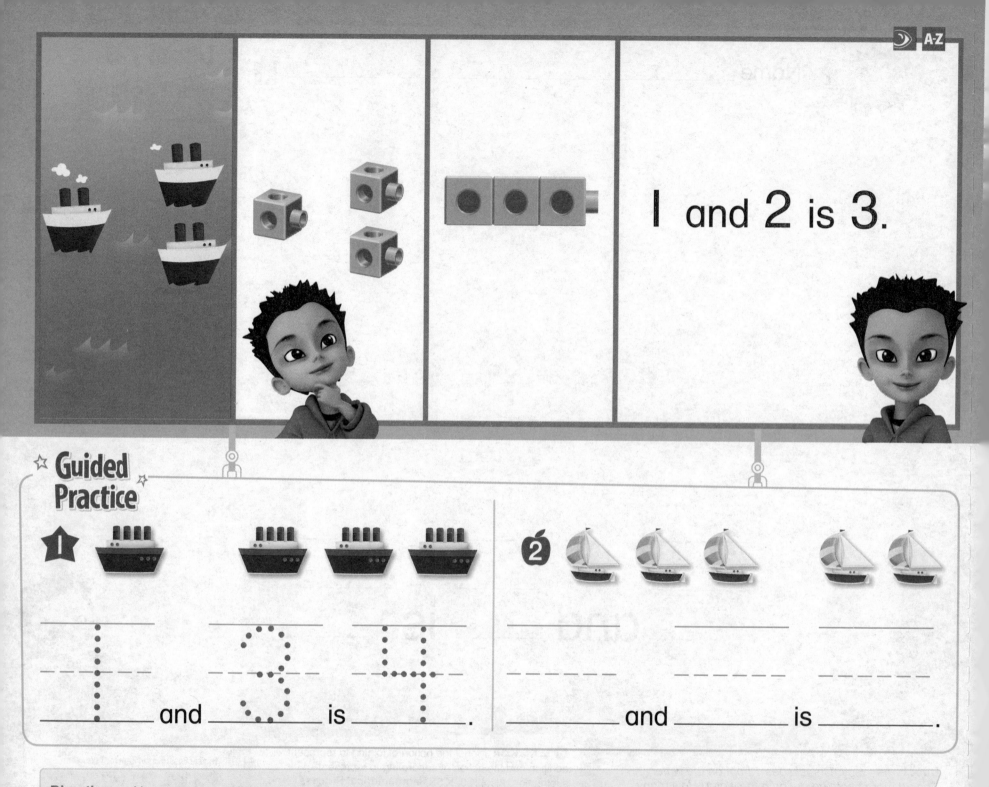

I and 2 is 3.

★ **Guided Practice**

① _____ and _____ is _____.

② _____ and _____ is _____.

Directions Have students use connecting cubes to model joining the groups, and then write a sentence that tells how many in all.

© Pearson Education, Inc. K

Topic 7 | Lesson 3

3

_____ _____ _____

- - - - - - - - - - - - - - - - - - -

_____ and _____ is _____ .

4

_____ _____ _____

- - - - - - - - - - - - - - - - - - -

_____ and _____ is _____ .

5

_____ _____ _____

- - - - - - - - - - - - - - - - - - -

_____ and _____ is _____ .

6

_____ _____ _____

- - - - - - - - - - - - - - - - - - -

_____ and _____ is _____ .

Directions Have students use connecting cubes to model joining the groups, and then write a sentence that tells how many in all.

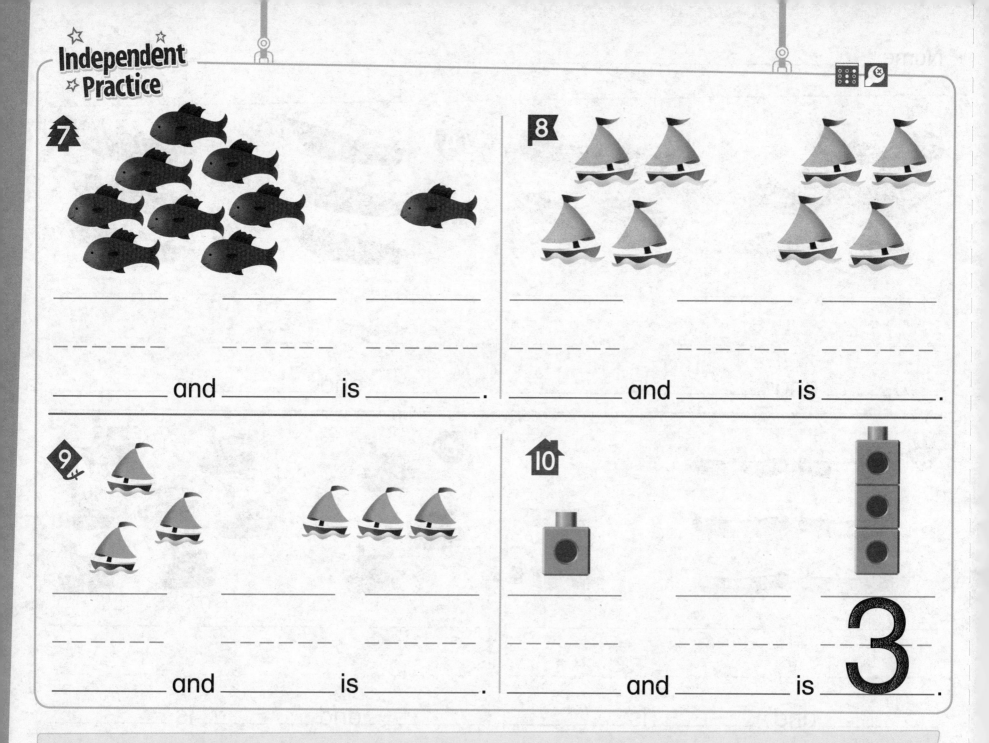

7

_____ _____

- - - - - - - - - - - - - - - - -

_____ and _____ is _____ .

8

_____ _____

- - - - - - - - - - - - - - - - -

_____ and _____ is _____ .

9

_____ _____

- - - - - - - - - - - - - - - - -

_____ and _____ is _____ .

10

_____ _____

- - - - - - - - - - - - - - - - -

_____ and _____ is _____ .

Directions Have students: 7–9 use connecting cubes to model joining the groups, and then write a sentence that tells how many in all; 10 draw the number of green connecting cubes needed to join the 1 green connecting cube to make 3 connecting cubes in all, and then complete the sentence.

Name _____

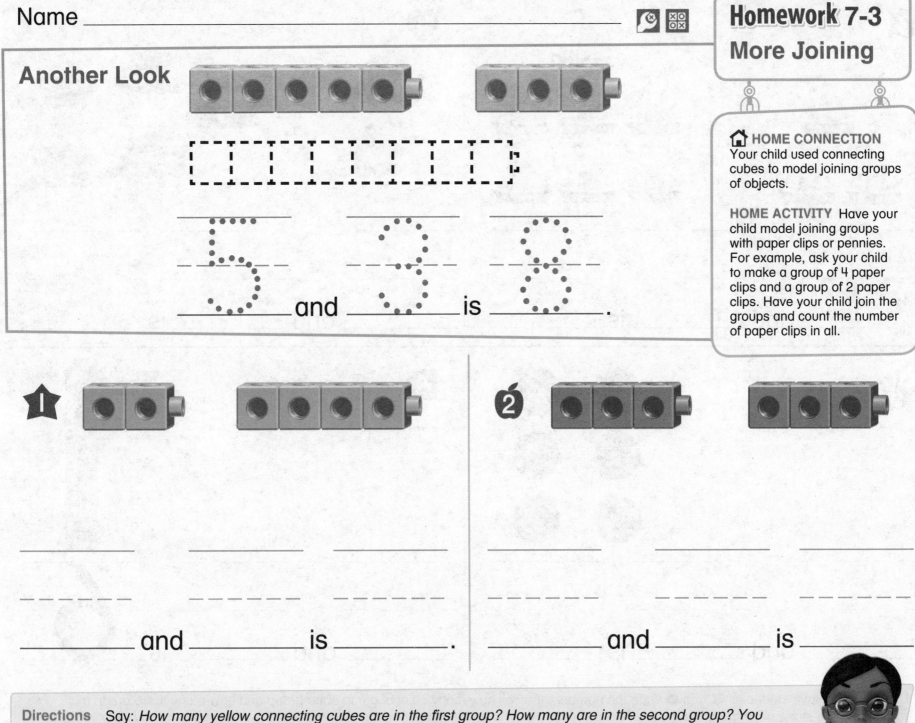

Another Look

5 3 8

_____ and _____ is _____.

🏠 **HOME CONNECTION**
Your child used connecting cubes to model joining groups of objects.

HOME ACTIVITY Have your child model joining groups with paper clips or pennies. For example, ask your child to make a group of 4 paper clips and a group of 2 paper clips. Have your child join the groups and count the number of paper clips in all.

⭐ 1

2

_____ and _____ is _____.

_____ and _____ is _____.

Directions Say: *How many yellow connecting cubes are in the first group? How many are in the second group? You can draw a picture to show joining 2 groups. Write a sentence that tells how many in all.* Then have students: ⭐–2 use connecting cubes or other objects to model joining the groups, and then write a sentence that tells how many in all.

3

_____ _____

_____ _____

_____ and _____ is _____ .

4

_____ _____

_____ _____

_____ and _____ is _____ .

5

_____ _____

_____ and _____ is _____ .

6

_____ _____

_____ and _____ is _____ .

6

Directions Have students: **3** and **4** write the numbers that tell how many objects are in each group and how many there are in all; **5** listen to the story, draw the other group of counters, and then write a sentence to match the story. Say: *There are some boats in the water. 6 more boats come. There are 9 boats in all.* **6** draw 2 groups of connecting cubes that equal 6 connecting cubes when joined together, and then complete the sentence.

   Topic 7 | Lesson 3

Name _____

★ TEKS K.3A Model the action of joining to represent addition and the action of separating to represent subtraction. Also, K.3, K.3B. Mathematical Process Standards K.1D, K.1F, K.1G.

Directions Say: *There are 4 crayons in a box. Daniel puts 3 red crayons in the box. How can you find how many crayons there are in all?*

Digital Resources at PearsonTexas.com

Solve   Learn   Glossary   Check   Tools   Games

Name

4 and 2

$4 + 2$

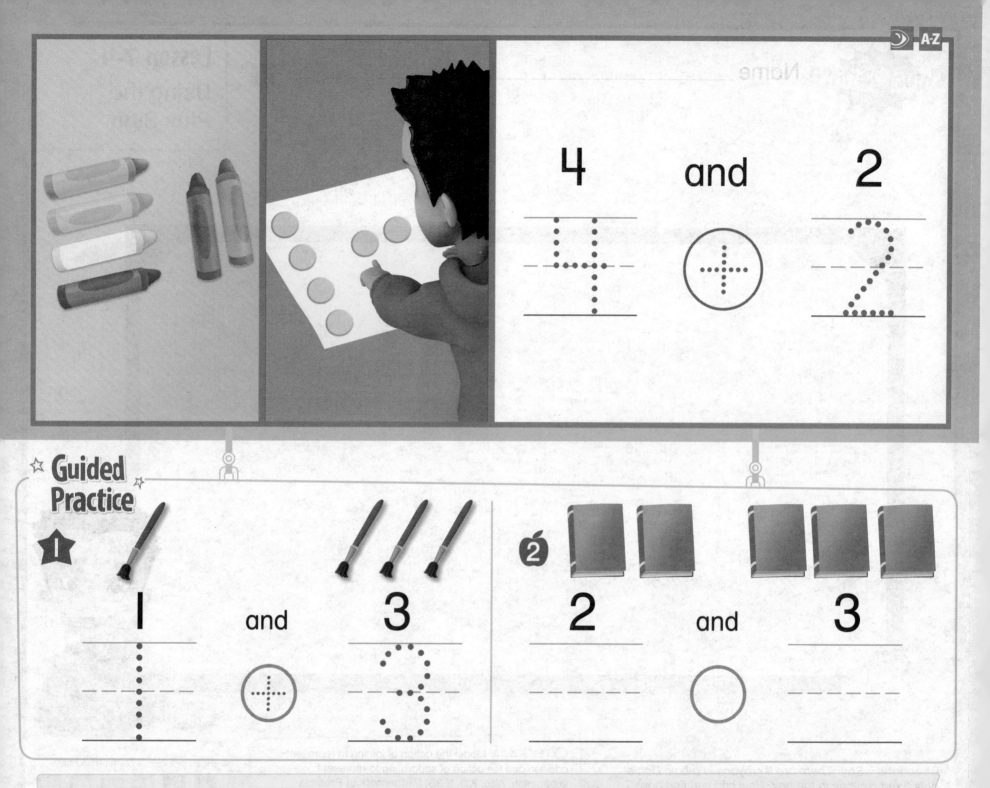

⭐ Guided Practice

1 1 and 3

$1 + 3$

2 2 and 3

2 ◯ 3

Name _____

3

3 and 4

◯

4

5 and 1

◯

5

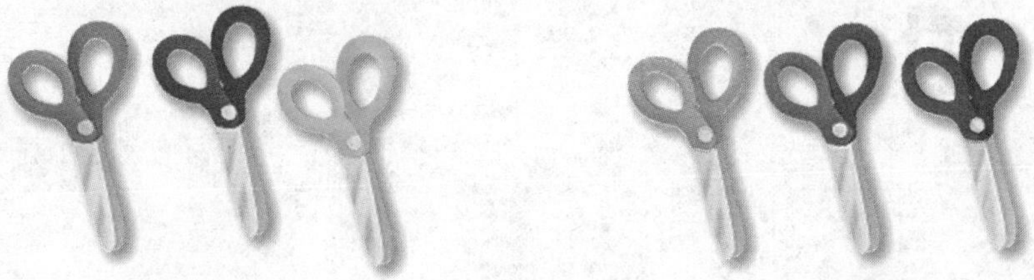

3 and 3

◯

6

2 and 1

◯

Directions Have students count the objects in each group, and then write the numbers and the plus sign to show joining the groups.

7

5   and   1

◯

8

2   and   5

◯

9

1   and   2

◯

10

◯

Directions Have students: **7–9** count the objects in each group, and then write the numbers and the plus sign to show joining the groups; **10** draw 2 groups of counters to show 5 in all, and then write the number of counters in each group and the plus sign to show joining the groups.

Name _____

Another Look

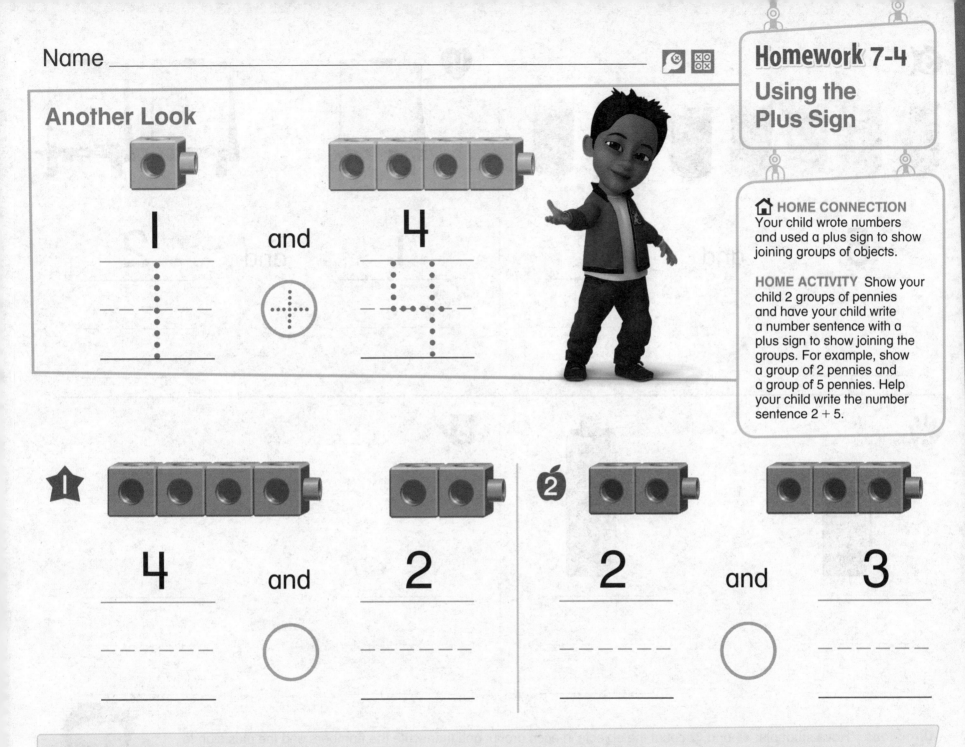

I

and

4

🏠 **HOME CONNECTION**
Your child wrote numbers and used a plus sign to show joining groups of objects.

HOME ACTIVITY Show your child 2 groups of pennies and have your child write a number sentence with a plus sign to show joining the groups. For example, show a group of 2 pennies and a group of 5 pennies. Help your child write the number sentence 2 + 5.

⭐

4

and

2

②

2

and

3

Directions Say: *You can use connecting cubes or other objects to show joining 1 and 4. Write the numbers and the plus sign to show joining the groups.* Then have students: ⭐ and ② count the objects in each group, and then write the numbers and the plus sign to show joining the groups.

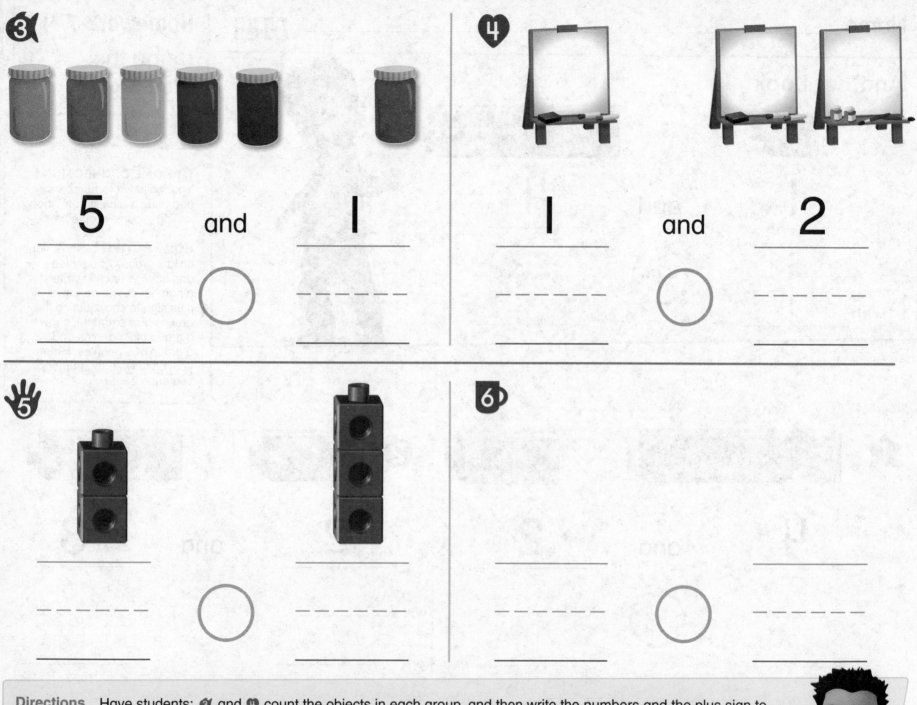

3

5 and 1

_ _ _ _ _ ○ _ _ _ _ _

4

1 and 2

_ _ _ _ _ ○ _ _ _ _ _

5

_ _ _ _ _ ○ _ _ _ _ _

6

_ _ _ _ _ ○ _ _ _ _ _

Directions Have students: **3** and **4** count the objects in each group, and then write the numbers and the plus sign to show joining the groups; **5** count the connecting cubes in each group, and then write the numbers and the plus sign to show joining the groups; **6** draw 2 groups of apples that make 6 apples in all when joined together, and then write the number of apples in each group and the plus sign to show joining the groups.

© Pearson Education, Inc. K

Directions Say: *Daniel counts 4 drums in a parade. Then he sees 1 more drum. What numbers do you add to find how many drums he sees in all? How can you show the adding?*

TEKS K.3A Model the action of joining to represent addition and the action of separating to represent subtraction. Also, **K.3, K.3B. Mathematical Process Standards K.1D, K.1G.**

Digital Resources at PearsonTexas.com

Solve Learn Glossary Check Tools Games

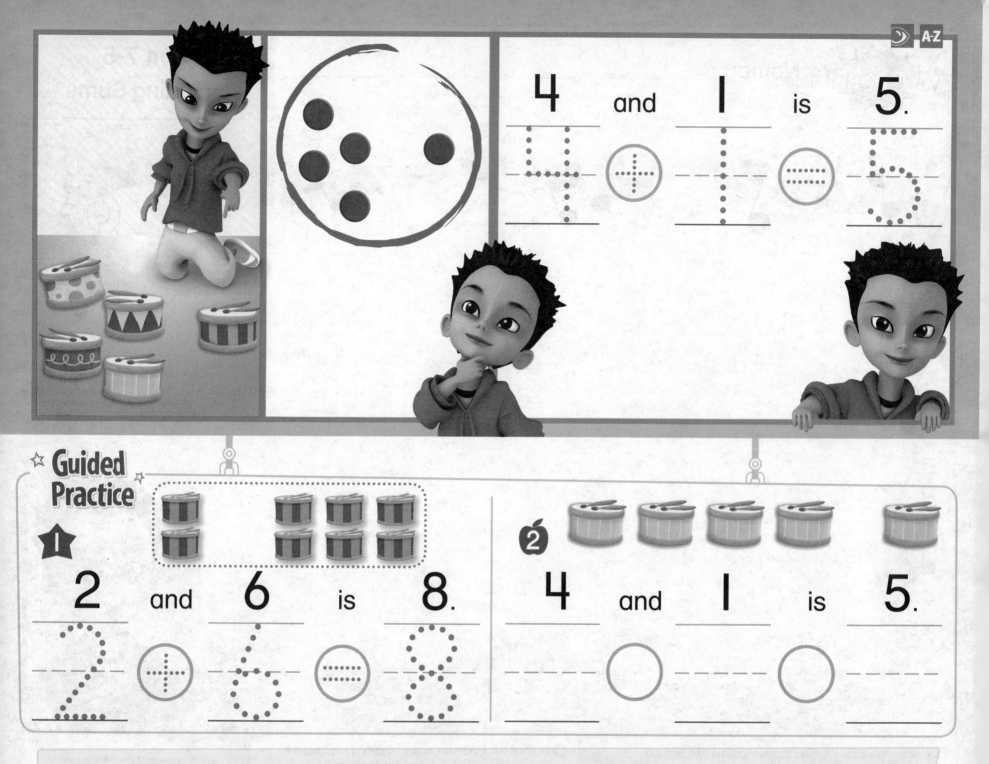

4 and 1 is 5.

Guided Practice

1 2 and 6 is 8.

2 4 and 1 is 5.

Directions Have students use counters to model joining the groups, circle the groups to join them, and then write a number sentence to find the sum.

© Pearson Education, Inc. K

Topic 7 | Lesson 5

Name _____

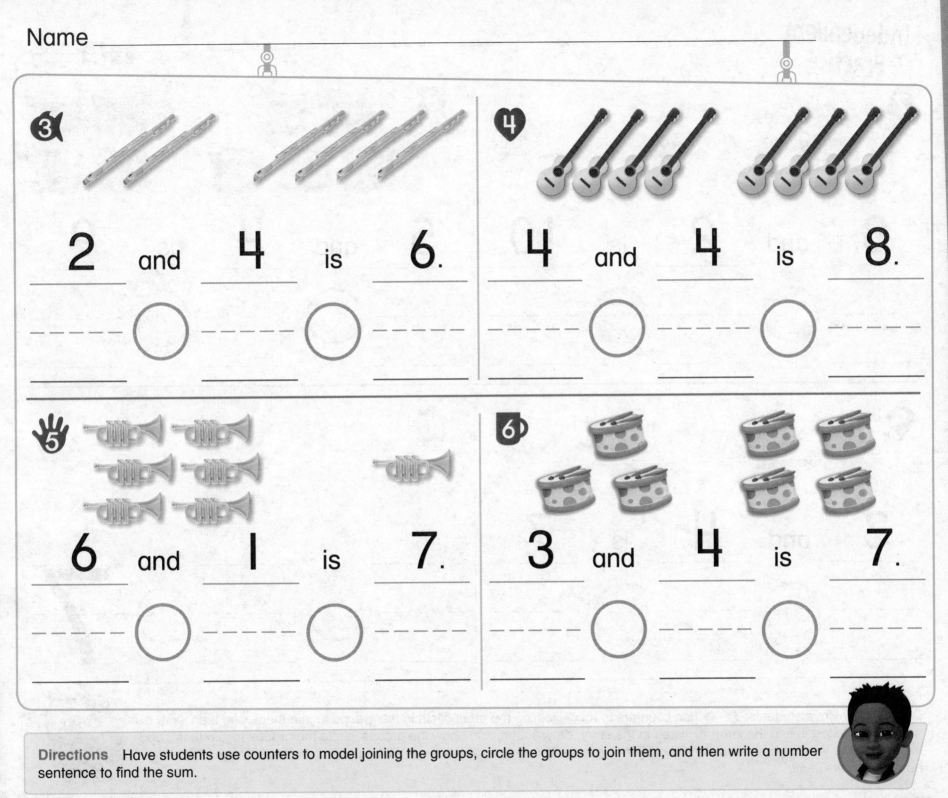

3

2 and 4 is 6.

◯ ◯

4

4 and 4 is 8.

◯ ◯

5

6 and 1 is 7.

◯ ◯

6

3 and 4 is 7.

◯ ◯

Directions Have students use counters to model joining the groups, circle the groups to join them, and then write a number sentence to find the sum.

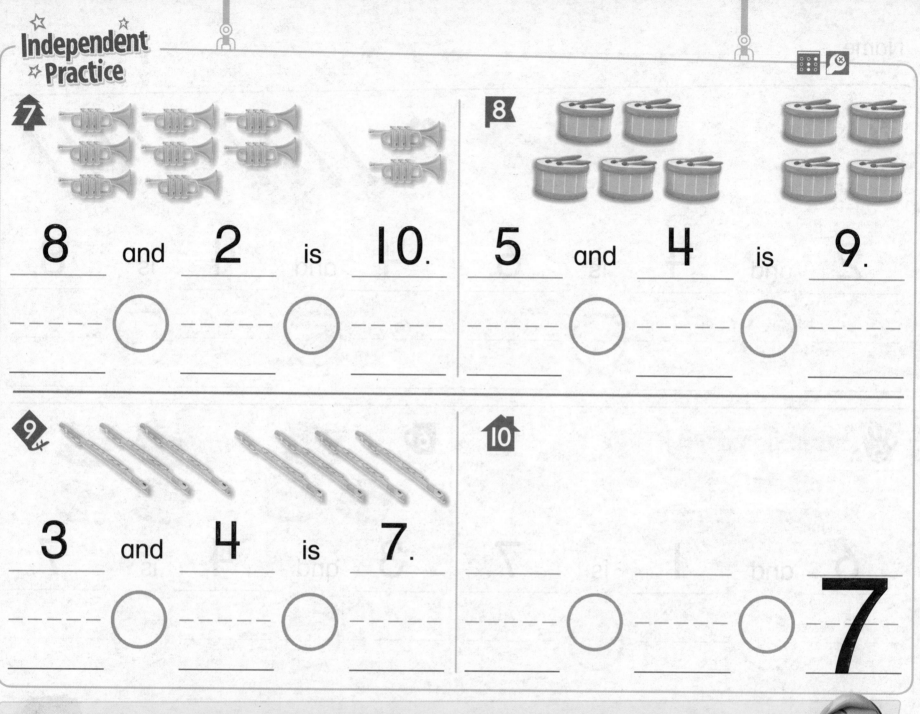

7 8 and 2 is 10.

8 5 and 4 is 9.

9 3 and 4 is 7.

10 7

© Pearson Education, Inc. K

Topic 7 | Lesson 5

Another Look

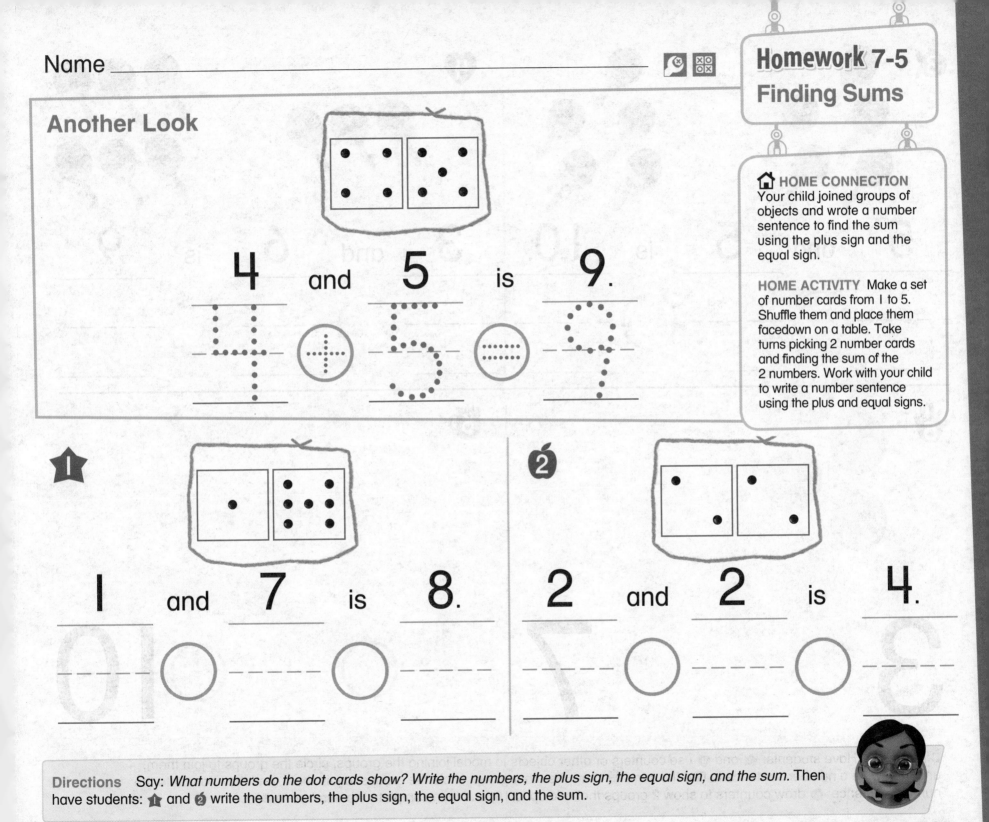

4 and 5 is 9.

🏠 **HOME CONNECTION**
Your child joined groups of objects and wrote a number sentence to find the sum using the plus sign and the equal sign.

HOME ACTIVITY Make a set of number cards from 1 to 5. Shuffle them and place them facedown on a table. Take turns picking 2 number cards and finding the sum of the 2 numbers. Work with your child to write a number sentence using the plus and equal signs.

⭐1

1 and 7 is 8.

🍎2

2 and 2 is 4.

Directions Say: *What numbers do the dot cards show? Write the numbers, the plus sign, the equal sign, and the sum.* Then have students: ⭐ and 🍎 write the numbers, the plus sign, the equal sign, and the sum.

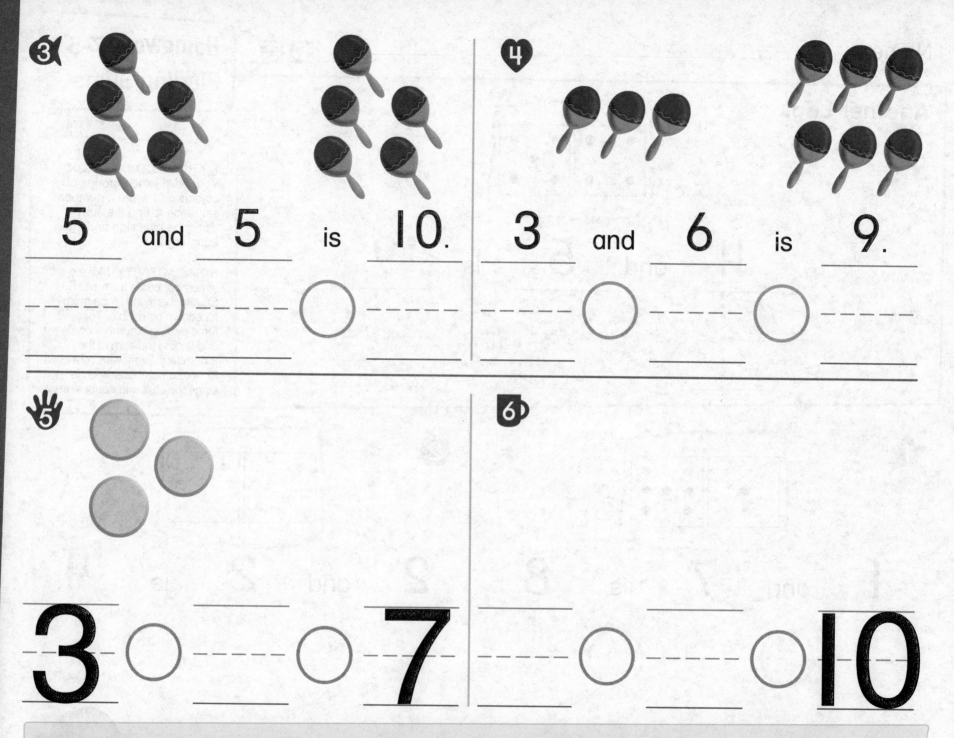

3 5 and 5 is 10.

4 3 and 6 is 9.

5 3 ◯ ─── ◯ 7

6 ◯ ─── ◯ 10

Name _____

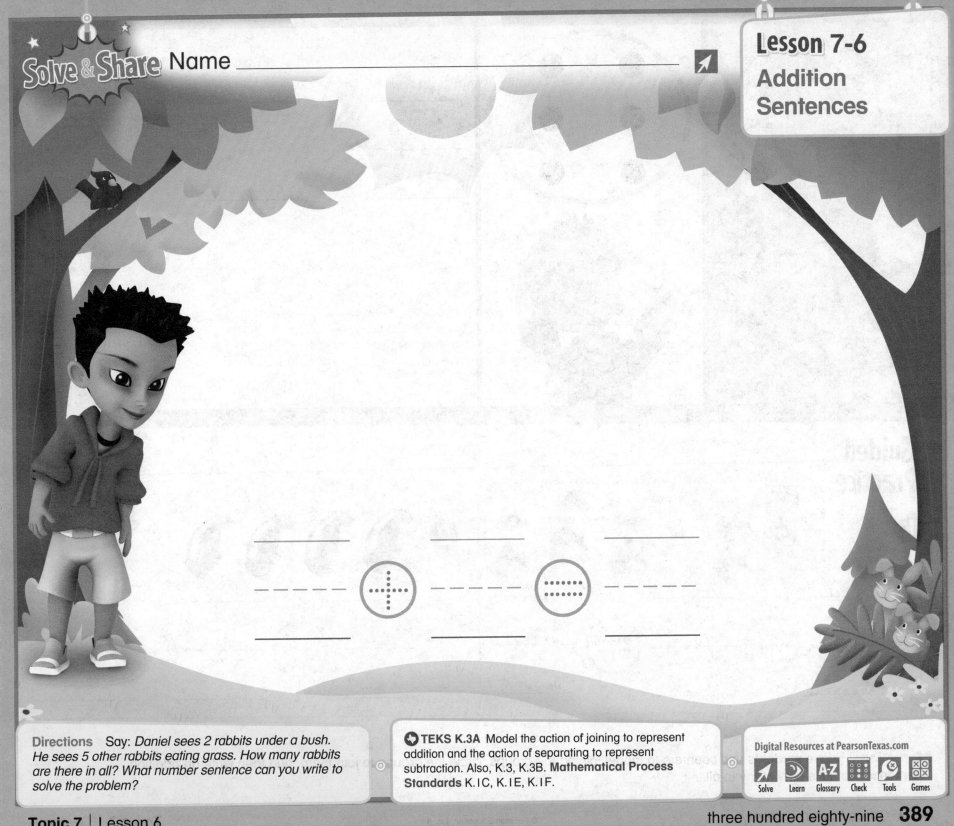

_____ _____ _____

- - - - - - $\oplus$ - - - - - - $\bullet$ - - - - - -

_____ _____ _____

Directions Say: *Daniel sees 2 rabbits under a bush. He sees 5 other rabbits eating grass. How many rabbits are there in all? What number sentence can you write to solve the problem?*

TEKS K.3A Model the action of joining to represent addition and the action of separating to represent subtraction. Also, K.3, K.3B. **Mathematical Process Standards** K.1C, K.1E, K.1F.

Digital Resources at PearsonTexas.com

Solve   Learn   Glossary   Check   Tools   Games

Guided Practice

1

2 + 3 = 5

2

◯ ◯

Directions Have students use counters to model joining the groups, circle the groups to join them, and then write an addition sentence that tells how many in all.

© Pearson Education, Inc. K

Topic 7 | Lesson 6

Name _____

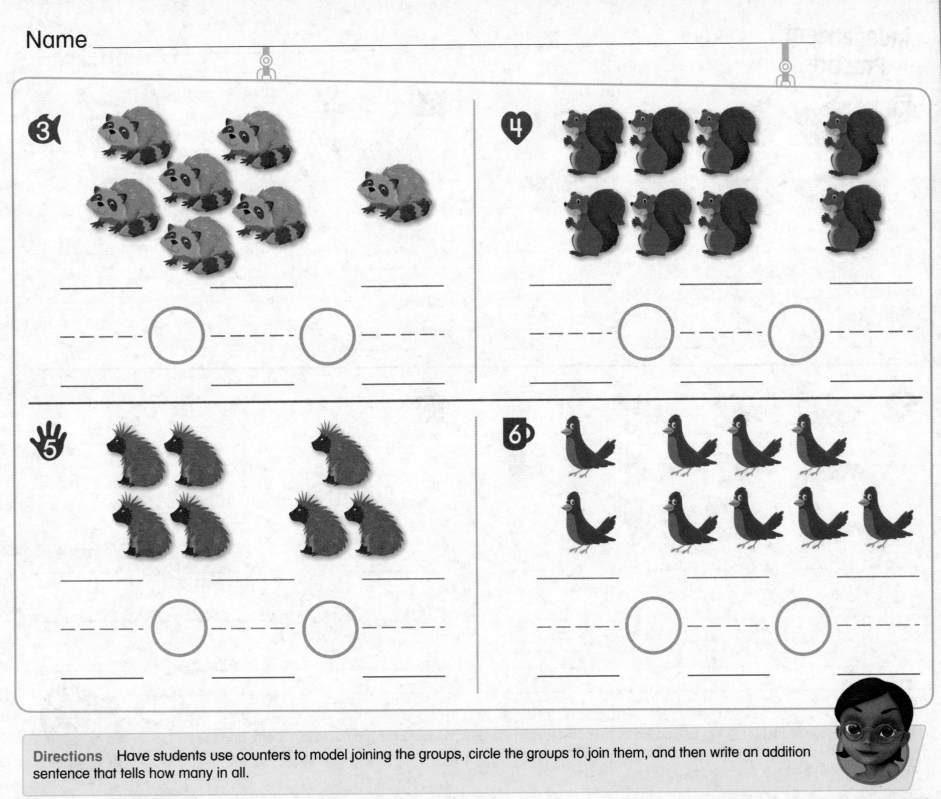

3

_____ _____
( ) — ( )
_____

4

_____ _____
( ) — ( )
_____

5

_____ _____
( ) — ( )
_____

6

_____ _____
( ) — ( )
_____

Directions Have students use counters to model joining the groups, circle the groups to join them, and then write an addition sentence that tells how many in all.

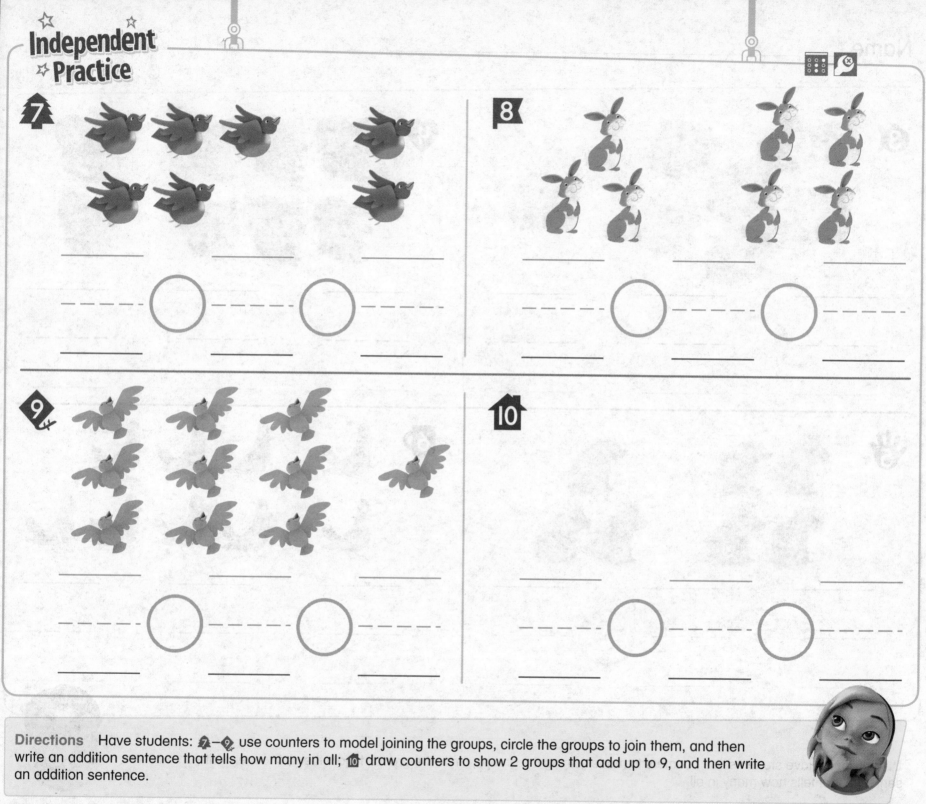

7

_____ ◯ _____
_____   _____

8

_____ ◯ _____
_____   _____

9

_____ ◯ _____
_____   _____

10

_____ ◯ _____
_____   _____

Directions   Have students: **7–9** use counters to model joining the groups, circle the groups to join them, and then write an addition sentence that tells how many in all; **10** draw counters to show 2 groups that add up to 9, and then write an addition sentence.

Topic 7 | Lesson 6

Another Look

$$4 \; \oplus \; 3 \; = \; 7$$

🏠 **HOME CONNECTION**
Your child joined groups of objects. He or she wrote plus signs, equal signs, and sums to complete addition sentences.

HOME ACTIVITY Make 2 groups of pennies and have your child write an addition sentence that shows joining the groups together. For example, show a group of 5 pennies and a group of 4 pennies, and help your child write $5 + 4 = 9$.

⭐ 1

② 2

Directions Say: *Make a group of 4 connecting cubes or other objects and a group of 3 connecting cubes or other objects. Now join the groups together to find out how many there are in all. Write the numbers, plus sign, equal sign, and sum to make the addition sentence.* Then have students: ⭐ and ② use cubes or other objects to model joining the groups, write the numbers that tell how many in each group, and then write the plus sign, the equal sign, and the sum to complete each addition sentence.

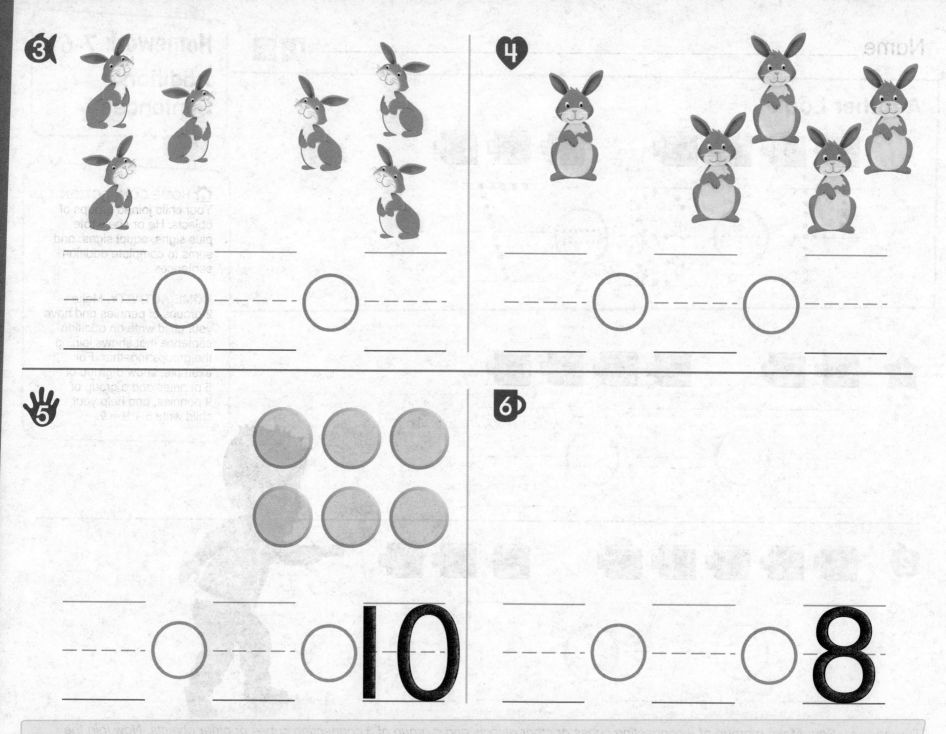

3 ◯ _ _ _ _ _ ◯ _ _ _ _ _

4 _ _ _ ◯ _ _ _ ◯ _ _ _

5 ◯ _ _ _ _ _ ◯ 10

6 ◯ _ _ _ _ _ ◯ 8

Directions Have students: **3** and **4** circle the groups to join them, and then write an addition sentence to tell how many in all; **5** draw the other group, circle the groups to join them, and then complete the addition sentence; **6** draw counters to show 2 groups that add up to 8, and then complete the addition sentence.

Directions Say: *Daniel's teacher is making name tags for her students. She made 3 name tags in the morning. She made 2 more in the afternoon. Now she has 5 name tags. How does Daniel's teacher know that she has made 5 name tags? Explain and then show how you know.*

⭐ **TEKS K.1G** Display, explain, and justify mathematical ideas and arguments . . . .
TEKS K.3C Explain the strategies used to solve problems involving adding . . . . Also, K.3. **Mathematical Process Standards** K.1C, K.1D, K.1F.

Digital Resources at PearsonTexas.com

Solve Learn Glossary Check Tools Games

7 in all.

4

3

4 ... 5 6 7

7 in all.

$4 + 3 = 7$

☆ Guided Practice

1

2 + 4 = 6

Directions Have students listen to the story, draw a picture to show what is happening, and then write an addition sentence. Then have them explain their work aloud. Say: *Daniel put 2 red crayons and 4 blue crayons on the table. Now there are 6 crayons in all. How can Daniel tell there are 6 crayons?*

© Pearson Education, Inc. K
Topic 7 | Lesson 7

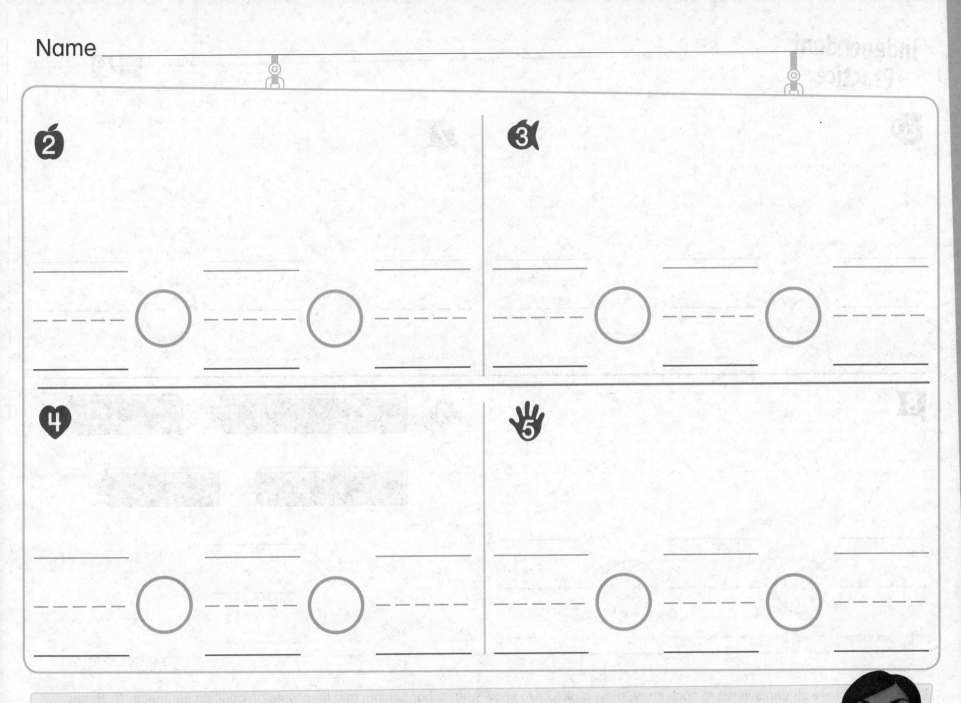

2

3

4

5

6️⃣

– – – – – ◯ – – – – ◯ – – – – –

7️⃣

– – – – – ◯ – – – – ◯ – – – – –

8️⃣

– – – – ◯ – – – – ◯ – – – –

9️⃣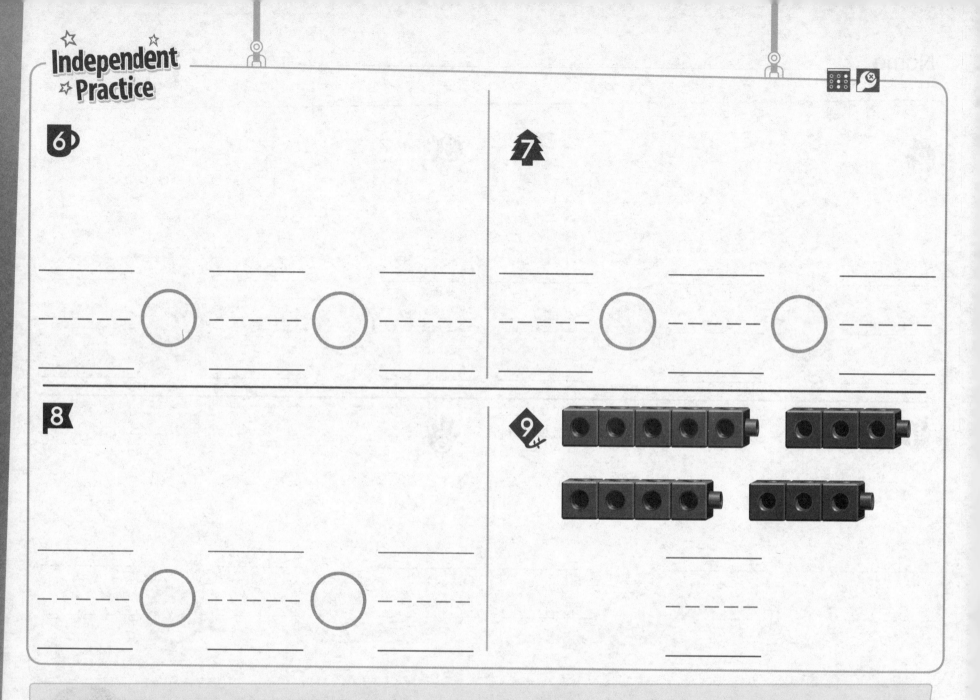

– – – – –

Directions Have students listen to each story, draw a picture to show what is happening, and then write an addition sentence. 6️⃣ *Benny puts 5 bananas in a bowl and 4 bananas on a plate. How many bananas does he have in all?* 7️⃣ *Kris eats 2 grapes at lunch and 6 grapes for her snack. How many grapes does she eat in all?* 8️⃣ *4 girls ride on a train. 2 boys join them. How many children are there in all?* Then have students: 9️⃣ listen to the story, circle the connecting cubes that show the story and tell why the other cubes do not show the story, and then write the number that tells how many in all. Say: *Jimmy picks 5 raspberries. Then he picks 3 more. How many raspberries does he have in all?*

© Pearson Education, Inc. K
Topic 7 | Lesson 7

Name _____

Another Look

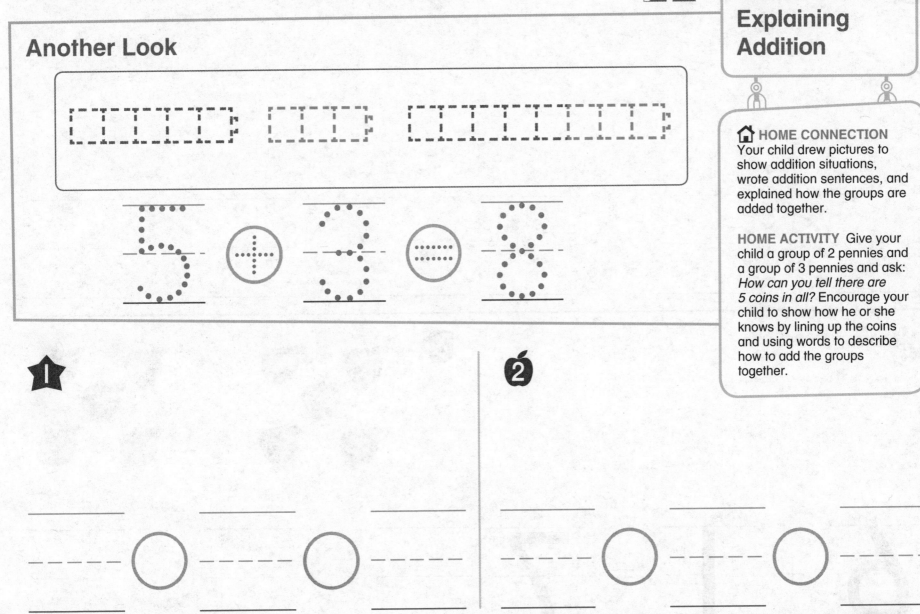

🏠 **HOME CONNECTION**
Your child drew pictures to show addition situations, wrote addition sentences, and explained how the groups are added together.

HOME ACTIVITY Give your child a group of 2 pennies and a group of 3 pennies and ask: *How can you tell there are 5 coins in all?* Encourage your child to show how he or she knows by lining up the coins and using words to describe how to add the groups together.

★ 1

🍎 2

Directions Say: *How can you explain the addition sentence* 5 + 3 = 8? Guide students to connect cubes or join other objects to model the addition. Encourage students to explain their thinking aloud. Then have students listen to each story, draw a picture to show what is happening, and then write an addition sentence. ★ *There are 2 cherries on a plate and 3 cherries in a bowl. How many cherries are there in all?* ② *There are 4 apples on the counter and 6 apples in a bag. How many apples are there in all?*

3 〇 〇

4 〇 〇

5 6 + 1 = 7

6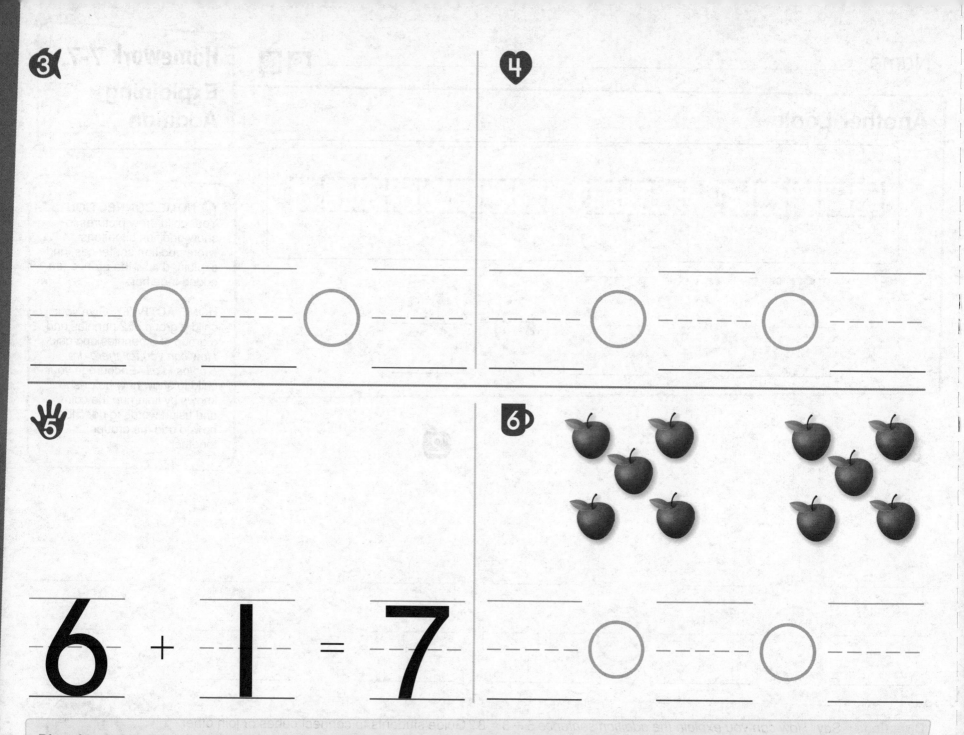

〇 〇

Directions Have students listen to each story, draw a picture to show what is happening, and then write an addition sentence. **3** *3 cardinals sit in a tree. 5 robins join them. How many birds are there in all?* **4** *4 rabbits look for food by the tree. 4 squirrels join them. How many animals are there in all?* Then have students: **5** tell a number story that matches the addition sentence, and then draw a picture to show what is happening; **6** tell a number story about the groups of apples, and then write an addition sentence that tells how many in all.

_____

- - - - - - - - - - -

_____

Directions Say: *Daniel sees a group of 3 fluffy, white clouds in the sky. Marta sees 1 other cloud. How many clouds do they see in all? Draw a picture to show what is happening, and then write the number that tells how many clouds in all.*

⭐**TEKS K.1D** Communicate mathematical ideas, reasoning, and their implications using multiple representations, including symbols, diagrams, graphs, and language as appropriate. Also, K.3, K.3A, K.3B. **Mathematical Process Standards** K.1A, K.1B, K.1F, K.1G.

Digital Resources at PearsonTexas.com

Solve Learn Glossary Check Tools Games

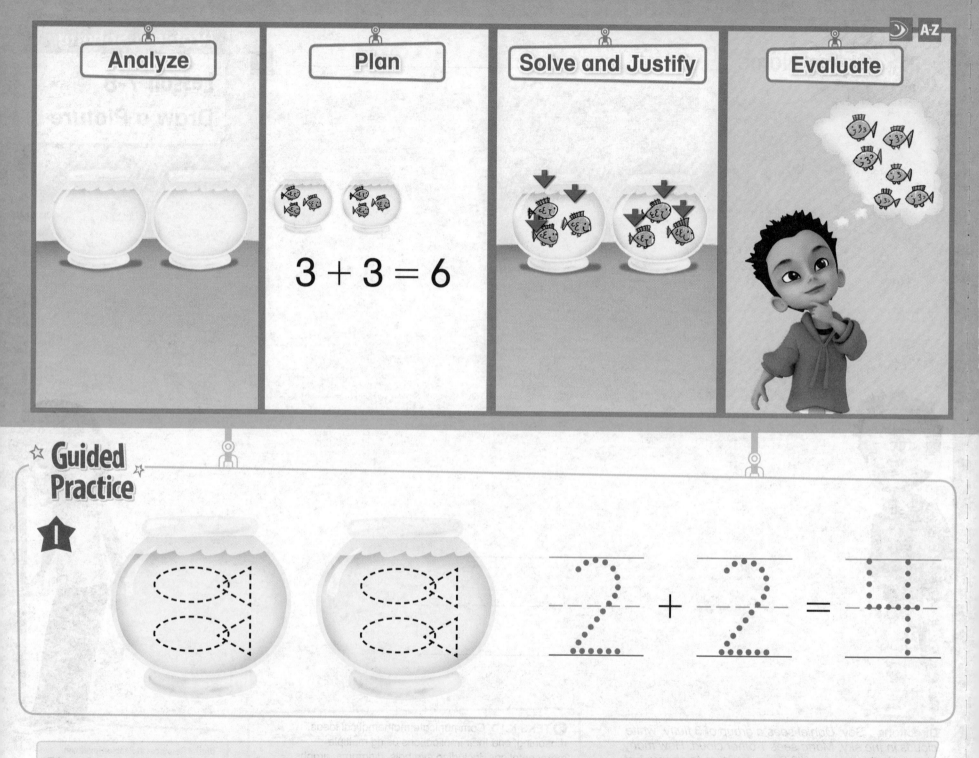

Analyze

Plan

$3 + 3 = 6$

Solve and Justify

Evaluate

☆ **Guided Practice** ☆

1

$2 + 2 = 4$

Directions Have students listen to the story, draw a picture to show what is happening, and then write an addition sentence.
Say: *Danny sees 2 fish in one bowl and 2 fish in another bowl. How many fish does he see in all?*

Topic 7 | **Lesson 8**

Name _____

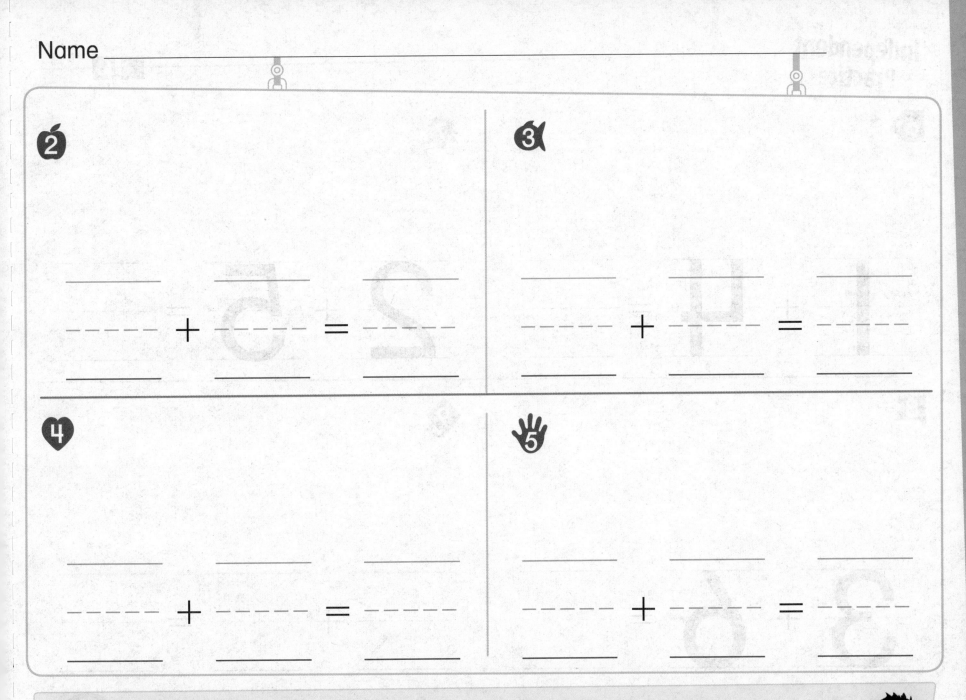

2

_____ + _____ = _____

3

_____ + _____ = _____

4

_____ + _____ = _____

5

_____ + _____ = _____

Directions Have students listen to each story, draw a picture to show what is happening, and then write an addition sentence. **2** *Julie sees 5 stones in one pail and 3 stones in another pail. How many stones does she see in all?* **3** *A hen laid 2 eggs one day and 3 eggs the next day. How many eggs did she lay in all?* **4** *Maria threw 5 baseballs in one inning and 2 in the next inning. How many baseballs did she throw in all?* **5** *Zak scored 2 goals playing soccer, and then he scored 4 more goals. How many goals did he score in all?*

6 $1 + 4 =$ _____

7 $2 + 5 =$ _____

8 $3 + 6 =$ _____

9 _____ $+$ _____ $=$ _____

Directions Have students: **6**–**8** draw counters to show each group, and then write the sum. Then have students: **9** listen to the story, draw counters to show what is happening, and then complete the addition sentence. Say: *Some balls were on the playground, and then 3 more balls were left there. Now there are 8 balls in all. How many were on the playground before?*

© Pearson Education, Inc. K

Topic 7 | Lesson 8

Another Look

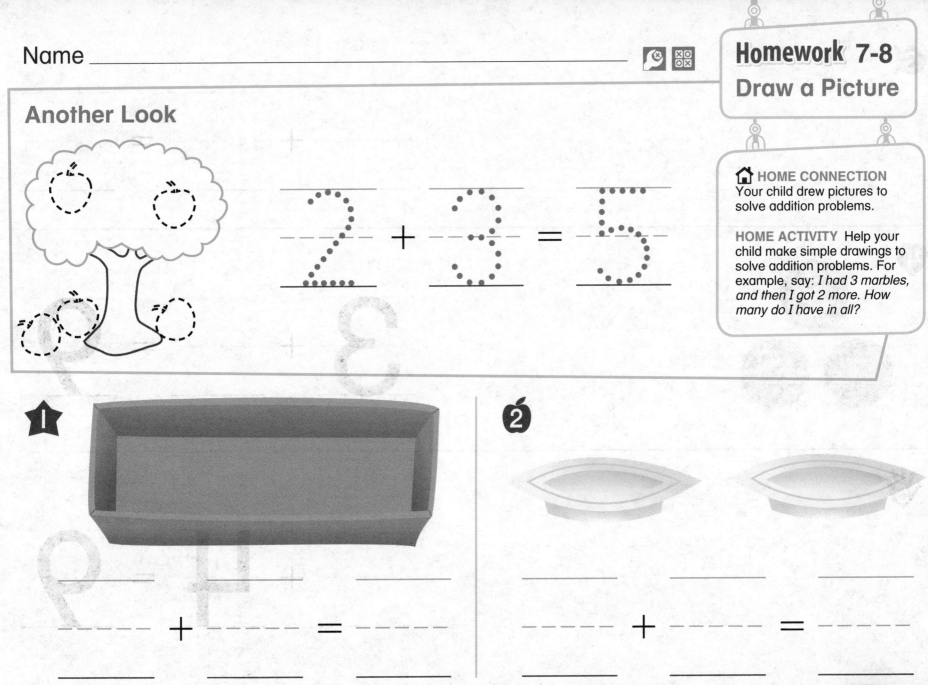

2 + 3 = 5

⭐①

___ + ___ = ___

②

___ + ___ = ___

Directions Say: *Marta found 2 apples on a tree. Then she found 3 more on the ground. How many apples did Marta find in all? Draw the apples, count the apples to find out how many in all, and then write an addition sentence.* Then have students listen to each story, draw a picture to show what is happening, and then write an addition sentence. ⭐① *There are 4 balls in the box. Pete puts 1 more ball in the box. How many balls are there in all?* ② *Maria has 3 oranges on a plate. Chris has 3 oranges on a plate. How many oranges do Maria and Chris have in all?*

3

___ ___ ___

___ + ___ = ___

___ ___ ___

4

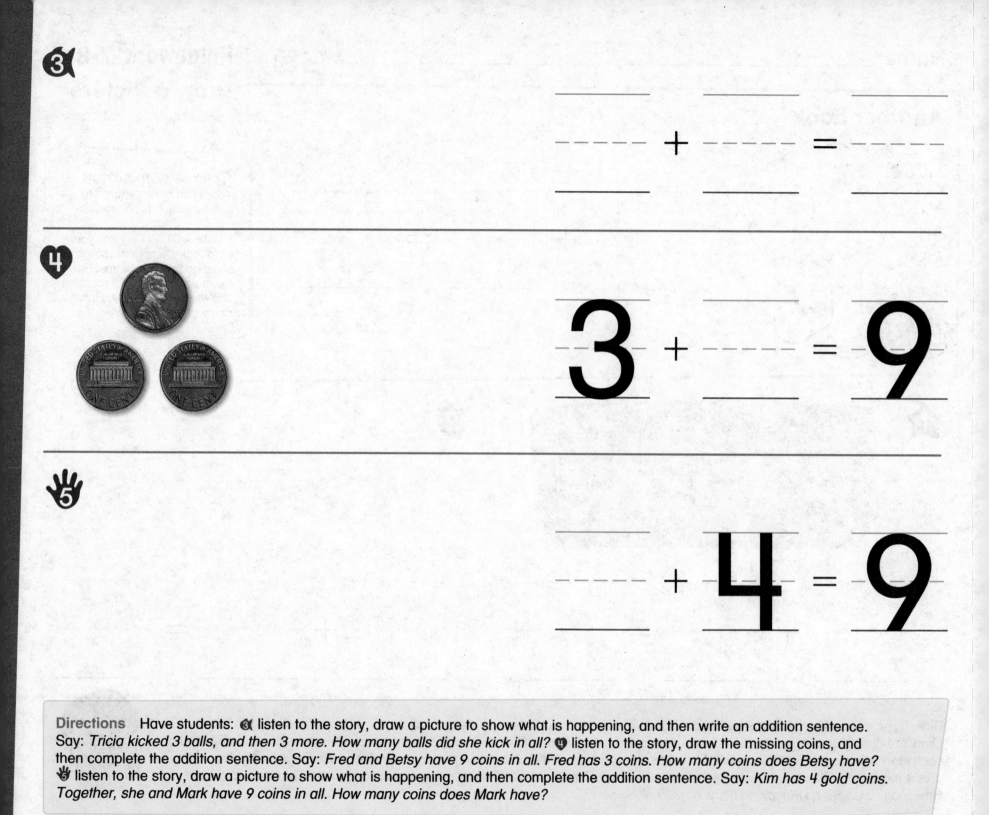

$3 + $ ___ $ = 9$

5

___ $ + 4 = 9$

Directions Have students: **3** listen to the story, draw a picture to show what is happening, and then write an addition sentence. Say: *Tricia kicked 3 balls, and then 3 more. How many balls did she kick in all?* **4** listen to the story, draw the missing coins, and then complete the addition sentence. Say: *Fred and Betsy have 9 coins in all. Fred has 3 coins. How many coins does Betsy have?* **5** listen to the story, draw a picture to show what is happening, and then complete the addition sentence. Say: *Kim has 4 gold coins. Together, she and Mark have 9 coins in all. How many coins does Mark have?*

Name _____

Set A _____

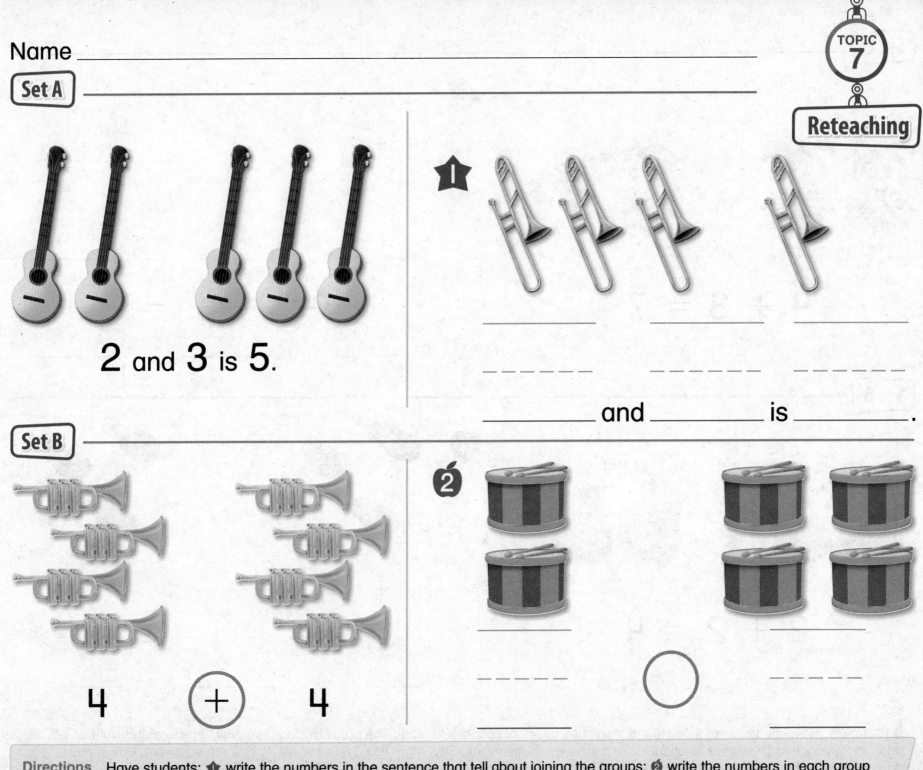

2 and 3 is 5.

⭐

_____ _____ _____

_ _ _ _ _   _ _ _ _ _   _ _ _ _ _

_____ and _____ is _____.

Set B

❷

4 ⊕ 4

_____   _____

_ _ _ _ _   ◯   _ _ _ _ _

_____   _____

Directions Have students: ⭐ write the numbers in the sentence that tell about joining the groups; ❷ write the numbers in each group and then write the plus sign to show joining the groups.

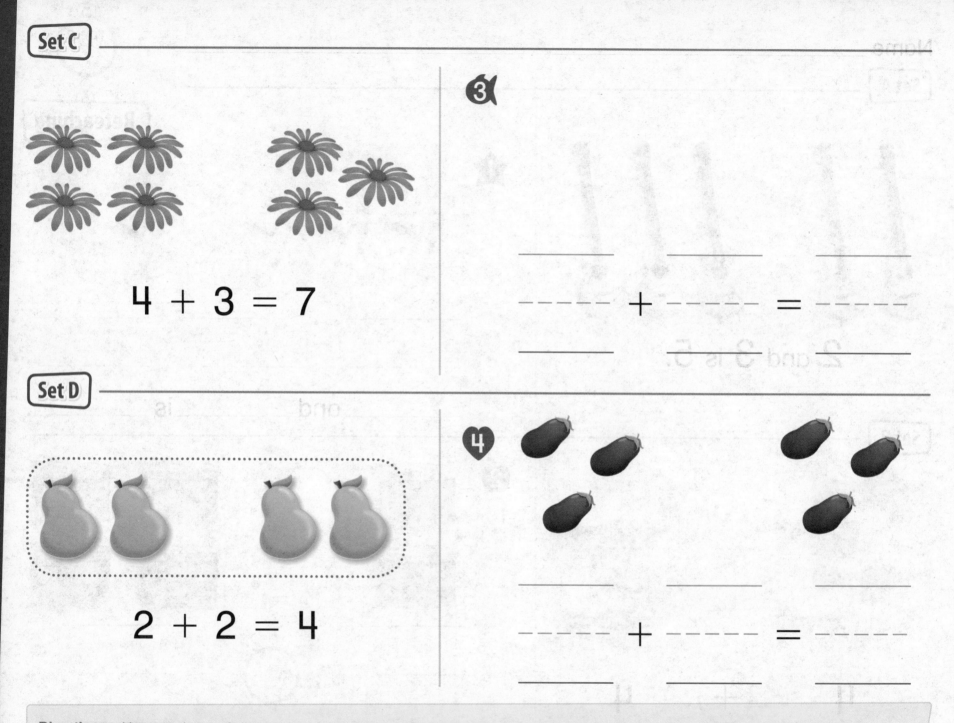

Set C

$$4 + 3 = 7$$

❸

_____ + _____ = _____

Set D

$$2 + 2 = 4$$

❹

_____ + _____ = _____

Directions Have students: ❸ listen to the story, use cubes or counters to model the problem, and then draw a picture and write an addition sentence to show their solution. Have them explain their work. Say: *Mark has 3 flowers. He picks 2 more flowers. How many flowers does he have in all?* ❹ use counters to model joining the groups, circle the groups to join them, write an addition sentence that tells how many in all, and then explain their work.

Name _____

1

1 in all.
○

4 in all.
○

6 in all.
○

8 in all.
○

2

1 and 4 is 5.
1 + 4 = 5
○

1 and 6 is 7.
1 + 6 = 7
○

1 and 5 is 6.
1 + 5 = 6
○

1 and 3 is 4.
1 + 3 = 4
○

3

2 and 2 is 4.
○

2 and 4 is 6.
○

2 and 6 is 8.
○

2 and 5 is 7.
○

4

3 + 4
○

3 + 1
○

4 + 0
○

4 + 1
○

Directions Have students mark the best answer. **1** *Jen puts 2 teddy bears on her bed. Then she puts 2 more teddy bears on her bed. How many teddy bears did she put on her bed in all?* Which tells how many in all? **2** *Tanya sees 1 scarecrow and then she sees 3 more. How many scarecrows does Tanya see in all?* Which number sentence tells the story? **3** Which sentence tells about joining the groups of tambourines? **4** Which tells about the picture?

Topic 7

four hundred nine **409**

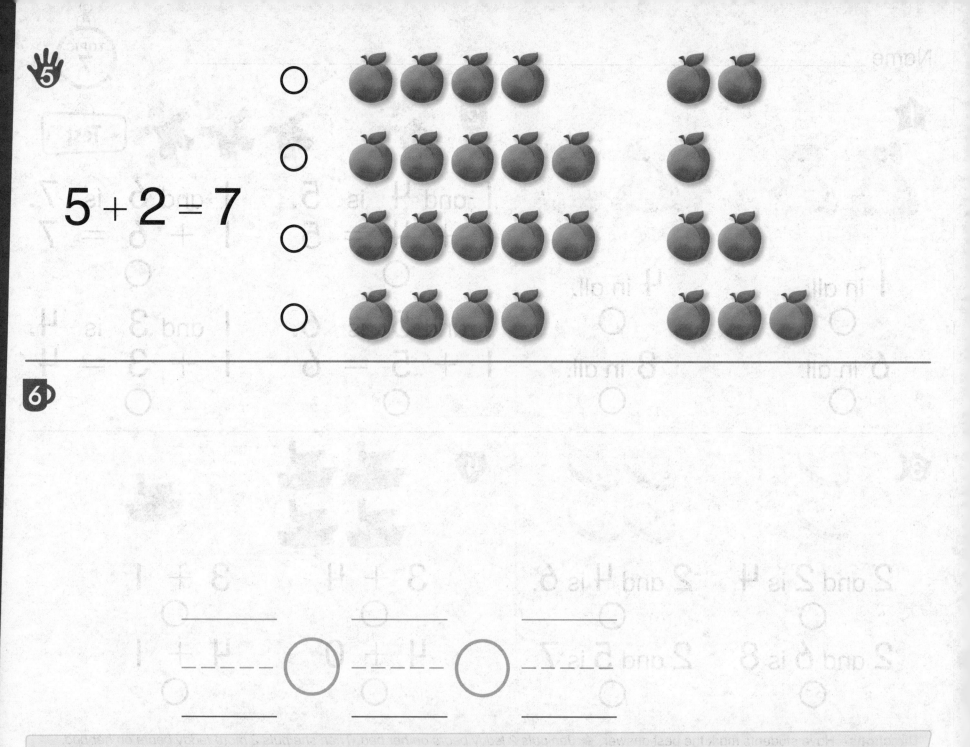

$5 + 2 = 7$

Directions Have students: ✋ mark the best answer. Which picture matches the addition sentence? ☕ listen to the story, use and then draw counters to show what is happening, and then write an addition sentence. Say: *There are 6 bunnies in a garden and 3 bunnies outside of the garden. How many bunnies are there in all?*

410 four hundred ten
© Pearson Education, Inc. K
Topic 7

Understanding Subtraction

Essential Question: What types of situations involve subtraction?

Math and Science Project: Magnets

Directions Read the character speech bubbles to students. **Find Out!** Have students find out about magnets and how they work with various materials. Say: *Talk to friends and relatives about magnets. Ask what types of things magnets attract.* **Journal: Make a Poster** Then have students make a poster. Have them draw a group of 5 paper clips, draw a magnet taking away 3 of the paper clips, and then tell a story about separating. Then have them write the number of paper clips that are left.

Name _____

Review What You Know

1 $3 + 6 = 9$

2 $4 + 1 = 5$

3 $2 + 5 = 7$

4

_____ _____ _____

_ _ _ _ _ _ + _ _ _ _ = _ _ _ _ _

_____ _____ _____

5

_____ _____ _____

_ _ _ _ _ _ + _ _ _ _ = _ _ _ _ _

_____ _____ _____

6

_____ _____ _____

_ _ _ _ _ _ + _ _ _ _ = _ _ _ _ _

_____ _____ _____

Directions Have students: **1** circle the plus sign; **2** circle the equal sign; **3** circle the sum; **4**–**6** count the objects in each group, and then write a number sentence that tells how many in all.

412 four hundred twelve   © Pearson Education, Inc. K   **Topic 8**

My Word Cards
Directions Have students cut out the vocabulary cards. Read the front of the card, and then ask them to explain what the word or phrase means.

A-Z

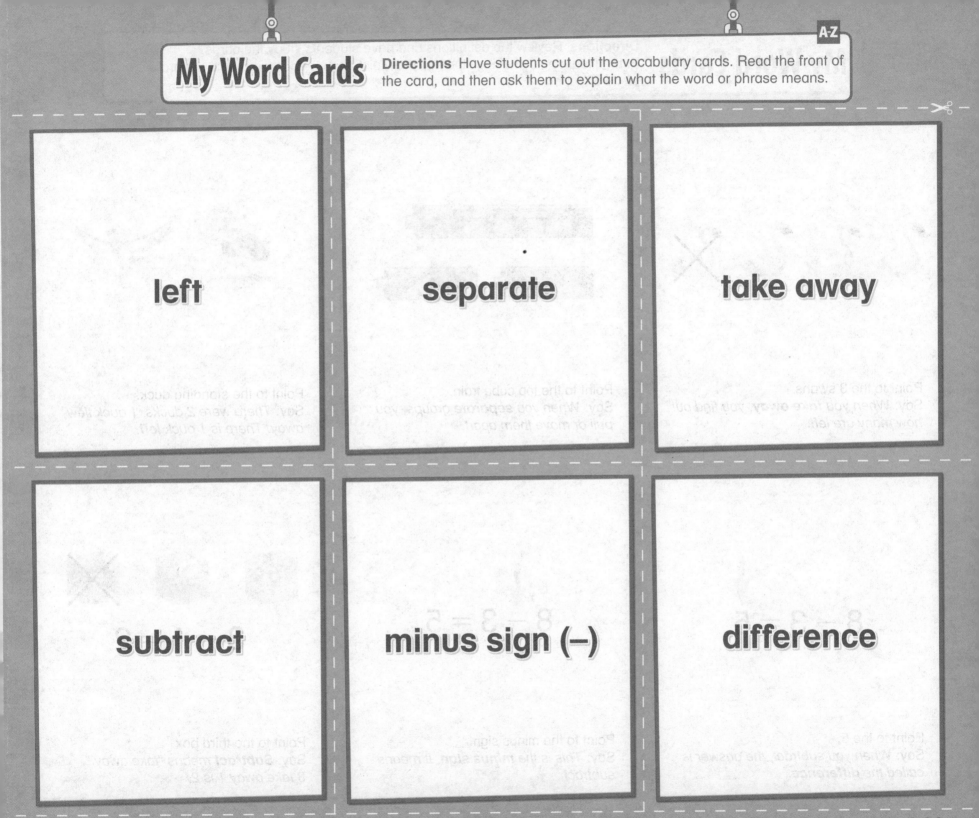

left

separate

take away

subtract

minus sign (−)

difference

My Word Cards

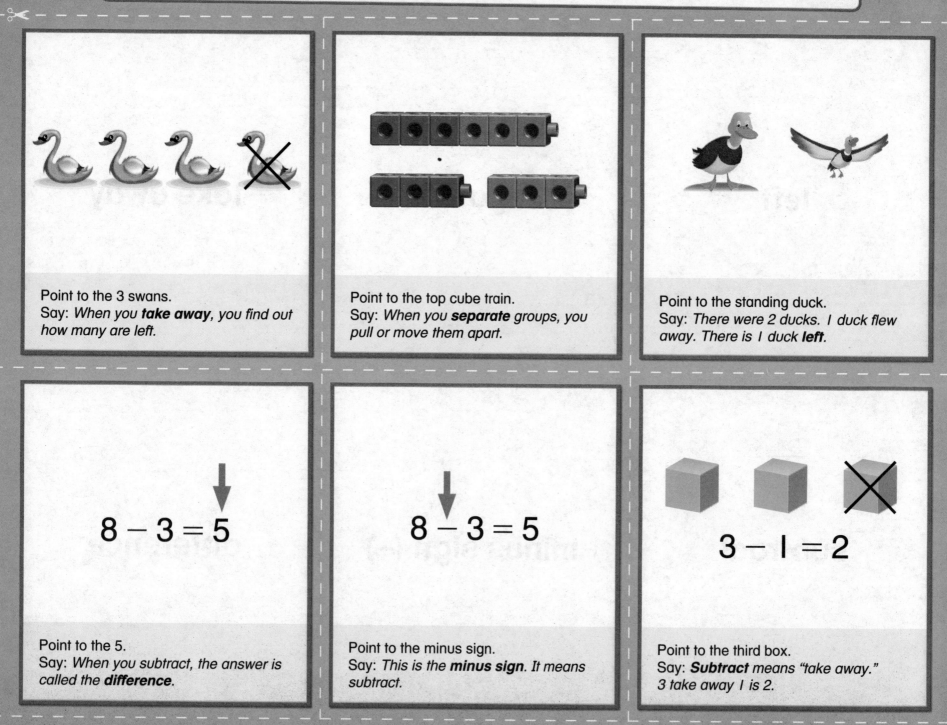

Point to the 3 swans.
Say: *When you **take away**, you find out how many are left.*

Point to the top cube train.
Say: *When you **separate** groups, you pull or move them apart.*

Point to the standing duck.
Say: *There were 2 ducks. 1 duck flew away. There is 1 duck **left**.*

$$8 - 3 = 5$$

Point to the 5.
Say: *When you subtract, the answer is called the **difference**.*

$$8 - 3 = 5$$

Point to the minus sign.
Say: *This is the **minus sign**. It means subtract.*

$$3 - 1 = 2$$

Point to the third box.
Say: ***Subtract** means "take away." 3 take away 1 is 2.*

My Word Cards

Directions Have students cut out the vocabulary cards. Read the front of the card, and then ask them to explain what the word or phrase means.

A-Z

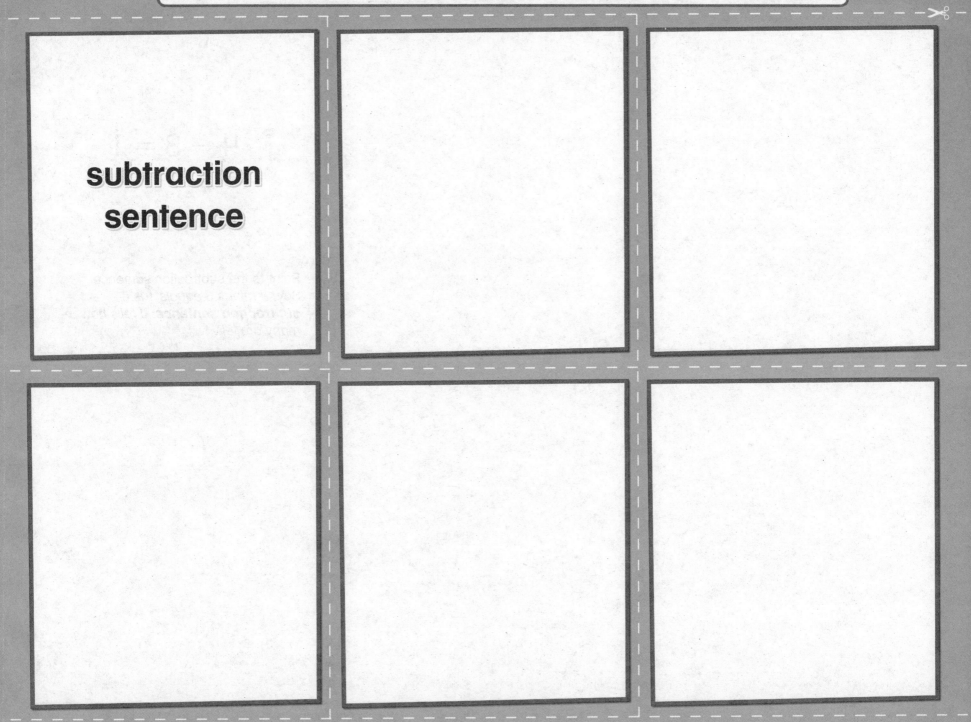

subtraction sentence

My Word Cards

Directions Review the definitions and have students study the cards. Extend learning by having students draw pictures for each word on a separate piece of paper.

$$4 - 3 = 1$$

Point to the subtraction sentence. Say: *4 minus 3 equals 1 is a* **subtraction sentence**. *It tells how many are left.*

© Pearson Education, Inc. K

_____

_ _ _ _ _ are left.

Directions Say: *Marta is watching bugs. She sees 4 ladybugs. Then 2 ladybugs crawl away. How can you find out how many ladybugs are left?*

⭐ **TEKS K.3B** Solve word problems using objects and drawings to find sums up to 10 and differences within 10. Also, K.3, K.3A. **Mathematical Process Standards** K.1D, K.1F, K.1G.

Digital Resources at PearsonTexas.com
Solve   Learn   Glossary   Check   Tools   Games

2 are left.

☆ Guided Practice ☆

1 _____ are left.

2 _____ are left.

Directions Have students listen to each story, count how many bugs are left, and then write the number that tells how many. **1** Marta sees 6 bumblebees. 3 bumblebees leave. How many bumblebees are left? **2** Marta sees 7 ladybugs. 2 ladybugs leave. How many ladybugs are left?

© Pearson Education, Inc. K

Topic 8 | Lesson 1

Name _____

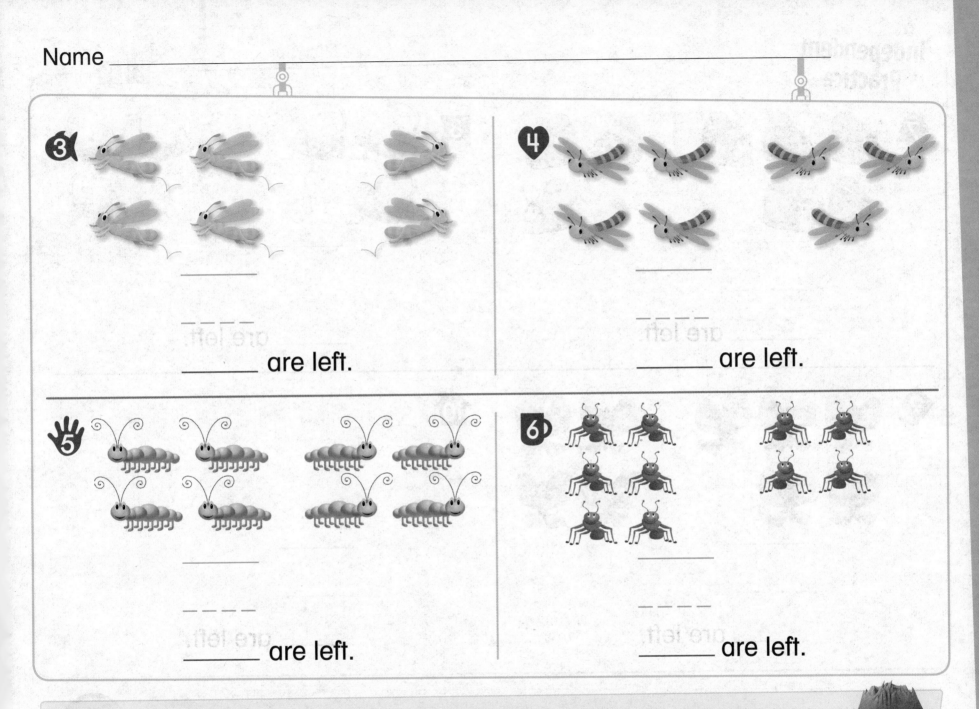

3 _____ are left.

4 _____ are left.

5 _____ are left.

6 _____ are left.

Directions Have students listen to each story, count how many bugs are left, and then write the number that tells how many. **3** *Alex sees 6 grasshoppers on the table. 2 grasshoppers hop away. How many grasshoppers are left?* **4** *Alex sees 7 dragonflies. 3 dragonflies fly away. How many dragonflies are left?* **5** *Alex sees 8 caterpillars resting on a branch. 4 caterpillars crawl away. How many caterpillars are left?* **6** *Alex sees 10 ants on a picnic blanket. 4 ants walk away. How many ants are left?*

7

_____

_ _ _ _

_____ are left.

8

_____

_ _ _ _

_____ are left.

9

_____

_ _ _ _

_____ are left.

10

_____

_ _ _ _

_____ are left.

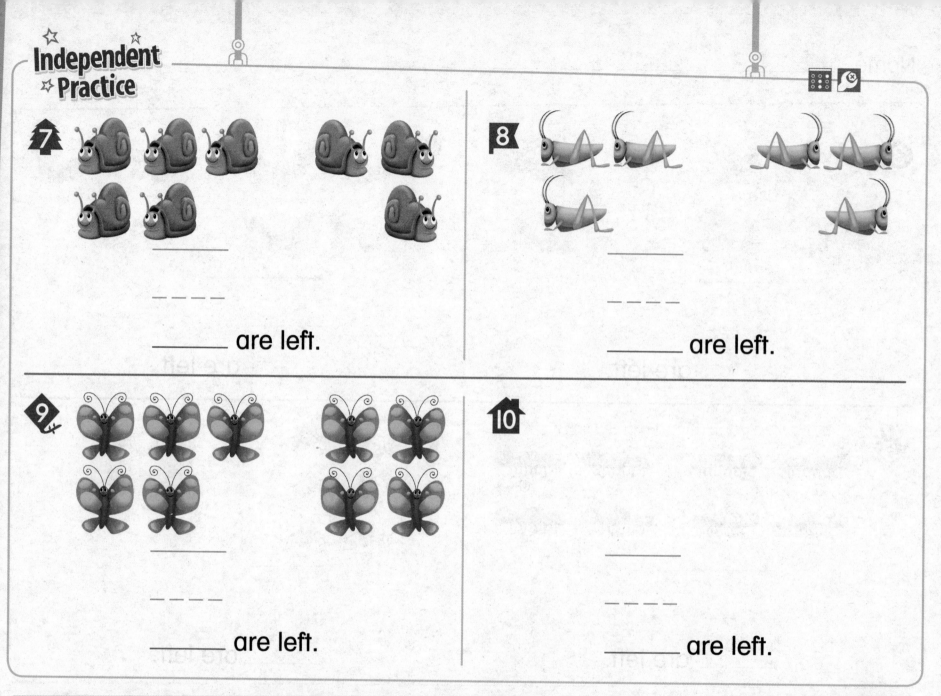

Directions Have students listen to each story, count how many are left, and then write the number that tells how many.
7 Emily sees 8 snails on the sidewalk. 3 snails slink away. How many snails are left? **8** Emily sees 6 grasshoppers in the grass. 3 grasshoppers hop away. How many grasshoppers are left? **9** Emily sees 9 butterflies in the garden. 4 butterflies flutter away. How many butterflies are left? Then have students: **10** listen to the story, draw a picture to show the story, and then write the number that tells how many are left. Emily sees 7 inchworms on a tree. 4 inchworms crawl away. How many inchworms are left?

Topic 8 | Lesson 1

Name _____

Another Look

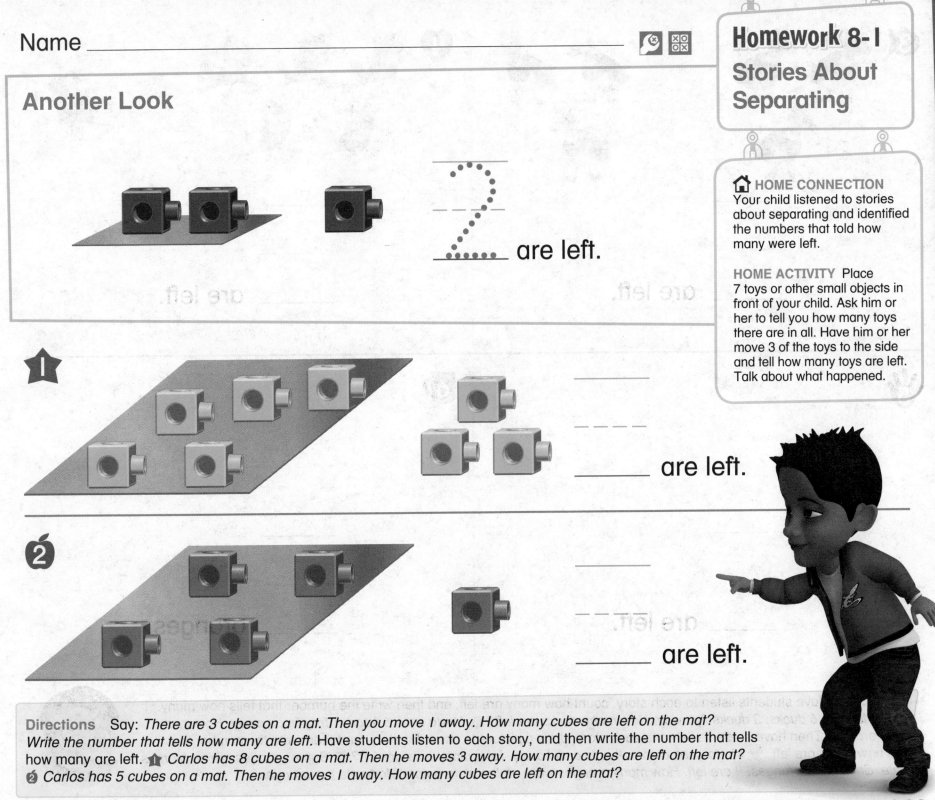

2 are left.

🏠 HOME CONNECTION
Your child listened to stories about separating and identified the numbers that told how many were left.

HOME ACTIVITY Place 7 toys or other small objects in front of your child. Ask him or her to tell you how many toys there are in all. Have him or her move 3 of the toys to the side and tell how many toys are left. Talk about what happened.

⭐ 1

_____ are left.

🍎 2

_____ are left.

Directions Say: *There are 3 cubes on a mat. Then you move 1 away. How many cubes are left on the mat?*
Write the number that tells how many are left. Have students listen to each story, and then write the number that tells
how many are left. ⭐ *Carlos has 8 cubes on a mat. Then he moves 3 away. How many cubes are left on the mat?*
🍎 *Carlos has 5 cubes on a mat. Then he moves 1 away. How many cubes are left on the mat?*

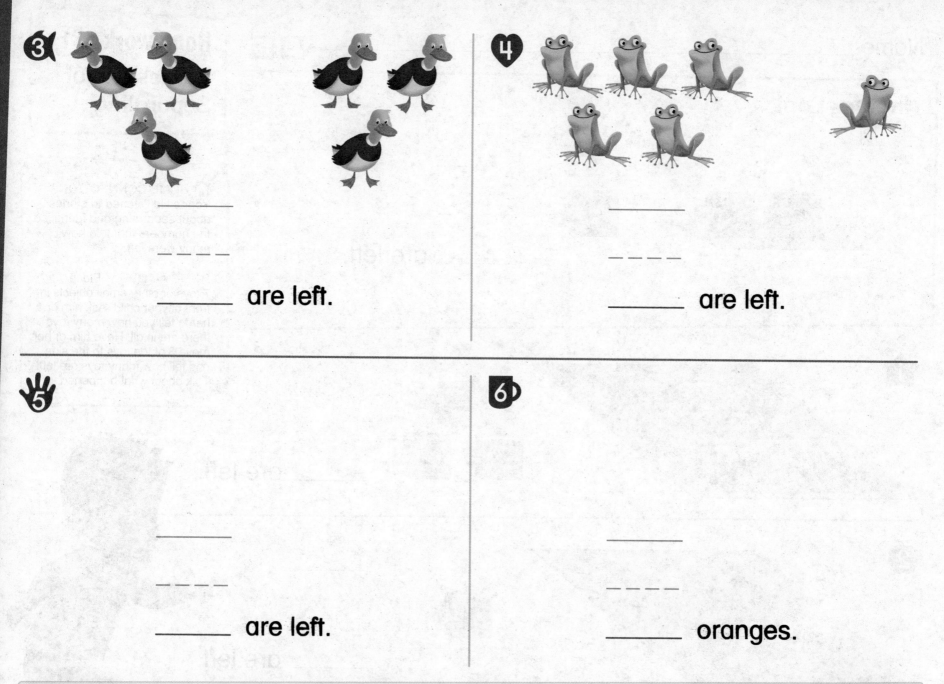

3

_____

_ _ _ _

_____ are left.

4

_____

_ _ _ _

_____ are left.

5

_____

_ _ _ _

_____ are left.

6

_____

_ _ _ _

_____ oranges.

Directions Have students listen to each story, count how many are left, and then write the number that tells how many. **3** _Marta sees 6 ducks. 3 ducks fly away. How many ducks are left?_ **4** _Marta sees 6 frogs. I frog hops away. How many frogs are left?_ Then have students listen to each story, draw a picture to show the story, and then write the number that tells how many are left. **5** _Marta sees 6 ants. 4 ants crawl away. How many ants are left?_ **6** _Some oranges are on Marta's plate. She eats 2 oranges. 4 are left. How many oranges were on the plate before Marta ate the oranges?_

Topic 8 | Lesson I

Name _____

_____

_ _ _ _ _

_____ are left.

Directions Say: *Marta sees 9 people riding in a van. The van stops and 2 people get out. How many people are left in the van? Use counters to show how you know.*

★ **TEKS K.1C** Select tools, including real objects, manipulatives, paper and pencil, ... and techniques, including ... number sense as appropriate, to solve problems. Also, K.3, K.3A, K.3B. **Mathematical Process Standards** K.1B, K.1F, K.1G.

Digital Resources at PearsonTexas.com

Solve Learn Glossary Check Tools Games

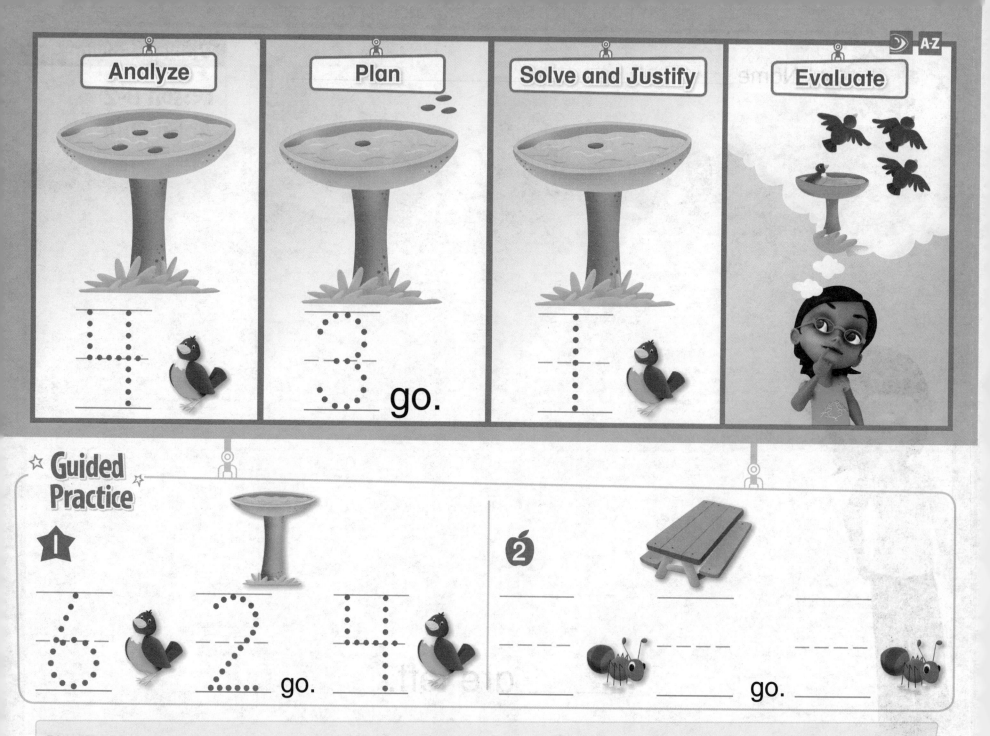

go.

☆ Guided Practice ☆

1

go.

2

go.

Directions Have students listen to each story and solve it by acting it out with counters or in another way they choose. Ask them to write each number in the story, and then write the answer at the end of the row. Have students explain their answers. ★ *There are 6 birds in the birdbath. 2 go away. How many birds are left in the birdbath?* ❷ *There are 9 ants on the table. 4 go away. How many ants are left on the table?*

Name _____

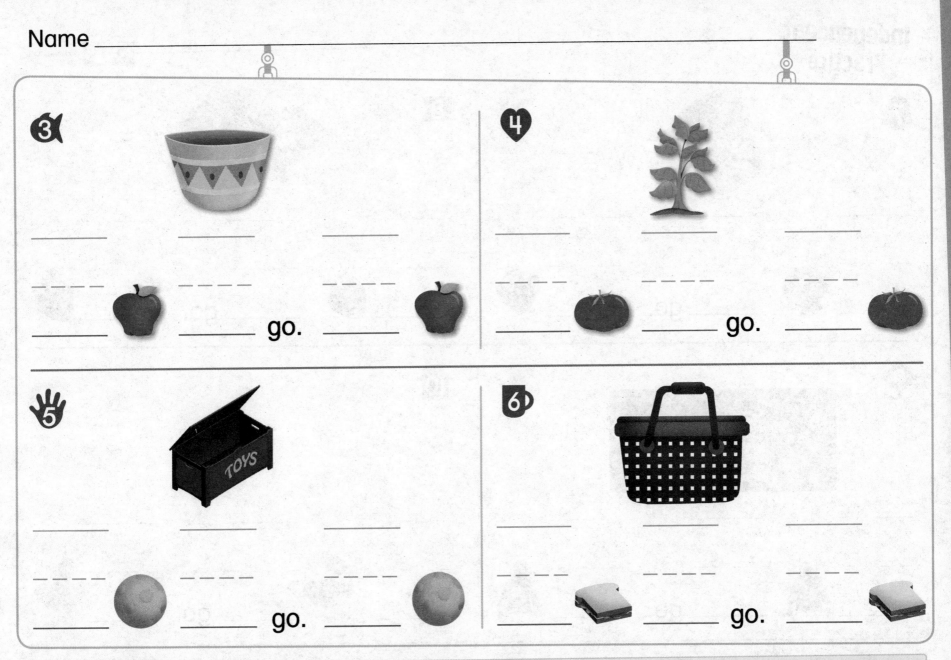

3 _____ _____ _____

_____ _____ go. _____

4 _____ _____ _____

_____ _____ go. _____

5 _____ _____ _____

_____ _____ go. _____

6 _____ _____ _____

_____ _____ go. _____

Directions Have students listen to each story and solve it by acting it out with counters or in another way they choose. Ask them to write each number in the story, and then write the answer at the end of the row. Have students explain their answers. 3 *7 apples are in the bowl. 2 apples go into lunchboxes. How many apples are in the bowl now?* 4 *6 tomatoes grow on a plant. 4 tomatoes go in a basket. How many tomatoes are left on the plant?* 5 *5 balls are in the toy box. 2 balls go outside. How many balls are left in the toy box?* 6 *9 sandwiches are in the picnic basket. 6 sandwiches go on plates. How many sandwiches are left in the picnic basket?*

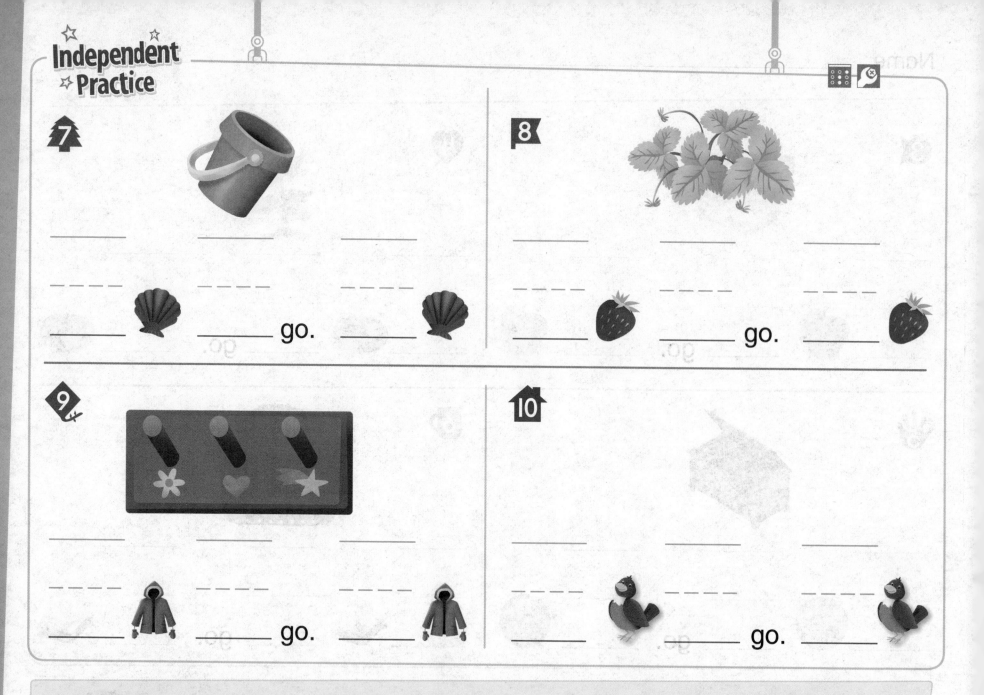

7 _____ _____

_____ 🐚 _ _ _ _ _ _ _____ go. 🐚

8 _____ _____

_ _ _ _ _ _ 🍓 _____ go. 🍓

9 _____ _____

_ _ _ _ _ 🧥 _____ go. 🧥

10 _____ _____

_ _ _ _ _ 🐦 _____ go. 🐦

Directions Have students listen to each story and solve it by acting it out with counters or in another way they choose. Ask them to write each number in the story, and then write the answer. Have students explain their answers. **7** 6 seashells are in the bucket. 3 go home with Alex. How many seashells are left? **8** 8 strawberries are on the plant. 2 strawberries go in a basket. How many strawberries are left on the plant? **9** 3 coats are on the hooks. 2 coats go home with children. How many coats are left on the hooks? Then have students listen to the story, and then write the numbers that tell the story. **10** 10 birds are in the tree. Some go away, and now there are 6 birds left. How many birds flew away?

© Pearson Education, Inc. K

Another Look

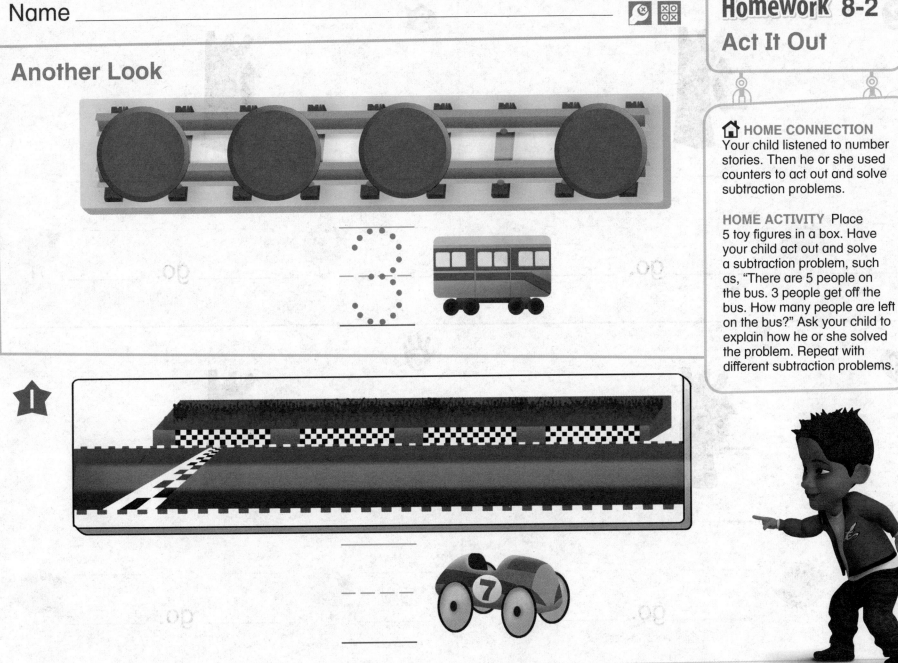

🏠 **HOME CONNECTION**
Your child listened to number stories. Then he or she used counters to act out and solve subtraction problems.

HOME ACTIVITY Place 5 toy figures in a box. Have your child act out and solve a subtraction problem, such as, "There are 5 people on the bus. 3 people get off the bus. How many people are left on the bus?" Ask your child to explain how he or she solved the problem. Repeat with different subtraction problems.

⭐ ①

Directions Have students listen to each story, solve it by acting it out with counters or other objects, and then write the number that tells how many are left. Say: *There are 4 train cars on the track. You take 1 train car off the track. How many cars are left on the track? How did you act out the problem to help you find the answer?* 🔺 *There are 6 race cars on the track. 4 race cars pull off the track. How many race cars are left on the track?*

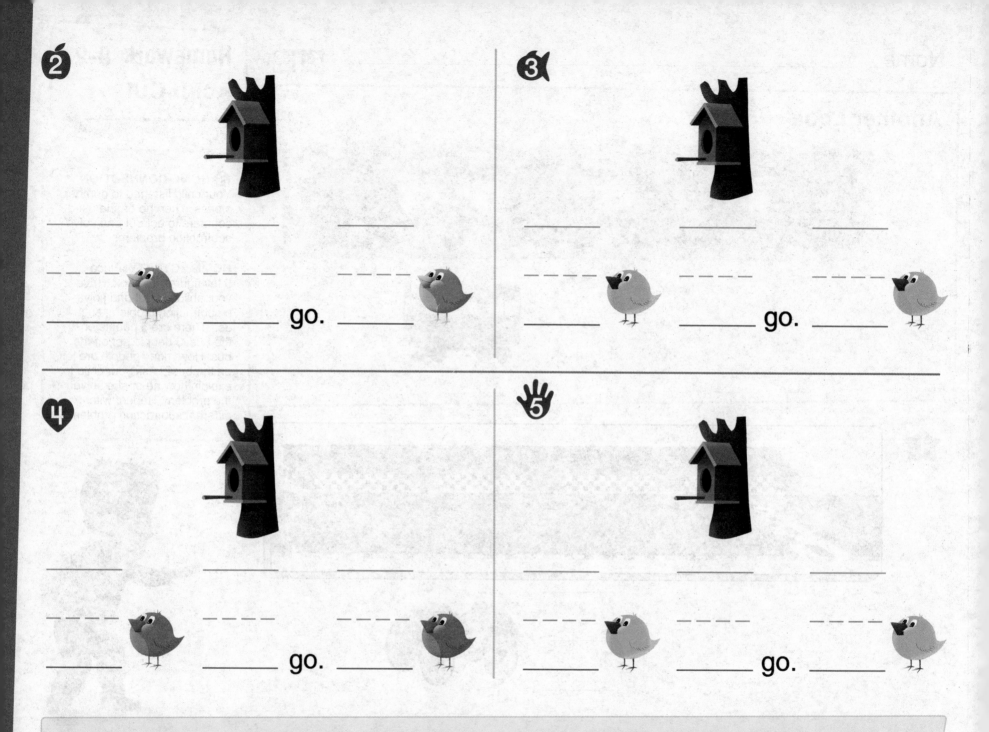

2

_____ _____ _____

- - - - - -   - - - - -
go. _____

3

_____ _____ _____

- - - - - -   - - - - -
go. _____

4

_____ _____ _____

- - - - - -   - - - - -
go. _____

5

_____ _____ _____

- - - - - -   - - - - -
go. _____

Directions Have students listen to each story and solve it by acting it out with counters or other objects. Ask them to write each number in the story, and then write the answer. **2** _8 birds are in the birdhouse. 7 go away. How many are left?_ **3** _6 birds are in the birdhouse, and 4 go away. How many are left?_ **4** _7 birds are in the birdhouse, and now there are 4. How many birds go away?_ **5** _Some birds are in the birdhouse. 2 go away, and now there are 4. How many were in the birdhouse before?_

Topic 8 | Lesson 2

Solve & Share   Name _____

_____ take away _____ is _____.

⭐ TEKS K.3B Solve word problems using objects and drawings to find sums up to 10 and differences within 10. Also, K.3, K.3A. Mathematical Process Standards K.1A, K.1C, K.1G.

Directions Say: *Marta sees 4 turtles in a pond. 1 turtle swims away. How many turtles are left?*

Digital Resources at PearsonTexas.com

Solve   Learn   Glossary   Check   Tools   Games

Topic 8 | Lesson 3

four hundred twenty-nine **429**

4 take away 1 is 3.

☆ Guided Practice ☆

1

3 take away 2 is 1 .

2

_____ take away _____ is _____ .

Directions Have students listen to each story, use counters to model the problem, draw Xs to show how many to take away, and then write the numbers to complete the sentence. **1** *Marta sees 3 beavers. 2 beavers swim away. How many beavers are left?* **2** *Marta sees 6 ducks. 3 ducks fly away. How many ducks are left?*

© Pearson Education, Inc. K

Name _____

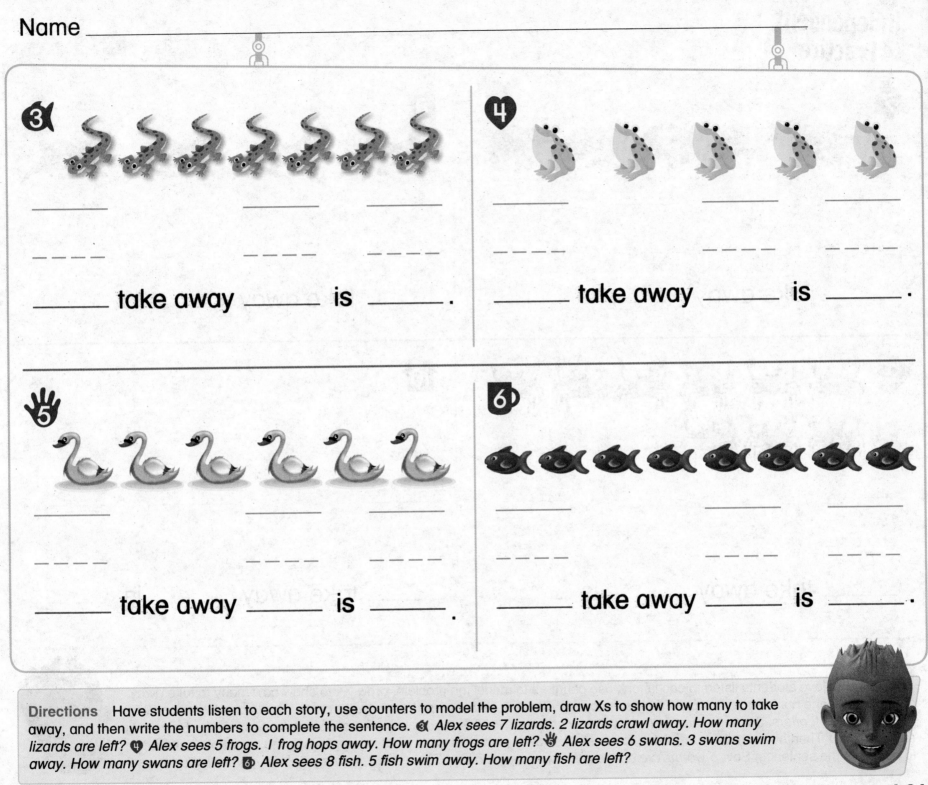

3 _____ _____

_____ take away _____ is _____ .

4 _____ _____

_____ take away _____ is _____ .

5 _____ _____

_____ take away _____ is _____ .

6 _____ _____

_____ take away _____ is _____ .

Directions Have students listen to each story, use counters to model the problem, draw Xs to show how many to take away, and then write the numbers to complete the sentence. **3** *Alex sees 7 lizards. 2 lizards crawl away. How many lizards are left?* **4** *Alex sees 5 frogs. 1 frog hops away. How many frogs are left?* **5** *Alex sees 6 swans. 3 swans swim away. How many swans are left?* **6** *Alex sees 8 fish. 5 fish swim away. How many fish are left?*

7

_____ _____

- - - - - - - - -

_____ take away _____ is _____ .

8

_____ _____

- - - - - - - - -

_____ take away _____ is _____ .

9

_____ _____

- - - - - - - - -

_____ take away _____ is _____ .

10

_____ _____

- - - - - - - - -

_____ take away _____ is _____ .

Directions Have students listen to each story, use counters to model the problem, draw Xs to show how many to take away, and then write the numbers to complete the sentence. **7** _Carlos sees 5 turtles. 1 turtle walks away. How many turtles are left?_ **8** _Carlos sees 4 otters. 3 otters swim away. How many otters are left?_ **9** _Carlos sees 9 crabs. 4 crabs crawl away. How many crabs are left?_ Then have students: **10** listen to the story, draw a picture to show what is happening, and then write numbers to complete the sentence. Say: _5 worms are on the hill. Some wiggle away. There are 3 worms left. How many wiggled away?_

Topic 8 | Lesson 3

Another Look

4 take away 1 is 3.

___ take away ___ is ___.

🏠 **HOME CONNECTION**
Your child listened to stories about take away and wrote numbers to tell how many in all, how many were taken away, and how many were left.

HOME ACTIVITY Place 5 pencils in a row. Tell your child to take away 2 pencils. Then have your child tell you how many pencils are left. Repeat the activity, using other numbers of pencils or objects.

⭐ 1

___ take away ___ is ___.

2

___ take away ___ is ___.

Directions Say: *Emily shows 4 counters. She takes away 1 counter. How many counters are left? Count and write the number that tells how many in all. Then draw Xs to show how many to take away, and write the number that tells how many are left. Then have students listen to each story, draw Xs to show how many to take away, and then write numbers to complete the sentence.* ⭐ *Emily shows 5 counters. She takes away 2 counters. How many are left?* 2 *Emily shows 6 counters. She takes away 2 counters. How many are left?*

Topic 8 | Lesson 3   Digital Resources at PearsonTexas.com   four hundred thirty-three **433**

3 _____ take away _____ is _____ .

4 _____ take away _____ is _____ .

5 _____ take away _____ is _____ .

6 7 take away 5 is _____ .

7 4 take away _____ is 2 .

Directions Have students listen to each story, draw Xs to show how many to take away, and then write numbers to complete the sentence. **3** _Marta sees 5 geese. 3 geese fly away. How many geese are left?_ **4** _Marta sees 6 fish. 1 fish swims away. How many fish are left?_ **5** _Marta sees 8 ducklings. 3 ducklings swim away. How many ducklings are left?_ Then have students: **6** and **7** draw counters and Xs to match the sentence, and then write the number that completes the sentence.

© Pearson Education, Inc. K

Directions Say: *There are 5 parrots in a tree. 2 parrots fly away. How can you find how many parrots are left?*

TEKS K.3A Model the action of joining to represent addition and the action of separating to represent subtraction. Also, K.3, K.3B. **Mathematical Process Standards** K.1C, K.1D, K.1F, K.1G.

Digital Resources at PearsonTexas.com

Solve Learn Glossary Check Tools Games

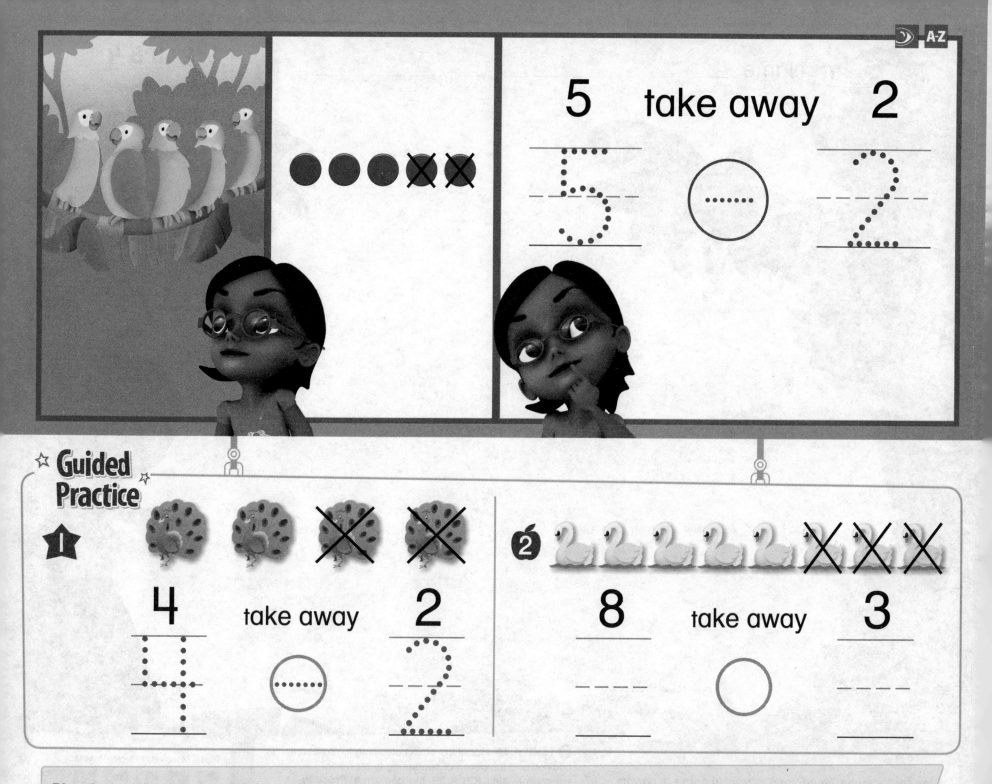

5 take away 2

5 ◯ 2

Guided Practice

1 4 take away 2

4 ◯ 2

2 8 take away 3

8 ◯ 3

Directions Have students count the birds and write the number that tells how many, and then write the minus sign and the number subtracted.

© Pearson Education, Inc. K

Name _____

3 🦅🦅🦅🦅🦅̷🦅̷

6   take away   2

_____   ⭕   _____

_____

4 🦩🦩🦩🦩̷🦩̷🦩̷

7   take away   3

_____   ⭕   _____

_____

5 🐧🐧🐧🐧🐧̷🐧̷🐧̷

8   take away   3

_____   ⭕   _____

_____

6 🦓🦓🦓🦓🦓̷🦓̷🦓̷🦓̷

9   take away   4

_____   ⭕   _____

_____

Directions Have students count the birds and write the number that tells how many, and then write the minus sign and the number subtracted.

🎄7

5   take away   I

_____ ◯ _____

- - - - -   - - - - -

🚩8

8   take away   5

_____ ◯ _____

- - - - -   - - - - -

9

6   take away   2

_____ ◯ _____

- - - - -   - - - - -

🏠10

9   take away   6

_____ ◯ _____

- - - - -   - - - - -

Directions Have students: 🎄—9 count the birds and write the number that tells how many, and then write the minus sign and the number subtracted; 🏠 listen to the story, draw counters and Xs to show the problem, and then write the numbers and the minus sign to solve. Say: *There were 9 birds. Some flew away. 3 are left.*

Another Look

6   take away   3

⭐ 1

7   take away   5

🍎 2

5   take away   4

Directions Say: *Write the number that tells how many counters in all and write the minus sign. How many counters are subtracted? Write the number that tells how many are subtracted. How many are left?* Then have students: ⭐ and 🍎 count the counters and write the number that tells how many, write the minus sign, and then count the counters that are taken away and write the number.

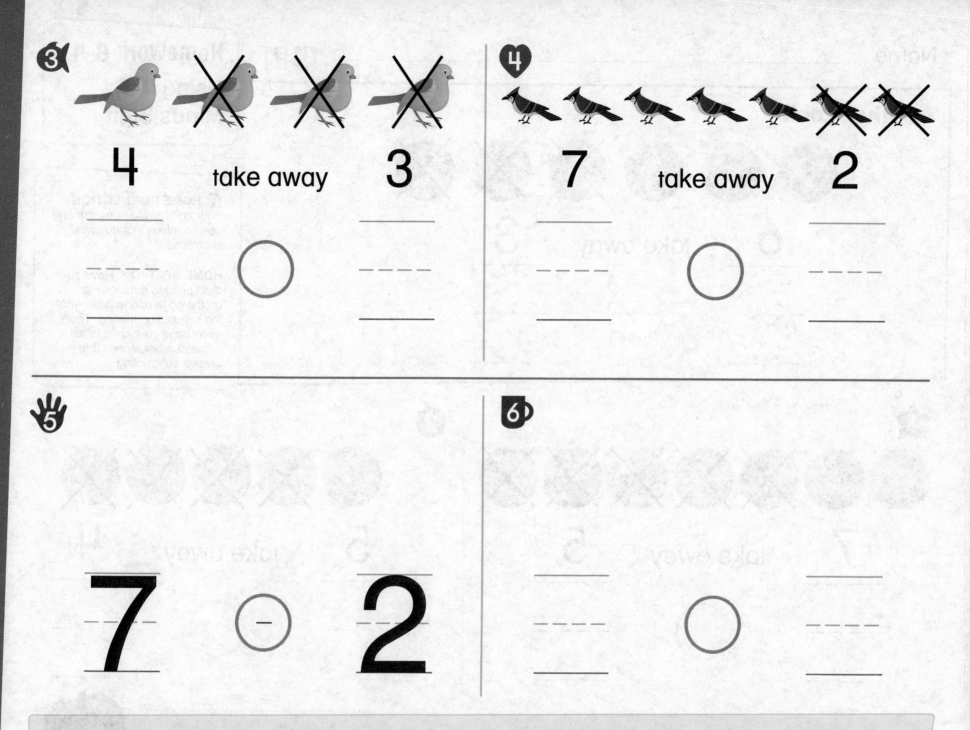

3 4 take away 3

◯ _ _ _

4 7 take away 2

◯ _ _ _

5 7 ⊙ 2

6

_ _ _ ◯ _ _ _

Directions Have students: **3** and **4** count the birds and write the number that tells how many, and then write the minus sign and the number subtracted; **5** draw a picture to match the number sentence; **6** listen to the story, draw counters and Xs to show what is happening, and then write the numbers and the minus sign. *There were 6 parrots in a cage. The zookeeper took some away for a show. Now, there are 2 left in the cage.*

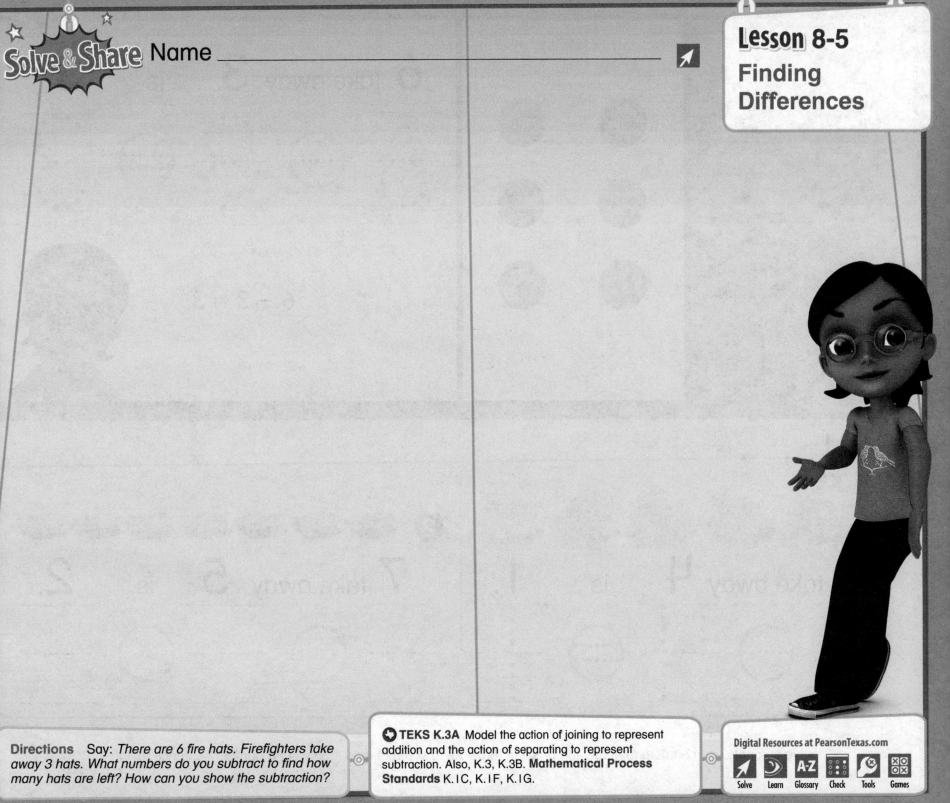

Directions Say: *There are 6 fire hats. Firefighters take away 3 hats. What numbers do you subtract to find how many hats are left? How can you show the subtraction?*

⭐ **TEKS K.3A** Model the action of joining to represent addition and the action of separating to represent subtraction. Also, K.3, K.3B. **Mathematical Process Standards** K.1C, K.1F, K.1G.

Digital Resources at PearsonTexas.com

Solve · Learn · Glossary · Check · Tools · Games

6 take away 3 is 3.

6 − 3 = 3

Guided Practice

1 5 take away 4 is 1.

2 7 take away 5 is 2.

Directions Have students use counters to model the problem, draw Xs to subtract, and then write a number sentence to find the difference.

© Pearson Education, Inc. K

3

8 take away 2 is 6.

_____ ◯ _____ ◯ _____

_ _ _ _ _ _ _ _ _ _ _ _

4

6 take away 5 is 1.

_____ ◯ _____ ◯ _____

_ _ _ _ _ _ _ _ _ _ _ _

5

9 take away 5 is 4.

_____ ◯ _____ ◯ _____

_ _ _ _ _ _ _ _ _ _ _ _

6

7 take away 2 is 5.

_____ ◯ _____ ◯ _____

_ _ _ _ _ _ _ _ _ _ _ _

Directions Have students use counters to model the problem, draw Xs to subtract, and then write a number sentence to find the difference.

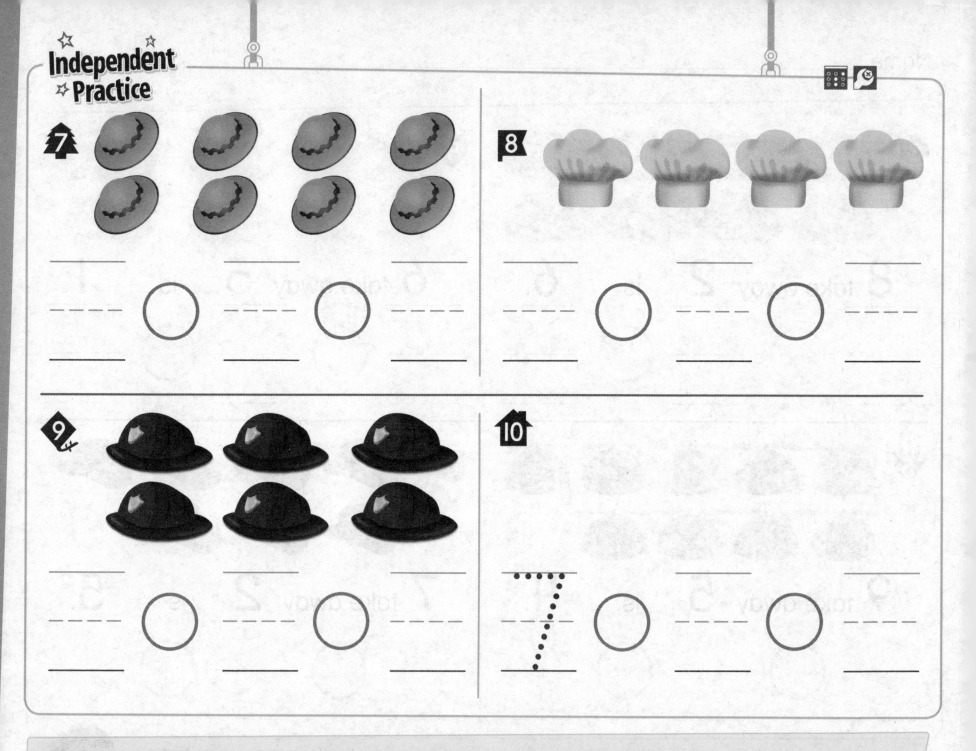

7 ⬭⬭⬭⬭ ⬭⬭⬭⬭

⭘ _____ ⭘ _____

8 🎩🎩🎩🎩

_____ ⭘ _____ ⭘ _____

9 🎩🎩🎩 🎩🎩🎩

⭘ _____ ⭘ _____

10

7 ⭘ _____ ⭘ _____

Directions Have students: **7**–**9** use counters to model the problem, draw Xs to subtract, and then write a number sentence to find the difference; **10** listen to the story, draw counters and Xs to show the problem, and then write a number sentence. Say: *There are 7 baseball caps. Some are worn to a game. There are 4 left. How many caps were worn to the game?*

Topic 8 | Lesson 5

Name _____

Another Look

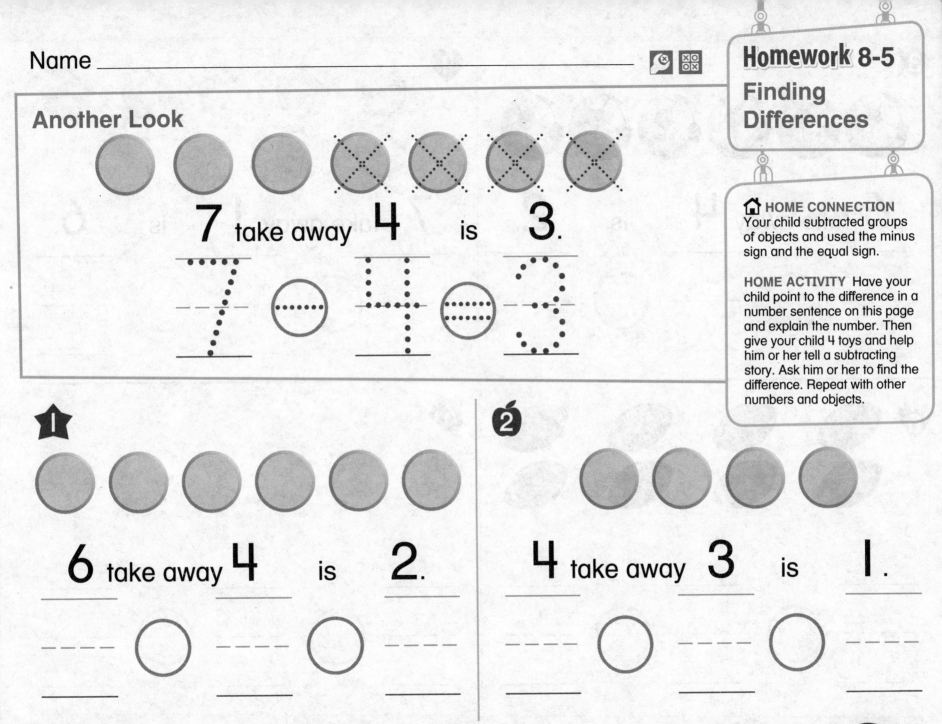

7 take away 4 is 3.

🏠 HOME CONNECTION
Your child subtracted groups of objects and used the minus sign and the equal sign.

HOME ACTIVITY Have your child point to the difference in a number sentence on this page and explain the number. Then give your child 4 toys and help him or her tell a subtracting story. Ask him or her to find the difference. Repeat with other numbers and objects.

⭐ 1

6 take away 4 is 2.

② 2

4 take away 3 is 1.

Directions Say: *What numbers are being subtracted? Draw Xs on the counters to show how many to take away, and then write the numbers, the minus sign, the equal sign, and the difference.* Then have students: ⭐ and ② draw Xs to show how many counters to take away, write the numbers, the minus sign, the equal sign, and the difference.

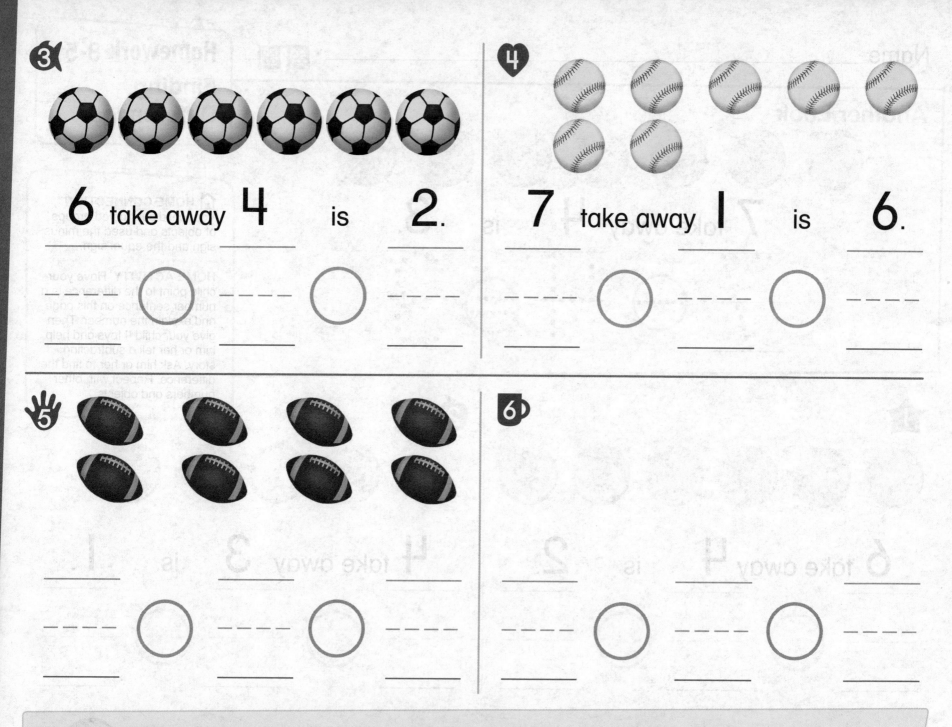

3

6 take away 4 is 2.

◯ ◯ ◯

4

7 take away 1 is 6.

◯ ◯ ◯

5

◯ ◯ ◯

6

◯ ◯ ◯

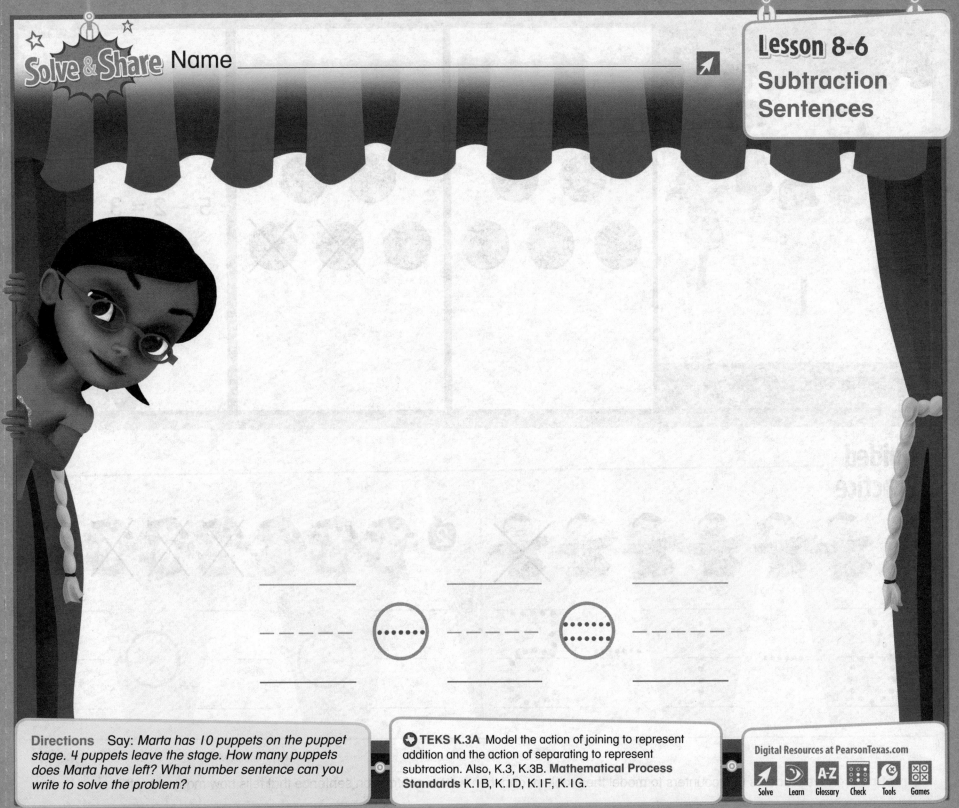

_____   _____   _____

- - - - - - - (••••••) - - - - - - - (••••••) - - - - - - -

_____   _____   _____

Directions Say: _Marta has 10 puppets on the puppet stage. 4 puppets leave the stage. How many puppets does Marta have left? What number sentence can you write to solve the problem?_

⊙ **TEKS K.3A** Model the action of joining to represent addition and the action of separating to represent subtraction. Also, **K.3, K.3B. Mathematical Process Standards K.1B, K.1D, K.1F, K.1G.**

Digital Resources at PearsonTexas.com
↗ Solve   ◐ Learn   A-Z Glossary   ⋯ Check   ⊕ Tools   ⊠ Games

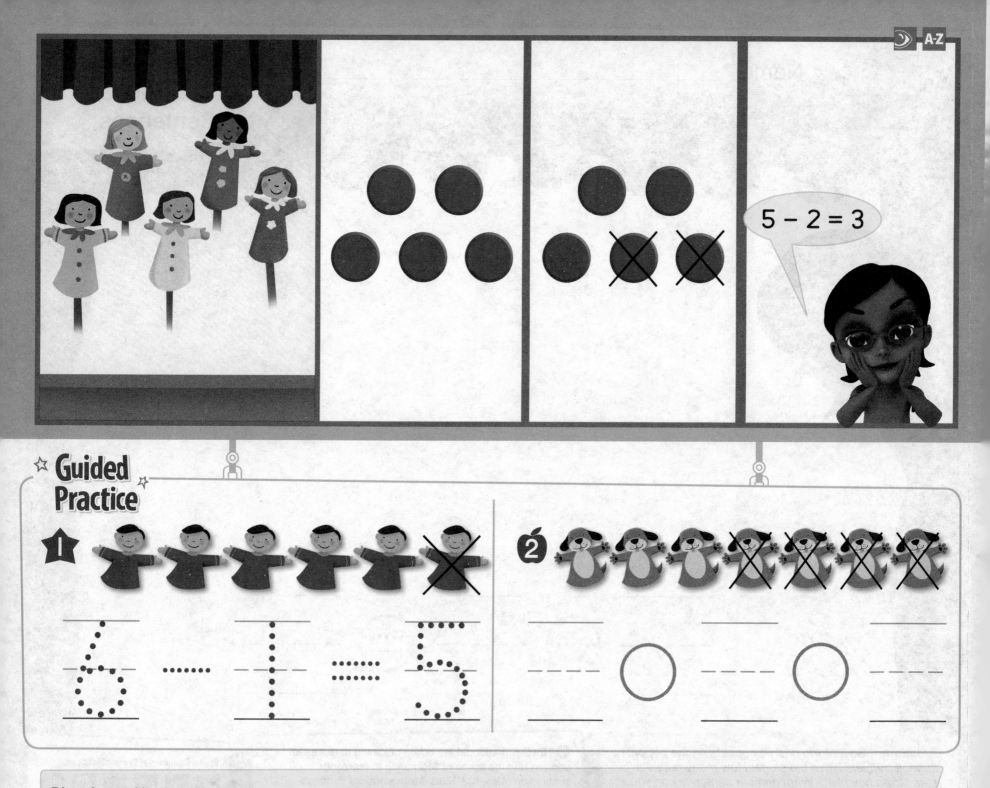

5 − 2 = 3

Guided Practice

1 6 --- 1 = 5

2 ◯ --- ◯ ---

© Pearson Education, Inc. K

Topic 8 | Lesson 6

Name _____

3

◯   ◯

4

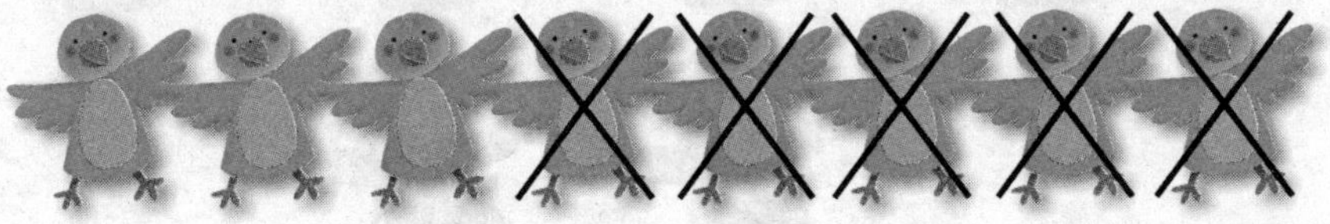

◯   ◯

5

◯   ◯

6

◯   ◯

Directions Have students use counters to model the problem, and then write a subtraction sentence that tells how many are left.

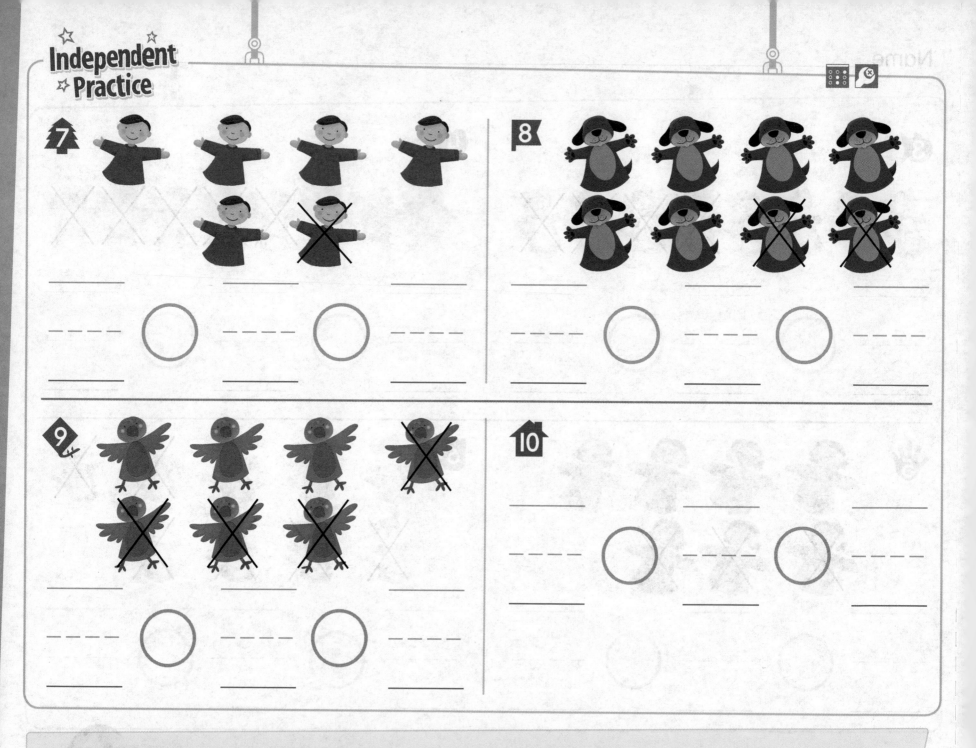

7

8

9

10

Directions Have students: 7–9 use counters to model the problem, and then write a subtraction sentence that tells how many are left; 10 listen to the story, and then write a subtraction sentence. Say: *Marta has 8 puppets for the puppet show. She takes away some puppets to be fixed. Marta has 5 puppets left for the show. How many puppets did she take away?*

Topic 8 | Lesson 6

Another Look

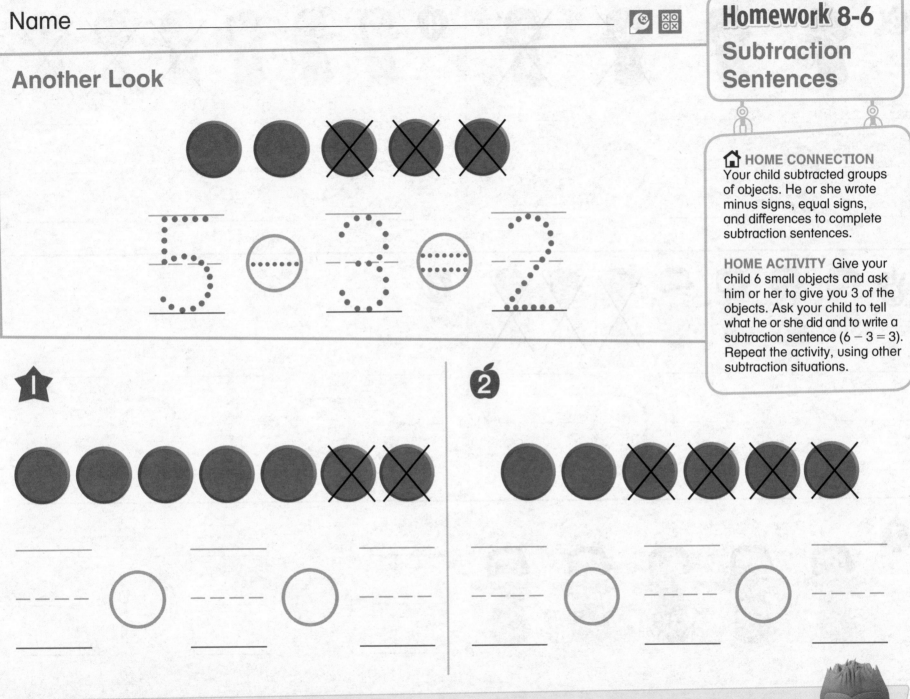

🏠 **HOME CONNECTION**
Your child subtracted groups of objects. He or she wrote minus signs, equal signs, and differences to complete subtraction sentences.

HOME ACTIVITY Give your child 6 small objects and ask him or her to give you 3 of the objects. Ask your child to tell what he or she did and to write a subtraction sentence ($6 - 3 = 3$). Repeat the activity, using other subtraction situations.

1

2

Directions Say: *How many counters are there in all? How many counters are being subtracted? Write the numbers, the minus sign, the equal sign, and difference to make the subtraction sentence.* Then have students: 1 and 2 write how many counters there are in all, the minus sign, the number subtracted, the equal sign, and the difference to complete each subtraction sentence.

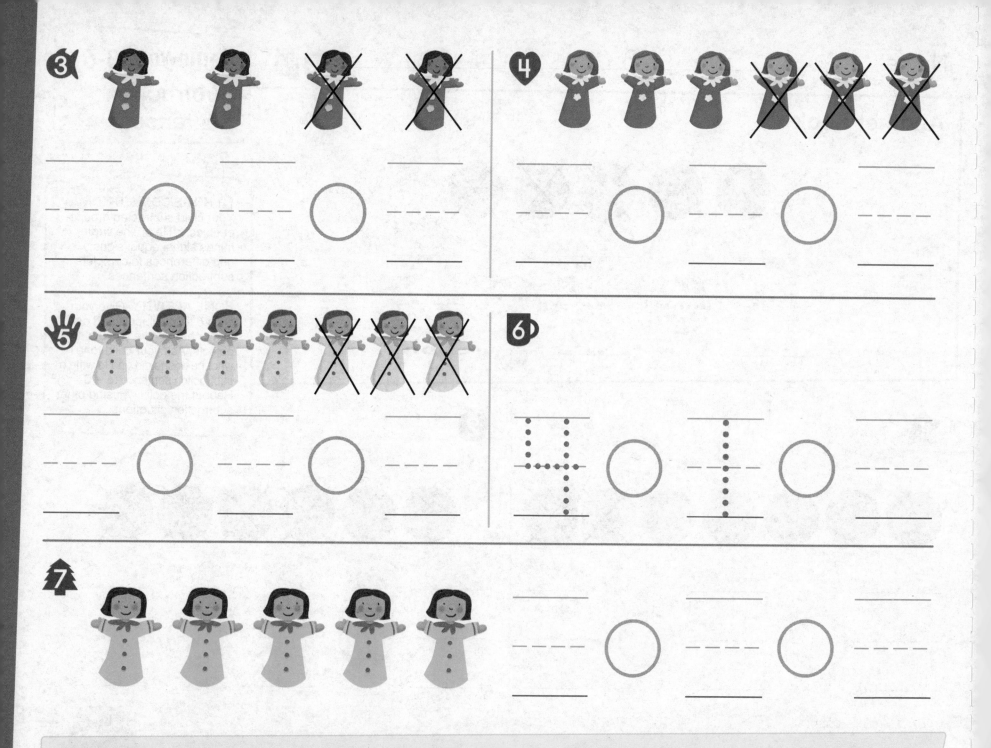

3 _____ ◯ _____ ◯ _____

4 _____ ◯ _____ ◯ _____

5 _____ ◯ _____ ◯ _____

6 _____ ◯ _____ ◯ _____

7 _____ ◯ _____ ◯ _____

Directions Have students: **3–5** write a subtraction sentence that tells how many are left; **6** draw a picture to show the subtraction, and then complete the subtraction sentence; **7** listen to the story, draw Xs to show what is happening, and then write a subtraction sentence. _Marta has some puppets. She gives 2 puppets to her brother. She has 3 left. How many puppets did she have before?_

Name _____

Directions Say: *Marta's dog, Spot, loves to eat doggie biscuits. There were 6 biscuits in a bag. One day, Spot ate 4 biscuits. Now there are only 2 biscuits left. How does Marta know that there are 2 biscuits left? Explain and then show how you know.*

⭐ **TEKS K.1G** Display, explain, and justify mathematical ideas and arguments .... **TEKS K.3C** Explain the strategies used to solve problems involving ... subtracting .... Also, K.3. **Mathematical Process Standards** K.1C, K.1D, K.1E, K.1G

2

X
3
X
X

2 are left.

1
2
3
4
5

2 are left.

$5 - 3 = 2$

☆ Guided Practice ☆

⭐ 1

6 ◯ 4 ◯ 2

Directions Have students listen to the story, draw a picture to show what is happening, and then write a subtraction sentence. Then have them explain their work aloud. Say: *Marta has 6 kittens. She gave them a big bowl of water to drink. But there was only room for 4 kittens at the water bowl. 2 kittens could not drink from the water bowl. How does Marta know that 2 kittens could not drink from the bowl?*

© Pearson Education, Inc. K

Name _____

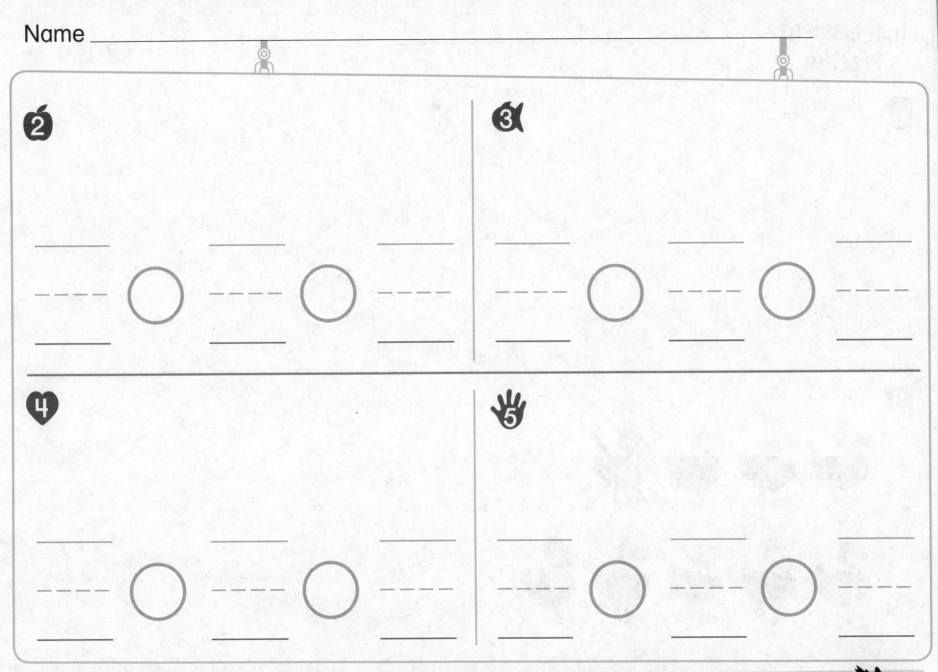

🍎 **2**

🎃 **3**

❤️ **4**

✋ **5**

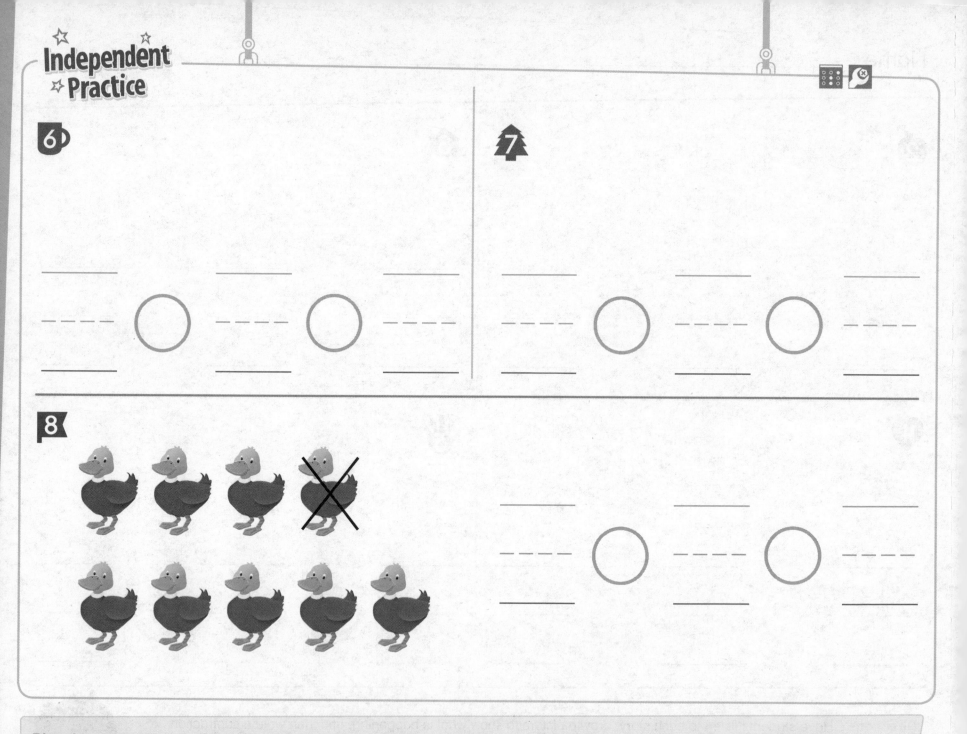

6

7

8

Directions Have students listen to each story, draw a picture to show what is happening, and then write a subtraction sentence.
6 *There were 6 birds in a birdbath. 4 flew away. How many are left?* **7** *There were 5 acorns under a tree. A squirrel took 3 acorns.*
How many are left? Then have students: **8** listen to the story, circle the picture that shows the story and tell why the other picture
does not show the story, and then write a subtraction sentence. *There were 4 ducks in a pond. I left. How many are left?*

456 four hundred fifty-six   © Pearson Education, Inc. K   **Topic 8** | Lesson 7

Another Look

$$5 \bigcirc 3 - 2$$

🏠 **HOME CONNECTION**
Your child drew pictures to show subtraction situations, wrote subtraction sentences, and explained how the groups are subtracted.

HOME ACTIVITY Give your child 7 small objects and ask him or her to give you 3 of the objects. Ask your child to tell you how many objects are left, and ask how he or she knows. Then ask your child to write a subtraction sentence (7 − 3 = 4).

⭐ 1

🍎 2

___ ◯ ___ ◯ ___

___ ◯ ___ ◯ ___

Directions Say: *There are 5 counters. Take 3 away. How many are left? You can draw counters and Xs to show what is happening. Write a subtraction sentence.* Then have students listen to each story, draw counters to show what is happening, and then write a subtraction sentence. ⭐ *There are 6 chipmunks. 4 run under a bush. How many are left?* 🍎 *There are 5 raccoons. 2 climb up a tree. How many are left?*

3

◯ ___ ◯ ___ ___

4

___ ◯ ___ ◯ ___

5

$6 - 5 = 1$

6

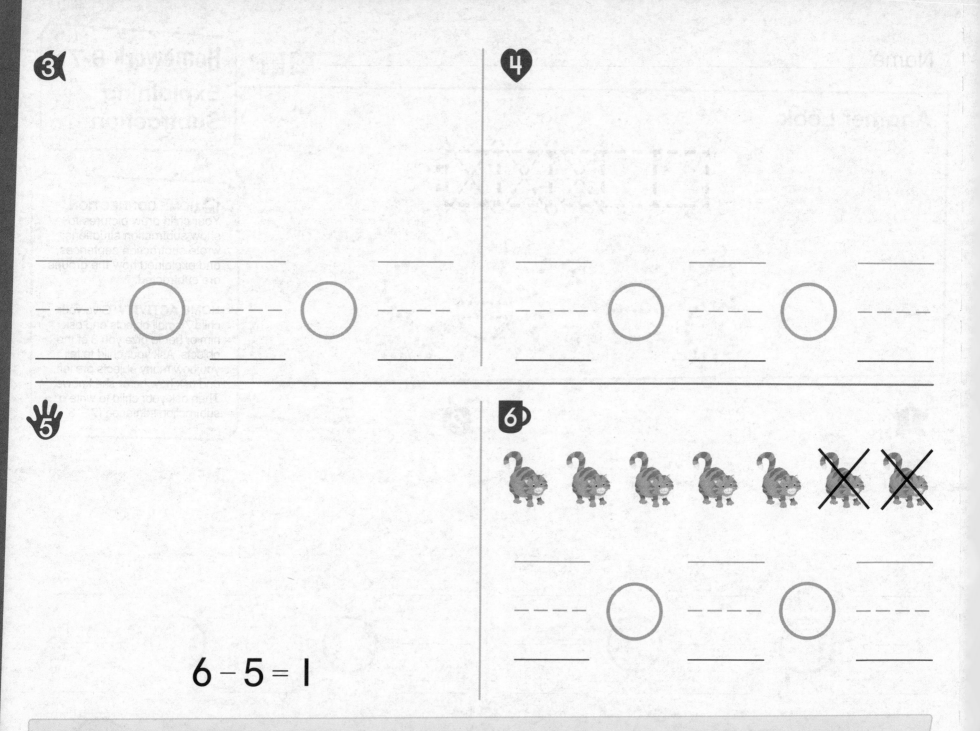

___

___ ◯ ___ ◯ ___

Directions Have students listen to each story, draw a picture to show what is happening, and then write a subtraction sentence.
3 *Marta has 9 dog biscuits. She gives her dog 5 biscuits. How many are left?* **4** *Marta buys 7 tennis balls. Her brother borrows 4 balls. How many are left?* Then have students: **5** *tell a number story that matches the subtraction sentence, and then draw a picture to show what is happening;* **6** *tell a subtraction story about the cats, and then write a subtraction sentence.*

© Pearson Education, Inc. K

Topic 8 | Lesson 7

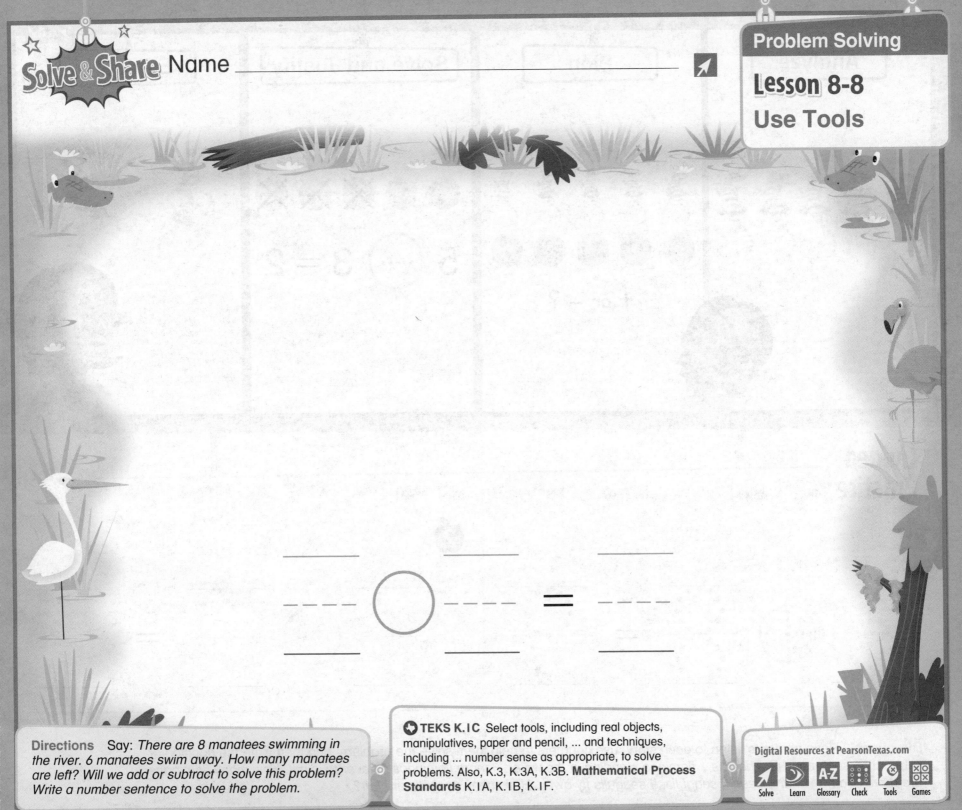

Solve & Share Name _____

_____ _____ _____

- - - - - ( ) - - - - - = - - - - -

_____ _____ _____

Directions Say: *There are 8 manatees swimming in the river. 6 manatees swim away. How many manatees are left? Will we add or subtract to solve this problem? Write a number sentence to solve the problem.*

★ **TEKS K.IC** Select tools, including real objects, manipulatives, paper and pencil, ... and techniques, including ... number sense as appropriate, to solve problems. Also, K.3, K.3A, K.3B. **Mathematical Process Standards** K.IA, K.IB, K.IF.

Digital Resources at PearsonTexas.com

Solve Learn Glossary Check Tools Games

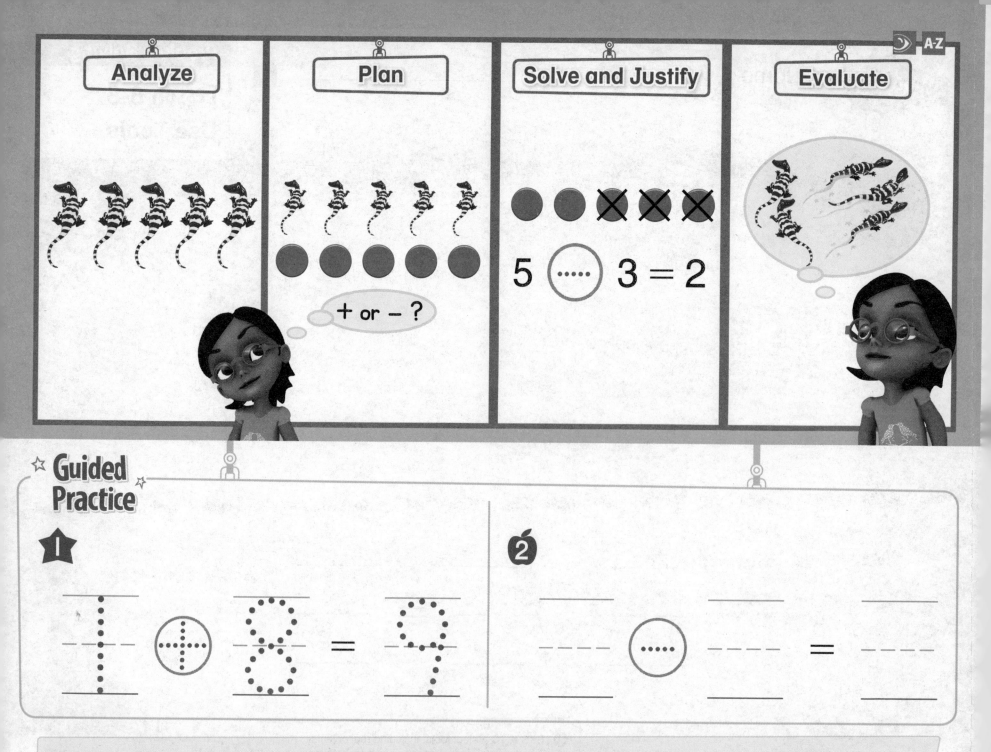

+ or – ?

5 (·····) 3 = 2

☆ Guided Practice

1

2

Directions Have students listen to each story, use counters to help them solve the problem, and then write the addition or subtraction sentence. **1** *There is 1 flamingo standing in the water. 8 more flamingos fly over to join it. How many flamingos are there in all?* **2** *Marta sees 7 seagulls. 4 seagulls fly away. How many seagulls are left?*

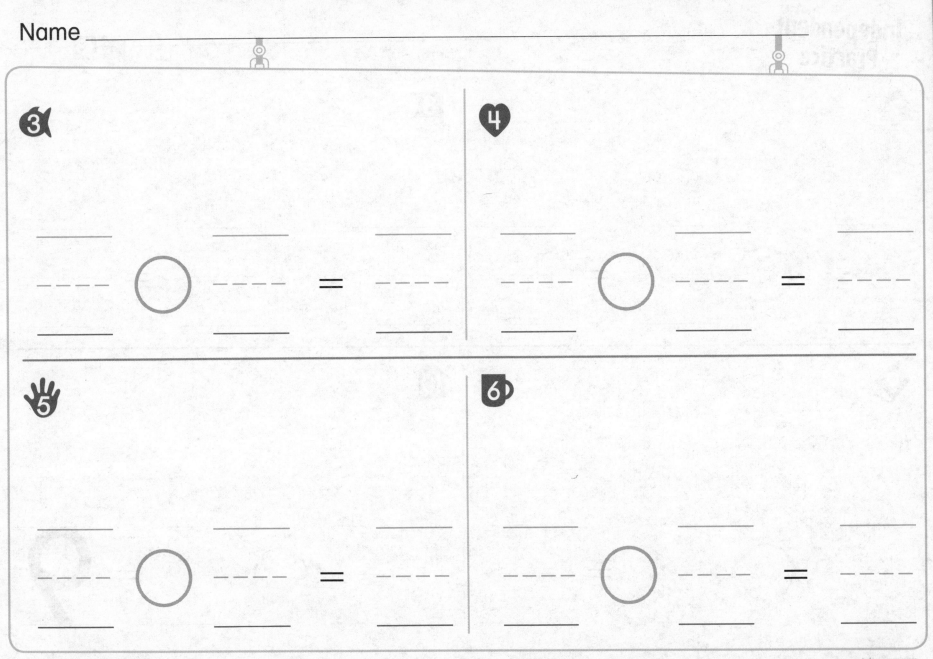

3

◯ = ___

4

◯ = ___

5

◯ = ___

6

◯ = ___

Directions Have students listen to each story, use counters to help them solve the problem, and then write the addition or subtraction sentence. **3** *There are 3 raccoons in a tree. 3 more raccoons climb the tree to join them. How many raccoons are there in all?* **4** *Marta sees 9 turtles swimming in a pond. 5 turtles dive under the water. How many turtles are left?* **5** *There are 7 beavers in the water. 4 beavers swim away. How many beavers are left?* **6** *Marta see 6 ducks in the lake. 2 more join them. How many ducks are there in all?*

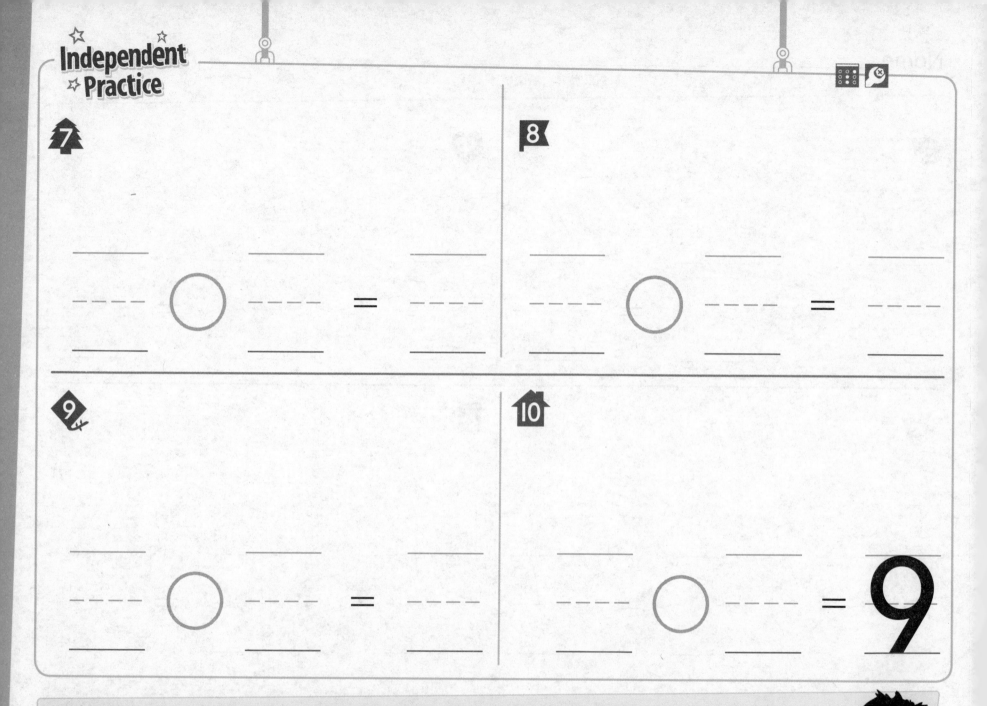

7

8

9

10

9

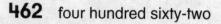

Name _____

Homework 8-8
Use Tools

Another Look

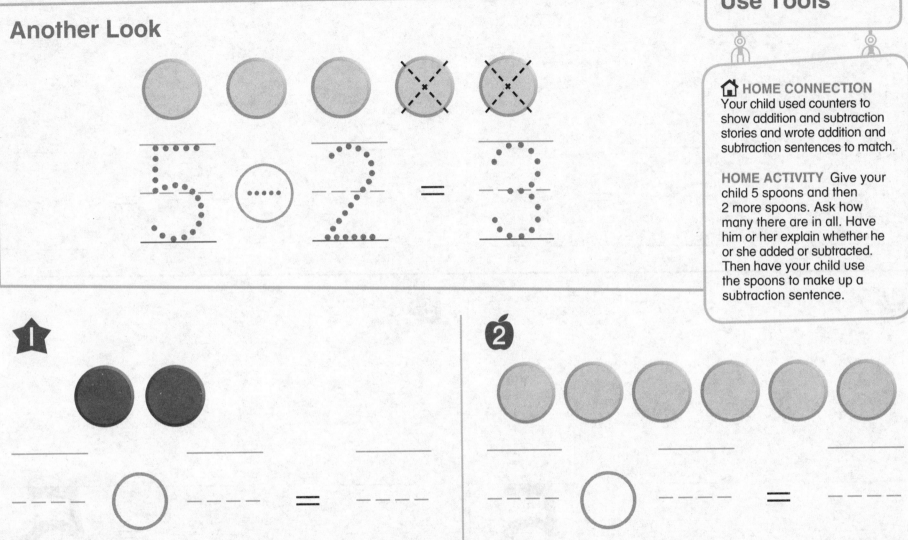

$5 - 2 = 3$

🏠 HOME CONNECTION
Your child used counters to show addition and subtraction stories and wrote addition and subtraction sentences to match.

HOME ACTIVITY Give your child 5 spoons and then 2 more spoons. Ask how many there are in all. Have him or her explain whether he or she added or subtracted. Then have your child use the spoons to make up a subtraction sentence.

1

2

_____ ◯ _____ = _____   _____ ◯ _____ = _____

Directions Say: *You can use counters to help you decide if a story is an addition or subtraction problem. Listen to this story: Emily built 5 sandcastles. Waves knocked down 2 of them. How many sandcastles are left? Model this story with counters. Did you add or subtract? Draw Xs on the counters to show subtraction and write the subtraction sentence. Then have students listen to each story, use counters or other objects to help them solve the problem, draw Xs on the counters shown that are subtracted or draw counters that are added, and then write the addition or subtraction sentence.* ⭐ *Emily saw 2 balls at the beach. Later that day, she saw 3 more balls. How many balls did Emily see in all?* ❷ *Emily had 6 sand shovels. Her brothers lost 3 of them. How many sand shovels are left?*

Topic 8 | Lesson 8   Digital Resources at PearsonTexas.com   four hundred sixty-three **463**

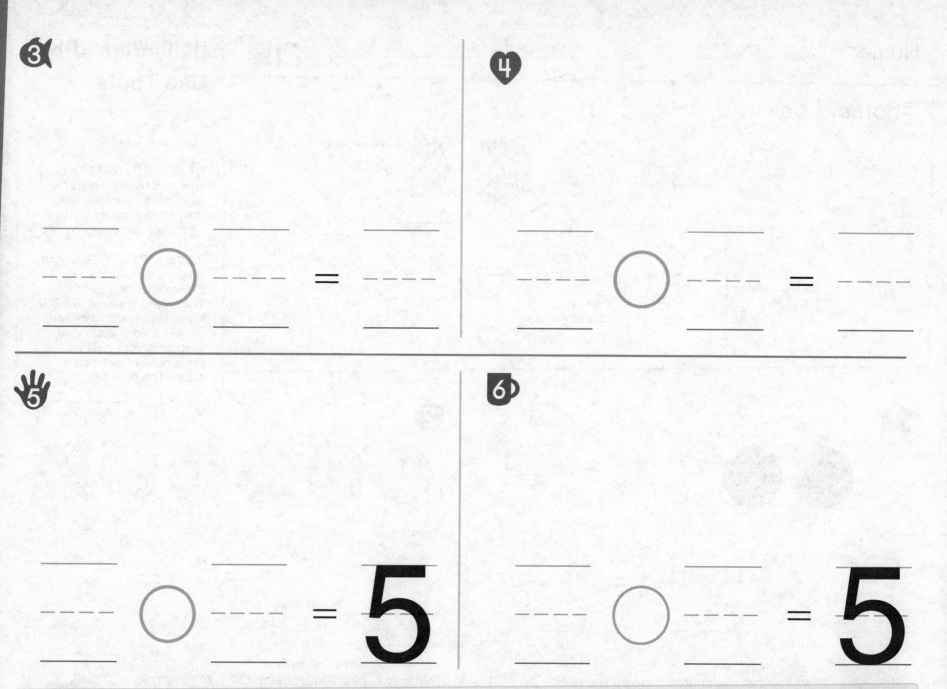

3

_____ ○ _ _ _ = _ _ _

_____   _____

4

_____ ○ _ _ _ = _ _ _

_____   _____

5

_ _ _ ○ _ _ _ = **5**

_____

6

_ _ _ ○ _ _ _ = **5**

_____

Directions Have students listen to each story, use counters or other objects to help them solve the problem, and then write the addition or subtraction sentence. ❸ *Marta picked 6 oranges. She ate 2 of them. How many oranges does Marta have left?* ❹ *There are 2 turtles in the pond. 3 more turtles swim over to join them. How many turtles are there in all?* Then have students use tools, such as counters, to: ❺ write an addition sentence where 5 is the sum; ❻ write a subtraction sentence where 5 is the difference.

Name _____

Set A _____

⭐ **1**

2 are left.

_____

_ _ _ _ _ _

_____ are left.

Set B _____

🍎 **2**

6 take away **2** is **4**.

_____   _____

_ _ _ _ _   _ _ _ _ _

_____ take away _____ is _____.

Directions Have students: ⭐ listen to the story, count how many bugs are left, and then write the number that tells how many. Say: *5 bees are on the flower. 1 flies away. How many are left?* 🍎 listen to the story, draw Xs to show how many to take away, and then write numbers to complete the sentence. Say: *4 seals are on the rock. 1 swims away. How many seals are left?*

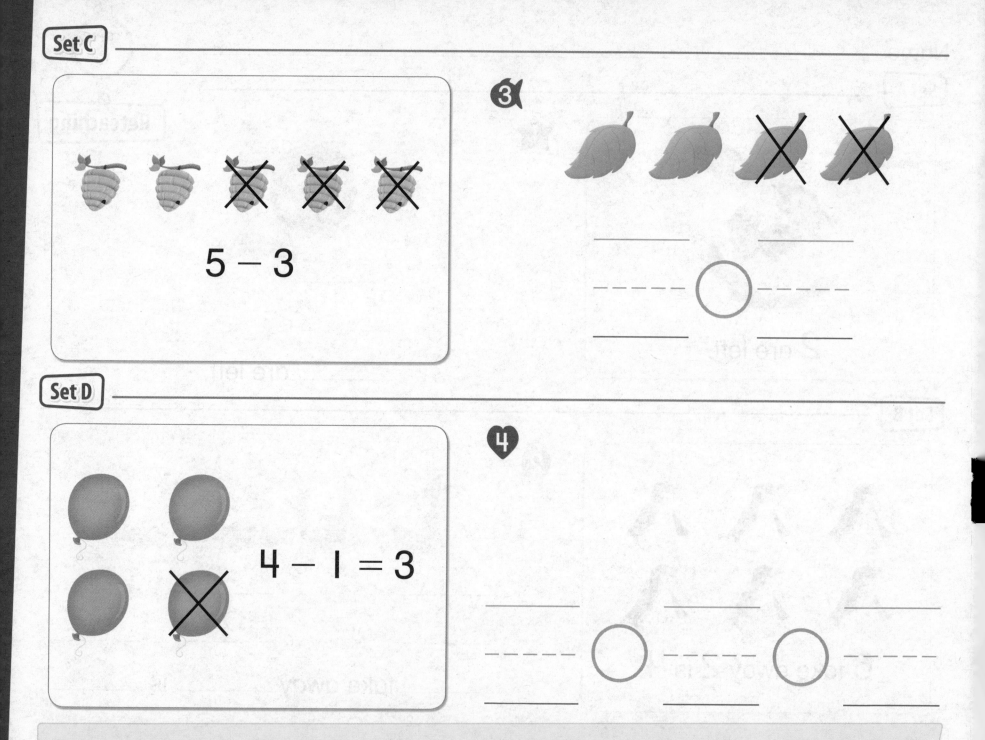

5 − 3

❸

4 − 1 = 3

❹

Directions Have students: ❸ count the leaves and write the number that tells how many, and then write the minus sign and the number subtracted; ❹ listen to the story, use cubes or counters to model the problem, and then draw a picture and write a subtraction sentence to show their solution. Have them explain their work. Say: *Lidia has 5 balloons. 2 balloons pop. How many balloons does she have left?*

Name _____

1

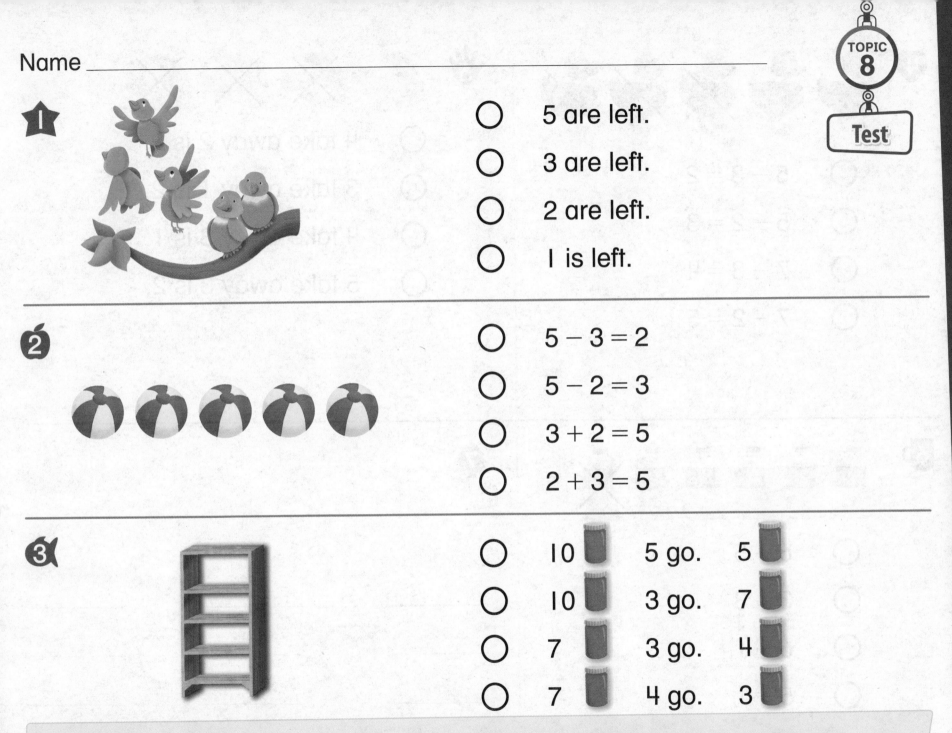

- ○ 5 are left.
- ○ 3 are left.
- ○ 2 are left.
- ○ 1 is left.

2

- ○ $5 - 3 = 2$
- ○ $5 - 2 = 3$
- ○ $3 + 2 = 5$
- ○ $2 + 3 = 5$

3

- ○ 10   5 go.   5
- ○ 10   3 go.   7
- ○ 7   3 go.   4
- ○ 7   4 go.   3

Directions   Have students mark the best answer. **1** *5 birds are on a branch. 3 of the birds fly away. How many are left on the branch?* **2** *There are 5 beach balls. 2 roll away. How many beach balls are left? Use counters or other tools to find the number sentence that matches the story.* **3** *There are 10 paint jars in the bookcase. 3 paint jars go with students. How many paint jars are left? Which matches the story?*

Topic 8   four hundred sixty-seven   **467**

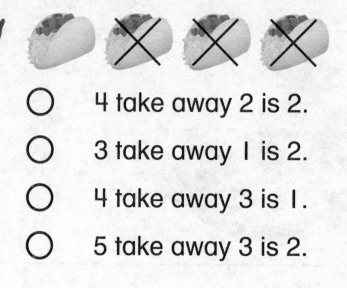

4

- ○ $5 - 3 = 2$
- ○ $5 - 2 = 3$
- ○ $7 - 3 = 4$
- ○ $7 - 2 = 5$

5

- ○ 4 take away 2 is 2.
- ○ 3 take away 1 is 2.
- ○ 4 take away 3 is 1.
- ○ 5 take away 3 is 2.

6

- ○ $6 - 5$
- ○ $3 + 3$
- ○ $6 - 1$
- ○ $5 - 1$

7

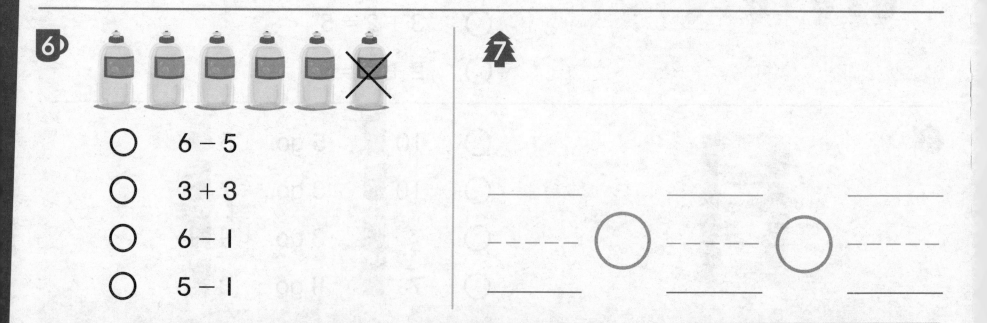

Directions Have students: **4** mark the best answer. Which subtraction sentence matches the picture? **5** mark the best answer. Which sentence matches the picture? **6** mark the best answer. Which matches the picture? **7** listen to the story, draw a picture to show what is happening, and then write the subtraction sentence. *There are 7 birds on a branch. 3 birds fly away. How many are left?*

468 four hundred sixty-eight

Topic 8

Glossary

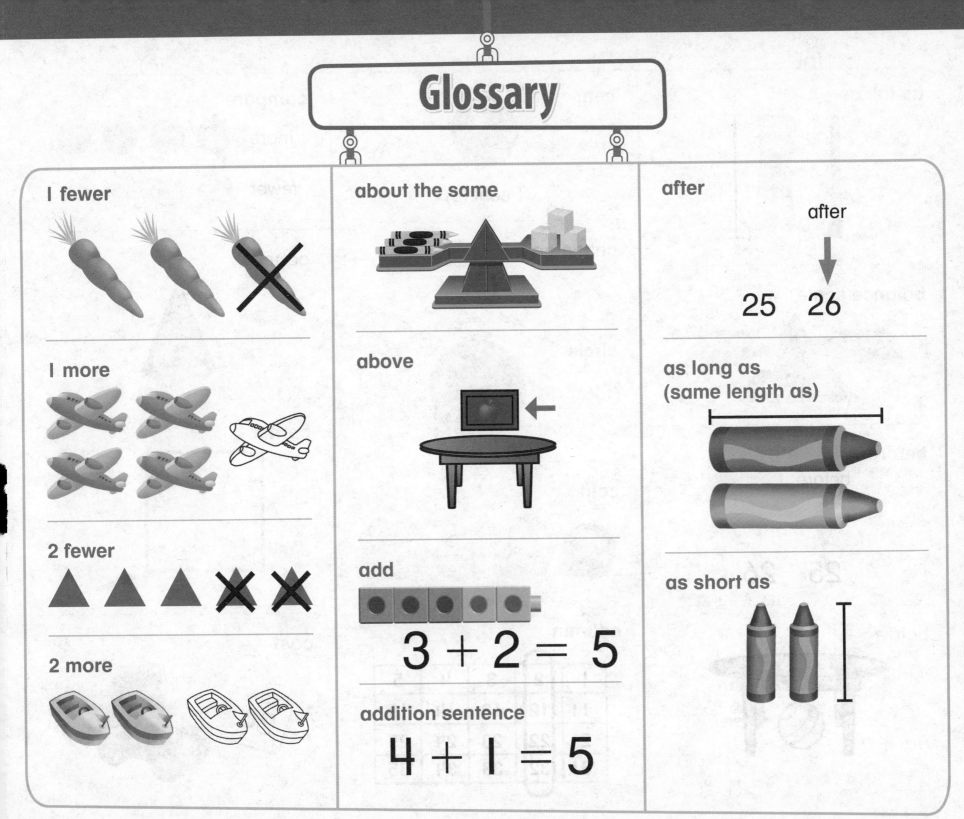

1 fewer

1 more

2 fewer

2 more

about the same

above

add

$$3 + 2 = 5$$

addition sentence

$$4 + 1 = 5$$

after

after

25 26

as long as
(same length as)

as short as

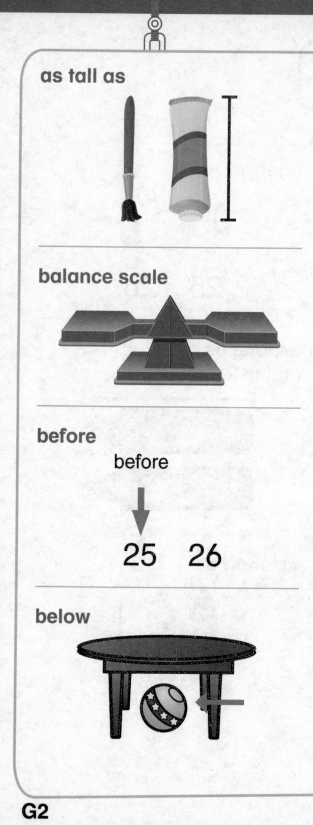

as tall as

balance scale

before

before

25 26

below

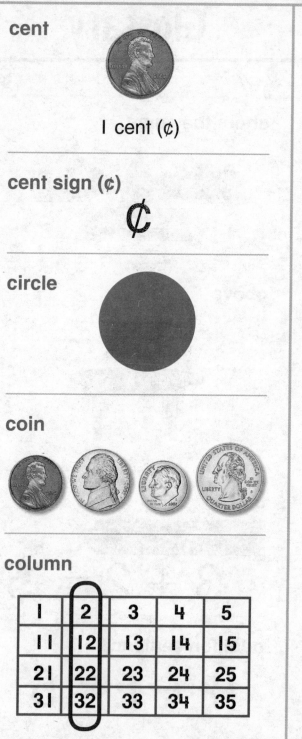

cent

I cent (¢)

cent sign (¢)

¢

circle

coin

column

1	2	3	4	5
11	12	13	14	15
21	22	23	24	25
31	32	33	34	35

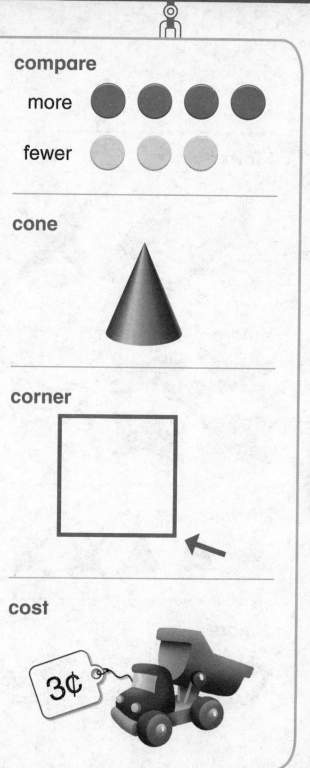

compare

more

fewer

cone

corner

cost

3¢

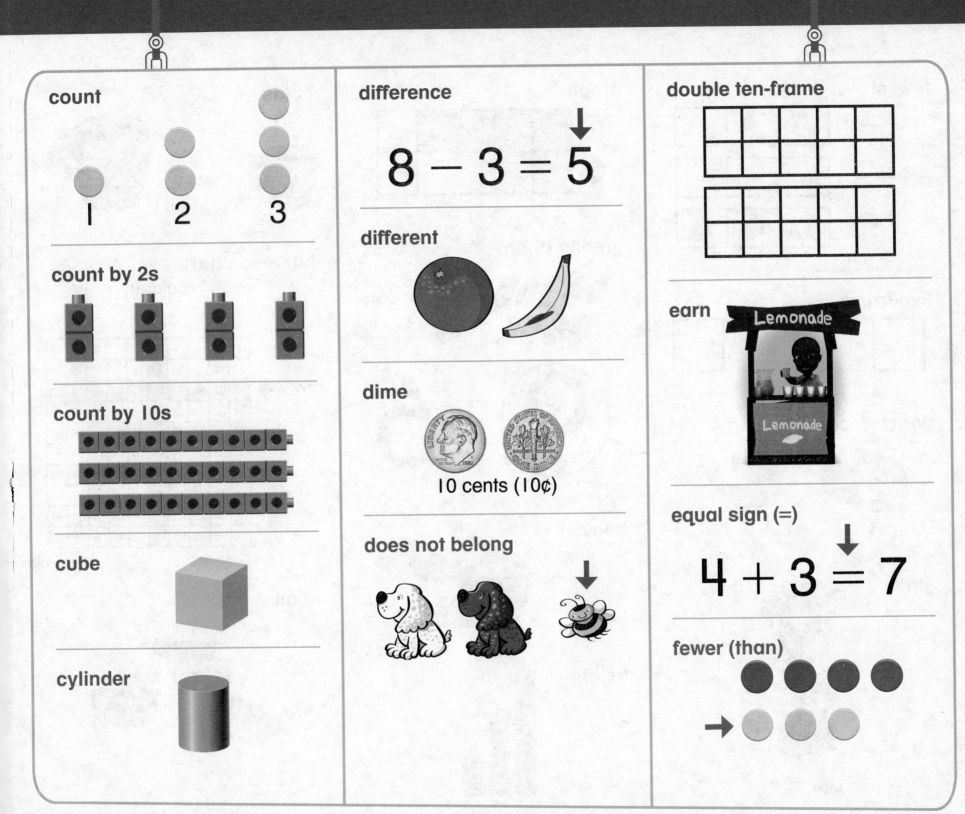

count

1 2 3

count by 2s

count by 10s

cube

cylinder

difference

$$8 - 3 = 5$$

different

dime

10 cents (10¢)

does not belong

double ten-frame

earn

Lemonade

Lemonade

equal sign (=)

$$4 + 3 = 7$$

fewer (than)

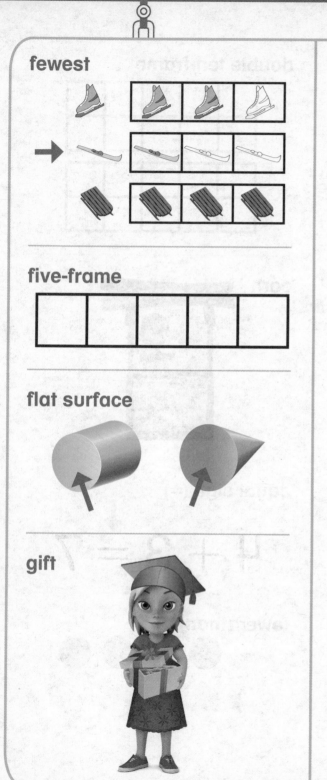

fewest

five-frame

flat surface

gift

graph

greater (than)

9 6

heavier

height

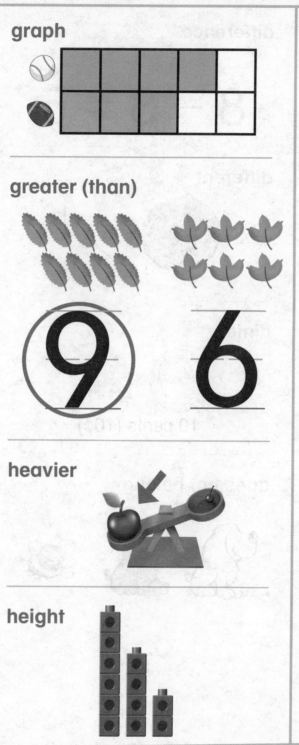

holds

hundred chart

column

1	2	3	4	5	6	7	8	9	10
11	12	13	14	15	16	17	18	19	20
21	22	23	24	25	26	27	28	29	30
31	32	33	34	35	36	37	38	39	40
41	42	43	44	45	46	47	48	49	50
51	52	53	54	55	56	57	58	59	60
61	62	63	64	65	66	67	68	69	70
71	72	73	74	75	76	77	78	79	80
81	82	83	84	85	86	87	88	89	90
91	92	93	94	95	96	97	98	99	100

row →

in all

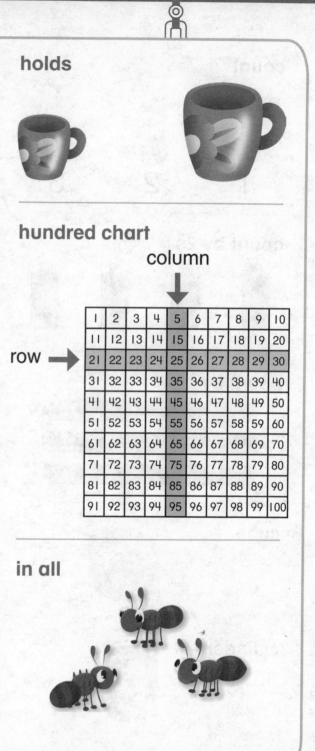

income

join

left

length

less (than)

lighter

longer

minus sign (−)

$$8 - 3 = 5$$

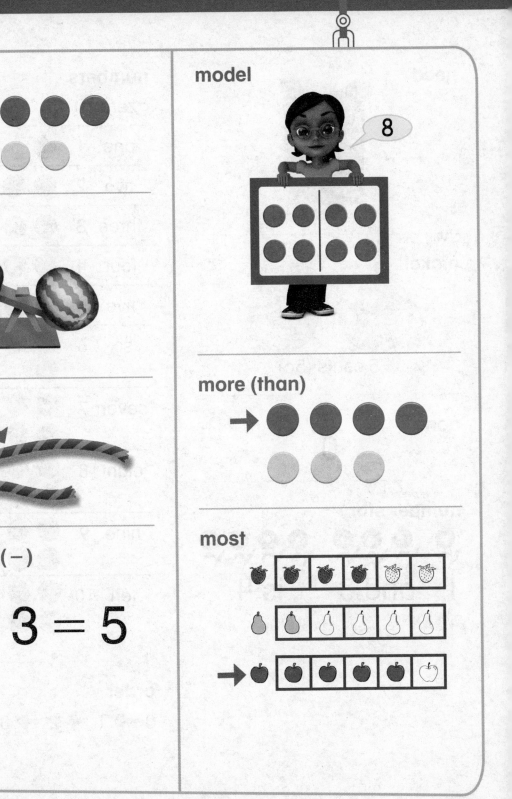

model

8

more (than)

most

need

nickel

5 cents (5¢)

none

0

number story

1 and 3 is 4.

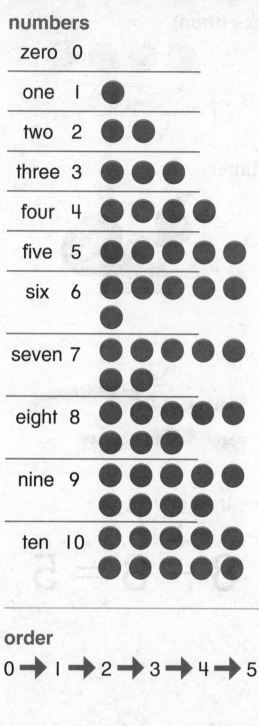

numbers

zero	0	
one	1	●
two	2	● ●
three	3	● ● ●
four	4	● ● ● ●
five	5	● ● ● ● ●
six	6	● ● ● ● ● ●
seven	7	● ● ● ● ● ● ●
eight	8	● ● ● ● ● ● ● ●
nine	9	● ● ● ● ● ● ● ● ●
ten	10	● ● ● ● ● ● ● ● ● ●

order

0 → 1 → 2 → 3 → 4 → 5

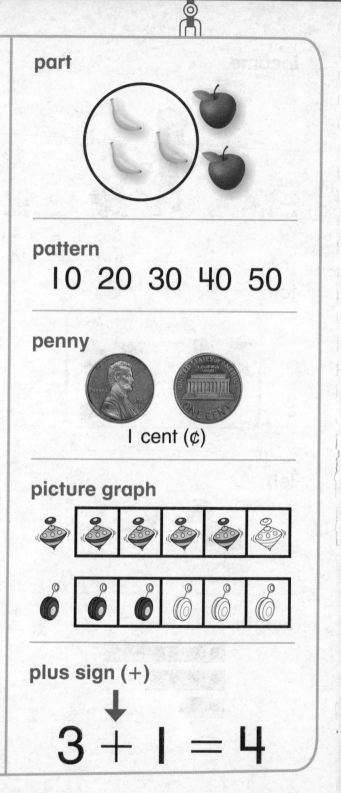

part

pattern

10 20 30 40 50

penny

1 cent (¢)

picture graph

plus sign (+)

↓

3 + 1 = 4

© Pearson Education, Inc. K

quarter

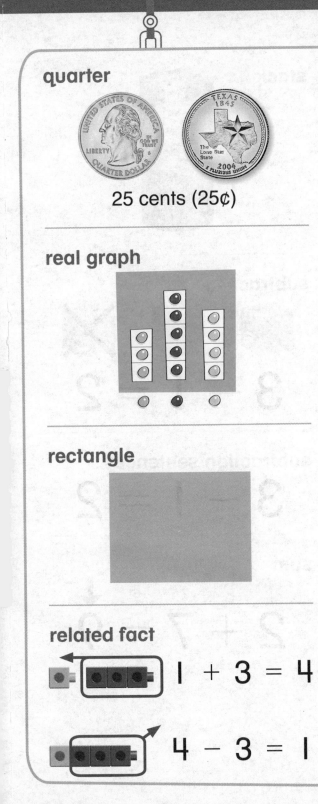

25 cents (25¢)

real graph

rectangle

related fact

$1 + 3 = 4$

$4 - 3 = 1$

roll

row

1	2	3	4	5
11	12	13	14	15
21	22	23	24	25
31	32	33	34	35

same (alike)

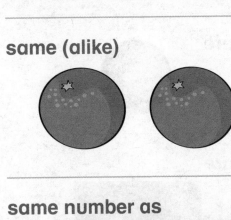

same number as

same shape

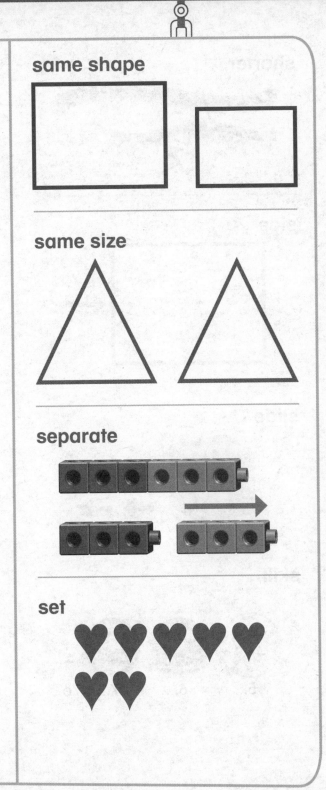

same size

separate

set

shorter

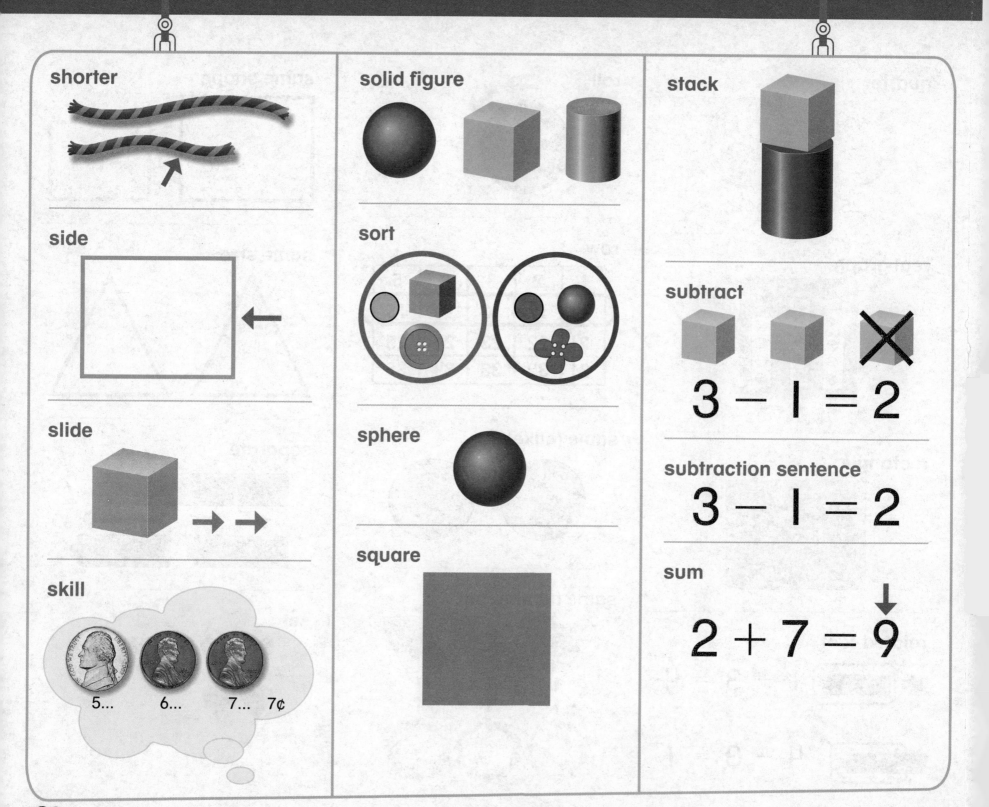

side

slide

skill

5... 6... 7... 7¢

solid figure

sort

sphere

square

stack

subtract

$$3 - 1 = 2$$

subtraction sentence

$$3 - 1 = 2$$

sum

$$2 + 7 = 9$$

Glossary

survey

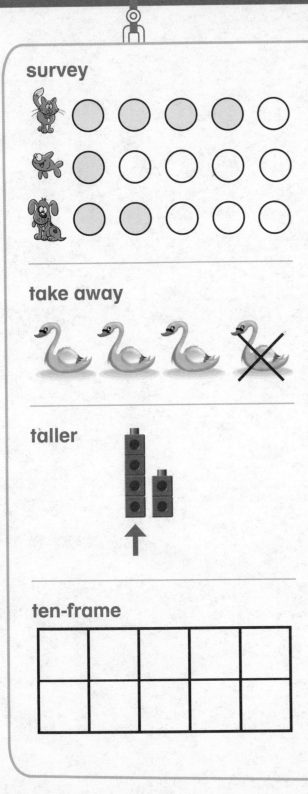

take away

taller

ten-frame

thirty

30

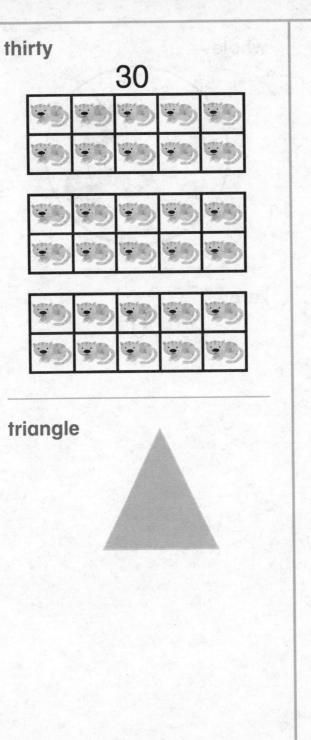

triangle

twenty

20

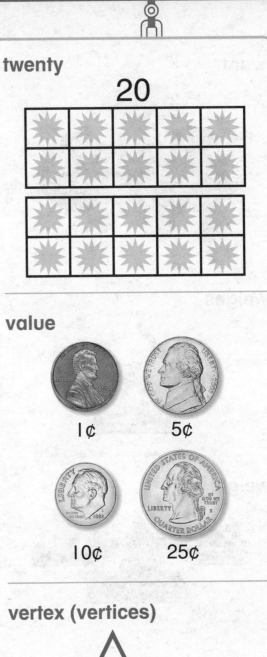

value

1¢   5¢

10¢   25¢

vertex (vertices)

want

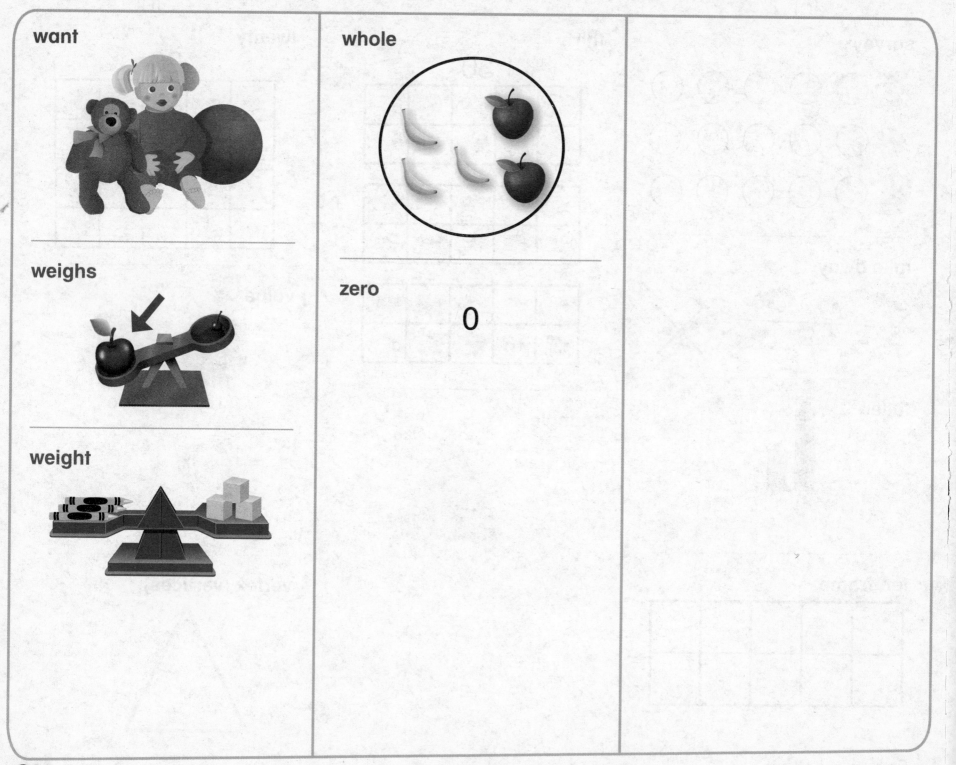

weighs

weight

whole

zero

0